The Chilean Economy

The Chilean Economy
Policy Lessons and Challenges

Barry P. Bosworth
Rudiger Dornbusch
Raúl Labán

editors

The Brookings Institution
Washington, D.C.

Copyright © 1994
THE BROOKINGS INSTITUTION
1775 Massachusetts Avenue, N.W., Washington, D.C. 20036

All rights reserved

Library of Congress Cataloging-in-Publication Data:

The Chilean economy : policy lessons and challenges / edited by Barry
P. Bosworth, Rudiger Dornbusch, and Raúl Labán.
  p. cm.
  Includes bibliographical references and index.
  ISBN 0-8157-1046-1 (pa)—ISBN 0-8157-1046-1 (cl)
  1. Chile—Economic policy—Congresses. 2. Chile—Economic
conditions—1973–1988—Congresses. 3. Chile—Economic
conditions—1988— —Congresses. I. Bosworth, Barry, 1942–
II. Dornbusch, Rudiger. III. Labán, Raúl.
HC192.C5195 1994   93-43252
                                                           CIP

9 8 7 6 5 4 3 2 1

Set in Times Roman
Composition by Graphic Composition, Inc.
  Athens, Georgia
Printed by R. R. Donnelley and Sons Co.
  Harrisonburg, Virginia

ᛒ THE BROOKINGS INSTITUTION

The Brookings Institution is an independent organization devoted to nonpartisan research, education, and publication in economics, government, foreign policy, and the social sciences generally. Its principal purposes are to aid in the development of sound public policies and to promote public understanding of issues of national importance.

The Institution was founded on December 8, 1927, to merge the activities of the Institute for Government Research, founded in 1916, the Institute of Economics, founded in 1922, and the Robert Brookings Graduate School of Economics and Government, founded in 1924.

The Board of Trustees is responsible for the general administration of the Institution, while the immediate direction of the policies, program, and staff is vested in the President, assisted by an advisory committee of the officers and staff. The by-laws of the Institution state: "It is the function of the Trustees to make possible the conduct of scientific research, and publication, under the most favorable conditions, and to safeguard the independence of the research staff in the pursuit of their studies and in the publication of the results of such studies. It is not a part of their function to determine, control, or influence the conduct of particular investigations or the conclusions reached."

The President bears final responsibility for the decision to publish a manuscript as a Brookings book. In reaching his judgment on the competence, accuracy, and objectivity of each study, the President is advised by the director of the appropriate research program and weighs the views of a panel of expert outside readers who report to him in confidence on the quality of the work. Publication of a work signifies that it is deemed a competent treatment worthy of public consideration but does not imply endorsement of conclusions or recommendations.

The Institution maintains its position of neutrality on issues of public policy in order to safeguard the intellectual freedom of the staff. Hence interpretations or conclusions in Brookings publications should be understood to be solely those of the authors and should not be attributed to the Institution, to its trustees, officers, or other staff members, or to the organizations that support its research.

Foreword

Over the past decade Chile has emerged as the nation with the fastest growing economy in Latin America. This surge of growth followed one of the most extensive economic reform programs ever undertaken in a developing country. Today Chilean policies are often held up to the countries of eastern Europe and much of the rest of Latin America as a model for economic stabilization and restructuring. Since the early 1970s Chile has experimented with a wide range of economic policies, all with a strong emphasis on economic liberalism. The country has gone through a major episode of economic stabilization to bring inflation under control; sharp reductions in trade restraints have opened the Chilean economy to the global trading system; and Chile has privatized state-owned enterprises and converted its social insurance system to a privately managed pension system.

This book reports on a joint undertaking by American and Chilean economists to examine the economic reforms that have been implemented in Chile during the past fifteen years. Each of the eight papers concentrates on a specific aspect of the Chilean economy or the reform program. These papers distill lessons from Chile's experience for other countries and examine the implications for the future evolution of the Chilean economy. The Brookings Institution, in cooperation with the Chilean research institution CIEPLAN, held a conference in April 1993 at which the individual studies were presented and discussed. This book comprises revised versions of the eight papers, the remarks of official commentators on each paper, and an introductory chapter in which the editors provide an overview of the main issues and summarize the papers and discussion. Because of time constraints, the manuscript was not subjected to the formal verification procedures established for research publications of the institution.

The editors wish to thank the many staff members at the Brookings Institution who contributed to the project: Hillary Sheldon provided valuable research assistance, Paige Oeffinger and Irene Coray organized the conference,

Deborah Styles edited the manuscript, Carlotta Ribar proofread it, Laura Kelly assisted with the verification, and Robert E. Elwood prepared the index.

Financial support for the project was provided by the Ford Foundation and the University of Miami, North-South Center.

The views expressed in this book are solely those of the authors and should not be ascribed to the organizations or persons acknowledged above, or to the trustees, officers, or staff members of the Brookings Institution.

BRUCE K. MACLAURY
President

January 1994
Washington, D.C.

Contents

Figures

Introduction

Barry P. Bosworth, Rudiger Dornbusch, and Raúl Labán

CHILE IS often presented as the model for the programs of economic restructuring, market liberalization, and stabilization that are being urged on other countries within Latin America and in Eastern Europe. It has also served as a social laboratory for some specific policies, such as privatization and social security reform, that are of interest in both developed and developing economies. For example, Chile has implemented the largest program of privatization of government-owned enterprises, and its social security system, based on privately managed individual retirement accounts, has attracted the attention of many observers. Furthermore Chile has emerged in the 1990s, after sixteen years of authoritarian rule, with a new democratic government, but now it must decide which direction it should take in its economic policies.

The advent of Chile as a paradigm of economic reform in the 1990s is a surprise, however. Many of the reforms were introduced in the 1970s. As recently as 1985, the published evaluations often concluded that the reforms had failed to achieve their primary objectives.[1] The initiation of the structural reforms and of the stabilization program in the mid-1970s, coupled with a severe shock in the terms of trade, led to a harsh recession in which unemployment rose to more than 15 percent of the work force at the same time that real wages declined by more than 15 percent during 1974 and 1975. The recession was followed by several years of strong economic recovery, precipitating premature claims of success for the economic program of the Pinochet government. Nevertheless, the unemployment rate remained high, with an average of 17.6 percent of the labor force for the period 1976–81, compared with an average of 6 percent during the 1960s, and the real wage was on average 6.3 percent lower during the period 1979–81 than it had been in 1970. The euphoria came to an abrupt end in 1981, when the economy again collapsed under the weight of an unsustainable accumulation of foreign debt and the shock of a dramatic change in the international economic environment. The resulting recession was among

---

1. See, for example, Edwards and Cox-Edwards (1987).

the most severe in all of Latin America: unemployment, including workers in special government-subsidized employment programs, rose to 30 percent of the labor force in 1983, with real wages declining more than 10 percent in that same year.

The more recent, positive view of the Chilean experience is the result of developments in the subsequent ten years. Since 1983 Chile has achieved a sustained strong expansion of its economy. The policies followed by the government over that period are universally extolled as an example of a pragmatic, outward-oriented economic growth program. What remains controversial is the question of why it took so long. Real wages have only recently recovered to the level of the early 1970s, and the unemployment rate reached levels consistent with those of the 1960s only by 1989. Should the Chilean experience with economic reform be interpreted as a single, though evolving experience in which the lags are inevitably long; or was the adjustment period abnormally lengthened by the severity of the initial disequilibrium and by major policy mistakes in the first ten years?

Some evidence suggests that stabilization and economic reform in Chile were accompanied by a worsening of the income distribution and an increase in poverty levels. An estimated 45 percent of the population was living below the poverty level in the mid-1980s. According to a September 1988 poll conducted by the CEP, by the end of the military regime poverty and low income levels were the principal reasons behind the vote for the "No" option in the plebiscite of October 1988, which cleared the way for presidential and congressional elections in 1989. How large were the welfare costs associated with economic transformation and stabilization in Chile? How were they spread over different social-economic groups? And how could they have been prevented or alleviated? These are all questions that should be answered before the Chilean experience with economic reform and stabilization can be evaluated completely.

This book is the result of a conference held at the Brookings Institution on April 22–23, 1993. The conference had two goals. The first was to review the history of economic reform in Chile and to assess the effectiveness of the individual policy measures. This is of primary value for a continuing discussion and debate about the design of optimal policies for economic stabilization and reform in other countries. The second goal of the conference more directly concerned the current economic situation and future challenges in Chile. Many of the original reforms have been largely completed, and for more than a decade Chile has been able to maintain a coherent macroeconomic policy with a slowly declining inflation rate.. That raises the question of the focus of economic policy in the 1990s. What must Chile do to sustain its growth in the future and to spread the benefits of that growth to a larger proportion of the population?

The remainder of this introduction provides a brief overview of economic events in Chile over the past two decades, highlights Chile's role in the debate over economic reform in Latin America, and summarizes the papers.

Background

lost decade

The 1980s have been characterized as the "lost decade" from the perspective of economic development in Latin America. Per capita incomes declined by approximately 10 percent after the debt crisis of the early 1980s. Many countries were overwhelmed by stagflation, unmanageable debt burdens, and the world's most unequal income distribution. The loss of confidence in the ability of governments to manage the economy resulted in a cutoff of funds from foreign creditors, large-scale capital flight, and a collapse of domestic investment.

The debate over what should be done has gradually coalesced around a reform of two central features of economic policy. First, steps must be taken to reduce the rampant inflation that plagued the region throughout the 1980s, largely as a result of delay in implementing the policies required to respond to the debt crisis. Countries have come to recognize that fiscal deficits are the driving force behind inflation and that those deficits must be eliminated by a policy that combines tax reform and reductions in government spending. Reconstruction of the tax system requires the introduction of a broad tax base combined with the lowest possible rates, the elimination of special provisions and exemptions, and greater efforts to ensure compliance. Reductions in spending should emphasize eliminating subsidies and privatizing those activities that can be more efficiently performed outside the government sector.

Second, the new growth strategies emphasize economic liberalization as a key feature of the structural adjustments required to restore economic growth. Trade liberalization is suggested both as a means of increasing competitive pressures and efficiency within the domestic economy and as part of a growth strategy that emphasizes expansion of the export sector. Opening these economies to international markets necessitates eliminating quotas and trade licensing and establishing a low and uniform tariff structure. Similarly, liberalizing the capital account and deregulating the domestic financial markets are viewed as ways to improve the efficiency with which capital is used and to provide a source of financing for new enterprises. State enterprises need to be privatized to sharpen the incentives for efficient management and to reduce the strains on public finances. Finally, liberalization involves adopting more favorable attitudes toward foreign direct investment. Foreign investment is important not just as a vehicle for capital inflows, but as a means of obtaining modern technology, management skills, and access to foreign markets.

Differences remain, however, within several areas of this broad consensus. They include questions about the sequence in which the various reforms should be introduced, the rate at which inflation targets should be reduced, exchange rate policy, and the extent to which domestic financial markets and international capital movements should be deregulated and decontrolled. They also include questions about the effect of these reforms on income distribution and which policy measures, if any, can be introduced in order to prevent those more vulnerable from bearing a disproportionate share of the required adjustment costs.

Chile stands out from the rest of Latin America both in the breadth of its reform program and in the extent to which it achieved a reversal of its history of declining economic performance. Because it introduced many of the reforms in the early 1970s, sufficient time has passed to make Chile an interesting case study of the problems and benefits of economic liberalization and macroeconomic stabilization. Rapid and sustained economic growth has occurred since the mid-1980s; unemployment has declined; and inflation, while still high by international standards, remains far below the rates that existed before 1975 and below the rates in other Latin American countries.

The gains in overall economic performance, however, involved substantial transitional costs, such as reductions in real wages and cutbacks in employment. The economic reforms of the 1970s also did not save Chile from the general collapse of Latin American economies in the debt crisis of the early 1980s. Today, the economic instability of the 1970s and early 1980s is attributed to unforeseen external shocks, the legacy of past conditions, and some initial mistakes that were made in the stabilization program during the 1970s. Most of the criticism of the program of economic liberalization is directed at the excessive speed with which some of the reforms were introduced and problems with the sequence in which they were undertaken and at the absence of mechanisms to shield lower income groups from the effects of these reforms and of the stabilization program.

Economic reform in Chile began with a highly distorted economy. In the 1950s and 1960s Chile followed a policy of isolating itself from the global economy. The average tariff level exceeded 100 percent, and both exports and imports had extensive nontariff barriers. During this period Chile suffered from an increasing degree of international financial repression, with the introduction of many restrictions on international capital mobility. Also during this period Chile was notable for chronic inflation, a relatively low rate of economic growth, and frequent economic crises. Popular dissatisfaction with the economy's performance was further fueled by a very unequal distribution of income and a highly monopolistic productive structure in both agriculture and industry.

The Allende government, which was in office from 1970 to 1973, pursued a socialist program of nationalizing industry, banking, and mining. It also accelerated a program of agrarian reform, eliminating the large estates but leaving a substantial amount of the land in state ownership. International trade was mostly taken over by the government. Large nominal wage increases were approved in combination with widespread price controls in the private sector and a freezing of prices for public services. The resulting sharp rise in real wages, a large increase in the budget deficit, and a rapid expansion of central bank credit initiated an economic boom in 1971 that quickly degenerated into an explosion of inflation, shortages, black markets, and huge losses in the state enterprises. By 1973 inflation had soared to an annual rate of 500 percent, the public sector deficit had reached 25 percent of GDP, and Chile had depleted its international reserves. The military seized the government in the fall of 1973.

1974–83

The Chilean economic adjustment program of the 1970s stands out as an example of a drastic and rapid reform process. The budget deficit was cut sharply from 25 percent of GDP in 1973 to 1 percent by 1975. A restrictive monetary policy pushed real interest rates above 50 percent a year. Price controls were lifted and subsidies eliminated in the domestic market. Quantitative restrictions on trade were eliminated, and tariffs were cut to a uniform 10 percent by 1979. The multiple exchange rate system was consolidated and combined with a large devaluation as an offset to the tariff reduction. The result was a post-liberalization surge of price inflation, which averaged 350 percent a year in 1974–75 before declining to 85 percent in 1977. The government also began a rapid privatization program in which more than 300 firms with a total book value of about $1 billion were returned to private ownership by the end of 1974.

In the rush to privatize the economy, the government paid little attention to issues such as the concentration of ownership of the newly privatized firms and banks, and it failed to establish a system of financial market supervision comparable to that of other market economies. Instead, it adopted an extreme laissez-faire approach, in which the government had little responsibility to su-

Figure I-1. Selected Economic Indicators, 1970–92

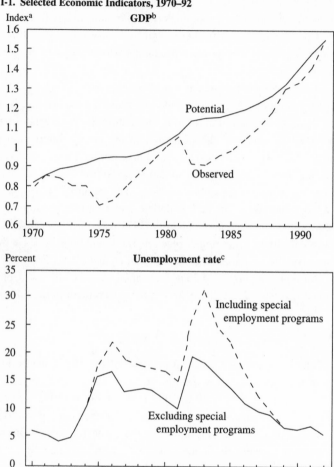

Index[a]   GDP[b]

Potential

Observed

Percent   Unemployment rate[c]

Including special
employment programs

Excluding special
employment programs

pervise individual markets or to adjust macroeconomic policies to changing circumstances. By 1980 only forty-three firms (including one commercial bank) remained under the control of the public sector, compared with the more than 500 firms under state control during President Allende's administration.

Chile was further affected in the early stages of the process by severe external shocks in the form of higher oil prices, the global recession of 1974–75, and a collapse of copper prices. Foreign exchange reserves were depleted by early 1975. The external factors, combined with the harsh domestic fiscal restraint, led to the 1975 recession in which unemployment rose to 15 percent of the work force (see figure I-1). A strong cyclical recovery began in 1976 that was to continue until 1982.

Figure I-1. (*continued*)

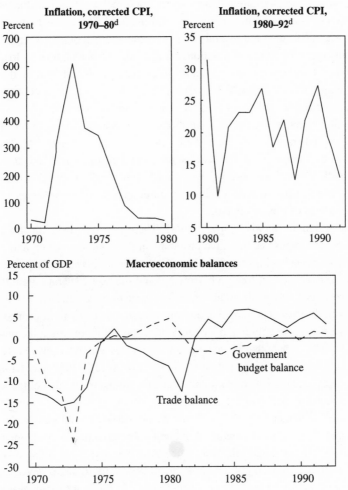

SOURCE: Central Bank of Chile.
a. 1980 = 1.
b. In 1977 prices.
c. Percent of labor force.
d. Annual percent change, December-December.

Exch rate desinflatio 1978 [handwritten margin note]

The year 1978 marked a major policy change as the government shifted to an emphasis on the exchange rate as the primary focus of its anti-inflation program. Chile introduced a system of preannounced fixed depreciations of the exchange rate, the *tablita* system, and followed that with adoption of a fixed nominal rate, tied to the U. S. dollar, in mid-1979. That lasted until mid-

1982. While the original intent of this program was to force domestic price inflation down to international rates, the major effect was to lower dramatically the costs of borrowing in foreign financial markets. The interest cost on such loans was the foreign interest rate plus the expected rate of depreciation. After an adjustment for domestic inflation, the real interest rate on foreign loans was negative throughout much of the period, compared with real rates on domestic bank loans, which averaged 15 percent in 1979–80 and 39 percent in 1981. The exchange rate policy, in combination with the government's policy of deregulating domestic financial institutions and removing controls on international capital transactions, unleashed a flood of foreign borrowing. The progressive overvaluation of the real exchange rate resulted in a steadily rising trade deficit, which reached 6.7 percent of GDP in 1980 and 12.9 percent in 1981, but this was financed without any drain on government reserves by enormous inflows of private capital.

The system began to collapse in 1981. The progressive overvaluation of the peso created intense competitive problems in the tradables sector, and several large firms went bankrupt in the midst of growing doubts about the sustainability of the trade deficit, foreign borrowing, and the exchange rate. Real interest rates rose as firms in financial difficulty tried to cover their losses through further borrowing. The global economic situation also began to change as interest rates rose sharply in the United States; the dollar, to which the peso was linked, rose against other currencies, and the world entered a severe recession. Foreign commercial banks cut off credit to Chile in early 1982, capital inflows fell sharply, and the government intervened to assume the burden of the foreign debts of a bankrupt financial system.

Domestic demand within Chile fell by an astounding 24 percent between 1981 and 1982, domestic output dropped by 14 percent, and open unemployment rose to 20 percent of the work force. Another 10 percent of the work force was enrolled in special public employment programs. A sharp devaluation of the currency added a large terms-of-trade loss. At this stage many evaluations concluded that the Chilean economic adjustment program had been a failure.

This major economic crisis, the worst since the 1930s, was partly the result of a combination of several external shocks—the drying up of voluntary external financing; the deterioration in the terms of trade; and the major increase in foreign interest rates. But the effect of external developments was exacerbated by the mishandling of several domestic policies: the fixed exchange rate policy coupled with mandatory indexation of wages at 100 percent of past inflation; the sweeping opening of the capital account at the time of the boom; the radical liberalization of domestic financial markets without the provision of proper regulations and controls; and the belief in the "automatic adjustment" mechanism, by which the market was expected to produce a quick adjustment to the new recessionary conditions without interference by the authorities.

1983–93

The past decade has witnessed a remarkable recovery of the Chilean economy from the 1982 economic collapse, but in many respects the challenges to policy were less than those faced ten years earlier. Inflation was in the range of 20 percent, the public sector budget was in surprisingly good condition, and the major problem was how to engineer an economic recovery from a deep recession—a condition on which there was vast international experience. The new features were how to deal with a domestic financial collapse and the massive level of foreign indebtedness resulting from the government's assumption of the private sector debts. Chile's foreign debt equaled 120 percent of GDP in 1985, and debt service absorbed 46 percent of export earnings.

After some false starts, the government adopted a pragmatic and orthodox macroeconomic policy beginning in 1985. The key feature was a large depreciation of the real exchange rate that initiated an export-led expansion, financed by a tight fiscal policy to raise domestic saving, which had fallen to a remarkable low of 1.6 percent of GDP in 1982. Chile's trade balance was reversed from a deficit equal to 13 percent of GDP in 1981 to a surplus that peaked at 6.6 percent in 1986 and averaged 4 percent a year in the 1987–92 period. The growth of GDP averaged 6.2 percent a year in the 1983–92 period, and unemployment had declined to below 5 percent of the labor force by 1992.

Starting in 1985, the government went through a second round of privatization to sell the firms that had been taken over in the 1982 financial collapse, it reversed the tariff increases that had been introduced during the crisis, and it rebuilt the financial system, establishing a greater supervisory role for the Central Bank. Chile also introduced some innovative debt conversion schemes to reduce its foreign debt by approximately 50 percent.

Today Chile has the most vibrant economy in Latin America, and its economic foundation is strong. The public sector budget is balanced, exports are growing vigorously, rates of domestic saving and investment are rising, the level of foreign debt is manageable, and inflation is declining slowly. The new democratic government also appears to have established a coherent rational process for formulating economic policy on a continuing basis. Nevertheless, Chile must still address a number of economic policy challenges to consolidate its development process. Among them are the achievement of sustainable future growth; reduced vulnerability to external shocks; the consolidation of recent gains in reducing inflation; the promotion of higher private saving; and the reduction of poverty, in which about 40 percent of the population is still living.

Evaluating the Chilean Reform Experience

Events since 1973 in Chile have long been viewed as one of the major case studies of economic adjustment. Chile's experience has taken on added interest in recent years because of some similarities between the initial conditions in 1973 and the current situation in eastern Europe: a severely distorted price structure, black markets, a repressed financial system, and a large deficit in the public sector budget. It offers pertinent lessons to other countries in the design of disinflation strategies, the role of trade liberalization, the implications of capital market deregulation, and the social welfare costs of economic adjustment. Chile has also attracted international attention for its reforms of the social security system and the privatization of state enterprises.

The eight papers presented at this conference examine distinct features of the Chilean experience with economic reform. The papers have some areas of overlap, however, and they reveal some significant differences of perspective on specific aspects of the economic reforms and causes of some of the problems that Chile encountered.

Lessons from the Chilean Stabilization and Recovery

Vittorio Corbo and Stanley Fischer focus on macroeconomic policies, arguing that the Chilean experience of the past twenty years should be interpreted as a successful application of an orthodox adjustment program. They also see, however, that the approach to policy in Chile in the years following the military overthrow of the Allende government has evolved through several distinct stages in which mistakes increased the costs of adjustment.

The inflation incorporated elements of both stock and flow disequilibriums. The stock disequilibrium, a money stock in excess of desired amounts, was evident in widespread rationing and black markets. A simultaneous flow disequilibrium, an excessive rate of money creation, was fueled primarily by a large public sector budget deficit financed through the Central Bank. The military government attacked the monetary overhang by immediately lifting domestic price controls and instituting a large real devaluation. The resulting one-shot rise in the price level was designed to reduce real money balances. Over a two-year period the government addressed the flow disequilibrium largely by eliminating the budget deficit in the public sector, reducing the need to finance the deficit through money creation.

These measures represented the core elements of a traditional disinflation program emphasizing demand management. They did achieve some success: after an initial surge, inflation declined from an annual rate of 600 percent in 1973 to 200 percent in 1976 and to below 100 percent in 1977. The government became increasingly concerned, however, about what it viewed as the slow pace of disinflation, despite the elimination of the fiscal deficit. The lack of confidence in the domestic currency was also evident in the extremely high levels of real interest rates.

The authors provide empirical evidence that the process of inflation in Chile embodied strong elements of inertia, and they are critical of the initial program for failing to deal with that aspect of the process. Indeed, many of the government's actions strengthened the inertia. By indexing public sector wages for past rates of inflation, the government encouraged the private sector to do the same. The inertia was reinforced by the practice of adjusting the exchange rate in line with past rates of inflation.

The issue of how best to deal with the inertia element of chronic inflation continues to be controversial. Some favor fixing the nominal exchange rate to provide a nominal anchor for the price system and to force a convergence of the domestic and foreign inflation rates. The adoption of a nominal exchange rate rule is seen as a signal of a sharp break with past practice; by imposing a constraint on future government actions, it should make the government's commitment to price stability more credible. If private agents can be persuaded to believe the commitment, price stability can be achieved with relatively low losses in transitional output.

Critics of nominal exchange rate targeting, however, doubt that there will be significant announcement effects of the policy shift. They argue further that fixing the nominal rate will have little effect until the appreciation of the real exchange rate translates into falling output in the tradables sector, higher unemployment, and excess capacity. Thus the costs of adjustment will fall disproportionately on the tradables sector, and the evident overvaluation of the real exchange rate will lead to expectations of further adjustments of the nominal rate and instability of capital flows. They suggest, instead, that exchange rate targeting should be limited to the early stages of sharp disinflation and that the problem of chronic inflation should be addressed with policies expressed as goals for the domestic economy: using the money supply as the nominal anchor, for example, and including more direct measures, such as temporary price controls or other incomes policies.

Corbo and Fischer are most critical of the decision to shift in 1978–82 to a stabilization program based on the exchange rate. Adoption of a fixed exchange rate dramatically increased the opportunities for arbitrage between foreign and domestic interest rates, leading to a surge of foreign borrowing that was used to finance a domestic boom. By maintaining the system of formal backward-looking indexation of wages, the government practically guaranteed a continuation of past inflation and a growing appreciation of the real exchange rate. But the enormous inflow of private capital, by providing the financing for a growing trade deficit, removed the balance of payments constraint that normally would have forced abandonment of the program.

The authors attribute the sustained expansion of the economy after 1985 to a shift of policy toward the promotion of export-led growth. Another effort at fiscal consolidation shifted the public sector balance from a deficit of 4.3 percent of GDP in 1984 to a surplus by 1988. The exchange rate underwent a sharp real devaluation, which allowed the fiscal restraint to translate into large trade surpluses throughout the last half of the 1980s. The authors also argue that the gains from the structural reforms of the 1970s, although they took a long time to materialize, were an important factor in the growth that occurred during the 1980s.

Corbo and Fischer suggest that achieving further reductions in the inflation rate to single-digit rates should be a major objective of future Chilean policy, but that objective should be secondary to a goal of maintaining a real exchange rate favorable to exports. To achieve this goal they propose adopting a crawling peg exchange rate with wide bands. Both the reference rate and the width of the band would be adjusted in the future on a basis consistent with a gradual reduction of the inflation rate.

At the conference, discussion centered on the reasons for the slow deceleration of inflation in the 1970s, despite the strong correction in the underlying fundamentals, and on the argument of Corbo and Fischer that adjustment necessarily takes a long time. In his comments Patricio Meller suggested that the liberalization of the domestic financial markets and the boom touched off by the large inflows of foreign capital were elements, in addition to the prevalence of backward indexation, that contributed to sustaining inflation.

There were significant differences about the role of backward-looking indexation versus a failure to achieve credibility of policy as explanations of the inertia of inflation. Corbo and Fisher argued that the government should have used incomes policies to break the momentum of the inflation process in the late 1970s. The extremely high level of real interest rates, however, seemed to suggest a credibility problem rather than just institutionalized inflation. Several participants argued that incomes policies would prevent the adjustments in labor markets that were necessary for the structural reforms to succeed. The participants did not fully resolve whether greater policy credibility was more effective than incomes policies in breaking the momentum of inflation.

Exchange Rate Policy and Trade Strategy

Foreign trade policies have long been at the center of the debate over optimal strategies for economic growth. While the classical arguments of comparative advantage dominated in the advocacy of free trade among developed economies, a strategy of import substitution and forced industrialization maintained a high degree of popularity until recently in many developing countries. In most cases the result has been steadily growing distortions of resource utilization, weak competitive constraints on domestic firms, and highly complex administrative controls on access to foreign exchange.

Chile is an important example of a country that undertook a sharp switch away from import substitution toward an outward-oriented policy of rapid trade liberalization. Rudiger Dornbusch and Sebastian Edwards review Chile's exchange rate and trade policies and conclude that, although Chile ultimately succeeded in creating an outward-oriented market economy, the lags in the reform process are long. Furthermore, opening the economy to international markets—particularly to flows of financial capital—can conflict in important respects with efforts to reduce domestic inflation. Unless exchange rate policies are closely integrated with domestic stabilization policies, the result can be collapse of the currency and of the economy. This is exactly what happened in Chile in the early 1980s.

The authors document the rapid pace at which Chile liberalized trade. By 1979 the government had eliminated all quotas and trade permits and had reduced tariffs to a uniform 10 percent. The average effective rate of tariff protection fell from 150 percent in mid-1974 to 50 percent by 1976 and to 14 percent in 1979.

Dornbusch and Edwards argue, however, that the rapid pace of trade liberalization was not a major factor in the subsequent recession. Instead, they point, as do Corbo and Fischer, to the decision to fix the nominal exchange rate in 1979 as the catalyst for the 1982 collapse. Beginning from high inflation, a fixed exchange rate reduces the cost of foreign borrowing and initiates a domestic spending boom. Unless they are restrained through an incomes policy, real wages rise and translate into further increases in consumer spending. The buildup of an overvalued currency and large trade deficits ultimately undermines confidence in the exchange rate and in an anti-inflation program. When this process is combined with an increasingly unfavorable external environment of rising global interest rates and recession, the 1982 collapse seems inevitable.

The 1982–83 economic collapse represented a major setback in the efforts to open the Chilean economy. The government reintroduced exchange rate controls and trade restrictions and assumed responsibility for the external debt of the private sector. In emerging from this crisis, Chile adopted a strategy much different from that of the 1970s. Exchange rate policy shifted away from an emphasis on reducing inflation to promoting trade competitiveness, and the real exchange rate was allowed to depreciate by nearly 30 percent between 1982 and 1986. The real devaluation was made possible domestically by the restraining effects of extreme unemployment and further efforts to raise national saving through a tightening of fiscal policy. Tariffs, which had reached an average level of 30 percent in 1985, were again reduced to 15 percent by 1988 and to a uniform 11 percent in the early 1990s. When capital began to return to Chile, the government aggressively intervened to prevent the inflows from translating into an appreciation in the exchange rate. The authors credit the exchange rate policy with initiating an era of export-led growth that has lifted Chile out of recession and contributed to substantial gains in productivity.

Several participants argued that the trade liberalization of the 1970s deserved greater emphasis as a factor in the turnaround of the Chilean economy. The extreme nature of the initial conditions, the influence of highly unfavorable external shocks, and policy mistakes all tended to slow the response to the liberalization reforms. Speakers disagreed about the relative effects of trade liberalization versus exchange rate devaluation in promoting an expansion of exports. It was noted that most of the export growth was in agricultural products, with smaller increases in manufactures.

The authors present evidence of a wide geographical distribution of Chile's exports, and this generated discussion about the desirability of Chile's entering into a free trade agreement with North America. Current trade with the United States is small, and Dornbusch and Edwards argue that Chile's future trade growth is likely to be associated with increased relations with other countries in the region rather than with an expansion of trade with a remote North American market. The rules of origin associated with such agreements are also seen as potential barriers to future growth of trade with countries outside the free trade area.

Capital Market Liberalization 3

Financial liberalization has both a domestic and a foreign component. Domestically, removing controls on interest rates and encouraging financial intermediaries are important to increasing domestic savings and using them efficiently. Liberalizing controls on capital inflows from abroad is often advocated as a means of increasing the supply of savings for domestic investment, and foreign involvement in the domestic market is seen as accelerating the growth of the institutions of an efficient capital market.

Chile is an illustration, however, of how advocating financial liberalization in both of these dimensions can easily go awry. In the first decade of reform, Chile freed up domestic interest rates and lending but failed to develop an effective system of financial supervision and regulation. In the early stages of an adjustment program, loan demand is likely to be highly unstable, and the high real interest rates that are typical can give rise to perverse motivations for loans. In Chile, there was inadequate monitoring of the creditworthiness of borrowers, and a large number of bad loans resulted. The banks were reluctant to recognize these losses and rolled the loans over in a continual Ponzi scheme that ended in a collapse of the banking system.

Liberalization of the foreign trade sector will generally require an offsetting depreciation of the currency. If, however, trade liberalization is quickly followed by opening of the capital account, the capital inflow generated by portfolio imbalances and large interest rate differentials will create short-term pressures for exchange rate appreciation. The appreciation will squeeze the tradables sector precisely during a difficult transition. In Chile, the initial trade liberalization of the mid-1970s was accompanied by a large depreciation, but the subsequent fixed exchange rate regime led to a progressive overvaluation camouflaged by large inflows of private capital. The large business conglomerates used their control of the banks to obtain low-interest foreign loans to relend at high rates in the domestic market.

The role of financial liberalization in adjustment programs is considered more cautiously as a result of the Chilean experience. Much greater emphasis is given to the need for a strong regulatory structure to foster the growth of a stable domestic financial system and the need for careful sequencing of the reform provisions. The opening of the external capital account in particular is an area in which governments should proceed cautiously and only after substantial progress has been made in restoring domestic balance and liberalizing the trade account.

Raúl Labán and Felipe Larraín examine the implications of liberalizing the capital account for the movements of capital between Chile and the rest of the world. They focus their analysis on the period after the debt crisis, when Chile gradually regained access to global capital markets. The resumption of large inflows after 1988 has revived memories of the 1978–81 period, when large capital inflows contributed to an overvalued exchange rate, a distorted domestic financial situation, and subsequent economic collapse.

How does the situation of the early 1990s differ from the earlier episode, and what should be the policy response? The phenomenon of large, but potentially destabilizing foreign capital inflows is a common important concern of many countries in the midst of major reform programs. High domestic interest rates during the transition, in combination with sudden shifts in investors' perceptions of the potential success of the reforms, give rise to volatile capital flows into domestic financial markets that are themselves still quite fragile.

Labán and Larraín address the major issues through two types of analysis. First, they compare the experience of 1989–92 with that of 1978–81 and argue that the later period displays a far smaller domestic interest rate premium, particularly after adjusting for the reserve requirements and taxes placed on capital inflows. The return on domestic deposits (adjusted for the exchange rate) exceeded foreign interest rates by about 20 percentage points in the early 1980s, compared with a differential of only about 5 percent in 1992. They attribute this difference to greater efforts in the second period to restrain capital inflows as part of a growth strategy of promoting exports by maintaining a highly competitive real exchange rate. Further, during the second period more capital inflows were absorbed in official reserves; consequently, the exchange rate was less overvalued.

Second, they provide estimates of an empirical model aimed at identifying the determinants of capital inflows. They find that the factors affecting short-term capital movements are much different from those for long-term capital. Short-term capital flows appear to reflect opportunities for arbitrage between domestic and foreign interest rates plus a country risk factor, which is measured by the ratio of foreign debt to GDP. Reserve requirements and the taxation of foreign credit have effectively restrained such inflows. Longer-term capital is responsive to more fundamental measures of domestic economic conditions, such as the domestic investment rate, the rate of economic growth, and the foreign debt ratio. In the aggregate, the resumption of capital inflows into Chile appears to be largely driven by the resolution of the country's foreign debt problem. This result is a sharp contrast with the conclusions of other specialists, who believe the large-scale return of foreign private capital to several Latin American economies in the late 1980s is the result of external developments in global capital markets. Such an interpretation leaves no role for reforms of national economic policies.

The empirical analysis also suggests that the domestic and foreign capital markets are not completely integrated. Thus, even though Chile is committed to specific exchange rate targets, the authorities have some room for maneuver in implementing domestic monetary policy.

Saving, Investment, and Economic Growth

In their paper Barry Bosworth and Manuel Marfán examine trends in saving and investment and the growth of the Chilean economy during the past two decades. They reach the surprising conclusion that there is little evidence that the reforms have had a significant effect on overall economic efficiency as measured by the growth in labor productivity. While the Chilean economy has grown at an annual rate in excess of 6 percent since 1983, much of that growth can be attributed to a cyclical recovery from the severe recession of the early 1980s. The growth in output was matched by increases in employment. Output per worker did not recover to the levels of 1980–81 until the beginning of the 1990s. While questions may be raised about the accuracy of the estimates of output per worker, a similar pattern of low-trend growth with large cyclical fluctuations is also evident in independent measures of average real wages.

Conclusions about the effect of the reforms on economic efficiency are complicated, however, by the severity of the disruptions in the economy over the past twenty years. The effects of the reforms are difficult to disentangle from the transitional costs of the economic stabilization program, and, as suggested in other papers in this volume, the adjustment lags may be longer than previously anticipated. Nor is it possible to develop a counterfactual case of what productivity growth would have been without the reforms. Furthermore, while the twenty-year trend is disappointing, productivity has shown much larger increases in the early 1990s.

In part the poor long-term trend performance can be attributed to a very low rate of capital accumulation during the period. Capital per worker has grown at an annual rate of only 0.5 percent, compared with 1.8 percent in the 1960s and an average near 4 percent annually in the high-growth economies of Asia. Domestic investment appears to have been adversely affected by the extreme volatility of output growth up to the mid-1980s and the very high level of real interest rates that accompanied the anti-inflation program. But, in addition, Chile experienced a dramatic decline in the rate of national saving. The estimated private saving rate averaged only about 5 percent of GDP in the first ten years of the Pinochet government. Higher rates of public sector saving and an enormous inflow of foreign savings financed the bulk of domestic investment in the 1973–83 period. Since the recession of 1983, the rate of private saving has steadily increased from a very low level, and the public sector has generated a consistent budget surplus.

The authors argue that previous low rates of investment can be adequately explained by the adverse economic environment; the more important limitation is the meager rate of domestic saving. Higher rates of saving could quite easily translate into higher domestic investment through reductions in real interest rates and would have the added benefit of reducing incentives for capital inflows and exchange rate appreciation.

Since Chile has used up most of the reserves of excess labor and capacity that were so apparent throughout the 1980s, the authors suggest that supply-side factors will exert a more constraining influence on growth in the future. On the basis of an estimated 1 percent annual growth in total factor productivity and 2.5 percent growth in effective labor supply, future growth of the Chilean economy is projected at approximately 4 percent a year. This growth appears to be consistent as well with the current rate of national saving, about 20 percent of GDP, which is sufficient to finance a matching 4 percent growth of the capital stock. Improvements in total factor productivity in the early 1990s provide the basis for somewhat higher projected growth rates, but such growth would require higher rates of national saving and capital formation.

The conference discussion focused on the estimates of productivity growth, with many participants holding to an optimistic assessment of future growth prospects based on productivity improvements in the most recent past. There was general agreement, however, that higher rates of saving and capital formation will be critical to sustaining high rates of output growth in the future and that promoting higher saving should be a major goal of government policy.

The Distribution of Income and Economic Adjustment

Critics of economic adjustment programs often charge that the costs fall heavily on the poor, and this frequently becomes a major political barrier to the adoption of such programs. Budget cuts, devaluations, wage freezes, and the transitional recessions that often accompany macroeconomic stabilization programs often do disproportionately affect lower-income groups, particularly in urban areas. But these same groups also lose from the economic instability that is the occasion for the programs, and they stand to gain the most from economic growth. Furthermore, the poor are seldom the beneficiaries of the subsidies, regulations, trade restrictions, and other measures that are often the target of economic liberalization programs. Thus the distributional effects of economic adjustment programs are not self-evident.

In this area also Chile is an instructive case because of the magnitude of the adjustment measures that it undertook and the severity of the two recessions that accompanied the reform program. Mario Marcel and Andrés Solimano examine the effects of the political and economic changes on the distribution of income. They report that the share of income going to the lowest four-fifths of the distribution, after rising in the 1971–73 period, fell substantially during the years of the Pinochet regime, more than reversing the increase that took place during the years of the Allende government. The decline was particularly pronounced for the middle class, defined as the third and fourth quintiles. The share of income going to the top quintile rose to 62 percent, compared with an average of 58 percent in the 1960s and 55 percent during the years of the Allende regime. In recent years the lowest portions of the distribution have regained most of their earlier loss, but at the cost of a continued decline in the income share of the middle class.

To account for this variation, the authors test the explanatory value of labor market, macroeconomic, and structural variables using annual data from the Survey of Household Incomes for Greater Santiago, undertaken by the University of Chile, for the years 1960 to 1992. They estimate regressions that relate the share of income received by each quintile to a measure of economic activity (unemployment rate, GDP growth, or capacity utilization), inflation, the minimum real wage rate, social expenditures, and education. Capacity utilization performs slightly better than the unemployment rate as an indicator of cyclical factors, but both measures suggest that recessions reduce the relative incomes of both low-income and middle-income groups and have the greatest effects on the very poor. Similar effects were obtained from changes in GDP, suggesting that growth was equalizing in Chile. Increases in the minimum wage had a positive effect on the income shares of both the low-income and middle-income quintiles, but the effect was more pronounced in the middle of the distribution. A shift term introduced for the period 1974–92 has a positive coefficient for the top fifth of the distribution and negative elsewhere, indicating some permanent gains for the top quintile, but the coefficient is significant only in the specification using growth of GDP to measure variations in activity.

These results suggest that the reforms had a possible lagged effect on income distribution. The restructuring of the economy during the Pinochet years caused employment and real wages to fall, which had significant negative effects on income distribution. But, because the reforms improved the outlook for sustained high growth, the long-term effects may be positive. If the economy continues to grow and redundant labor is used up, labor will have more bargaining power, and real wages and income distribution should improve.

Significantly, there is some evidence that targeted social programs can alleviate some of the transitional costs for the poorest groups in society. Increases in social expenditures have had positive effects on the share of income going to the lower four-fifths of the distribution. While the Pinochet government did sharply reduce budget outlays for social programs, it did make some effort to focus the remaining programs more tightly on the poorest groups, and it expanded such spending during the periods of most severe recession.

One surprising observation was that inflation lessened inequality. The authors offered several possible explanations. First they tested for a nonlinear relationship between inflation and income distribution by including in the model a dummy for annual inflation greater than 40 percent. The coefficient of this variable was negative for the lower and middle quintiles, but statistically insignificant. They also suggested that inflation may have a positive effect if the additional government revenue leads to greater spending on social programs. In the general discussion John Williamson proposed to correct for this by deducting the amount of the inflation tax from income shares and eliminating double counting. If the inflation tax is actually regressive, then subtracting the income lost would worsen the income distribution. Finally, in Chile's history years of high inflation have coincided with times when other factors had strong positive effects on equality. Since during the period the rate of inflation had few sharp peaks, the regressions may not have enough observations to separate accurately the influence of inflation from the influence of other factors.

Another unexpected finding was that education did not have a strong effect on income distribution in Chile. Research on other countries has found it to be an important factor. In her discussion of the paper, Eliana Cardoso related this result to the methodology of the paper and suggested that using alternative measures of inequality, such as the Theil index, would have made it possible to examine the influence of the cyclical factors within subgroups with the same level of education. The influence of slowly changing factors such as education may be overwhelmed in a time-series analysis that is dominated by cyclical factors.

Whether the reforms developing countries are encouraged to implement cause rising inequality is an important question. Chile carried out many of these reforms, and Chilean income distribution deteriorated. This paper suggests that the deterioration may be the result of the transitional effects of the macroeconomic crises rather than of structural reforms such as trade liberalization or deregulation. Furthermore, social programs seem to have a role in alleviating the regressive effects, and the paper provides evidence that they can be effective.

Conference participants noted that the results of the paper refer only to urban workers in greater Santiago and that the data could be misleading about the income distribution of the entire country. There was also general agreement that the Chilean experience indicated that targeted social programs could be an effective means of ameliorating the transitional effects of economic adjustment on the poorest sectors at relatively low fiscal costs. The distribution of income worsened by even larger amounts in Latin American countries that did not attempt economic adjustment or attempted more populist approaches to reform. The conference participants generally agreed with the current government's efforts to expand some of the social programs, noting that income inequality was a problem that should be addressed more actively in the future.

Social Security Reforms

Countries around the globe are encountering problems with administering and financing their social security systems. Financing difficulties have become more severe as a result of slower economic growth, demographic trends, and maturation of systems with unrealistic benefit commitments. There is also a growing recognition of the inequalities and anomalies built into the system of benefit payments to different categories of workers because of a weak linkage between their contributions and their ultimate benefits. Furthermore, deficiencies in record-keeping and compliance create strong incentives to avoid the system by shifting employment into the informal sector.

Chile's privatization of its social security system is the most dramatic and widely discussed alternative to the traditional defined-benefit systems. The paper by Peter Diamond and Salvador Valdés-Prieto provides a detailed description and evaluation of the new system. The cornerstone is a defined-contribution retirement pension based on a mandatory contribution equal to 10 percent of wages, with a legal maximum of about U.S.$1,500 monthly. In addition, workers pay a fee of about 3 percent of wages to finance the disability pension and to cover administrative costs. Workers' individual accounts are managed by private pension funds subject to government oversight. Benefits are based on the accumulated value of each worker's investment account at the time of retirement (with the exception that there is a guaranteed minimum). Any shortfall between the minimum pension and the accrued benefit is financed out of general revenues. The minimum pension is the only provision for redistribution toward low-wage workers. Contributions and benefits are exempt from the income tax, and workers can make additional voluntary contributions, which are subject to income taxation only when they are withdrawn.

The authors argue that the major benefits of the new system are the consistent treatment of all workers, insulation of the system from politics, increased worker confidence that they will receive future benefits, and a large boost to the development of domestic capital markets. The authors also highlight several problems that need to be addressed in Chile, however, problems that will limit the feasibility of the system in other countries. First, the old pension system has a large transitional fiscal cost that must be covered when payroll tax revenues are redirected into the new system. Second, the administrative charges of the private fund managers have been very high compared with those in other countries. And third, converting accumulated wealth into retirement income requires the existence of an annuities market. Imperfection in the annuities market and problems of adverse selection will further raise the cost of operating the system.

The conference discussion emphasized the confluence of factors that contributed to the success of the conversion in Chile but that would make it more problematic in other countries. The growth of the private funds occurred after Chile had instituted a system of strong regulation and supervision of the domestic financial system. If the private pension system had existed prior to the 1981–82 financial collapse, the outcome might have been different. The Pinochet government also covered the fiscal costs of taking over the old pension program by making severe cuts in other programs, and the high level of real interest rates contributed to the new system's popularity among workers.

Privatization and Regulation

Eduardo Bitran and Raúl Sáez assess the privatization of state-owned enterprises (SOEs) and highlight some lessons learned from the divestiture process. Most of the sixty-seven SOEs existing in 1970 reflected the standard justifications for state operation—natural monopolies, the provision of public goods, and political pressure to provide employment opportunities in depressed areas. Between 1970 and 1973, the Allende government greatly expanded the number of SOEs—to 529—through nationalizations and outright seizures. The share of SOEs and government administration in GDP rose from 14 percent in 1965 to 39 percent in 1973. The military government, driven by the need to reduce the enormous fiscal costs of operating losses from the SOEs, made it an immediate goal to reform the SOE sector. To accomplish this goal the government raised prices to cover costs, eliminated subsidies, and privatized enterprises.

The authors focus on state divestiture of three types of SOEs: tradable and competitive enterprises, financial institutions, and public utilities. The first and second types underwent two periods of privatization. Episode one was initiated in 1973, but was partially undone by the crisis of 1982, during which several bankrupt firms were returned to the government. Episode two was a revised privatization program that was implemented after 1984.

Privatization began with the return of seized enterprises to the original owners, who agreed not to take legal action against the state because of the expropriations. Next, nationalized enterprises were offered for sale. In many cases the privatizations were financed with low down payments and government loans to the new owners. In addition, the new owners of the privatized banks used them as a source of funds to finance additional purchases of SOEs. The result was a highly concentrated pattern of ownership by a few highly indebted conglomerates, and a commingling of financial and nonfinancial institutions. Because of their excessive reliance on debt and joint ownership, many of these conglomerates failed during the 1982 crisis, and the firms reverted to state control.

Learning from these bankruptcies, the government sought during episode two to ensure more diffuse ownership and less indebtedness. The government offered no credit for purchases, except for the sale of small packages of shares in financial institutions to individuals. It encouraged foreign participation by allowing foreign investors to exchange debt, at prices more favorable than those in the secondary market, for shares in the new enterprises. Finally, it enacted legislation to restrict insider trading, to guarantee the rights of minority shareholders, to prevent banks from taking equity positions, and to regulate loans to affiliated parties.

The authors point out that the emphasis on diffuse ownership in the second episode could create new problems by making it difficult for shareholders to exert control over management. They argue that the abuses of conglomerates are more effectively controlled by preventing the joint ownership of financial and nonfinancial enterprises.

The privatization of public utilities and other natural monopolies was attempted only in the 1980s because of the more complex issues involved in such divestitures. The authors argue that privatization must be planned with careful attention to the special characteristics of each industry. The firms should be restructured to promote competition whenever possible, and a strong regulatory system should be in place prior to privatization. If these issues are postponed, uncertainties about their resolution will reduce the sale price, and future reform will be made difficult by its effect on property rights.

Bitran and Sáez are critical of the failure to establish a strong independent regulatory system, free from political influence. They focus on the electric and telecommunications industries to provide examples of the issues raised by privatization of public utilities. They believe that restructuring of these firms would have offered substantial opportunities to expand competition. The emphasis on diffusion of ownership allowed one holding company to exert control over a significant share of the electrical industry with minority ownership.

Chile privatized because it was more optimistic about the ability of government to regulate than to operate enterprises. Yet privatization also raises problems for which there are no simple solutions, particularly in the area of natural monopolies. For example, the growth of conglomerates in the 1970s was strongly influenced by the government's privatization policies, and the conglomerates were an important factor contributing to the 1982 economic collapse. Popular capitalism may safeguard against the formation of conglomerates, but the diffusion of ownership, if carried too far, inhibits control of the firms by stockholders. Vertical and horizontal integration increases operational efficiency but can reduce the efficiency generated by competition.

The privatization program made an important contribution to the public finances in part through the revenues that were generated from sales of the firms, but more important by relieving the public budget of the need to finance the investments and in some cases the operating losses of the firms. Privatization also reduced political pressures to provide subsidies through artificially low prices for publicly provided goods and services.

The Political Economy of the Reform Process

In the concluding paper Andrés Velasco examines the political and economic factors that made possible such a thorough transformation of the Chilean economy. A simple answer might be that dictatorships can do whatever they want, but that does not explain why Chile adopted a set of reforms that were not to the clear benefit of major interest groups of either the left or the right. While many of the reforms have long been advocated by economists, measures such as trade liberalization, the elimination of subsidies, and restrictive macroeconomic policies imposed large costs on interest groups that one might have expected to be supporters of the Pinochet regime. Velasco argues that the reform program must have been seen as the outgrowth of a breakup of a past political process in which economic policy was the product of a convoluted interaction among vested interest groups, each seeking state intervention to its own advantage, and not simply as a backlash against the populist policies of the Allende government.

Historically Chilean economic policy reflected an alliance of business, the middle class, and state bureaucrats, who pursued an inward-looking policy of industrialization. The policies of an interventionist government, highly sensitive to the concerns of domestic interest groups, exerted increased influence on resource allocation, with a resulting growth of economic inefficiencies and inequities. The Allende government pushed this process to a crisis by bringing in new interest groups, the rural and urban poor, with whom the traditional interests had difficulty reaching an accommodation, and by circumventing the traditional avenues of compromise in favor of a more ideological approach to policy.

Velasco suggests that the breakup of the traditional political system and the shock of the global recession of the mid-1970s provided the military regime with an unusual degree of autonomy in the design and implementation of economic policy. The major interest groups on both the right and the left were unable to provide an alternative. Furthermore, the traditional interest groups were sufficiently alarmed by the Allende experience to be willing to forgo a return to the status quo of the late 1960s. Having learned that they could not guarantee their own control of state institutions, they saw a reduced role for the state as the most effective response to the threat of control by others. The severity of the recession strengthened the argument that drastic reforms were required.

As evidence of a primary focus on a reduced role of the state, Velasco cites the emphasis on private property rights in the 1980 constitution, the ban on nontariff barriers, the removal of executive discretion in the setting of tariffs, the privatization of the social security system, and the establishment of an independent central bank. The trade reforms and the independent central bank are particularly noteworthy in limiting the access of business groups to state protection and credit. Thus, while the reforms were expected to reduce government control of private sector activities, they also effectively limited the power of private sector interests to manipulate government policy.

Several participants at the conference noted that Velasco's emphasis on factors other than the dictatorship in the success of the reform movement in Chile gave hope that countries with democratic governments could implement economic adjustment programs. The new democratic government has, in fact, tended to extend and strengthen the earlier reforms. Pessimism arises from the recognition that economic reform is often counter to the interests of powerful interest groups that prefer to maintain the status quo, and Chile gives evidence that reform involves major transition costs and that the benefits take many years to materialize.

Implications for the Future of Economic Reform

In general, the conference participants believed that the turnaround of the Chilean economy is a successful example of an outwardly oriented economic policy that emphasized conventional approaches to macroeconomic stabilization and the strengthening of competition through liberalized markets. At the same time, the papers identified significant mistakes that raised the transition costs and from which other countries could learn important lessons in designing their own programs. Furthermore, with many of the reforms fully implemented and recovery from the 1982–83 recession complete, Chile needs to shift the direction of its policies to a greater emphasis on the supply-side determinants of economic growth.

In retrospect, Chile placed too little importance in the 1970s on the need for close supervision and regulation of domestic financial markets. The growth of large conglomerates that intermingled financial and nonfinancial enterprises was an important factor in the 1982 financial collapse. Furthermore, liberalization of the financial market needs to be preceded by macroeconomic stabilization. Efforts to establish open financial markets in the presence of high inflation are likely to result in excessive speculation and financial instability.

While there was strong support for a rapid liberalization of the current account through the removal of tariffs and other controls on trade, the opening of the economy to external capital transactions was viewed as a more risky undertaking in the early years of a stabilization program and before the establishment of a strong domestic financial system. In this respect, the Chilean experience was seen as implying that the sequence in which markets are liberalized is important to the ultimate success.

The privatization process was a third area of liberalization where there was concern that the initial program was undertaken with excessive haste. The Chilean officials paid too little attention to the effects of the privatizations on competition, failing to implement an adequate regulatory framework for privatized natural monopolies, and to the importance of a strong financial structure in the newly privatized firms.

Chile's decision to adopt a fixed nominal exchange rate as a tool of its anti-inflation policy in the late 1970s was generally viewed as the greatest mistake of the macroeconomic stabilization program. There was some difference of view as to whether such a program could have succeeded if it had been combined with an incomes policy aimed at breaking the indexation and inertia of the domestic inflation process. Most participants believed it important to distinguish between the use of a nominal exchange rate target as part of a program to counter a hyperinflation and its use in Chile to suppress a cycle of high but stable inflation. Most of the participants favored a long-term exchange-rate policy that emphasized competitiveness and promoted export growth.

Finally the process of economic adjustment in countries with a history of severe inflation and distortions of markets appears, on the basis of the Chilean experience, to involve long lags and significant adjustment costs that cannot be fully avoided. There is some evidence that the effects of some of these transitional costs on the poorest segments of society can be mitigated. Governments will come under intense pressure during the transition period, as major vested interests will lose from both the stabilization program and liberalization of markets.

For Chile itself, the outlook seems relatively bright. It has undergone a remarkable economic transformation from an import-substituting economy with extensive state intervention to an open, market-oriented economy. It has successfully restored democratic government, and in the first few years that government has affirmed its commitment to an economic strategy that continues to emphasize open markets and a pragmatic and very orthodox approach to fiscal-monetary policy. But the transition to open markets and the recovery from a deep economic recession are both largely complete. Now Chile needs to shift the focus of its economic policies to sustaining growth over the long term.

First, Chile cannot continue to base its growth strategy on redundant supplies of labor, and it will need to pay more attention to increasing the quality of its work force and expanding capital formation as the basis for future gains in living standards. Present rates of national saving are sufficient to support a future growth rate of only about 4 percent a year. Because a heavy reliance on inflows of foreign saving limits exports and is a potential source of financial instability, the promotion of domestic saving should be a central goal of economic policy in Chile. Second, inflation remains relatively high, and the task of reducing it to international levels without precipitating a recession remains a major task of macroeconomic policy. And third, Chile's success has attracted considerable amounts of international capital, but those capital inflows create pressures on the exchange rate that conflict with an earlier strategy of using an undervalued real exchange rate to promote export-led growth. In the short run, those pressures have been offset by Central Bank interventions to sterilize a large portion of the capital inflows, but such interventions become increasingly ineffective in the longer term.

Reference

Edwards, S., and A. Cox-Edwards. 1987. *Monetarism and Liberalization: The Chilean Experiment.* Cambridge, Mass.: Ballinger.

1 Lessons from the Chilean Stabilization and Recovery

Vittorio Corbo and Stanley Fischer

THE PURPOSE of this chapter is to evaluate Chile's experience in stabilizing its economy over the past twenty years. During this period Chile had to struggle with the stabilization of very high inflation in 1973, with persistent but declining double-digit inflation between 1976 and 1982, and with continued moderate inflation in the decade after 1982. Stabilization also had an external dimension, the reduction of high current account deficits. The restoration of the external balance to manageable levels was a major goal of policy when the military government took over in 1973, following the sharp drop in the terms of trade in early 1975, and again after the external debt crisis of 1982–83.

We study the recent Chilean stabilization experience in the context of seven issues. First, why did inflation explode after price controls were lifted in the last quarter of 1973? This issue has two aspects: the extent of the money overhang and the alternatives for dealing with it—shock treatment or a gradual stabilization program. Given the political will to carry out a sharp reduction in the public sector deficit, the choice should depend on the government's ability to coordinate the evolution of the key nominal prices.

A second and related issue is the extent to which there was a monetary crunch and therefore shock treatment rather than a gradual approach to stabilization in the 1974–76 period.

The third question concerns the sources of Chile's inflationary inertia. Two possible sources need to be analyzed: slowly adjusting inflation expectations and inertia resulting from the behavior of the exchange rate and wage adjustment.

Fourth, we address the reasons for the failure of the exchange rate based stabilization program of 1978–82. Here we pay special attention to the role of exchange rate policy in the stabilization effort and in the crisis of 1982.

We thank J. Cauas, J. A. Fontaine, A. O. Krueger, and P. Meller for their comments and M. Alier and J. Davidovich for very efficient research assistance.

A fifth issue—one that is surely of the widest interest—is how Chile was able to pull out of the 1982–83 crisis and then initiate a phase of export-led growth. A key factor in the turnaround was the real devaluation, which provided a radical change in price incentives in favor of tradable activities. The question is how Chile was able to achieve a 113.1 percent real devaluation between 1981 and 1990 while maintaining a moderate rate of inflation.

In 1990 a coalition of parties from the center and the left came to power. As the coalition's economic team included many critics of the economic policies of the previous government, there was naturally some uncertainty about the policies of the new government. A particular concern was that the new government would implement populist policies. To maintain the macroeconomic achievements of the previous government, the new government had to convince the private sector that these were its intentions. In addition, the Central Bank, which had become legally independent in December 1989, wanted to demonstrate its independence in practice. Accordingly the new government in its first year implemented a stabilization program aimed at reducing the accelerating rate of inflation that it had inherited. Restrictive monetary policy was the main instrument it used to effect this. The sixth issue that we will investigate is whether this was the correct way to reduce inflation in early 1990.

In recent years, several countries that have reduced inflation to the range of 10 to 15 percent a year have been attempting to reduce their inflation further, to single-digit and even international levels. In the past three years, Chile has announced and pursued a goal of gradually reducing inflation toward international levels. The issues and problems associated with pursuing this objective are different from those encountered in reducing triple-digit annual inflation. We therefore analyze this problem in a separate section.

The Economic Background

As a consequence of the trade and industrial policies of the preceding forty years, the Chilean economy was practically isolated from the world economy by the end of 1973.[1] The average nominal import tariff was 105 percent; tariffs ranged from nil for some inputs and essential consumer goods to 750 percent for goods considered as luxuries. There were also many nontariff barriers, such as a requirement for a ninety-day non-interest-bearing deposit amounting to ten times the import value, import and export quotas, and prior approval for all

1. For economic policies in Chile up to 1973 see Universidad de Chile (1963), Corbo (1974), and Ffrench-Davis (1973). For economic policies during the Allende regime see Cauas and Corbo (1972), Bitar (1986), and Larraín and Meller (1991).

types of imports. Not surprisingly, the few imports that resulted were mostly intermediate goods, followed by capital goods and a few essential consumer goods. Copper was the principal export, making export earnings almost entirely dependent on copper prices.

During the Allende administration (November 1970–September 1973), international trade was taken over almost entirely by the government. By 1973, six widely different exchange rates prevailed; the ratio between the highest and the lowest was 52:1. As a direct result of the system of protection, export activities were heavily taxed. Private capital inflows were almost nonexistent.

During the socialist administration of Allende, the government also directly or indirectly took control of a substantial part of productive activities. The agrarian reform, initiated in the Alessandri administration (1958–64) and intensified during the Frei administration (1964–70), was drastically accelerated during the Allende government, with the result that practically all large estates were dismembered. The banking system was nationalized.[2]

In other sectors of the economy private businesses were taken over by workers' councils. Alternatively, the government bought company shares to extend what was then called the area of social property. Multinationals were expropriated, in some cases—copper enterprises, for example—without compensation. This brought the government into conflict with various foreign governments, especially with the United States.

On the macroeconomic front, the Allende government pursued populist policies. In 1971 current government spending grew by 12.4 percent in real terms, and the fiscal deficit reached 10.7 percent of GDP. Fueled by this aggressive expansion of demand, GDP grew 9 percent in real terms in 1971 (see table 1-1). In the same year, the money supply grew by 66 percent in real terms—a result of the large growth in high-powered money to finance the rising public sector deficit and the inertia of prices.

Measured inflation in 1971 was relatively low, but price controls and commodity and factor market rationing became widespread. During the following two years, the government continued its expansionary policies and intensified price controls. Consequently the fiscal deficit rose from 2.7 percent of GDP in 1970 to almost 25 percent of GDP in 1973. Because this deficit was financed mostly by borrowing from the Central Bank and because imports were controlled, pressures on domestic prices rose. The government tried to contain inflation by means of still tighter price controls, a policy that resulted in active

2. As the government could not pass the required expropriation law to take over the property of the banks from the previous shareholders, it offered attractive prices to buy the shares in the open market. This process took place mostly in 1971. By 1972 almost all the banking system was in public hands.

Table 1-1. Macroeconomic Indicators, 1960–92
Percent unless otherwise specified

Years	Growth of GDP	Growth of real domestic expenditure	Trade deficit[a,b]	Current account deficit[a]	Public sector deficit[a,c]	Price of copper[d]	Inflation[e]	Unemployment rate[f]	Real exchange rate[g]	Real interest rate[h]
1960	n.a.	n.a.	2.9	3.8	4.6	30.8	5.5	7.1	78.6	…
1961	4.8	6.1	4.3	5.5	4.5	28.7	9.6	8.0	72.6	…
1962	4.7	2.5	1.4	3.0	5.8	29.3	27.7	7.9	69.7	…
1963	6.3	5.8	2.5	4.3	4.9	29.3	45.4	7.5	79.4	…
1964	2.2	2.9	0.9	2.7	3.9	44.1	38.4	7.0	71.3	…
1965	0.8	0.4	−0.8	1.3	4.1	58.7	25.8	6.4	74.9	…
1966	11.2	16.5	−1.1	1.4	2.5	69.5	17.0	6.1	78.4	…
1967	3.2	0.6	−1.4	1.6	1.3	51.1	21.9	4.7	82.5	…
1968	3.6	4.8	−0.8	2.0	1.5	56.1	27.9	4.9	88.9	…
1969	3.7	5.8	−2.3	0.6	0.4	66.6	29.3	5.5	93.5	…
1970	2.1	1.8	−0.7	1.2	2.7	64.2	36.1	5.7	93.4	…
1971	9.0	9.7	1.0	2.1	10.7	49.3	28.2	3.9	85.6	…
1972	−1.2	1.0	3.5	3.9	13.0	48.6	255.4	3.3	64.7	…
1973	−5.6	−6.2	1.9	2.7	24.7	80.8	608.7	5.0	74.4	…
1974	1.0	−2.4	−0.7	0.4	3.5	93.3	369.2	9.5	122.7	…

Year										
1975	-12.9	-20.8	2.0	5.2	0.9	55.9	343.3	14.8	147.1	…
1976	3.5	0.2	-4.3	-1.7	-0.6	63.6	198.0	12.7	124.1	…
1977	9.9	14.2	1.8	3.7	-0.1	59.3	84.2	11.8	100.0	16.3
1978	8.2	9.7	3.3	5.2	-1.5	61.9	37.2	14.2	111.4	18.9
1979	8.3	10.5	2.8	5.4	-3.3	89.8	38.9	13.6	112.2	15.6
1980	7.8	9.3	4.2	7.1	-4.5	99.2	31.2	10.4	97.2	10.1
1981	5.5	11.6	10.3	14.5	-0.8	78.9	9.5	11.3	84.5	14.7
1982	-14.1	-24.1	1.9	9.2	3.5[8.8]	67.1	20.7	19.6	94.2	15.6
1983	-0.7	-4.6	-2.7	5.4	3.2(7.5)	72.2	23.1	14.6	113.1	11.2
1984	6.3	8.5	1.1	10.7	4.3(9.1)	62.4	23.0	13.9	118.2	9.2
1985	2.4	-1.9	-2.8	8.3	2.5(9.8)	64.3	26.4	12.0	145.2	9.1
1986	5.7	5.3	-3.8	6.9	2.1(5.0)	62.3	17.4	8.8	159.7	9.1
1987	5.7	7.3	-4.1	4.3	0.2(1.5)	81.1	21.5	7.9	166.6	7.6
1988	7.4	8.9	-7.2	0.7	-0.1	117.9	12.7	6.3	177.6	7.4
1989	10.0	12.2	-3.6	3.1	-1.2	129.1	21.4	5.3	173.5	8.9
1990	2.1	0.1	-2.9	2.8	0.7	120.9	27.3	5.7	180.1	12.7
1991	6.0	4.5	-4.9	-0.2	-1.0	106.1	18.7	5.5	169.9	8.5
1992	10.4	13.2	-2.1	1.7	-0.5	103.6	12.7	4.5	156.7	8.3

SOURCES: For growth of GDP, growth of real domestic expenditure, trade deficit, current account deficit, public sector deficit, unemployment rate, and real interest rate, Central Bank of Chile, *Indicadores Económicos y Sociales*. Monthly Bulletin for years since 1988. For nonfinancial public sector (public sector deficit), *Indicadores Económicos y Sociales* and, from 1974, T. Flores, "Sector Público No Financiero," PIMA, Instituto de Economía, Universidad Católica de Chile. For corrected CPI, CIEPLAN. For real exchange rate, Central Bank of Chile Real Exchange Rate corrected by CIEPLAN CPI.

a. Percent of GDP.
b. Computed with national account information at current prices.
c. The figures in parentheses include an estimate of the quasi-fiscal subsidies channeled through the Central Bank (Larrañaga 1989).
d. U.S.$ per pound.
e. Percent change in CPI, December-December.
f. Percent of labor force.
g. Increases indicate a real depreciation of the domestic currency.
h. Indexed interest rates on one- to three-year loans. For the period 1977–80, figures correspond to the indexed interest rate on 90- to 365-day loans.

black markets, where consumer goods were available at prices many times the official price. At the same time, enterprises faced a chronic shortage of basic inputs at official prices. As a result, black markets also emerged for inputs.

The Allende government's expansionary policies caused a progressive deterioration of the current account deficit, which reached 3.9 percent of GDP in 1972 (see table 1-1). The government used the large foreign reserves it had inherited from the Frei administration to finance the current account deficits of 1971 and 1972, and by August 1973 the reserves were exhausted. Since the government's populist policies made it difficult to obtain foreign financing, the stage was set for a major balance of payments crisis.

The government that took power in September 1973 inherited an economy closed to international trade, dominated by the public sector, and experiencing severe macroeconomic imbalances in the form of accelerating inflation and a current account deficit close to 3 percent of GDP without access to foreign financing and without international reserves. Relative prices were severely distorted, and the production and distribution of goods were determined mainly by bureaucratic rules. The labor market was dominated by a few organizations that were fighting for political objectives rather than for the well-being of the workers. The country had practically no foreign exchange reserves, and the nonfinancial public sector had a deficit of close to 25 percent of GDP (see table 1-1).

Macroeconomic Developments in the Past Twenty Years

The Chilean economy grew modestly in the year after the coup, but then experienced a deep recession in 1975. Thereafter the economy recovered and grew rapidly until 1981, when a new crisis developed. After a costly adjustment effort, growth resumed in 1984. The average growth rate between 1984 and 1992 was 6.9 percent; growth in 1992 was 10.4 percent (see figure 1-1).[3]

Inflation was at three-digit annual levels until 1976, averaging 296 percent for the period 1974–76. From 1977 to 1980 inflation averaged 46.5 percent a year (see figure 1-2). Annual inflation temporarily reached 9.5 percent in 1981 and then hovered around 20 percent a year for the period 1982–92. However, as shown in figure 1-2, quarterly inflation was much more variable. The lowest levels of inflation during these years were reached in both 1988 and 1992.

---

3. For economic policies and performance during this period see Corbo (1985a), Edwards and Cox-Edwards (1987), Harberger (1985), Fontaine (1989), Meller (1990), Meller (1992), and Rosende (1987). For details of the fiscal adjustment, see Corbo (1990).

Figure 1-1. Annual Growth of Real GDP, 1970–92

Percent

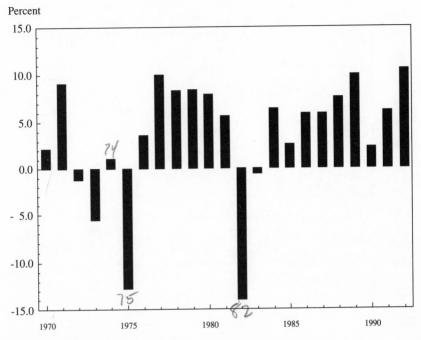

SOURCE: National Accounts, Central Bank of Chile.

The new government undertook a massive fiscal adjustment in 1974, cutting subsidies and introducing a value added tax. The fiscal deficit declined from nearly 25 percent of GDP in 1973 to only 4 percent in 1974. Despite this massive adjustment, the economy grew, mainly because the government removed widespread controls and production rebounded from its state of virtual collapse at the end of the Allende regime.

The recession of 1975 had three major causes. The first was the large drop in the terms of trade, with copper prices falling by about 45 percent in real terms (see table 1-1) and the price of oil rising by a factor of three. The cumulative effect was a drop in the terms of trade of close to 40 percent. A second factor was the severe adjustment program (beyond that of 1974), in the form of restrictive fiscal and monetary policy, that was introduced in April 1975. The program had three goals: to stop inflation; to make it possible to service the external debt; and to reduce an emerging current account deficit that could not be financed externally at that time. A third cause of the recession was the large jump in the price level that had followed the lifting of price controls. Prices in Chile had been controlled since 1952, and removal of the controls

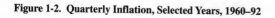

Figure 1-2. Quarterly Inflation, Selected Years, 1960–92

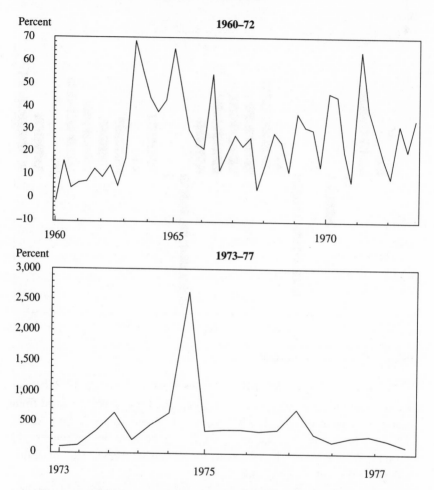

without any attempt to coordinate the private sector response produced a price increase that made fiscal and monetary policy more restrictive than expected.[4]

In 1976 the economy was still experiencing high inflation (198.3 percent a year) and high unemployment (15 percent) and had only U.S.$107.9 million in international reserves, equivalent to less than one month of imports. Nonetheless, as the reforms progressed and their credibility was enhanced, the economy started to grow. Growth in GDP was 3.5 percent in 1976, 9.9 percent in 1977, and 8.2 percent in 1978 (see table 1-1).

4. Ramos (1986). Short-term costs as a consequence of the restructuring called for by the trade liberalization policies were not important in 1975 as the reduction in import barriers was

Figure 1-2. (*continued*)

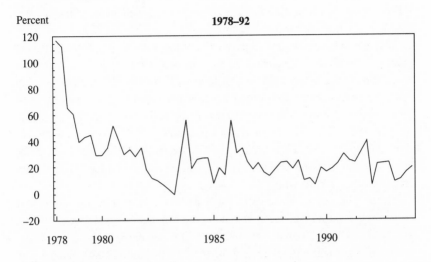

Percent   **1978–92**

Source: Corrected CPI of CIEPLAN.

With the resumption of growth, the reduction of inflation became the main priority of the economic team. The slow progress in reducing inflation, despite a budget that was already in surplus starting in 1976 (see table 1-1), persuaded the policymakers that it would take more than further fiscal tightening to reduce inflation. In February 1978 an active crawling peg exchange rate regime was introduced with the goal of reducing inflation by slowing the rate of nominal devaluation. This policy culminated in the fixing of the exchange rate in June 1979, even though domestic inflation for that month was still running at an annual rate of 37 percent.

The objective of achieving a stable real exchange rate consistent with the macroeconomic fundamentals conflicted with the use of the nominal exchange rate as an anchor for the price level while nominal wages and most financial contracts were fully indexed to past inflation. The natural result of this conflict was a rapid real appreciation of the exchange rate. The exchange rate policy, in conjunction with a domestic financial liberalization carried out while the financial system was poorly regulated and supervised, had severe repercussions on the macroeconomic front: it was one of the main causes of the boom that developed in the following years and of the deep recession in 1982–83.

---

more than compensated by a sharp real devaluation. Corbo (1985a) and de la Cuadra and Hachette (1992).

The boom resulted from the drastic reduction in the cost of foreign borrowing implied by the real appreciation of the exchange rate. The bust came when, following the drastic decline in the availability of foreign loans, a sharp depreciation of the currency was called for.

With the introduction in February 1978 of the crawling peg formula for the nominal peso-dollar exchange rate, the cost of foreign borrowing decreased from 22.6 percent a year in the fourth quarter of 1977 to 10.2 percent a year in the first quarter of 1978 and became negative from then until the last quarter of 1980.[5] This reduction in borrowing costs unleashed a large increase in capital inflows, which caused domestic real interest rates to fall. Inappropriate regulation and supervision of the banking system exacerbated the traditional problems of moral hazard associated with deposit insurance and facilitated the increase in foreign borrowing.

The drop in real peso and dollar interest rates and the large increase in real credit fueled a rapid increase in real domestic expenditure, which rose by 10.5 percent in 1979, 9.3 percent in 1980, and 11.6 percent in 1981. Meanwhile, growth of GDP reached 8.3 percent in 1979, 7.8 percent in 1980, and 5.5 percent in 1981 (see table 1-1).

The widening gap between the rate of growth of real domestic expenditure and real GDP, which was reflected in the larger trade deficit and financed by an increase in foreign borrowing, built up demand pressures in the market for nontradable goods. The trade balance deficit rose from 2.8 percent of GDP in 1979 to 4.2 percent in 1980 and to 10.3 percent in 1981. While increased expenditures on tradable goods caused imports to rise and exports to fall, the rise in expenditures on nontradable goods resulted in a rise in their prices. Consequently the real exchange rate appreciated by 24.1 percent between 1978 and 1981 (table 1-1).

With the emergence of a large trade deficit and unfavorable external shocks in 1981 (a decline in the terms of trade and a sharp increase in international interest rates), doubts arose about the sustainability of the current policies, and in particular about the continuation of the fixed exchange rate policy. As shown in table 1-2, there was a positive external shock of 1.2 percentage points of GDP in 1980, a negative shock equivalent to 0.5 percentage points of GDP in 1981, and a large negative shock equivalent to 3.8 percentage points of GDP in 1982. Private capital flows turned around in the face of these shocks, and a period of capital flight began late in 1981.

As a result of these events, the Chilean policymakers were faced with the

5. Corbo (1985a).

Table 1-2. External Shocks, 1977–83

Characteristics of shocks	1977–79	1980	1981	1982	1983
Total external effect (TXE)[a]	0.00	1.20	−0.52	−3.80	−3.37
Terms of trade effect (TTE)[a]	0.00	1.04	−0.55	−1.87	−0.88
Real interest rate effect $(RIRE)$[a]	0.00	0.16	0.03	−1.92	−2.49
Price of exports (PX)	1.0000	1.1049	0.9424	0.7437	0.7175
Price of imports (PM)	1.0000	1.0501	0.9715	0.8495	0.7849
Average real interest rate of foreign debt (RIR)	−0.0018	−0.0056	−0.0026	0.0451	0.0590
Ratio of foreign debt to GDP (FD/GDP)	0.4104	0.4020	0.4761	0.7047	0.8816
Ratio of exports to GDP (X/GDP)	0.2149	0.2282	0.1642	0.1936	0.2404
Ratio of imports to GDP (M/GDP)	0.2415	0.2698	0.2675	0.2125	0.2132

SOURCE: Authors' calculations.
a. Percent. The indicators TXE, TTE, and $RIRE$ were calculated with the following formulas:
$TXE = TTE + RIRE$
$TTE = (PX_t/PX_o - 1) * (X/GDP)_o - (PM_t/PM_o - 1) * (M/GDP)_o$
$RIRE = - (RIR_t - RIR_o) * (FD/GDP)_o$
where the period 0 is the average 1977–79.

need to adjust the current account deficit even before the international debt crisis broke in August 1982 (see figure 1-3). The adjustment was made through a deep cut in total domestic expenditures, brought about by a sharp increase in real interest rates and a credit crunch. As the nominal exchange rate was fixed and wages were indexed by law to past inflation, the relative price of nontradables—the reciprocal of the real exchange rate—was very inflexible. Accordingly, the cut in domestic expenditures reduced the output but not the price of nontradables.

Eventually, in June 1982, in the midst of a severe recession—a 14.1 percent drop in GDP in 1982 and a more than 10 percentage point increase in the unemployment rate—the fixed exchange rate policy had to be abandoned and compulsory wage indexation eliminated. A series of nominal devaluations took place.[6]

At the trough of the 1982–83 depression, the liberalization policies of the previous eight years were under attack on every front: entrepreneurs' associations were asking for protection for import-competing sectors; unions were asking for employment policies to decrease unemployment; highly indebted families and firms were asking for debt relief; and banks were asking for a

6. For a short period the exchange rate was allowed to float.

Figure 1-3. Current Account Deficit, 1970–92

Percent of GDP

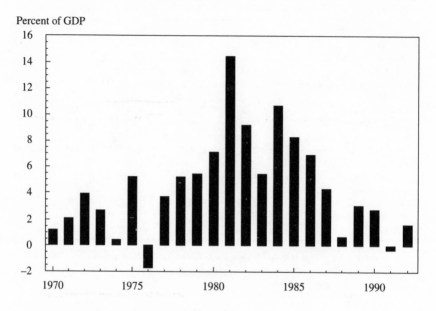

SOURCE: Computed with National Accounts information at current prices.

bailout to solve their increasing problem of nonperforming loans. Popular discontent was growing. Monthly days of protest, which began to claim many lives, expressed this discontent. There were dissenting views within the government about the causes of the recession and the way out of it. Not surprisingly, at the end of 1983, the Pinochet government was searching for a policy to pull the economy out of recession.

Although it made concessions, the government adhered to the main thrust of its policies. It accommodated the pressures for protection by raising the maximum tariff to 20 percent in March 1983 and to 35 percent in September 1984 but turned down the request for a differentiated tariff structure. It maintained free access to foreign exchange for dividends and capital remittances associated with direct foreign investment and the service of foreign debt. From the beginning the government developed a strategy of renegotiating the foreign debt, but with the declared goal of servicing it in full and, eventually, reestablishing full access to international capital markets. On this point, Chile took a very different route from that taken by many other heavily indebted countries.

Much had to be done to renegotiate domestic debt and to rescue the banking system. During the period of the sharp recession, in order to prevent widespread bankruptcies, the government introduced a comprehensive program to rescue financially distressed institutions. It bought their nonperforming loans, paying with Central Bank bonds. Commercial banks were supposed to buy back their loans with their profits; they were not allowed to distribute dividends to the previous shareholders until their loans had been redeemed. Similarly, the Central Bank during this period acquired the external debt of the rescued commercial banks. These rescue programs were financed through a large increase in domestic debt and also, in later years, through external borrowing as the international financial institutions resumed lending to Chile.

The public sector deficit as a percentage of GDP also increased in these years, as social programs were introduced to assist the unemployed and tax revenues suffered from the recession. As shown in table 1-1, the public sector deficit reached 4.3 percent of GDP in 1984, while the unemployment rate peaked at 19.6 percent of the labor force in 1982 and remained in the double digits well into 1985.[7]

The size of the nonfinancial public sector deficit does not tell the whole story of the public finances, as the Central Bank was also experiencing heavy losses from its programs to rescue financially distressed financial institutions and private sector borrowers. In 1985 alone, these Central Bank losses were estimated to be as high as 7.8 percent of GDP.[8]

The increase in the current account deficit in 1984 to 11 percent of GDP forced further contraction of fiscal policy in 1985 and a tightening of credit. These policy changes were introduced early in 1985 by the new minister of finance, Hernán Büchi, who had been a junior member of the liberal economic team during the 1974–81 period. Büchi presided over the second restructuring of the Chilean economy from 1985 onward. The government's comprehensive adjustment program aimed to restore both macroeconomic balance and economic growth in a situation of restricted access to foreign borrowing. The tradable sector (exportable and efficient import competing sectors) was expected to be the engine of growth. Incentives were expected to come from a reduction in tariff levels and a sharp real devaluation. The government would assist by taking an active role in promoting Chilean exports in international markets.[9]

The real exchange rate more than doubled between 1981 and 1990 as a result of the large nominal devaluations, the reduction in the average tariff (to 30 percent in March 1985, to 20 percent in June 1985, and to 15 percent in

7. Including workers engaged in emergency public works programs, the unemployment rate in 1983 was close to 30 percent of the labor force.

8. Larrañaga (1989).

9. A clear statement of the main thrust of the Economic Recovery Program appears in Büchi (1985).

Figure 1-4. Real Exchange Rate, 1970–92

Index[a]

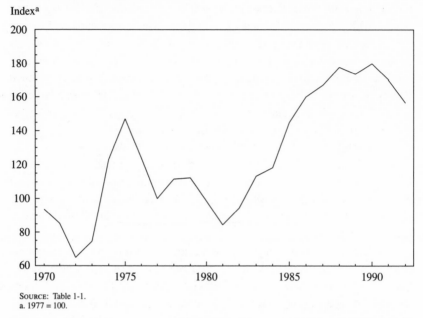

Source: Table 1-1.
a. 1977 = 100.

January 1988), and the supportive macroeconomic policies of the time (see table 1-1 and figure 1-4). This new policy changed incentives drastically in favor of export-oriented activities, initiating a period of export-led growth. As the export-led process gained momentum, the export-oriented sectors began to realize large increases in efficiency through improvements in quality control, better marketing, and new technologies.

Following the implementation of this adjustment program, Chile entered a period of export-led growth that lasted well into the 1990s. Growth in GDP reached 6.3 percent in 1984, declined to 2.4 percent in 1985, and then increased to 5.7 percent in 1986. In the same years inflation reached 23.0 percent in 1984, 26.4 percent in 1985, and 17.4 percent in 1986 (table 1-1 and figure 1-2). In the meantime, the unemployment rate, which had reached close to 20 percent in 1982 (counting those in emergency public works programs as employed), was reduced to 8.8 percent by 1986.

Vigorous growth continued after 1986 partly because, as the debt crisis was increasingly left behind, the positive results of the policy reforms of the previous twelve years started to emerge. With the economy by now delivering growth of more than 5 percent a year and with the unemployment rate coming down rapidly, public support for the economic policies began to increase. When the new coalition government came to power in March 1990, it wisely

Figure 1-5. Public Sector Deficit, 1970–92

Percent of GDP

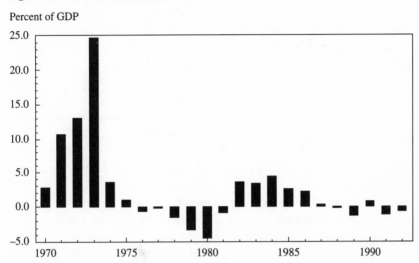

SOURCE: Table 1-1.

decided to maintain the market-oriented, open-economy policies of the past administration. Its main departure from the policies of the previous government has been its concern for improving access to education and health for the poorest groups in the population. To accomplish this objective, it promptly negotiated with the opposition a temporary tax reform that raised government revenues by around 2.8 percent of GDP to finance a similar increase in social sector expenditures.

Attempts to Achieve Stabilization

Chile has a long history of inflation. In the 1960s inflation averaged 24.3 percent a year. In the early 1970s, under the populist policies of the Allende government, inflation accelerated, reaching an annual rate of approximately 463 percent in August 1973, the month before Allende's fall. Foreign reserves were running down, and the current account deficit reached 2.7 percent of GDP. Underlying the acceleration of inflation and the balance of payments crisis of that period was a consolidated nonfinancial public sector deficit of close to 25 percent of GDP (see figure 1-5).

Among the main objectives of the military government that took power in September 1973 were the elimination of the severe and pressing macroeconomic disequilibriums that it had inherited and the reestablishment of a market economy. Toward this end, reforms were introduced in eight main areas:

(1) an initial stabilization program to reduce an inflation rate that was reaching 1,000 percent a year; (2) profound public sector reforms aimed at permanently eliminating the public sector deficit and reducing government distortions; (3) trade reforms to provide appropriate incentives to export-oriented and import-competing activities; (4) a social security reform to change a bankrupt pay-as-you-go pension system into a system based on individual capitalization; (5) financial sector reform to improve the efficiency of financial intermediation; (6) reform of the labor market to facilitate industrial restructuring and the drastic but essential reallocation of labor from the highly protected, import-competing sectors toward the export-oriented activities; (7) a comprehensive privatization program to get the state out of the activities that the private sector could undertake and to expand activities where the public sector has a central role to play, as in the provision of basic health, education, and nutrition for the poorest groups in the population; and (8) reforms of social sectors to improve the incentive system in the production and provision of social services and to target the provision of social programs to the poorest groups in the population.[10] To achieve these goals, the government would have to revise public sector responsibilities and sharply curtail the size of the public sector and its participation in economic activities.

In an effort to allow the price system to return to operation, the government preceded these reforms with a liberalization of markets. The monetary expansion and the price controls of the Allende years had resulted in a money overhang. The first decision the military government had to make was how to deal with the money overhang. Two possibilities were open: the first, to introduce a capital levy, and the second, to allow a jump in the price level. The authorities chose the second option. As a result of the price liberalization, inflation temporarily increased to an annual rate of 2,600 percent between the third and fourth quarters of 1973.

From the beginning the new economic authorities thought that the high fiscal deficit and the associated increase in money supply were at the root of the high inflation. They also believed, however, that because of inflation inertia inflation should be reduced only gradually. Despite a drastic fiscal adjustment, which cut the budget deficit by 21 percentage points of GDP in just one year, the rate of inflation in 1974 was still 369 percent. Monetary policy in this period was supposed to be geared to provide enough liquidity to support the price increases resulting from higher costs.[11]

Early in 1975 two developments prompted the government to change its

10. Corbo (1993).

11. It should be mentioned that existing fiscal accounts showed a public sector deficit of 10.5 percent of GDP for 1974. The fiscal adjustment of 1974 was, therefore, done in that context.

stabilization strategy in favor of a less gradual approach. First, a drastic worsening of the terms of trade (a reduction in the copper price of almost 45 percent in real terms and the persistence of the oil price increase of the previous year) suggested that the resultant current account deficit would be difficult to finance. Second, the government was unhappy with the pace at which inflation was being reduced. Indeed, monthly inflation even intensified in early 1975, reaching 17 percent in February and March when devaluation was accelerated to deal with the worsening of the current account.

The acceleration of inflation (inflation for January-April was 90 percent) prompted the preparation of a more radical fiscal adjustment. The new program, announced in April 1975, included a further fiscal adjustment in the form of a 10 percent temporary hike in income taxes, a 10 percent additional consumption tax on luxury items, a reduction of between 15 and 25 percent in budgeted expenditures on goods and services by public entities and public enterprises, and the elimination of all exemptions to the value added tax. Money growth was expected to decelerate along with the reduction of the deficit in the nonfinancial public sector.

To support the new export-led growth strategy, and as a response to the sharp fall in the terms of trade, the fiscal and monetary corrections were accompanied by an aggressive crawling peg policy geared to achieving and sustaining a higher real exchange rate. Also, starting in October 1974, public sector wages were indexed to provide full compensation for the previous period's inflation. At the same time the government mandated wage adjustment for the private sector based on past inflation.[12] These exchange rate and wage adjustment mechanisms built inflationary inertia into the economy.

The government announcement of the new measures included an explicit statement providing for full deposit insurance, thus setting the stage for undue risk taking by financial intermediaries: "All financial operations of the banking system as well as of the Savings and Loan Associations are guaranteed by the Central Bank, which has been financing the Savings and Loan deficits and shall continue to do so whenever this should be required."[13]

As a result of the substantial fiscal correction, the nonfinancial public sector deficit was reduced by a further 2.6 percentage points of GDP in 1975, in spite of the sharp recession (see table 1-1). The size of the fiscal correction and the

12. At the beginning, to avoid large increases in real wages while inflation was being sharply reduced, the size of the adjustment did not compensate fully for past inflation.

13. Causs (1979, p. 161). This latter announcement, introduced during a major crisis and when bank regulation and supervision were extremely weak, exacerbated moral hazard problems in the financial system. Problems related to moral hazards were one of the important causes of the financial crisis of the early 1980s.

accompanying monetary squeeze in the presence of inflation inertia magnified the effects of the drop in the terms of trade.[14] The current account deficit for 1975, which in early 1975 had been expected to be $2 billion for the year, turned out to be only $492 million at year's end. However, inflation for the year was 343.3 percent, only marginally below the 369.2 percent of 1974. The costs of reducing inflation and the external deficit in terms of the drop in GDP and the resulting increase in unemployment proved very high.

Unhappy with the progress in reducing inflation, and observing a surplus of $148 million in the current account of the balance of payments in 1976, the Central Bank undertook a revaluation of 10 percent in June 1976 and again in March 1977. Inflation declined rapidly, but it was still 198 percent in 1976 and 84.2 percent in 1977. The unemployment rate came down to 12.7 percent in 1976 and to 11.8 percent in 1977.

Late in 1977 a debate began to emerge in government circles on the dynamics of inflation and the slow pace at which it was being reduced. At the center of the debate was the role of the exchange rate policy in the perpetuation of inflation. In an influential paper, Barandiarán questioned the exchange rate policy that was being followed.[15] He recommended a passive crawling peg policy in the form of a forward-looking preannounced devaluation schedule, at a decreasing rate, as a vehicle to shape inflation expectations and to provide a nominal anchor for the evolution of the price level. Another group was in favor of moving toward a flexible exchange rate with monetary aggregate targets.[16]

An important shift in stabilization policy in the direction of Barandiarán's proposal occurred in February 1978 when the government instituted a system of preannounced rates of devaluation of the peso. This policy culminated in June 1979 in a fixed exchange rate of 39 pesos to the dollar, a rate that was maintained until June 1982. The government believed that the crawling peg, and a fortiori the fixed exchange rate, would reduce inflation both by shaping expectations about inflation and by directly influencing the prices of tradable goods (import-competing and exportable goods) on all domestic prices.

However, the indexation system for wages and financial contracts was not changed when the exchange rate policy was changed. Since October 1974

14. According to the old public sector deficit figures, the fiscal correction was even more severe, with a reduction in the deficit from 10.5 percent of GDP in 1974 to 2.6 percent of GDP in 1975. Ministerio de Hacienda (1982).

15. Barandiarán (1977).

16. McKinnon (1988) describes the options for slowing down inflation that were considered at the time.

wages had been indexed to past inflation with full compensation for increases in the CPI. The new labor code of 1979 also ensured that, for workers subject to collective bargaining, the lowest wage offered would be equal to the previous wage augmented by the CPI change since the last wage contract. Full indexation to the CPI applied also, on a voluntary basis, to financial contracts, to house rentals, and to many other private contracts. This extensive indexing, in the context of declining inflation with a fixed exchange rate, was bound to result in a slow pace of reduction of inflation and an appreciation of the real exchange rate (see figure 1-4).

Another problem of the post-1975 period was the high real interest rates that followed the deregulation of the domestic financial system. In response to these high real rates, pressure started to build for the liberalization of capital inflows so that domestic firms could borrow at lower foreign rates. Following the introduction of the forward-looking devaluation schedule, the initial spread between the domestic interest rate and the foreign interest rate—adjusting for the expected rate of devaluation—increased the incentives to bring capital into Chile. Weak financial regulations and institutions, in the presence of full deposit insurance, resulted in undue risk taking in the financial system. The result was—as elsewhere in Latin America—large capital inflows, an expenditure boom, and a sharp real appreciation. Lax lending practices by the private financial system financed a boom in expenditures that resulted in a deficit in the trade balance of 10.3 percent of GDP in 1981.

This was also a year in which the public sector had a surplus of 0.8 percent of GDP, down from a surplus of 4.5 percent of GDP in 1980. The decline in the public sector surplus was due mostly to the transitory cost of a change in the social security system.

After three years in which the exchange rate was fixed, inflation declined to a single-digit annual level in 1981. But this achievement, which brought with it a 25 percent real appreciation, did not last long. When external financing was drastically reduced in 1982, the economic authorities decided to use a hands-off policy to allow the textbook automatic adjustment mechanism to accommodate domestic expenditures to a much reduced level of foreign financing.

The reduction in expenditures required a large real depreciation to avoid unemployment in the nontradable sector. With the nominal exchange rate fixed, this adjustment could be made only through differentially lower inflation in Chile than abroad. But the indexed wage adjustment mechanism implied substantial rigidity in the adjustment of the real exchange rate. The method selected to stabilize the external account thus became very costly. GDP dropped

14.1 percent in 1982, and the unemployment rate increased 8.3 percentage points between 1981 and 1982.[17]

The sharp recession proved to be too much for the poorly regulated financial system. As a major financial crisis unfolded early in 1983, the government had to intervene to rescue the financial system, to support financially distressed firms and households, and to assist the unemployed. As a result, the public sector deficit, including the quasi-fiscal deficit of the Central Bank, showed a large increase.

The Central Bank played an essential role in rescuing the financial system and in distributing substantial subsidies to the private sector during the crisis. The Central Bank was able to use its access to domestic and foreign financial markets to finance its rescue operations. As a result, the expenses associated with the rescue of troubled financial institutions, stemming from the financial crisis of 1983, were not financed by printing money but instead by issuing domestic and foreign interest-bearing liabilities of the Central Bank. Even when the public sector deficit (including the quasi-fiscal deficit of the Central Bank) was running close to 10 percent of GDP in 1985, the Central Bank tapped domestic and external financial markets to obtain nonmonetary financing by issuing its own debt. As the initial debt of the public sector was very small and the risk of lending to a bankrupt private sector very high, domestic real interest rates did not increase much.[18] From then on, Chile initiated a second fiscal adjustment, as drastic as that undertaken in the period 1974–76.

Once the financial crisis was under control, Chile faced the problem of achieving a turnaround in its trade balance while creating the conditions for sustainable growth. By 1984 the nonfinancial public sector deficit had reached 4.3 percent of GDP; the losses the Central Bank incurred to support the financial system and private borrowers have been estimated at another 4.8 percent of GDP.[19]

The stabilization program put in place in 1985 was part of a broader structural adjustment program aimed at restoring the trade balance to a sustainable level and maintaining the microeconomic and institutional reforms introduced in the preceding ten years. The program included a sharp fiscal adjustment assisted by an exchange rate policy that facilitated the increase in the real exchange rate toward its higher equilibrium level. The exchange rate policy intro-

17. Of course we are not claiming that the entire decline in output was due to the overvaluation of the exchange rate.

18. In this period Chile also initiated a monetary policy based on real interest rate targeting instead of monetary targeting. Fontaine (1989).

19. Larrañaga (1989).

duced was again a crawling peg, but now it was passive and retroactive, adjusting the exchange rate for the differential between domestic and foreign inflation. This system is similar to the one that existed up to February 1978; it differed in having some additional flexibility built in with the introduction of an exchange rate band around the target exchange rate.

The last stabilization episode of interest is the current struggle to reduce inflation to the levels of industrial countries. Inflation has come down from 27.3 percent in 1990 to 18.7 percent in 1991 and to 12.7 percent in 1992. The nonfinancial public sector has a surplus, and the authorities have announced their decision to reduce the inflation rate gradually toward international levels. As the economic system currently lacks an explicit nominal anchor for the price level, discussion has centered on how best to achieve the desired reduction in inflation. The issue of how to reduce a 10–25 percent a year inflation rate to the levels of industrial countries is an important question, which is being asked by policymakers in many other countries.[20] We will return to it.

Issues Underlying Stabilization

In this section we turn to some of the questions raised in the introduction.

Dealing with a High Open and Repressed Inflation

Was there a money overhang in 1973? To answer this question we estimated a money-demand equation for the period 1960.1 to 1970.4. The money-demand equation is standard for a country with interest-rate controls.[21] The equation is a semi-logarithmic function given by

$$\ln m_t = a_0 + a_1 \ln y_t^p + a_2 R_t + a_3 \ln m_{t-1},$$

where

m = the stock of real balances, measured as M1 divided by the CPI;
y^p = permanent income, computed as the predicted value of y_t in a four-period autoregressive model of GDP;
R = the cost of holding money, measured as the contemporaneous inflation rate.

The estimated equation, with standard errors in parentheses, is

20. Dornbusch and Fischer (1993).
21. By now there is considerable literature on demand for money equations for Chile. See in particular Corbo (1982b), Matte and Rojas (1989), and Herrera and Vergara (1992).

$$\ln m_t = -3.288 + 0.397 \ln y_t^p - 0.508 R_t + 0.808 \ln m_{t-1}.$$
$$\quad\quad (1.211)\quad (0.145)\quad\quad (0.206)\quad\quad (0.078)$$

$R^2 = 0.973$; Durbin-Watson $= 1.98$; Period $= 1960.1–1970.4$

Using the above equation, plus the observed values of income and inflation and the observed evolution of the price level, we obtained dynamic simulations of the quantity of money demanded for the period 1971.1 to 1973.2.

The estimated values indicate a money overhang of 44 percent of the existing level of the money supply in 1971, of 63 percent of the money supply in 1972, and of 96 percent of the money supply in the first half of 1973. The money-demand equation estimated on the basis of data from the relatively low-inflation 1960s could conceivably give a misleading impression about the extent of the money overhang at the end of three years of high inflation. To deal with this possibility, we also computed the size of the money overhang implied by a money-demand equation estimated over the period 1975.1 to 1982.1, when inflation was high.[22] The estimated values of the money overhang from this equation are 109 percent for 1971, 145 percent for 1972, and 156 percent for the first half of 1973.

Both estimates for 1973—96 percent and 156 percent—indicate the presence of a substantial money overhang when the military government took power. Two aspects of stabilization must be considered in such circumstances: first, the elimination of the money overhang (a stock problem); and second, elimination of the public sector deficit that is the cause of the money buildup (a flow problem).

Elimination of the money overhang can in principle be achieved through a once-and-for-all increase in the price level or through monetary reform. At the end of World War II, most European countries used the route of a monetary reform.[23] The option of allowing a jump in the price level runs the risk of starting a chain reaction of increases in other prices, initiating a lengthy process of inflation. The risk is higher for countries with a long history of inflation.

The Chilean authorities decided to allow the price level to jump. When price controls were lifted in late 1973, the price level jumped by a factor of 2.3 between the third and fourth quarters of 1973. Since price controls were re-

---

22. The estimated demand for money equation is given by:
$$\ln m_t = -4.149 + 0.623 \ln y_t^p - 0.651 R_t + 0.482 \ln m_{t-1}.$$
$$\quad\quad (2.772)\quad (0.306)\quad\quad (0.151)\quad\quad (0.146)$$
$R^2 = 0.965$; Durbin-Watson $= 1.91$

23. Dornbusch and Wolf (1990).

moved before a clear fiscal program had been announced or put in place, a high inflation process did get under way. With no active fiscal policy, and with an exchange rate policy that, after an initial devaluation, was geared to keeping the newly achieved real exchange rate stable through nominal devaluations, high inflation was bound to continue.

Shock Treatment versus Gradualism

For countries suffering from hyperinflation and an unsustainable balance of payments situation, as Chile was in late 1973, gradual stabilization was not a real option. The balance of payments crisis had to be addressed from the beginning, and therefore a comprehensive and immediate stabilization package was the only realistic stabilization option.[24]

Although Chile was an inflationary country, annual inflation had usually hovered in the range of 20 to 30 percent. The inflation levels of 1972–73 were without parallel in Chilean history. Because of its chronic inflation, however, Chile had developed indexation mechanisms to deal with the uncertainty associated with unpredictable levels of inflation. These indexation mechanisms had built in enough inertia in the dynamics of inflation to make any shock treatment in the form of a monetary crunch difficult to sustain because of the excessive unemployment it would cause.

As we saw in the previous section, the stabilization program that Chile introduced included a sharp fiscal adjustment, a cut in the budget deficit of 21.2 percentage points of GDP in just one year, and some elements of a monetary crunch. Sjaastad and Cortés, Lagos and Galetovic, and Corbo and Solimano have found that there was a monetary crunch in 1974–75 and especially following the acceleration of inflation in the second quarters of 1975 and 1976.[25] However, the PPP (purchasing power parity) exchange rate rule and the indexation of wages introduced in October 1974 reinforced the indexation mechanisms already in existence in the Chilean economy and ensured that the pace of inflation reduction would be slow. The unemployment cost was correspondingly high.

The experience of the past twenty years shows that the adjustment would have been less costly if the massive fiscal adjustment and associated monetary crunch had been accompanied by incomes policies to break the inflationary

24. Bruno and others (1988 and 1991); Dornbusch and Fischer (1986); Dornbusch, Sturzenegger, and Wolf (1990); and Sargent (1982).
25. Sjaastad and Cortés (1978), Lagos and Galetovic (1990), and Corbo and Solimano (1991).

inertia.[26] Part of this coordinated adjustment would have involved using the exchange rate as a nominal anchor. Income policies to accompany the fiscal adjustment would have provided some breathing space for the fiscal adjustment to take effect. The use of a heterodox policy would most likely have accelerated the reduction of inflation and diminished the cost in unemployment.

One could argue that the use of incomes policies was not an option in 1973 as the country had already overused and abused price controls in the previous two years without much result. Furthermore the country had no track record that would have given it credibility about the seriousness of the proposed fiscal adjustment. We doubt that the approach used in 1973 produced better results than a more coordinated approach would have attained. But in any case, the argument that there was no track record for fiscal policy was no longer valid in early 1975, when the stabilization program was revised to increase the size of the fiscal correction. At that time a coordinated heterodox stabilization—which paid attention to wages as well as the exchange rate—would very likely have helped bring down inflation more rapidly.

The Sources of Inertia

It is generally accepted today that there was much inertia in inflation in the Chilean economy after 1974. By inertia we mean, of course, that inflation was slow to respond to contractionary policy.[27] Corbo built a model of Chilean inflation to study inflation dynamics.[28] From a model estimated for the period 1974.1 to 1983.2, he found that Chilean inflation, for that period, had considerable inertia. Up to early 1978, inertia came from both the exchange rate rule and the indexation of wages. Starting in February 1978, with the introduction of an exchange rate based stabilization program, the first source of inertia was eliminated, but wage indexation remained as an important cause of inertia.

Corbo and Solimano investigated the dynamics of Chilean inflation in this period using a small structural model.[29] For this purpose they estimated, for the period 1976.1 to 1989.1, a three-equation quarterly model of the type used by Bruno and Fischer and Fischer.[30] The model includes a price equation, an output-growth equation, and a wage equation. Corbo and Solimano found that

---

26. Kiguel and Liviatan (1988).

27. We do not here go into the question of whether inflation responded asymmetrically to increases and decreases in demand.

28. Corbo (1985b).

29. Corbo and Solimano (1991).

30. Bruno and Fischer (1986), Fischer (1986), and Fischer (1988).

the slow pace of disinflation in the 1975–78 program was due in large part to the exchange rate and wage rules that were in place.

From a counterfactual simulation they concluded—as should have been expected—that the aggressive nominal devaluations of 1975, introduced to produce a real devaluation in response to the severe external shocks of that year, slowed down the pace of disinflation. Using the same model, they found that the forward-looking exchange rate policy introduced in February 1978 had a major part, in conjunction with the indexed wages, in producing the real appreciation of 1978–81.

Edwards examines the question of inertia in the context of the use of the exchange rate as a nominal anchor.[31] He uses a reduced form of an Australian model.[32] In the reduced form, inflation is a function of lagged inflation (which comes from the wage and exchange rate equations of his structural model), foreign inflation, and the rate of change in domestic credit. Edwards also introduced a dummy variable, which takes the value of one during the fixed exchange rate period. The dummy variable interacts with the coefficient of the lagged inflation variable to allow for a reduction of inertia following the fixing of the exchange rate. The estimation results lead Edwards to conclude that the Chilean economy displayed considerable inertia during this period. He also finds that the coefficient of lagged inflation did not decrease following the fixing of the exchange rate.

We pursue here the key question of the causes of the inertia by estimating a small structural model like that used in Bruno, Corbo, and Corbo and Nam.[33] The model is given by the following set of equations:

$$(1\text{-}1) \qquad \hat{p}_t = \alpha_0 + \alpha_1 P\hat{E}XT_t + \alpha_2 P\hat{E}XT_{t-1} + \alpha_3 \hat{E}_t + \alpha_4 \hat{W}_t + \alpha_5 \hat{M}_{t-1}$$

$$(1\text{-}2) \qquad \hat{E}_t = \beta_0 + \beta_1 \hat{P}_{t-1} + \beta_2 P\hat{E}XT_{t-1} + \beta_3 DI_t$$

$$(1\text{-}3) \qquad \hat{W}_t = \gamma_0 + \gamma_1 \hat{P}_{t-1} + \gamma_2 \frac{1}{U_t}$$

$$(1\text{-}4) \qquad \hat{M}_t = \hat{P}_t + \hat{L}(y_t, R_t, M_{t-1}/P_{t-1}),$$

where

$(\hat{\ })$ = quarterly rate of change
P = consumer price index
$PEXT$ = external prices in dollars
E = exchange rate in pesos to the dollar

31. Edwards (1992).
32. Dornbusch (1980).
33. Bruno (1978), Corbo (1985b), and Corbo and Nam (1992).

Table 1-3. Parameter Estimates, Quarterly Inflation Model, February 1974–January 1982

Price equation		*Exchange rate equation*		*Wage equation*	
α_0	−0.004 (0.016)	β_0	−0.043 (0.032)	γ_0	−0.015 (0.085)
α_1	−0.147 (0.291)	β_1	1.055 (0.104)	γ_1	0.953 (0.089)
α_2	0.052 (0.289)	β_2	0.085 (0.661)	γ_2	0.439 (1.027)
α_3	0.441 (0.068)	β_3	−0.209 (0.076)	...	...
α_4	0.283 (0.070)	...	...	...	...
α_5	0.263 (0.073)	...	...	...	...
R^2	0.948	R^2	0.790	R^2	0.800
Durbin-Watson	2.60	Durbin-Watson	1.65	Durbin-Watson	2.83

SOURCE: Authors' calculations. The numbers in parentheses are the estimated standard errors.

W = average wage rate

M = money supply M1

L = real money demand

y = real income

R = nominal interest rate

U = unemployment rate

$D1$ = dummy variable that takes a value of one in a quarter following a large nominal appreciation. It takes the value of one in 1976.3 and 1977.2, and zero otherwise.

Equation 1-1 is the price equation, while equation 1-2 describes the PPP exchange rate rule. Equation 1-3 describes the wage indexation rule, and equation 1-4 represents the demand for money.

The model was estimated with quarterly data for the period 1974.2 to 1982.1. The results of the estimation appear in table 1-3.

The estimated exchange rate and wage equations indicate a strong response of the nominal exchange rate and wages to lagged inflation.[34] Substituting equations 1-2, 1-3, and 1-4 into equation 1-1, we obtain the following expression for the coefficient of lagged inflation: $\alpha_3\beta_1 + \alpha_4\gamma_1 + \alpha_5$. Replacing the

---

34. Some aspects of the estimated equations stand out. We are surprised that foreign prices in dollars (*PEXT*) have so little apparent effect on both domestic inflation and the exchange rate; perhaps the relative stability of the foreign price series makes it difficult to estimate the coefficient reliably. The statistical insignificance of the unemployment rate in the wage equation is also surprising.

estimated values from the structural model, we obtain an estimated value for this expression of 0.998.

From these results we conclude that inflation indeed shows strong inertia. Further, given its weight in the price equation, most of the inertia comes from the coefficient of lagged inflation in the exchange rate equation. However, the contribution of the coefficient of lagged inflation in the wage equation to the inertia in overall inflation is not small.

These results confirm the view that the PPP exchange rate rule was a major source of inertia. A review of the empirical work on this topic, however, along with the new evidence presented here, shows that the wage indexation rule also played an important part in producing inflationary inertia.

The Exchange Rate Based Stabilization Program (1978–82)

Unhappy with the slow pace at which inflation was being reduced, the government authorities in February 1978 initiated an exchange rate based stabilization program. This program lasted four years. Its role in the Chilean crisis of 1982 has been the subject of heated debate.[35] The question is essentially whether the program was bound to fail or whether it succumbed to minor design flaws that were exacerbated by major external shocks.

There is no question that a forward-looking exchange rate adjustment at a decreasing rate could and did slow the rate of inflation. The real dispute is over the roles of wage indexation and poor financial regulation. Even with β_1 (in equation 1-2) equal to zero, the limit of the crawling peg policy when the exchange rate is fixed, the coefficient of lagged inflation in the reduced form inflation equation derived from the model presented in table 1-3 is equal to 0.53. That means that inertia remains and that, without a change in the wage rule, the stabilization based on a crawling peg exchange rate with a decreasing crawl was bound to result in a real appreciation.

Our results confirm that the inconsistency between the forward-looking indexing of the nominal exchange rate at a decreasing rate and the backward-looking indexing of nominal wages contributed much to the real appreciation and to the ultimate crisis that built up during this period.

At the same time, the opening of the capital account without appropriate regulation and supervision of the financial system, in a system with full deposit insurance, exacerbated problems of moral hazard and led the banks to pursue

35. Corbo (1985b), Corbo and de Melo (1987), Edwards and Cox-Edwards (1987), Morandé (1988), and Valdés (1992).

risky lending financed by a boom in foreign borrowing. This borrowing was also encouraged by the change in the exchange rate rule, as it increased the spread between domestic interest rates and the expected devaluation-augmented foreign interest rate. The large increase in foreign borrowing fueled a boom in private expenditure and a real appreciation.

With the trade balance deficit reaching 10.3 percent of GDP in 1981, the obvious unsustainability of the expenditure boom set in motion a sharp drop in the availability of external financing. This led to a large increase in domestic real interest rates and a drop in the rates of growth of expenditures and GDP—and ultimately to the abandonment of the exchange rate policy on June 14, 1982, almost two months before Mexico's crisis.

It could be claimed that the 1982 crisis was caused by external shocks. Corbo and de Melo, using an econometric model, show that external shock was important, but they can only account for a slowdown in the rate of growth of GDP of 2.1 percent for the period 1981–83 rather than the actual rate of −3.4 percent.[36]

Thus we conclude that the inconsistency between the exchange rate and wage adjustment rules, combined with the weak regulation and supervision of the financial system, bears most of the blame for the macroeconomic difficulties of the period.[37]

Recovery and Real Devaluation (1983–89)

The Chilean success story is the story of the last decade, in which the economy appears to have achieved sustained growth. How were the turnaround and the accompanying real devaluation achieved and maintained?

In an open economy, the definition of the real exchange rate that is most relevant for resource allocation is the relative price between tradables and nontradables. This relative price is obtained from the market clearing condition in the market for nontradable goods. Starting with the Australian model developed by Salter and extended by Dornbusch, Rodriguez obtained the following expression for the equilibrium real exchange rate:

$$\ln RER_t = \alpha_o + \alpha_1 TS_t + \alpha_2 \ln(PX/PM)_t + \alpha_3 (GOV/GDP)_t,$$

36. Corbo and de Melo (1989).
37. We are struck also by the difficult dynamics confronted by policymakers then and now who have embarked on a stabilization program whose success depends completely on not changing the nominal exchange rate. The more they demonstrate their commitment to their policy, the greater the costs if they fail, for the real exchange rate is becoming further out of line. Thus a policy of this sort is likely to end in a crisis—with a bang rather than a whimper.

where *RER* is the real exchange rate, *TS* is the trade surplus as a share of GDP (that is, $TS = (Q-E)/Q$, where Q is nominal GDP and E is nominal domestic expenditures), *PX/PM* are the terms of trade between exportables and importables, and *GOV/GDP* is the share of government expenditures in GDP.[38] If we assume that the composition of government expenditure is more intensive in nontradables than is the composition of private expenditures, then the share of government expenditures in total expenditures is another determinant of the equilibrium real exchange rate. In this model the expected signs are a_1 positive, a_2 ambiguous, and a_3—the coefficient of the share of government expenditures in GDP—negative.

In this model an increase in the equilibrium real exchange rate must accompany an increase in the size of the trade surplus to avoid excess supply in the market for nontradable goods. Structural measures are the fundamental determinants of the equilibrium real exchange rate through their effects on the trade surplus. For example, a liberalization of the labor market that facilitates resource reallocation across sectors results in a higher value of output; if expenditures do not increase as much as output, it results also in a higher *TS*. To eliminate the excess supply of nontradable goods, a higher value of the equilibrium real exchange rate is required, that is, a real depreciation. A fiscal adjustment that results in an increase in the public sector surplus increases the difference between nominal output and nominal domestic absorption and therefore requires a real depreciation.

We estimate the equation using annual data for the period 1974–90. The result, with estimated *t*-coefficients in parentheses, is:

$$\ln RER_t = 1.88 + 2.05TS_t + 0.001 \cdot \ln (PX/PM)_t + 0.55(GOVS/GDP)_t + 0.59 \ln RER_{t-1}$$
$$\quad (1.93) \quad (2.70) \quad\quad (0.005) \quad\quad\quad\quad (0.26) \quad\quad\quad\quad\quad (3.80)$$

$$R^2 = 0.84; \text{Durbin-Watson} = 1.88; \text{Years} = 1974\text{–}90.$$

The coefficients of the share of the trade surplus in GDP and of the lagged value of the real exchange rate are highly significant. The coefficient implies that an increase in the trade surplus of one percentage point of GDP requires a two percent real depreciation the same year and an accumulated real depreciation of five percent. We conclude from this empirical result that the evolution of the trade surplus is the most important factor in the evolution of the real exchange rate.

Of course the trade surplus itself is another endogenous variable, determined at the macroeconomic level by the difference between the value of output and the value of domestic expenditures. To complete the model one must

38. Salter (1959), Dornbusch (1980), and Rodriguez (1991).

explain the evolution of the ratio of the trade surplus to GDP. This ratio is explained by aggregate demand variables. The variables to include here are the primary deficit relative to GDP, the domestic interest rate, and the level of capital inflows relative to GDP.

Now we use this framework to discuss how Chile was able to achieve a large real depreciation in the period 1981–89. As we saw earlier, following the large increase in fiscal and quasi-fiscal expenditures at the time of the financial crisis in 1982, a radical fiscal adjustment took place. As shown in table 1-1, the public sector deficit, including the losses of the Central Bank, reached a peak in 1985 and then began to drop off sharply. The increase in the overall deficit at that time was due mostly to the losses of the Central Bank. The losses the Central Bank sustained as a result of its role in supporting the financial system and other debtors have been estimated at 5.3 percent of GDP in 1982, 4.3 percent of GDP in 1983, 4.8 percent of GDP in 1984, 7.3 percent of GDP in 1985, 2.9 percent of GDP in 1986, and 1.3 percent of GDP in 1988.[39]

The reduction in government expenditures and quasi-fiscal subsidies contributed to a drastic cut in the public sector deficit (including the quasi-fiscal deficit of the Central Bank). This deficit declined to only 1.2 percent of GDP in 1988. The large fiscal adjustment resulted in a rapid turnaround of the trade deficit, by eight percentage points of GDP between 1984 and 1988. In accordance with the model presented above, this improvement in the trade balance could account for a real depreciation of 17.0 percent in the short run and of 42 percent in the long run.

The observed real depreciation between 1984 and 1988 was 50.3 percent. In recent years the maintenance of a surplus has been facilitated by the creation of a copper stabilization fund. The main purpose of this fund is to avoid spending temporary improvements in the terms of trade resulting from temporary increases in copper prices. The flow contribution to the copper stabilization fund, as a share of GDP, was 0.1 percent in 1987, 3.4 percent in 1988, 4.1 percent in 1989, and 2.5 percent in 1990. These are substantial additions to public sector savings.

If we compare 1981 with 1989, we find that the turnaround of the trade balance was 13.9 percentage points of GDP, while the real devaluation was 58.5 percent (table 1-1). For this period, the expenditures and GDP developments that contributed to the observed improvement in the trade surplus account for a real devaluation of 28.4 percent in the short run and of 69.5 percent in the long run.

What made it possible to obtain a large real devaluation without accelerat-

---

39. Larrañaga (1989) and Marshall and Schmidt-Hebbel (1991).

ing inflation? The main factors were the combination of the large fiscal adjustment, the elimination of wage indexation in 1982, and the persistence of considerable unemployment, at least until 1987. In fact, unlike the governments of some other Latin America countries, Chilean authorities did not have to use inflationary acceleration to erode real wages in order to make them consistent with a higher real exchange rate.[40]

The credibility of the government's anti-inflationary stance is another factor that could have contributed to the low inflation that accompanied the real devaluation. This credibility would have derived from the overall consistency of macroeconomic policies and from the government's persistence with its basic market-oriented policies. As a result, expectations of inflation may have been low.[41] In other words, the public believed the government's reluctance to use the inflation tax (and acknowledged its proven willingness and political ability to cut current public spending), and this perception gave rise to an anti-inflationary bias in the system.

The sustained real depreciation was one of the key factors behind the recovery and growth record of the post-1984 period. Non-copper exports and efficient import-competing activities responded rapidly to the higher real exchange rate and the modest increase in tariffs that took place after 1983 (figure 1-4). It is also worth noting that the policy of preventing the very high real interest rates that have been seen in other stabilizations (table 1-1) was another important element behind the recovery of private investment and the resumption of growth after 1984.

Other factors that contributed to the recovery and growth of the Chilean economy after 1984 are: the increased microeconomic efficiency of the economy as a result of the institutional and microeconomic reforms of the previous decade; the existence of a core of innovative entrepreneurs and of a nondistorted labor market, with a large pool of unemployed labor and some unused capacity until 1987; the relative absence of distortions in commodity markets; the access to external financing from international financial institutions in the early stages of the adjustment; the favorable copper prices in 1988–89, which provided a cushion for the external sector and improved public finances; the support provided by an increase in the share of public investment in GDP and a recovery in private investment starting forcefully from 1987; and the existence of an efficient network to cushion the impact of the adjustment on the

40. As indexation had been suspended and unemployment was high, nominal wages did not adjust fully to the large initial nominal devaluation in 1982.

41. The comparison of one-year nominal interest rates with CPI-indexed interest rates indicates a drop in expected annual inflation from 30.2 percent in the first half of 1985 to 29.2 percent in the second half of 1985 and only 14.3 percent in 1986.

poorest group in the population, which helped make the difficult adjustments more acceptable.[42]

A final observation concerning the strong real performance of the Chilean economy after the crisis of 1982–83: as Chile had by 1983 eliminated most of the major trade and factor market distortions, the correction of the misalignment in the key relative prices, the real exchange rate, and the real interest rate was likely to result in a large export and output response. The Chilean experience supports the view that restoring macroeconomic balance, reducing major distortions, and gaining access to appropriate external financing are key ingredients for restoring sustainable growth.[43]

The Stabilization Program (1990)

The democratic government that came to power in March 1990 inherited an accelerating rate of inflation (figure 1-2), which had reached 27.3 percent in 1989, the highest level since 1980. The new government, which was expected to increase attention to social issues, faced the immediate task of slowing down inflation and conveying the message that maintenance of macroeconomic balance would be one of its main objectives.

The newly independent board of the Central Bank implemented from the beginning an aggressive stabilization program based on a sharp increase in real (CPI-indexed) interest rates on Central Bank paper. Real interest rates on ten-year Central Bank paper were raised 230 basis points, from 6.9 to 9.2 percent a year.

The resultant slowdown in real expenditures contributed to a reduction in growth of GDP, to an increase in the trade balance surplus, and to lower inflation. However, in a world of increasingly integrated capital markets, a high real interest rate policy pulls in foreign capital that tends to offset the desired contractionary effects of the increase in the interest rate. Not surprisingly, in 1990 the Central Bank ended up accumulating $2.4 billion in reserves. The issuing of Central Bank debt to finance the reserve accumulation increased Central Bank losses, as the Central Bank in effect borrowed at high domestic interest rates to invest abroad at lower rates (adjusted for changes in the exchange rate).

This episode and Chilean macroeconomic management in 1991 and 1992 (see below) illustrate that monetary policy alone has a limited effectiveness in pursuing simultaneous inflation and exchange rate objectives. We believe that

42. Solimano (1989).
43. Corbo and Fischer (1992).

fiscal policy should have been used more actively during this period of anti-inflationary policy.

Single-Digit Inflation

The Chilean government has declared as a long-term goal of policy that it will reduce inflation to the levels of leading industrial countries. So far, however, the inflation rate has continued in the moderate range of 12 to 30 percent a year.[44] At the end of 1992, as the real exchange rate appreciated, it seemed that the inflation rate might decline to less than 10 percent. The recent worsening of the current account has made that prospect more remote, however.

Given Chile's remarkable real economic performance, the questions arise whether and why the government should even attempt to reduce the inflation rate below the range to which it has been confined for the past decade, and if so, how.[45]

The general arguments in favor of low inflation are well known.[46] They start from the welfare costs of inflation, computed as the area under the demand-for-money curve. The ratio of currency to GDP in Chile is low by international standards, for 1992 about 2.6 percent; the ratio of total non-interest-bearing monetary assets held by the public to GDP is about 4.6 percent. Using a demand-for-money equation (M1) of the form reported above, but estimated for the period 1983.4 to 1992.2, this cost of inflation—which includes the shoe-leather costs—amounts in the Chilean case to less than one percent of GDP.[47] This is very small by international standards. The cost of distortions associated with the failure to adapt domestic institutions, including taxation, to inflation must be added. These costs, which include menu costs, result from institutional nonadaptation and would be relatively low in the highly indexed Chilean system. In addition, there are other costs associated with the greater relative price variability and greater uncertainty about future price levels that are associated with higher inflation rates. While we are unaware of formal evidence on the relationship between relative price variability and inflation in the

44. Dornbusch and Fischer (1993).

45. Annual inflation has been in the range of 14.7–30.7 percent since 1982, when it was 9.9 percent.

46. Fischer and Modigliani (1978).

47. This statement is based on an estimate of the relevant area under the demand curve for non-interest-bearing money (M1), for a decline in the nominal interest rate from 5.5 percent a quarter to 2 percent a quarter. The estimated demand-for-money equation is given by:

$$\ln m_t = -2.36 + 0.357 \ln y_t^p - 0.026 R_t + 0.712 \ln m_{t-1}.$$
$$(0.958)\ (0.120) \qquad (0.005) \qquad (0.111)$$

$$R^2 = 0.894; \text{Durbin-Watson} = 2.17$$

Table 1-4. Quarterly Inflation Rate, 1984–91
Percent

Country	Average (AVπ)	Standard deviation (SDπ)	$\dfrac{AV\pi}{1+SD\pi}$
Canada	1.07	0.47	1.07
Chile	4.88	2.08	4.78
Colombia	5.70	2.36	5.57
France	0.92	0.42	0.92
Germany	0.48	0.50	0.48
Italy	1.64	0.71	1.63
Japan	0.46	0.71	0.45
United Kingdom	1.41	0.97	1.40
United States	0.97	0.42	0.96

SOURCE: International Financial Statistics, IMF, various issues.

Chilean case, we would be surprised if this relationship does not hold for Chile too.

The inflation rate in Chile has been quite variable over the past decade, implying considerable uncertainty about future price levels. Examination of figure 1-2 shows three episodes of high inflation within the past decade and sizable swings in the quarterly inflation rate. In fact, the variability of quarterly inflation in Chile in the past decade has been exceptionally high by international standards. A comparison between Chile and other countries shows that the variability of inflation in Chile is among the highest (table 1-4). The economic costs of this uncertainty are mitigated by widespread indexation, but some costs remain.

The arguments for seeking to reduce the inflation rate are conceptually clear, even if they cannot all be quantified; they are the traditional shoe-leather and menu costs of inflation, plus costs associated with unnecessary variability in relative prices and uncertainty about future price levels, which are greater at higher inflation rates. These benefits of lower inflation must be weighed against the loss in seigniorage that the government would experience if inflation were lower. In recent years, the Chilean government has collected 0.7 percent of GDP in seigniorage revenue. This seigniorage arises from the inflation tax and income growth. With income growing at, say, 7 percent a year and with an estimated long-run income elasticity of money demand of 1.25, about 0.5 percent of GDP in seigniorage derives from growth. Therefore, the government would lose very little seigniorage revenue from stabilizing inflation. The flow loss of seigniorage must also be weighed against the stock gain as the public increases its real holdings of non-interest-bearing government liabilities as inflation comes down. The crucial costs of reducing inflation are thus the likely recessionary consequences of any attempt at stabilization.

Two basic strategies for reducing inflation can be envisaged. The first would be fully orthodox, tightening monetary and fiscal policy and relying on reductions in aggregate demand. The second would be heterodox, using, in addition to the orthodox tools, the nominal anchor of the exchange rate and agreements with the labor unions and industry to attempt to reduce the inflation rate at lower cost.[48] In either case, the stabilization attempt would probably slow growth, though the first scenario would probably slow it more.

A stabilization based on the exchange rate would, quite likely, cause a real appreciation for a period. Given what appear to be relatively small benefits of reducing current levels of inflation and the possible costs of transition, we do not believe the balance of the argument favors a resolute attack on inflation no matter what the condition of the economy. Chile's economic successes in the past decade owe much to the absolute commitment to maintaining a real exchange rate favorable to exports, and that commitment should not be abandoned just to accelerate the rate of disinflation.

Before turning to our recommended anti-inflationary policies, we digress briefly to examine current Chilean monetary policy. It is remarkable that Chilean monetary policy has operated for the past decade without an explicit nominal anchor. Monetary policy targets both the real exchange rate and the inflation rate. The main instrument of monetary policy has been the ninety-day real interest rate on Central Bank liabilities. The real interest rate is adjusted when inflation rises and when the real exchange rate moves away from its target level. Sometimes the two objectives come into conflict, and the Central Bank implicitly trades off between them. Recently, for instance, the real exchange rate has been allowed to appreciate as capital flowed in at the set level of the real interest rate.[49]

When changes in the real interest rate are infrequent, as is the case at present, nothing ties down the inflation rate except the stickiness of prices in responding to changes in aggregate demand. As we show in a simple model in the appendix, under plausible conditions the price level becomes a random walk in such a system, while the inflation rate is determinate. However, changes in expectations of price setters, or any arbitrary change in their price-

---

48. In correspondence, John Williamson—a student of Fritz Machlup—has pointed out that *heterodox* is the wrong word for the concept to which it has been applied over the past decade. "Hetero" means "other," which gives *heterodox* the connotation of "other than orthodox," rather than the intended "orthodox plus." The right word, suggested to us by Enrico Perotti, would appear to be *polydox*, where "poly" means "many."

49. There was much less possibility of conflict between the two objectives in the 1980s, when Chile's access to international capital markets was severely curtailed. Then the link between domestic and international interest rates was broken, and the Central Bank could set real interest rates without affecting the level of capital inflows.

setting behavior, would change the inflation rate. Thus in a fundamental sense, the stated current operating rules of the Chilean monetary authority do not place constraints on the inflation rate. In practice, it appears that the Central Bank has operated with a target range for the inflation rate as well as the exchange rate and has given more weight to the inflation target than to the real exchange rate target. When the inflation rate has moved above an acceptable range, the Central Bank has reacted by increasing the real interest rate or undertaking a revaluation. This ensures that the inflation rate will return to its target range, if necessary through a slowdown of economic activity.

With the recent emergence of current account deficits, the Central Bank has also stated that one of its objectives is to maintain the current account deficit below 4 percent of GDP. The Chilean Central Bank is implicitly operating with target ranges (or upper limits) for the inflation rate, for the real exchange rate, and for the current account deficit as a share of GDP. Indeed, sometimes the inflation target becomes quite explicit. Thus in its annual reports to Congress the Central Bank announces inflation targets and also publicizes the progress made in achieving this target.

Of course monetary policy alone cannot achieve so many objectives (the inflation rate, the real exchange rate, and the size of the current account deficit). But that does not necessarily mean the Central Bank should confine itself to a single objective. In the first place, the objectives are linked. For instance, the bank has a real exchange rate target in part because it aims to control the current account to avoid an excessive buildup of foreign debt. Furthermore, the bank is fully capable of trading off among these objectives in setting monetary policy.

Nonetheless macroeconomic policy in Chile in the past few years would have been more effective if the work of monetary policy had been shared with a more active fiscal policy. In particular, through its effects on aggregate expenditures, fiscal policy could provide an additional instrument for pursuing the three targets of macroeconomic policy. Furthermore, when monetary policy rather than fiscal policy is used to reduce aggregate demand, any reduction in demand must come from the crowding out of private expenditures, in particular the most interest-elastic component, which is private investment. The crowding out of private investment affects long-term growth prospects.

Anti-Inflationary Policy

Turning now to anti-inflationary policy, we argue that the costs of inflation in Chile do justify an attempt to bring down the inflation rate. But in the still heavily indexed Chilean economy, the policy should be a gradual one. Chile should attempt to move gradually to a lower inflation rate, by making use of favorable shocks when they occur and by locking in the resultant gains. In particular, we recommend that Chile adopt an active crawling peg exchange rate, with the central reference rate crawling at a gradually declining rate and with a wide band on either side of the target rate. This crawling band would be similar to the diagonal band Israel adopted at the end of 1991. The rate of crawl would be adjusted approximately annually, and the central parity could, if necessary, be adjusted as well. Such adjustments are the equivalent of devaluations and revaluations within an adjustable peg system; recent European experience suggests that it would be expensive to rule them out even though they reduce the commitment benefit of the exchange rate peg.

This proposal raises at least two questions. First, why is the exchange rate commitment so weak? Surely, if Chile is serious about reducing inflation, it should make a much firmer commitment. The commitment is weak because we do not believe that Chile should trade in its commitment to a pro-export exchange rate policy for an anti-inflationary policy. The Chilean economy has lived moderately well with inflation; the patient is not really sick from inflation, and there is no case for drastic treatment. However, since inflation is mildly debilitating, a concerted effort to take every opportunity to reduce it, with the goal of bringing inflation down to international levels over a period of years, is certainly warranted. The crawling band gives that opportunity.

Second, is any nominal targeting possible in an economy that is so heavily indexed? Preserving the distinction between financial indexation and wage indexation, we strongly recommend against any attempts to ban indexation in the long-term financial markets. Indexation has been instrumental in promoting the development of a long-term capital market even while there has been uncertainty about long-term inflation prospects, and it should be permitted to continue to serve that function until private agents are sufficiently confident to do without it. Currently indexation is forbidden in financial contracts of less than ninety days. If the inflation rate comes down and becomes more stable, we would recommend the extension of this ban to six months and then a year, but not to longer-term loans. We recommend using a ban rather than relying purely on markets to make the switch away from indexation because it is quite likely there are dual equilibriums in which everyone operates either with indexed contracts or with nominal contracts, and markets may have difficulty switching from one equilibrium to the other.

Wage indexation is not an insuperable obstacle to stabilization provided that the reduction in inflation is gradual and that productivity growth continues at a reasonable rate, making room for real wage increases. To the extent that government decisions affect nominal wages, for instance in setting the minimum wage and in reaching wage agreements with government employees, these contracts should be based on the nominal inflation that is implicit in the rate of crawl of the exchange rate. If a decision is ever made to try to move inflation down by 5–6 percent within a year, then it will be necessary to reach an agreement with labor that prevents the familiar real wage increase that follows from ex-post backward indexation in a context of declining inflation.

Circumstances in 1992 were exceptionally favorable to the adoption of a crawling band. If the system had been put in place during the year, we believe it would by now have been operating well. However, the 8.9 percent real appreciation during that year, the recent worsening of the terms of trade, the deterioration of the trade account, and the proximity of elections suggest that this is not the best time to move to a new system. Nonetheless, given the flexibility that can be built into the system by starting with wide bands and by adjusting the reference rate occasionally if necessary, we do recommend introducing a crawling band with an exogenous and decreasing rate of crawl for the reference rate. To be specific, given the expected inflation rate of 12 percent in Chile and about 3 percent among its trading partners, we recommend a crawl of the central peg at 9 percent a year, starting from the current nominal rate.[50]

Given the uncertainty about the behavior of the current account, a band of plus or minus 8 percent on either side of the peg would be warranted. Both the central rate and the width of the band would be reassessed at the end of the year. Any adjustments in either should attempt to avoid discrete changes in the exchange rate. The intention would be to reduce both the crawl, to perhaps 7 percent, and the bands, to, say, 6 percent in either direction, for 1994.

The introduction of a crawling band exchange rate in a system with free capital flows puts limits on the movement of domestic nominal interest rates. In the absence of risk premiums, and with no uncertainty about exchange-rate movements relative to the reference rate, the domestic nominal interest rate would be exactly equal to the foreign rate plus the rate of crawl. In practice, the domestic nominal interest rate would have some room to move, derived from both risk premiums and expected exchange-rate movements within the band. With the nominal interest rate given and with expected inflation closely related to the rate of crawl, the real interest rate is also constrained.

The question then is how the Central Bank would conduct monetary policy in the new system. The answer is twofold: first, when there is a nominal exchange rate target, the quantity of money must adapt to demand; and second, the existence of the bands still leaves room for movements in interest rates. To

---

50. The relevant nominal rate is the observed rate rather than the central point of the present exchange rate band.

adapt the quantity of money to demand, the Central Bank will have to conduct open market purchases and sales that will keep nominal interest rates at the level implied by the exchange rate policy. On the second point, the bands exist precisely because the exchange rate may have to move relative to the reference rate; this flexibility needs to be exploited by the monetary authority, by adjusting nominal interest rates. Ultimately the rate of crawl would decline to zero, but we would recommend maintaining the bands at 5 percent in each direction to give some room for the exchange rate to respond to movements in the terms of trade and capital flows. Maintenance of such an exchange rate commitment would require a more active use of fiscal policy than has been seen in the past three years.

Conclusions

Two decades after the start of the economic reform process in 1973, Chile is the major success story of orthodox adjustment policies. Starting in 1973, Chile undertook a big-bang fiscal policy and liberalized prices; then in 1974 it started a gradual trade liberalization program that by 1979 had resulted in a uniform 10 percent tariff. Later it aggressively deregulated markets and carried out large-scale privatization. As a result of external shocks, the flawed exchange rate based stabilization strategy of 1978, and an ill-fated financial liberalization, it had again to undertake a drastic fiscal stabilization from 1982 to 1986.

The Chilean experience provides many lessons to countries pursuing comprehensive reforms. It supports the view that maintaining the basic macroeconomic balances is a necessary condition to promote a supply response. The far-reaching microeconomic reforms of the 1970s, which began the creation of an outward-oriented market economy, were almost destroyed in the macroeconomic crisis of 1982–83. Once the macroeconomic situation was brought under control, the conditions were created for growth to resume.

The recent Chilean experience is also enlightening on how to carry out a financial liberalization and to coordinate it with stabilization. Chile began to deregulate the financial markets quite early in the reform process, while inflation was at the three-digit annual level and while radical reforms were causing major changes in relative prices. This deregulation, coupled with weak regulation and supervision of financial institutions and full deposit insurance, led to high real interest rates and the eventual collapse of the financial system.

Two lessons emerge here. First, extensive liberalization of financial markets should not take place until significant progress has been achieved in stabilization and in the adjustment of relative prices. Second, deregulation in the presence of implicit or explicit deposit insurance and in the absence of adequate regulation and supervision of financial intermediaries is a recipe for disaster. Thus any major deregulation should wait for the development of adequate regulation and supervision capabilities.

One lesson of the Chilean adjustment program is that targeted anti-poverty programs work.[51] Such programs are fully justified on their own terms. In addition, by cushioning the poorest groups in the population from some of the short-term costs of adjustment, they can provide much-needed breathing space to give the reforms time to bear fruit.

The growth payoff to the Chilean reforms took many years, and its success was not guaranteed. Indeed, as late as the mid-1980s, the Chilean reform program was seen by many as a failure. Only with the string of high-growth years in the second half of the 1980s, the return in 1989 of a democratic government that confirmed the main thrust of the market-oriented policy reforms implemented in the previous fifteen years, and the crucially important stabilization of 1990 and subsequent stellar growth performance could the success of the economic reforms be considered deep-seated. Thus one crucial but politically unpalatable lesson from the Chilean experience is that the returns realized from structural reforms take a long time to materialize.[52] However, the maturity period can be shortened if lessons are learned from the mistakes of others, including Chile. Judging from the Chilean case, the reforms more than justify the initial investment once they do materialize. We do not in this paper address the question of whether democracies are capable of sustaining such long-maturity adjustment programs. We believe that the answer is yes.

Comment by Anne O. Krueger

The economic performance of the Chilean economy in recent years has been remarkable. It has attracted the attention of all who are concerned with improving the economic prospects of those in many of the developing countries where living standards have risen little, if at all, in recent years. Quite clearly the Chilean macroeconomic experience has been a crucial, although by no means the only, ingredient of the entire reform program. I was pleased,

---

51. Castañeda (1992).

52. This is a sober and disappointing lesson for many countries in eastern Europe and the former Soviet Union that are trying to make a transition to a market economy.

therefore, to be asked to read and comment on the paper by Vittorio Corbo and Stanley Fischer. Since much of what I know about the Chilean reforms is based on the research undertaken by people present at this conference, it is fortunate that the conference topic is not only the Chilean economy, but the lessons for other countries that can be derived from Chile's experience. For I have little to contribute to the masterful analysis of Corbo and Fischer with regard to the essentials of the Chilean experience with stabilization and recovery.

Several issues associated with deriving lessons for other countries merit attention, and I will focus on those. First, there are four implications, or nuances, in the paper that I wish briefly to question. Second, I want to challenge the authors' conclusion that the Chilean experience suggests that a successful transition to growth necessarily takes a long time.

Let me turn first to the questions. Here I do not wish to quarrel with the authors' conclusions so much as I want to assert that I do not find the case as they have made it convincing, or that I believe their conclusions need qualification.

The first such issue pertains to the role in Chile's success of the opening of the trade and payments regime. Corbo and Fischer give little prominence to the opening of the trade and payments regime in the turnaround of the Chilean economy, yet it clearly played a major role. If I perform the mental experiment of an economic policy regime after 1973 that followed the budget and monetary policies actually pursued, but with no change in the preexisting trade and payments regime, I find it inconceivable that the outcome of the policy changes would have been anywhere near as favorable as it was. Indeed it is relatively straightforward to imagine the entire reform process foundering on balance of payments difficulties. An important question is the role of the trade and payments regime in the success story, both as a provider of incentives for more efficient allocation of resources through shifts toward export industries and a more competitive environment and as an enabler to avoid the earlier balance of payments crises, which served as a constraint on growth. There is also a set of interesting and important questions as to the converse: could the Chilean economy have experienced the turnaround it did if the trade and payments regime had been altered but the macroeconomic stabilization was less successful than in fact was the case?

A second question concerns the role of the nonperforming assets in the Central Bank's portfolio as a policy problem and as a constraint on alternative courses of action. Here is a hypothesis at least worth examining, that had the Central Bank portfolio not included nominal assets with little or no value, macroeconomic stabilization could have taken place much faster.

Third, I am not persuaded that the authors' endorsement of incomes policy is validated by the Chilean experience. There are several questions. One is the extent to which such policies in fact contributed to stabilization in Chile: at least during the late 1970s, there was some discussion as to the maintenance of real wages and the effects of such a policy on the level of unemployment. Another is whether an incomes policy that was successful under the Pinochet government could have been as effective under a different form of government, given the political economy considerations that surround the determination of incomes policies. In addition, one can imagine an economy initially in difficulty because of a high real wage; depending on the extent of such a wage's inconsistency with full employment or realization of comparative advantage in exporting, an incomes policy could prevent the emergence of those new economic activities upon which resumption of growth must depend.

Fourth, I am not sure that a *tablita* is a sound policy prescription. We know that there are many countries in which stabilization efforts have been undermined by difficulties as the real exchange rate appreciated when the rate of inflation exceeded the rate of exchange rate depreciation. While inertia in inflation is clearly important, I would hope that future research could shed light on the causes of inertia. If understanding of the reasons for the tendency for inflation to persist improved, it should be possible to find policy prescriptions to mitigate the inertial component of inflation that would be less dangerous to the entire reform program than a solution such as a *tablita*.

All of the above are really qualifications to the authors' argument. My remarks will focus, however, on yet another question. To what extent does the Chilean experience show that successful transitions must necessarily involve many years before growth accelerates? Based on my knowledge of Chile, a strong case can be made that a number of factors made the Chilean transition far longer than might be expected under other circumstances. These include the initial conditions under which the policy changes occurred, the evolution of the world economy, and even the policy responses themselves.

I will sketch the argument that Chile's very long transition was unique and cannot be used as a basis for concluding that transitions must always take such a long time. (Turkey, for instance, began changing policies in 1980 and achieved an average annual rate of growth of 5 percent in the latter half of the 1980s.) A starting point is to note the extreme dislocations of the Chilean economy in 1973: many industries had been nationalized; real wages had been increased sharply; the (suppressed) annual rate of inflation was many hundreds of percent; failure to adjust the nominal exchange rate and a large fiscal deficit had led not only to a large current account deficit but also to a sharp reduction in Chile's foreign exchange reserves and in its ability to borrow abroad. The latter implied that there had to be a very sharp reduction in real expenditures rapidly. Arguably, Chile's economic plight was significantly worse than that of many countries when reform programs are launched.

To assess the gravity of the situation, we really need a counterfactual: how would the major aggregates of the Chilean economy have evolved over the next few years in the absence of any policy reform program? Another way of phrasing the question is to ask how much future real output had already been mortgaged under earlier economic policies. It is highly likely that there would have been an intolerable reduction in real output and living standards. Set against that counterfactual, the economic performance of the next several years might be judged to be far more satisfactory.

However, the influence of external factors also contributed to the long, drawn-out period before resumed growth could be sustained. The deterioration in Chile's terms of trade in the 1974–75 worldwide depression (and again in 1981–82) clearly aggravated the situation. The difficulties inherited in 1973 were in spite of the commodity price boom. When commodity prices fell, they significantly exacerbated the severity of economic difficulties.

Finally, it is certainly arguable, as Corbo and Fischer do, that the *tablita* of exchange rates in the 1970s was a serious policy mistake. To the extent that inflation was inertial, the inevitable real exchange rate appreciation that resulted would in any event have led to the need for further stabilization and reform. In fact that policy mistake, too, was compounded by the precipitate drop in copper prices in the early 1980s, which left Chile highly vulnerable to rising world interest rates. The debt crisis then further complicated economic management.

Not only did initial conditions, policy mistakes, and worldwide economic conditions each slow down the response to policy reform. They interacted with each other so that the timing of declines in the price of copper exacerbated policy problems, first with respect to the initial adjustment in 1974–75 and then with respect to the negative effect of the *tablita*.

Had the copper price and the real exchange rate remained fairly constant during the 1970s, the response to the changes in economic policy might have been much more rapid. Had they been, the difficulties of the early 1980s would have been far less severe. Perhaps Chile's economic growth under this scenario would have been sufficient in the late 1970s to offset the effect of worldwide recession in 1980–83.

To develop a sufficiently plausible model to provide a confident estimate of the counterfactual under alternative policies and world conditions is far beyond the capabilities of the economics profession at the present time. In the absence of such a model, however, it is as wrong to conclude that all turnarounds must inevitably take a long time as it is to conclude that the Chilean case was exceptional.

The question as to the minimum essential time for realization of sustained rapid growth after policy reform is an important one. It is to be hoped that further research on those factors contributing to the long turnaround time in Chile will shed light not only on the question, but also on ways of shortening that essential minimum.

Comment by Patricio Meller

This paper highlights the key issues related to stabilization of inflation in Chile. I agree with many of the points made in the paper, but I will focus my comments on areas of disagreement. I will address five issues.

The Mystery of the Slow Reduction of Inflation in 1973–81

After the 1973 coup, the government made reducing inflation its main objective. Measures taken to achieve that goal were: drastic reduction of the fiscal deficit, from 25 percent of GDP in 1973 to almost 0 percent in 1976; real wage contraction on the order of 15 percent to 30 percent (1973–75); implementation of structural reforms such as price liberalization (1974), trade reform (1974–79), liberalization of the domestic capital market (1975–76), and privatization (1974–76); and the use of appreciations in the (nominal) exchange rate (1976–77) to break inflationary expectations.

As a result of the above measures, GDP contracted by −13 percent (1975), unemployment rose from 4 percent (1973) to 20 percent (1976), and inflation diminished from 370 percent (1974) to 84 percent (1977).[53]

From 1978 on (up to 1982), the (nominal) exchange rate was used as the anti-inflation tool; in 1978 the *tablita* system set future values for the exchange rate, and in 1979 (June) a fixed exchange rate was established. At the same

53. Unemployment figures include people receiving unemployment compensation in the so-called Minimum Employment Programs. See Jadresic (1986). Inflation figures include the Cortázar-Marshall (1980) revision. Figures for inflation correspond to annual values.

time, the capital account was liberalized (1979–82). Now inflation diminished from 38 percent (1978) to 9.5 percent (1981).

It took *eight years* to bring inflation down to the single-digit level. The main explanation given relates to the inconsistency of the policies that the government followed from 1978 on; while the exchange rate was indexed forward, wages were readjusted on the basis of backward indexation. Corbo and Fischer found that the inflationary inertia resulting from the wage rule had a weight coefficient that was one half of the weight coefficient of the exchange rate rule. The period of policy inconsistency (1978–81) coincides with the period in which inflation was reduced to the single-digit level. The real issue thus is how to explain the drop in inflation despite the existence of that policy inconsistency.

Two main factors, in my opinion, contributed to the slow reduction of Chilean inflation. The first is the supply shock caused by the liberalization of the domestic capital market. Nominal and real interest rates were quite high; for example, the average annual real interest rate was more than 30 percent in the 1976–82 period. The second factor concerns the liberalization of the capital account; the large inflow of external credit generated a sharp and sustained increase of domestic expenditure. Corbo and Fisher do not examine the role of these two factors.

The Role of the Exchange Rate as the Nominal Anchor, 1978–82

First of all, the exchange rate as a nominal anchor works, but too slowly, to combat inflation. The main problem, however, is the generation of a trade disequilibrium. Chilean experience shows that if the current account deficit is higher than 5 percent of GDP for three to four years or higher than 10 percent of GDP for two years, the probability of a balance of payments crisis is quite high with or without the existence of a fiscal surplus or of a balance of payments surplus.

Corbo and Fischer consider the fixed nominal exchange rate the main factor in the 1982 external (and internal) disequilibrium crisis. If, however, a free exchange rate policy had been in effect when the capital account was liberalized, the level of appreciation could have been higher. In other words, the main problem is not exactly the nominal anchor, but the liberalization of the capital account.

When a fixed exchange rate is used as the nominal anchor, the prevailing level of domestic inflation does make a difference. In 1979, Chilean inflation was 39 percent; some critics pointed out that the level of domestic inflation was too high to fix the exchange rate and that the adjustment would not be instantaneous. A strange explanation by official economists was that the level of external inflation that was relevant for Chile was 35 percent, and some Central Bank calculations supported this.

The Effect on Inflation of the Sharp Devaluations in the 1980s

Corbo and Fischer ask how the devaluation of the real nominal exchange rate was achieved. This question misses some key discussion related to stabilization policies, however.

The prevailing opinion during 1981–82 was that devaluation was useless, because all increases in the nominal exchange rate would translate into inflation of price levels. In fact, Corbo wrote a very important and influential econometric paper showing that the Chilean economy was homogeneous of degree one with respect to the exchange rate.[54] Moreover, Corbo and Fischer have shown that most of the inflationary inertia comes from the nominal exchange rate.

Therefore the key question is really why the sharp increases of the exchange rate did not have an inflationary effect. The explanation is related to the complementary policies used in an almost closed monetarist economy: tight controls of capital movements, deindexation of wages (1982), tight monetary policy, and heavy fiscal adjustment. Some economic indicators provide an idea of the deep adjustment: GDP fell -16 percent (1982–83), real wages decreased by -20 percent, and unemployment increased up to 30 percent (1982) and remained above 24 percent for three years (1983–85).

Credibility and Structural Reform

Corbo and Fischer's explanation for the low inflation in the 1980s is that high credibility induced by sharp fiscal adjustment generated lower inflationary expectations. Let us review the more general issue of the role of credibility. Sargent has pointed out that to stop inflation "it would require far more than a few temporary restrictive fiscal and monetary actions; . . . it would require a change in the policy regime."[55] This idea in Latin America has come to mean that a change of the policy regime will be accompanied by implementation of

---

54. Corbo (1982a). In a later paper, Corbo (1985a) shows that the Chilean economy is not homogeneous of degree one with respect to the exchange rate.
55. Sargent (1982, p. 42).

Table 1-5. Annual Inflation, 1975–78
Percent

Year	Official CPI[a]	True CPI	Estimated CPI[b]
1975	341	341	341
1976	174	198	244
1977	63	84	114
1978	30	37	88

SOURCE: Cortázar (1983).
a. Based on cheating.
b. Based on true CPI assuming same wage indexation rule.

deep structural reforms (liberalization, privatization, and so forth), and this is the mechanism to stop inflation.

In the 1970s Chile experienced significant changes in government and in policy and undertook a huge fiscal adjustment; each of these changes exceeds by far what is usually required to achieve credibility. Nonetheless, it took eight years for inflation to come down. During the 1980s the political regime did not change, the economic model collapsed, and no major changes of policy were introduced; none of these would help credibility. Nonetheless, inflation stayed at a relatively low level.

A clear lesson is that there are many good reasons for making structural reforms in a Latin American economy; stating that structural reforms increase credibility and in this way help reduce inflation (in the short or medium term) is not one of them.

Cheating

There was cheating in the measuring of official inflation during 1976–78 (see table 1-5). Cheating helped to bring down inflation. Corbo and Fischer do not mention this issue of cheating; moreover, some of the tables show the official CPI. If this official CPI is used to deflate some variables, it generates variables with errors for the econometric estimation.

The lesson from the Chilean experience should not be that cheating helps to bring down inflation. In this case, cheating meant that every agent was using an underestimate of inflation for its indexation readjustment rule; since each one was indexing by less than 100 percent with respect to backward inflation, this was equivalent to an income policy where all use the same "reduced" (arrived at by cheating) inflation level.[56] In short, unexpectedly, monetarist economists used income policy to reduce inflation, and it worked.

56. Cortázar (1983).

Appendix: Chilean Monetary Policy

In this appendix we explore the issue of the determinacy of the price level when monetary policy attempts to fix the real interest rate. For simplicity the analysis is conducted for a closed economy. At the end we comment briefly on how the analysis would change for an open economy. Assume the demand for money function is:

(1A-1) $m_t - p_t = y_t - \alpha i_t + \varepsilon_t,$

where m, p, and y are logarithms and where we assume

(1A-2) $i_t = r^* + p_{t-1} - p_{t-2}.$

Equation 1A-2 is the real interest rate rule, with r^* the target real rate, and $(p_{t-1} - p_{t-2})$ is the most recently observed inflation rate.[57] For convenience we can assume that y_t is constant and equal to $y^* = r^* = 0$. Then

(1A-1') $m_t - p_t = -\alpha(p_{t-1} - p_{t-2}) + \varepsilon_t.$

As it stands, equation 1A-1' cannot determine the price level. It is simply an equation for the real money supply, and m_t and p_t could take any values as long as their difference is determined by equation 1A-1'. There are two ways out of this indeterminacy. At the formal level, the authorities could fix either m_t or p_t as a nominal target, and the price level would then be determinate. But equation 1A-1' is implausible because it is hard to believe that the price level reacts one-for-one to the money stock in the current period. Suppose, alternatively, that the price level is predetermined through the goods market. Specifically, assume that prices are set on the basis of the excess demand for goods in the previous period and that demand is determined by wealth (in this case real balances). We can write:

(1A-3) $p_t = p_{t-1} + \Theta(y_{t-1}^d - y^*) + u_{t-1} = p_{t-1} + \beta(m_{t-1} - p_{t-1}) + u_{t-1},$

where y^d is aggregate demand, given by

$$y_t^d = y_{t-1}^d + (\beta/\Theta)(m_t - p_t) + y^*.$$

Since the price level is predetermined, and for tractability, we replace the interest rate rule (1A-2) by

---

57. For tractability, we simplify here by assuming that money demand adjusts completely, within one period, to changes on the right hand side of equation 1A-1. Partial adjustment would be handled by including a term γm_{t-1} on the right hand side of 1A-1. While the simplification helps keep the dynamics manageable, the lagged adjustment term should be included in general, especially for understanding why the money stock has been so variable in Chile.

(1A-2′) $i_t = r^* + p_t - p_{t-1} = p_t - p_{t-1}.$

Now putting the pieces together (equation 1A-2′ in equation 1A-1′, and then substituting equation 1A-1 lagged into equation 1A-3), we have the equation for the price level:

(1A-4) $p_t - p_{t-1} = -\alpha\beta(p_{t-1} - p_{t-2}) + \beta\varepsilon_{t-1} + u_{t-1}.$

This implies that the price level is a random walk but that the inflation rate is not. Writing Π for the inflation rate, we have

(1A-5) $\Pi_t = -\alpha\beta \, \Pi_{t-1} + \beta\varepsilon_{t-1} + u_{t-1}.$

Assuming that $\alpha\beta$ is less than one in absolute value, this is a stable equation for the inflation rate:

(1A-6) $0 < \alpha\beta < 1.$

Equation 1A-5 implies that the inflation rate tends to oscillate in response to a shock. The mechanism is that a demand shock today increases the price level and thus the inflation rate. This in turn leads the monetary authority to reduce real balances, which tends to reduce aggregate demand, pushing the price level down in the next period and setting up a stable oscillation. The conclusion in this extremely simplified example, in which the price level is predetermined, is that the real interest rate rule does make the price level indeterminate but does not make the inflation rate indeterminate or unstable. Note that the determinacy of the inflation rate comes from the stickiness of the price adjustment process (equation 1A-3). To apply such an analysis to an open economy, like that of Chile, it would be necessary to include the exchange rate. We suspect that as long as the exchange rate was being set by a rule similar to equation 1A-2, intended to keep the real exchange rate constant, a similar analysis would apply.

References

Barandiarán, E. 1977. "Una Nota sobre Política Cambiaria." Documento 50. Santiago: Departamento de Estudios Empresas, Banco Hipotecario de Chile, processed.

Bitar, S. 1986. *Chile: Experiments in Democracy.* Philadelphia: Institute for the Study of Human Issues.

Bruno, M. 1978. "Exchange Rates, Import Costs, and Wage-Price Dynamics." *Journal of Political Economy* 86 (June): 379–403.

————. 1991. "High Inflation and the Nominal Anchors of an Open Economy." Princeton Essays in International Finance 183. International Finance Section. Princeton, N.J.: Princeton University.

Bruno, M., and S. Fischer. 1986. "The Inflationary Process: Shocks and Accommodation." In *The Israeli Economy: Maturing Through Crises,* edited by Y. Ben-Porath, 347–74. Harvard University Press.

Bruno, M., and others, eds. 1988. *Stopping High Inflation.* MIT Press.

———. 1991. *Lessons of Economic Stabilization and Its Aftermath.* MIT Press.

Büchi, H. 1985. "Chile's Economic Strategy." Remarks to the World Bank's Advisory Committee (March). New York.

Castañeda, T. 1992. *Combating Poverty. Innovative Social Reforms in Chile during the 1980s.* San Francisco: ICS Press.

Cauas, J. 1979. "The Government Economic Recovery Program." Text of the Address to the Nation by the Minister of Finance. April 24, 1975. In *Chilean Economic Policy,* edited by J. C. Méndez, 155–63. Santiago: Ministry of Finance.

Cauas, J., and V. Corbo. 1972. "La Economía Chilena en 1971 y Perspectivas para 1972." Series Informes de Coyuntura 1. Instituto de Economía. Santiago: Universidad Católica de Chile.

Corbo, V. 1974. *Inflation in Developing Countries.* Amsterdam: North Holland Publishing Co.

———. 1982a. "Inflación en una economía abierta." *Cuadernos de Economía* 56 (April): 5–15.

———. 1982b. "Monetary Policy with an Overrestricted Demand for Money Equation." *Journal of Development Economics* 10 (February): 119–31.

———. 1985a. "Reforms and Macroeconomic Adjustment in Chile during 1974–84." *World Development* 13 (August): 893–916. Oxford: Pergamon Press Ltd.

———. 1985b. "International Prices, Wages and Inflation in Open Economy." *Review of Economics and Statistics* 67 (November): 564–73.

———. 1990. "Public Finance, Trade, and Development: The Chilean Experience." In *Fiscal Policy in Open Developing Economies,* edited by V. Tanzi, 131–43. International Monetary Fund.

———. 1993. "Economic Reforms in Chile: An Overview." Paper presented at the Eastern Economic Association Meetings (March), Washington, D.C.

Corbo, V., and J. de Melo. 1987. "Lessons from the Southern Cone Policy Reforms." *World Bank Research Observer* 2 (July): 111–42.

———. 1989. "External Shocks and Policy Reforms in the Southern Cone: A Reassessment." In *Debt Stabilization and Development,* edited by G. Calvo and others, 235–58. Oxford and New York: Blackwell.

Corbo, V., and S. Fischer. 1992. "Adjustment Programs and Bank Support: Rationale and Main Results." In *Adjustment Lending Revisited,* edited by V. Corbo, S. Fischer, and S. Webb, 7–17. The World Bank.

Corbo, V., and S. Nam. 1992. "Recent Experience in Controlling Inflation." In *Structural Adjustment in a Newly Industrialized Country: The Korean Experience,* edited by V. Corbo and S. Suh, 95–114. Johns Hopkins University Press.

Corbo, V., and A. Solimano. 1991. "Chile's Experience with Stabilization Revisited."

In *Lessons of Economic Stabilization and Its Aftermath,* edited by M. Bruno and others, 57–91. MIT Press.

Cortázar, R. 1983. "Salarios nominales e inflación: Chile 1974–1872." *Colección Estudios CIEPLAN* 11 (December): 85–112.

Cortázar, R., and J. Marshall. 1980. "Indices de precios al consumidor en Chile 1970–78." *Colección Estudios CIEPLAN* 4 (November): 159–201.

de la Cuadra, S., and D. Hachette. 1992. *The Chilean Trade Liberalization Experience.* Santiago: Editorial de Economía y Administración. Universidad de Chile.

Dornbusch, R. 1980. *Open Economy Macroeconomics.* New York: Basic Books.

Dornbusch, R., and S. Fischer. 1986. "Stopping Hyperinflations: Past and Present." *Weltwirtschaftliches Archiv* 122 (April): 1–14.

———. 1993. "Moderate Inflation." *World Bank Economic Review* 7 (January): 1–44.

Dornbusch R., F. Sturzenegger, and H. Wolf. 1990. "Extreme Inflation: Dynamics and Stabilization." *Brookings Papers on Economic Activity 2*: 2–84.

Dornbusch, R., and H. Wolf. 1990. "Monetary Overhang and Reforms in the 1940s." MIT, Department of Economics. Processed.

Edwards, S. 1992. "Exchange Rates and Nominal Anchors." NBER Working Paper 4246. Cambridge, Mass.: National Bureau of Economic Research (December).

Edwards, S., and A. Cox-Edwards. 1987. *Monetarism and Liberalization: The Chilean Experiment.* Cambridge, Mass.: Ballinger.

Ffrench-Davis, R. 1973. *Políticas Económicas en Chile 1952–1970.* Santiago: Editorial Nueva Universidad.

Fischer, S. 1986. "Contracts, Credibility, and Disinflation." In *Indexing, Inflation, and Economic Policy,* S. Fischer, 221–45. MIT Press.

———. 1988. "Real Balances, the Exchange Rate, and Indexation: Real Variables in Disinflation." *Quarterly Journal of Economics* 103 (February): 27–50.

Fischer, S., and F. Modigliani. 1978. "Towards an Understanding of the Costs of Inflation." *Weltwirtschaftliches Archiv* Band #114: 810–32.

Fontaine, J. A. 1989. "The Chilean Economy in the 1980s: Adjustment and Recovery." In *Debt Adjustment and Recovery,* edited by S. Edwards and F. Larraín, 208–33. Oxford and New York: Blackwell.

Harberger, A. C. 1985. "Observations on the Chilean Economy, 1973–1983." *Economic Development and Cultural Change* 33 (April): 451–62.

Herrera, L. H., and R. Vergara. 1992. "Estabilidad de la Demanda de Dinero, cointegración y política monetaria." *Cuadernos de Economía* 86 (April): 35–54.

Jadresic, E. 1986. "Evolución del empleo y desempleo en Chile, 1970–85. Series anuales y trimestrales." *Colección Estudios CIEPLAN* 20 (December): 147–94.

Kiguel, M., and N. Liviatan. 1988. "Inflationary Rigidities and Orthodox Stabilization Policies: Lessons from Latin America." *The World Bank Economic Review 2* (September): 273–98.

Lagos, L. F., and A. Galetovic. 1990. "Los Efectos de la Indización Cambiaria y Salarial en el Control de la Inflación: El caso de Chile 1975–1981." *Cuadernos de Economía* 82: 357–79.

Larraín, F., and P. Meller. 1991. "The Socialist-Populist Chilean Experience: 1970–1973." In *The Macroeconomics of Populism in Latin America,* edited by R. Dornbursch and S. Edwards, 175–214. The University of Chicago Press.

Larrañaga, O. 1989. *El Déficit del Sector Público y la Política Fiscal en Chile, 1978–1987.* Santiago: ECLA.

Marshall, J., and K. Schmidt-Hebbel. 1991. "Macroeconomics of Public Sector Deficits: The Case of Chile." WPS 696. Washington, D.C.: The World Bank.

McKinnon, R. 1988. "Financial Liberalization and Economic Development." Occasional Papers 6. San Francisco: International Center for Economic Growth (ICEG).

Matte, R. E., and P. Rojas. 1989. "Evolución Reciente del Mercado Monetario y una Estimación de la Demanda por Dinero en Chile. *Cuadernos de Economía* 78 (Agosto): 195–216.

Meller, P. 1990. "Chile." In *Latin American Adjustment: How Much Has Happened?* edited by J. Williamson, 54–85. Washington D.C.: Institute for International Economics.

———. 1992. "Adjustment and Equity in Chile." Paris: OECD Development Center.

Méndez, J. C. 1979. *Chilean Economic Policy.* Santiago: Ministry of Finance.

Ministerio de Hacienda. 1982. "Exposición Sobre el Estado de la Hacienda Pública." Santiago: Dirección de Presupuestos.

Morandé, F. 1988. "Domestic Currency Appreciation and Foreign Capital Inflows. What Comes First? (Chile, 1977–1982)." *Journal of International Money and Finance* 7: 447–66.

Ramos, J. 1986. *Neo-conservative Economics in the Southern Cone of Latin America, 1973–83.* Baltimore: Johns Hopkins University Press.

Rodriguez, C. 1991. "The Macroeconomics of Public Sector Deficits: The Case of Argentina." WPS 696. Washington, D.C.: The World Bank.

Rosende, F. 1987. "Ajuste con Crecimiento: El Caso Chileno." Documento de Investigación 32. Santiago: Banco Central de Chile.

Salter, W. E. G. 1959. "Internal and External Balance: The Role of Price and Expenditure Effects." *The Economic Record* 35 (August): 226–38.

Sargent, T. 1982. "The Ends of Four Big Inflations." In *Inflation: Its Causes and Effects,* edited by R. Hall, 41–98. Chicago: The University of Chicago Press.

Sjaastad, L., and H. Cortés. 1978. "The Monetary Approach to the Balance of Payments and Interest Rates in Chile." *Estudios de Economía,* no. 11 (I Semester): 3–58.

Solimano, A. 1989. "How Private Investment Reacts to Changing Macroeconomic Conditions. The Case of Chile." WPS 212. Washington, D.C.: The World Bank.

Universidad de Chile. 1963. *La Economía Chilena en el Período 1950–1963.* Santiago: Instituto de Economía.

Valdés, S. 1992. "Financial Liberalization and the Capital Account: Chile, 1974–84." Santiago: Universidad Catolica de Chile.

2 Exchange Rate Policy and Trade Strategy

Rudiger Dornbusch and Sebastian Edwards

CHILE'S economic policy during the past twenty years has been a textbook example of an open economy. In the early 1980s, liberalization and a policy of fighting inflation without proper attention to stable financing and competitiveness caused a collapse of the currency and of the economy. Since 1983 economic policy has been inspired by the lessons of that failure and thus has been outstandingly successful.

In judging the success one must bear in mind that the country had a fiercely repressive dictatorship and mass unemployment. As shown in figure 2-1, for most of the past twenty years Chilean output was far below potential. At its peak, in the mid-1980s, unemployment had affected almost a third of the labor force. These facts do not belittle the accomplishments, but they do place in perspective the applicability of the Chilean experience to other political situations or to countries with a lower tolerance for repression.

Disturbances to the Chilean economy and opportunities that are relevant to the external sector and to management of the exchange rate include:

—the political turmoil, including populism, associated with the Allende years;

—the trade liberalization of the Pinochet regime, including a temporary reversal of the policy of the early 1980s;

—major budget cutting;

—the world debt crisis, credit rationing, and the return of Chile to the world capital market;

—major shifts in commodity prices and the resulting variations in the terms of trade;

—a disinflation program based on the exchange rate;

—the achievement of star-performer status in the 1990s.

Chile has emerged from these disturbances with a far stronger economy than it had in the early 1970s. Few doubt that the accomplishments are by now irreversible. But what comes next? For the second time in two decades, one speaks of a Chilean "miracle."

Figure 2-1. Actual and Potential GDP, 1970–92

Billion 1977
CH$

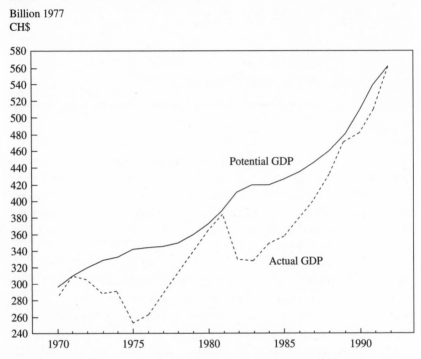

SOURCES: International Monetary Fund, *International Financial Statistics* (various issues), and Marfán and
Artiagoitia (1989).

Two further points deserve notice in this connection: even with the significant progress that was made in the 1980s, per capita consumption today is not
much higher than it was in 1970. That point is significant because it suggests
that the time necessary for successful reform to translate into a rise in the standard of living is long unless there are no adverse shocks. The other point is
that Chile has successfully opened its economy and created stable institutions
to support a market economy. Even so, while investment has increased in the
past few years, the investment ratio remained below 20 percent until 1991.
Such a low investment ratio obviously raises the question where increases in
per capita income will come from. In the past, high rates of productivity
growth have accomplished this goal. But that cannot be expected to last indefinitely unless new policy initiatives open new sources.

Do trade and exchange rate policy offer hope for further rounds of such
gains, or can they become a vehicle for improving the performance of investment, including foreign direct investment? An immediate approach to answer-

Figure 2-2. Real Exchange Rate, 1970–93

Index[a]

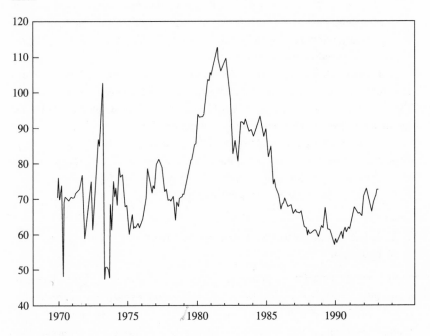

SOURCE: J. P. Morgan, unpublished data
a. 1980–82 = 100.

ing this question is to evaluate the possibilities of joining NAFTA and to expand trade relations with the Mercosur.

An Overview

Figure 2-2 shows the Chilean real exchange rate. The series shown is the J. P. Morgan measure of nonfood manufacturing prices in Chile relative to a group of forty trading partners.[1]

We can distinguish the following four periods:

1. The Allende and post-coup years, 1970–79. In this period the exchange rate was caught between inflation fighting and the need to restore and expand competitiveness in the face of a dramatic deterioration in the terms of trade— lower copper prices and higher prices for oil—and a major trade opening.

1. The real exchange rate is defined as the ratio of domestic prices to partners' prices in a common currency. Thus a rise in the ratio corresponds to a real appreciation.

2. In 1979–82, the Pinochet government embarked on an ambitious strategy of disinflation based on the exchange rate. External borrowing played a central role in financing the resulting trade imbalance and capital flight. The government persistently and stubbornly, as is common in such instances, denied reality. Ultimately, of course, the program crashed in 1982–83. A major real depreciation restored competitiveness.

3. In 1984–91, the government followed a clear strategy of progressive undervaluation of the currency. Year after year the real exchange rate depreciated. The depreciation of the dollar in world markets and mass unemployment, at the outset, helped support the gain in competitiveness.

4. The political opening called for higher real wages. The strong trade performance and readily available capital inflows accommodated a real appreciation. Major productivity gains in 1989–92 supported very high growth.

We now review these episodes in more detail.

Trade Liberalization and Accommodation of Inflation

In the early 1970s the socialist government of Allende precipitated an economic crisis. Populist policies from deficit financing to currency overvaluation and the response of controls and rationing caused diminished output, an exchange crisis, and acute inflation. In September 1973, the constitutional government of Chile, having brought the economy to the brink and beyond, was overthrown in a violent coup.

The policies of the next six years focused on five areas: restoring a vigorous private economy; deregulating (a spinoff of which was a dramatic trade opening); balancing the budget; fighting inflation; and alleviating the foreign exchange crisis.

We focus on trade liberalization and the exchange rate policy. In the area of trade, the government removed *all* quotas and permits. This was a drastic step in view of the fact that 50 percent of tariff positions required official approvals.[2] Prohibitions were reduced from 187 to only 6 by 1976; import deposits, similarly, were phased out by 1976. The government also rationalized the tariff structure. Maximum tariffs were reduced, enhancing uniformity. Table 2-1 shows that by 1979 the program was complete, with the move to a uniform 10 percent tariff.

The post-coup period was characterized by a pragmatic exchange rate policy that complemented the liberalization of trade restrictions. The multiplicity

2. See Hachette (1991, p. 42).

Table 2-1. Trade Liberalization

Condition	12/73	6/74	6/76	6/79
Maximum tariff	220	140	65	10
Percent covered	8	14.4	0.5	99.5
Effective rate of protection	151.4	51.0	19.7	13.6

Source: Edwards and Cox-Edwards (1987).

of rates was quickly reduced to only two, a tourist rate and a general rate for foreign transactions. Following an initial 300 percent devaluation, the exchange rate was depreciated at a pace sufficient to ensure no loss of competitiveness and to maintain a concern for inflation. Several maxi-devaluations and a 10 percent appreciation reflected the vagaries of the external balance, the increasing normalization of the economy, and relations with the world capital market.[3]

The normalization of external credit relations during the period after the coup is apparent from the prices of defaulted Chilean bonds, which rapidly rose as investors watched the Chilean miracle unfold and understood that the dictator might well have to seek favor with foreign bondholders.

The Overvaluation of 1979–82

Marked recovery, following the 1975 crash in output, did not occur until 1977. By 1979, normalization had gone far enough to make inflation the leading issue. Inflation continued, at 33 percent, fueled by indexation and inertia, with depreciation steadily compensating for inflation.

The background for the overvaluation of 1979–82 has two chapters. First was the trade liberalization that we reviewed in the preceding section. The other critical ingredient was a policy to stop depreciating the *nominal* exchange rate in an effort to bring an end to a vicious cycle of inflation and depreciation. Whether one appeals to the "law of one price" or simply to a Taylor-style model of rational expectations in the overlapping wage-setting process, accommodating exchange rate policy cannot fail to perpetuate an inflation process. Accordingly, the decision to stop depreciating and to peg the currency at thirty-nine pesos to the U.S. dollar in 1979 was the decisive step. Perhaps that strategy might have worked in a setting of incomes policy, as in Mexico in the late 1980s. But in Chile, as table 2-2 shows, with inflation still at 33 percent and with full wage indexation, wage inflation and the fixed rate inevitably built up

3. For details of the exchange rate policy see de Gregorio (1986) and Ffrench-Davis (1979).

Table 2-2. Inflation and Depreciation, 1979–83
Percent a year, except as noted

Characteristic	1979	1980	1981	1982	1983
Wage increase	47.8	46.9	30.3	9.7	13.7
Inflation	33.3	35.7	21.1	8.7	28.0
Depreciation[a]	14.9	0	0	30.5	54.9
Real exchange rate[a,b]	77.2	94.3	108.0	97.7	100.5

SOURCE: Authors' calculations.
a. Relative to the U.S.$.
b. Index: 1980–82=100.

a growing tension. Ultimately, with zero inflation virtually in sight, the scheme collapsed in August 1982.

Explaining Overvaluation

The real appreciation has two explanations. One focuses on indexation and inertia, the other is an equilibrium theory of the real exchange rate under the pressure of capital inflows.

The equilibrium theory is decidedly classical—new or old. This interpretation is possibly appropriate because at the end of the 1970s Chile returned to the world capital market or, to put it better, the world capital market turned on to Chile. It is always appropriate, at this stage of the discussion, to quote Taussig on capital flows—too much or too little, never the right amount.

> The loans from the creditor country . . . begin with a modest amount, then increase and proceed crescendo. They are likely to be made exceptionally large amounts toward the culminating stage of a period of activity and speculative upswing, and during that stage become larger from month to month so long as the upswing continues. With the advent of crisis, they are at once cut sharply, even cease entirely.[4]

In this scenario an *autonomous* capital inflow translates into an increase in absorption. With an increase in demand relative to available output, the prices of nontraded goods rise relative to tradables, as does the full employment wage. The capital flow itself would be explained by renewed access to world capital markets and the resulting relaxation of credit constraints in the domestic economy. The link from capital inflows to spending can be based on cost of capital arguments or on an expansion of credit and reduced credit rationing.

The scenario ends with the sudden withdrawal of capital. The resulting cut

4. Taussig (1928, p. 130).

in spending and financing forces a sharp real depreciation. A major inflation or a sharp drop in output would not be part of this story and hence puts this interpretation in question.

The alternative hypothesis focuses on pricing based on costs and fixed exchange rates and wages. The simplest model is an acceleration Phillips curve, where inflation increases when wage increases and depreciation outpace the prevailing rate of inflation. A simple model helps formulate the problem of real currency appreciation.[5] Let P, W, and E be the log level of prices, wages, and the exchange rate, and lowercase letters stand for their rates of change, with π the rate of inflation. The unemployment rate (or the GDP gap) is represented by y.

$$(2\text{-}1) \quad \dot{\pi} = (1 - \alpha)(w - \pi) + \alpha(e - \pi)$$

$$(2\text{-}2) \quad w = \pi - \sigma y$$

$$(2\text{-}3) \quad y = \Theta(i^* + e + \Delta - \pi) - \lambda(E - P) + f$$

$$(2\text{-}4) \quad CA = \mu(E - P) + \beta(i^* + \Delta + e - \pi) + \delta f,$$

where i^* and i are foreign and domestic interest rates and Δ denotes the political risk premium. Fiscal restraint is denoted by f, and CA stands for the current account surplus.

Equation 2-1 represents a standard accelerations pricing equation: inflation has inertia.[6] Deceleration is only possible if wage inflation or the rate of currency depreciation can be brought down below the prevailing rate of inflation. Equation 2-2 describes wage inflation. The rate of increase of wages, because of explicit or implicit indexation, is equal to the rate of inflation, but with an adjustment for cyclical conditions. In the third equation, the unemployment rate is determined by real interest rates and by the level of competitiveness.

Figure 2-3 shows the phase diagram of this model, using equation 2-3 and the combination of equation 2-1 and equation 2-2:

$$(2\text{-}5) \quad \dot{\pi} = \tau(e - \pi) + (1 - \alpha)\lambda(E - P) - (1 - \alpha)\Theta(i^* + \Delta);$$
$$\tau = [\alpha - (1 - \alpha)\Theta] > 0.$$

The diagram is drawn for a given rate of depreciation, e_o, and it is assumed that the term τ is positive.

Consider now a program of disinflation. Starting in a steady state at point A, the government reduces the rate of depreciation to zero and sustains the

5. See, among others, Dornbusch (1993) and Edwards (1989, 1993a). Edwards (1993a) proposes a very detailed model that embodies an explicit role for expectational mechanisms.
6. See Dornbusch and Fischer (1993) and the references given there.

Figure 2-3. Disinflation

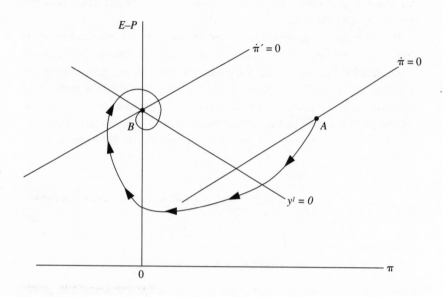

now fixed exchange rate. The new long-run equilibrium is at point B, where inflation has come down to zero.

The immediate effect of the rate fixing is to cut nominal interest rates and hence the real interest rate, so that demand increases. Higher demand next leads to real appreciation. There is a boom (see figure 2-1 above, with 1981 the boom year). The instant rise in the level of demand, output, and employment gradually wears off. Ultimately the loss in competitiveness returns the economy to normal levels of output and then creates a recession. The economy will return to full equilibrium, with reduced inflation, only after deflation has restored the initial level of competitiveness. Protracted unemployment is the rule. Moreover, in the early phases of the adjustment program, the current account turns toward deficit.

The highly stylized model captures the patterns of the adjustment process. It shows in particular that on the way to full disinflation, high unemployment and large deficits constitute major confidence obstacles to the continuation of the program. And if confidence does break down, so does the financing of external imbalances. Interest rates will soar, output will fall faster, and ultimately the program will be abandoned.

Table 2-3. External Debt, 1978–82
Billion U.S.$

Type	1978	1979	1980	1981	1982
Total	7.4	9.4	12.1	15.7	17.3
Long-term	6.3	7.7	9.5	12.8	14.0
Short-term	1.1	1.6	2.6	3.0	3.3

SOURCE: World Bank, *World Debt Tables* (various years).

Back to Facts

Whether the classical equilibrium model is the right approach or, as we believe, the inertia factor matters little for the rest of the story. Record high world interest rates, world recession, credit rationing, and loss of confidence all built up into a gigantic wave that crashed on the prospects of sustaining the fixed par. Moreover, for many observers that outcome was all too obvious. Table 2-3 shows the rapid accumulation of debt, including liabilities to official institutions, in the 1978–82 period.

Accordingly a situation developed in which all those who thought the rate would go, and possibly with it trade liberalization, borrowed to buy dollars or durables. All those who maintained confidence lent in pesos. Deposit rates in 1980–82 averaged 37.4 percent (1980), 40.8 percent (1981), and 47.8 percent (1982). In the light of the fixed exchange rate, until June 1982, Chile was clearly a gambling parlor. The annualized real deposit rate for 1981 was 28.7 percent.

The trade balance (see figure 2-4) reached unprecedented deficit levels. At the same time, because of tightened U.S. monetary policy, the interest burden increased sharply while the deterioration in the terms of trade reduced the purchasing power of exports.

The temporary stabilization was accompanied by a consumption boom—a pattern that by now has become a common feature of such programs. In the period 1978–81, real consumption increased by 26 percent. That might be thought of as the Diaz Alejandro effect—rising real wages spill over into increased spending. Much of the rise in spending, of course, falls on imported consumer goods, including, notably, consumer durables. Constant peso imports increased by 68 percent over this period. Consumer goods imports in dollars doubled over this period.

In June 1982 the peso peg was abandoned. Trade restrictions returned, exchange control came back, a debt crisis erupted (see table 2-4), and the prosperity of 1981 gave way to a disastrous collapse of economic activity. Mass unemployment ensued.

Figure 2-4. Trade Balance, 1970–92

Billion U.S.$

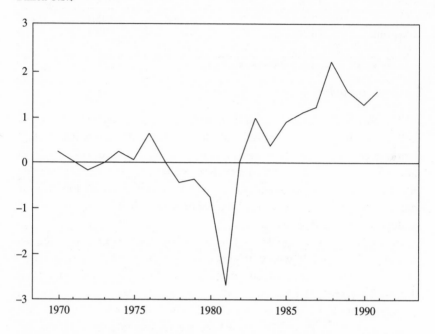

SOURCE: International Monetary Fund, *International Financial Statistics* (various issues).

After the Collapse

The immediate aftermath of the 1982 crisis was a setback on all fronts (see table 2-5). Exchange control was introduced, trade restrictions returned, and annual appointments had to be made with the commercial banks to work out debts. Special arrangements for dollar debtors were set up. Bankruptcy was the rule. The confidence, exuberance, and arrogance of policymakers had vanished.

Regaining Competitiveness

For our purposes the most interesting aspect of this crisis period is the behavior of the real exchange rate. Indexation still prevailed. Even so, the real exchange rate depreciated in 1982–86 by nearly 30 percent. How was that possible?

The substantial gain in competitiveness has two explanations. First, the ex-

Table 2-4. The Payments Crisis of 1981–82
Billion U.S.$

Category	1979	1980	1981	1982
Balance of payments	1,047	1,244	766	−1,165
Current account	−1,169	−1,971	−4,733	−2,304
Financial services	−675	−930	−1,453	−1,921

SOURCE: Central Bank of Chile (1989).

Table 2-5. The Adjustment of the Early 1980s

Category	1981	1982	1983	1984	1985	1986
Growth	5.5	−14.1	−0.7	6.4	2.5	5.6
Unemployment	11.1	22.1	22.2	19.3	16.3	13.5
Real wage	9.0	0.3	−10.9	0.2	−4.5	2.0
Real exchange[a]	108	98	101	90	80	69

SOURCE: Edwards and Cox-Edwards (1987).
a. Index: 1980–82=100.

treme levels of unemployment put a significant damper on wage settlements. Jadresic has shown that unemployment exerts a depressing effect on wages; he estimates that a 10 percent increase in the unemployment rate will reduce the real wage by 2 percent.[7] The doubling of the unemployment rate, not counting the employment in low-paying public works programs, clearly helps explain how real depreciation was possible.

After 1985 the large decline of the dollar in world markets helps explain the gain in competitiveness. In these years Chile steadily depreciated in nominal terms on the dollar and thus gained in terms of its real effective exchange rate. Even though the nominal exchange rate policy helps explain mechanically the gain in competitiveness, it is essential to recognize the role of unemployment in accommodating so sharp a real depreciation.

On the domestic side the reduction of government spending offset the expansion of exports and net exports (see figure 2-5). While exports as a share of GDP rose from 20 to 33 percent in the 1980–92 period, government consumption declined steadily, from 12 to 8.6 percent. The large real depreciation thus facilitated the retrenchment required in the accommodation of so large a spending shock.

The Return of External Capital

The second aspect of the post-collapse years is the treatment of external capital. Chile was part of the Latin American debt crisis. Like other countries

7. See Jadresic (1992).

Figure 2-5. Exports and Government Consumption, 1976–92[a]

Percent of GDP

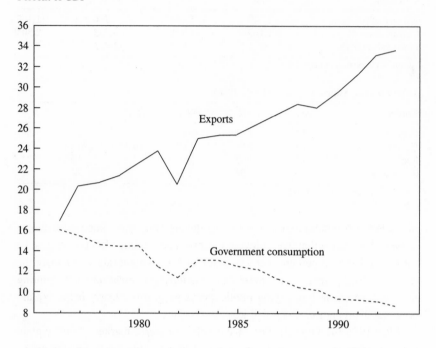

SOURCES: International Monetary Fund, *International Financial Statistics* (various issues), and Central Bank of Chile.
a. 1977 CH$.

in the region, Chile was unable to meet its debt service, and, as a result, its bonds started trading at a discount and external credit dried up. More rapidly than other countries, Chile made an effort to restructure its external liabilities.

Starting in 1983, agreements with the commercial banks stretched maturities and created more favorable terms. A generous debt-equity swap program and a debt-repatriation scheme allowed investors to take advantage of the discounts in secondary markets to repatriate public debt.

The return to the world capital market had a clear implication for both real wages and the real exchange rate, making both less vulnerable and removing the necessity to live closely by an external constraint. Real appreciation was, therefore, within limits, a possibility.

As institutions were strengthened in the transition to democracy, Chile's external credit became stronger. By 1993 bond ratings had recovered and even reached BBA levels.

Figure 2-6. Average Tariff Rate, 1980–92

Percent

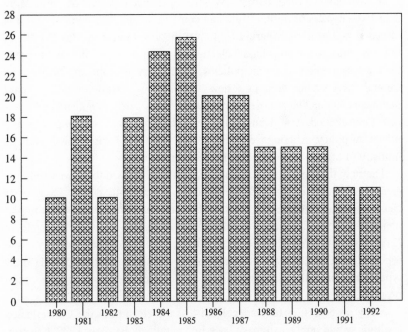

SOURCES: de Gregorio (1986) and International Monetary Fund, *International Financial Statistics* (various issues) and *Direction of Trade Statistics* (various issues).

As the domestic economy recovered, trade was liberalized. In the immediate aftermath of the collapse and increasingly until 1985, protection returned (see figure 2-6). By 1985 the average tariff was up to 26 percent. But that did not last long. By 1988 tariffs had already been brought down to 15 percent; they declined further to 11 percent in 1991 as the new democratic government took office.

The model of a very open economy is one of the lasting accomplishments of the past two decades. Combined with strong growth in the world economy, it was one of the important elements in the strong expansion of the Chilean economy in the second half of the 1980s.

The Period 1989–93

The past four years mark the shift in Chile from a perception that all is well until further notice to the clear-cut recognition that all is well and very unlikely to unravel. Democracy is firmly in place, with no threat to economic institutions and accomplishments; growth is strong; real wages have been rising. What comes next is the only interesting question.

In December of 1989, Patricio Aylwin was elected president of Chile. More than sixteen years of military rule had come to an end, and a broad coalition of center and center-left parties took over the government in March 1990. A few days prior to the presidential election, as a way to ensure the continuity of the market-oriented economic policies, the military government reformed the Central Bank statute, creating a new "autonomous" institution whose board members could not be removed for ten years.[8] This newly established independent Central Bank was given the responsibility to conduct exchange rate and monetary policy. Although consultation between the Central Bank and the ministry of finance was expected, it was not required.

The new democratic government of President Aylwin took over amid increasing speculation on the future direction of economic policy. Three areas caused special concern: (1) whether the policies of fiscal austerity implemented by the military regime during most of its rule would be maintained; (2) the extent to which the structural reforms engineered by the military—and especially the opening of international trade—would be continued; and (3) the type of measures that the government would implement to pursue its social programs.

Many observers, in fact, speculated that the election of the Concertacion coalition would imply a slippage back into populism. By early 1990, however, perceptive analysts understood that the incoming government was not going to tamper with the main elements of the market reforms. If anything, the new authorities were ready to move even further in some areas, such as the opening of the economy and the reduction of import tariffs.[9] In fact, the incoming administration soon decided to slash import tariffs by one-third (see the discussion below).[10]

Minister of Finance Alejandro Foxley clearly stated the Aylwin government's decision to maintain the main aspects of the market reforms. In a 1990

8. Of course, the law establishes a number of limited circumstances—including corruption and other forms of misconduct—under which members of the board can be relieved of their functions.

9. The Aylwin government reduced import tariffs to a uniform 11 percent and has declined to participate in new regional integration efforts for fear that they would be "too protectionist." See chapter 5 for further details.

10. In an incisive article, Fontaine (1989) has argued that by 1989 the majority of Chilean voters were still skeptical about the merits of the market-oriented reforms. He says that the process of convergence and synthesis began with the intellectual elites of the Socialist and Christian Democrat parties.

interview he said: "Preserving the former government's achievements means maintaining an open economy fully integrated into world markets, dynamic growth in exports, with a private sector fully committed to the task of [economic] development."[11]

Although once in power the leaders of the new democratic Chilean government firmly supported some of the fundamental market reforms of the 1970s and 1980s, they still had some important disagreements with the former rulers regarding the role of social oriented and redistributive policies. Foxley was equally clear on this point in the 1990 interview: "Remedying the former government's shortcomings means recapturing the balance between economic growth and the deteriorated conditions of the middle and, above all, the lower classes."

In seeking funding for new social programs, the new Chilean government strongly and decisively rejected traditional formulas based on inflationary finance. Instead, the new administration made it clear from day one that the only way to increase social spending without generating unsustainable macroeconomic pressures was to find solid sources of government revenues. The new government continued the policy of targeting programs for the poor, avoiding blanket subsidies that had historically benefited the middle and upper classes.

An important political decision made by the new government was to address head-on, and during the first year of its administration, two critical economic reforms: a tax package aimed at funding the new social programs and a reform of the Pinochet labor law, which had been criticized by union leaders and some political commentators. Government officials were careful to explain that these two pieces of legislation constituted the *only* important changes to the economic model of Pinochet. In this way, and especially by tackling these issues early, the government sought to minimize possible negative effects on private investment associated with policy uncertainty. This strategy is clearly discussed in a perceptive document by Minister of the Presidency Edgardo Boeninger: "The administration first undertook the task of implementing reforms producing either uncertainty or cost increases in the economy (tax reform and changes in labor legislation). These have now [March 1991] been mostly completed, enabling the government to guarantee full stability of the rules of the economic game for the rest of its term, thus facilitating dynamic behavior by business."[12]

11. *Newsweek* (Latin American edition), March 26, 1990.
12. See Boeninger (1991, pp. 35–36).

Trade Policy after 1989: Further
Liberalization, Productivity Gains, and
Export Booms

For decades Chile's international trade was severely repressed. In 1973 import tariffs averaged 105 percent and had great variability, with some goods subject to nominal tariffs of more than 700 percent and others fully exempt from import duties. A battery of quantitative restrictions were also applied, including outright prohibition of some imports and deposits of up to 10,000 percent that had to be posted before certain items could be imported.[13] These protective measures were complemented with a highly distortive multiple exchange rate system consisting of fifteen different rates. By August of 1975, all quantitative restrictions had been eliminated, and the average tariff had been reduced to 44 percent. This tariff reduction process continued until June of 1979, when all tariff items but one (automobiles) were set at 10 percent. In the mid-1980s, in the midst of the debt crisis, temporary tariff hikes were implemented; by 1987, however, a uniform level of 15 percent had been firmly established. The combination of increased competition and an aggressively depreciated real exchange rate (after 1984) helped create a dramatic expansion in exports.

In spite of what pundits had predicted, the new democratic administration of President Patricio Aylwin decided to continue the opening process. In June of 1991, the administration reduced import tariffs even further to a uniform 11 percent, and it has firmly pushed for the creation of a free trade zone with the United States.

The relaxation of trade impediments has had a fundamental effect on the Chilean economy. Recent evidence strongly suggests that the increased foreign competition has been associated with strong growth in productivity. For example, labor productivity in the Chilean manufacturing sector increased at an average annual rate of 13.4 percent during the early phase of the trade reforms.[14]

Table 2-6 contains data on the change in aggregate total factor productivity growth in the period following the implementation of trade liberalization reform in Chile and in five other Latin countries. The table shows that Chile experienced the fastest increases in total factor productivity growth in the post-reform period, followed by Costa Rica. These productivity gains have been uneven across sectors, however, with some of them experiencing rapid growth

13. See de la Cuadra and Hachette (1990).
14. See Edwards and Cox-Edwards (1987).

Table 2-6. Change in Total Factor Productivity Growth, 1978–91[a]
Percent

Country	1978–82 compared with 1987–91	Country	1978–82 compared with 1987–91
Argentina	1.91	Costa Rica	3.25
Bolivia	0.11	Mexico	−0.32
Chile	4.96	Uruguay	2.02

SOURCE: Martin (1992).
a. For all countries but Chile, computed as the difference of total factor productivity growth for 1987–91 and 1978–82. For Chile the prereform period is 1972–78.

while others have stagnated severely.[15] The results for Chile in table 2-6 coincide with those obtained by Edwards, who found that in the late 1970s, after the trade reforms had been completed, total factor productivity growth was approximately three times higher than the historical average.[16]

The story of Chile's success in the past few years is largely the story of the boom in agricultural exports. During the 1960s Chile was a net importer of agricultural goods. Today, exports from the agriculture, forestry, and fishing industries are increasingly important in the Chilean economy. In 1970 Chile exported U.S.$33 million in agriculture, forestry, and fishing products; by 1991 this figure had jumped to U.S.$1.2 billion. Notice that this figure excludes those manufactured goods based on the elaboration of products from these sectors. Chile's success in the agriculture sector is not limited to fruits, however. Production has also increased significantly in more traditional crops—many of which are mostly devoted to domestic consumption. Much of Chile's increased agricultural production has been the result of rapidly improving productivity.[17]

After 1984 the trade reform was supported by a strongly depreciated real exchange rate, which provided a significant degree of competitiveness to Chilean exports. Between 1982 and 1988, the real exchange rate was devalued by approximately 80 percent.

Starting in 1985 the government introduced a novel nominal exchange rate system, characterized by a crawling band. The main purpose of this policy was to maintain the international competitiveness of Chilean exports. By adopting this system, the authorities explicitly relegated to a second plane in the policy agenda the rapid convergence of domestic inflation to "world levels." The new economic team placed growth (led by vigorous exports) at the center of its program. Initially the width of the nominal exchange rate band was $+/-2$ per-

15. See Fuentes (1992).
16. See Edwards (1985) and Agacino, Rivas, and Roman (1991).
17. Edwards (1993b).

Table 2-7. Exchange Rate Bands, Selected Intervals, 1985–92
Percent

Period	Band
January 1985–December 1987	2
January 1988–June 1989	3
June 1989–January 1992	5
January 1992–	10

SOURCE: Authors' calculations.

cent around a moving reference rate. In January of 1988, the width of the band was increased to $+/-3$ percent and again increased to $+/-5$ percent in June 1989.

Exchange Rate Policy after 1989

By late 1989 the Chilean economy was showing clear signs of overheating—inflation climbed to 30 percent, imports grew at 35 percent, and GDP grew at 10 percent (see figure 2-1 on potential and actual GDP). The incoming government, and especially the newly appointed Central Bank, soon decided to control expansion of aggregate demand. In the first half of 1990, interest rates were hiked by more than 3 percentage points in real terms (yields on ten-year Central Bank notes increased from 6.9 percent to 9.7 percent in real terms), and credit policy became increasingly tight.

Although these measures were successful in curbing inflation, they had an unwanted side effect: the increase in interest rate differentials attracted considerable inflows of short-term capital, making monetary management particularly difficult. In addition, the realization that the new authorities would not alter the fundamental course of economic policy made Chile an increasingly attractive place for international speculators and investors. In 1990 alone, international reserves increased by almost 90 percent.[18]

The rapid accumulation in international reserves put increasing pressure on the exchange rate, which rapidly moved to the floor of the band (see table 2-7). The Central Bank reacted to these events by engaging in massive sterilization operations and relaxing the requirements for moving capital out of the country. Although these policies had short-term effects, capital movements did not subside. On the contrary, during 1991 and 1992, capital flew in record amounts to Chile. A strong performance in export growth added to the sense that the country was suffering from exchange overabundance. The real exchange rate began to experience a process of steady real appreciation.

18. See Bianchi (1992) for a fascinating insider's account of this period.

An important question the authorities had to address was whether this situation of "overabundance" would be sustainable or if a decline in the level of funds available would occur in the near future. The government and the public became particularly concerned about the real exchange rate, as they remembered that the 1981–82 collapse had been preceded by a steep degree of real depreciation. This time, however, the situation was different. Interest rates were not as high as in the early 1980s; the financial sector was much stronger; and exports were growing rapidly.

Nevertheless the nature of these capital inflows remains a question. Whether these capital movements are temporary—and thus subject to sudden reversals, as in 1982—is particularly important in evaluating their possible consequences. In a recent study, Calvo, Leiderman, and Reinhart argue that the most important factors behind the generalized inflow of resources are external.[19] Their empirical analysis suggests that the recession in the industrialized world and the reduction in U.S. interest rates are the two catalysts of these movements of capital. These authors suggest that once these world economic conditions change, the volume of capital flowing to Latin America will be reduced. At that point the pressure over the real exchange rate will subside, and the real exchange rate will have to be depreciated.

During much of 1991 the Central Bank tried different ways to tackle the appreciation forces: capital mobility was increased, pension funds were allowed to invest a (small) percentage of their portfolio in foreign securities, the correction for world inflation to compute the reference rate was suspended, and the Bank engaged in heavy sterilization.[20] In spite of all these efforts, capital continued to flow into the country, and the nominal rate remained at the floor of the band.

In late 1991 the authorities changed their diagnosis regarding the nature of the external imbalance. Increasingly the Central Bank argued that the country had gone through a structural change and that the increases in productivity, the change in the terms of trade, and Chile's reduced country risk had generated a shift in the equilibrium real exchange rate. Continuing to battle these forces was deemed ineffective and counterproductive. In January of 1992 the reference exchange rate was revalued by 5 percent, and the width of the band was increased to 10 percent. The Central Bank committed itself not to intervene more intensively to support the new rate. Later in the year the authorities implemented a series of additional measures aimed at alleviating the pressure on

19. Calvo, Leiderman, and Reinhart (1993).

20. An unwanted consequence of this was that the Central Bank incurred large losses. It paid high interest rates on its own paper and obtained a modest yield from its reserves. A similar situation occurred in Colombia during this period.

the exchange rate, including reserve requirements (30 percent) on short-term capital movements and replacement of the dollar peg with a basket peg with respect to the dollar (50 percent), the deutsche mark (30 percent), and the yen (20 percent). The purpose of this last measure was to alter the arbitrage relationships and to discourage capital inflows.

The actual nominal rate appreciated after the exchange rate adjustment of January 1992, but from then on remained within the band. This measure generated significant political problems, as exporters—and especially agricultural exporters—argued for compensation and increased protection. In line with its announcements, however, the government did not give in, maintaining its policy of openness.

By and large our discussion shows that after 1989 the Chilean authorities continued the pragmatic exchange rate policy initiated in 1985. It made an effort to maintain competitiveness and to avoid overvaluing the exchange rate. Not surprisingly, the authorities found that a high degree of capital mobility makes it extremely difficult if not impossible to manage the money supply under anything like fixed rates. The pragmatic approach showed clearly in the government's refusal to use the nominal exchange rate as an anchor in an effort to bring inflation down at any cost. The democratic government understood that after decades of frustration and stagnation, vigorous and sustainable growth, combined with increasing real wages and social programs, was a priority. Inflation control is occurring gradually, without jeopardizing the achievements in exports and productivity.

Lessons and Policy Challenges Ahead

In this concluding section we highlight some of the conclusions to be drawn from the Chilean experience, and we look to the challenges ahead.

The Costs and Continuity of Reform

Two lessons stand out. First, continuity in policies ultimately must count for a lot. Second, the costs of transition have been huge. Chile has undergone a radical transformation in its economic structure and, indeed, in the way government is viewed in the economy. After two decades of experimentation, we see a modern and market-oriented economy where the role of government is targeted toward market failures, not pervasive intervention. Around the world the trend toward such a transformation is under way, but it is fair to say that in Chile the process has gone further and deeper than in most other economies. Such a prominent and unchallenged role for the market and for market-

Table 2-8. Growth and Share of Investment in GDP, 1985–92
Percent

Period	Growth	Investment
1985–89	7.8	16.4
1990–92	6.1	21.0

SOURCE: Central Bank of Chile (1989).

oriented policy surely makes up in part, at least, for any other shortcomings such as size and location.

Closely connected to this first point is the exorbitant cost of modernizing the economy. We must be careful in this judgment because the sheer loss in output documented in figure 2-1 cannot be uniquely ascribed to modernization. Some of it is due to the monstrously incompetent overvaluation strategy of the late 1970s, some to the decline in real export prices, some to the debt crisis and the accompanying credit rationing. In fact, one might even ask whether the modernization per se had any cost at all or, going further, whether it might have restrained the costs of the various shocks. It would be wrong to take this view. The overvaluation of the 1970s was part of the same policy approach, except that it failed. The immense fiscal contraction reflected in the decline of the share of government spending is part of the strategy and, in the end was a success, though it was not along the way.

On the side of costs one must also note that, perhaps inevitably, the modernization has translated into a long period of sharply reduced real wages. Thus output was lost and redistribution of income was an important part of the transition. Only by 1990 was the real wage back to its 1970 level. Was such a large cut in real wages—presumably the counterpart of a real depreciation— necessary to accomplish the transformation? And if it was a necessary investment, when will the investors realize the dividends?

Investment and Productivity

In the late 1980s reform in Chile paid off. The growth rate of output rose to Asian levels. The great puzzle was to identify the sources of growth. For the time being, the explanation must be a sharp increase in total factor productivity attendant upon reform and the option of an outward-oriented trade strategy. Investment is so far *not* the explanation. As the data in table 2-8 show, the investment rate, on current data, did not rise to even close to 30 percent of GDP, as is common in high-growth economies.

We have no doubt that high growth of measured total factor productivity is always the bonus of an aggressive modernization strategy. Catching up comes

Table 2-9. Exports and Imports, 1970–91
Percent of GDP, 1977 pesos

Period	Exports	Imports
1970–79	15.7	23.4
1980–91	26.9	25.2
1991	33.0	27.7

SOURCE: Central Bank of Chile (1989).

easiest when countries internationalize in their allocation of resources and in their mind-set. But one would expect that substantial investment is a sine qua non to harvest these productivity gains. The full explanation of the Chilean growth miracle must wait until the publication of the new national accounts data. Apparently these new series report far higher investment rates than were reported in the current (1977-based) data.

Trade Strategy

Chile has undertaken a radical trade opening in the past two decades, abandoning quotas, reducing tariffs to a moderate 11 percent rate, and encouraging trade to become a far more important part of economic activity. Table 2-9 shows that the ratio of exports to GDP tripled between 1970 and 1992. On the surface, as an experiment in trade opening, the Chilean strategy was altogether successful. The success can be measured in three complementary ways:

—trade has increasingly become a source of growth;

—trade widening has supported a strategy of retrenching the role of government;

—a flexible and large trade sector affords an important shock absorber for external shocks and a mechanism that avoids bottlenecks.

One might argue whether, at the margin, the strategy was phased in with the right timing and whether it went far enough or too far. The truth is that we have no very good way to answer these questions. Harberger-style wisdom is probably the right answer in two ways: first, use any opportunity you get because another one is almost never around the corner; second, any external protection scheme that is cluttered is bad, ipso facto.

Going beyond the accomplishments, what are the next challenges? The Chilean government has expended great energy in getting on the list for early adherence to NAFTA, and it has been successful in making its point. Of course NAFTA is not here quite yet, and much of the Clinton administration's commitment to Chile may be lip service. Certainly Chile has no constituency that would push the issue, quite unlike Mexico or Brazil. Chile is a small, remote,

Table 2-10. Directions of Trade, 1991
Percent of total

Location	Exports	Imports
United States	17.7	20.6
European Community	31.9	18.3
Japan	18.2	8.4
Western Hemisphere	14.4	27.1

SOURCE: International Monetary Fund (1993), *Direction of Trade Statistics Yearbook*, pp. 2–7.

open economy that trades little with the United States (see table 2-10). From the U.S. perspective, it is hard to make the case that vital national interests are involved in securing free trade with Chile.

The attempt to join NAFTA might be interpreted as a broader attempt to put Chile on the map as a place for high value-added manufacturing. In this sense, NAFTA partnership might draw foreign direct investment and build up the next decade's sources of growth.

A more plausible strategy is emerging in the market. The Chilean business community, with the experience of reform in business, trade, and finance, is doing increasing business in the neighboring economies. That is the natural place for Chilean growth, not a grand U.S. strategy. The very fact that this regional activity is so strong underlines the point that the market is a lot better than activist, interventionist governments in guessing where the brightest prospects are.

The Capital Account

The winner's curse is the capital account. Capital is internationally mobile, and the rest of the world's pockets are very deep relative to a small economy's capital market and absorptive capacity. The credit rationing of the early 1980s meant a dramatic shock to the economy, with a collapse in output and in real wages. The return to the capital market, and the preferred status incumbent on very successful reform, have brought an overabundance of credit and capital. The capital account has started wagging the economy, and a growth-oriented real exchange rate strategy conflicts with the pressure for real appreciation that comes from capital inflows.

Chile has coped with the capital inflow problem for the most part by regulating the ability to import capital and by regulating capital outflows. It has also used the crawling peg with a band, but not with much success. As we saw, the rate is mostly at the strong end, so the scope for variation within the band does not play much of a role. In fact, the possibility of a shift of the band as a result of appreciation presumably offsets the chances of within-band depreciation.

Could Chile have used a very different strategy, namely a capital inflow tax? Of course there are administrative difficulties. But when all is said and done, a tax, and possibly a variable one, is probably an effective and market-oriented means to moderate an excessive enthusiasm of the world capital market. The consideration is important because of the possibility that this enthusiasm may cool off, perhaps because of trouble in Mexico or Argentina. Because the effects of contagion are important, less dependence on external capital and its vagaries is desirable, and a capital inflow tax is probably the only means of achieving that.

We Are All Reformers

Chile of all Latin American countries best documents how much of a shift in thinking has taken place. In the 1970s orthodoxy was tantamount to Pinochet, Chicago, conservatism, and antisocial policy. Today, in the aftermath of some tempering of the policies, but mostly in view of the sheer success of these policies and of the pressure of world opinion, Chile has espoused these policies and rejected populism and interventionism. There is nothing wrong with this; on the contrary, we applaud the flexibility with which Chilean policymakers in the democratic camp have enlisted market forces and ideas to promote aggregate growth and thus gain room to pursue social improvements.

Comment by Susan M. Collins

This paper reviews the Chilean experience since the early 1970s and successfully explains developments and infers lessons. The concluding discussion of lessons and policy challenges is especially useful. Much has happened in Chile during the past two decades, and the paper tries to cover a lot of ground. Not surprisingly, some issues are only partially developed. My comments will focus on some of the loose ends and speculate about how key issues might have been expanded.

The first section of the paper briefly reviews the period after the coup. This period featured aggressive management of the exchange rate and a major liberalization of trade. The discussion, however, makes little attempt to explore the extent to which exchange rate policy and trade strategy generated the revival of growth or the implications of those policies for factor productivity. I believe these questions are of special interest because Chile went through another cycle, ten years later, that is similar in some respects: from a sharp decline in output and high unemployment in 1982 to recovery in the midst of a major real depreciation and trade liberalization. The authors stop short of exploring whether these policies play similar roles in both episodes.

Turning to a discussion of the 1979–82 experience with fixing the nominal exchange rate in an attempt to bring down inflation, the paper suggests two explanations for the large real appreciation that occurred and for the initial boom followed by a slowdown and eventual collapse of output and of the exchange rate regime. The first explanation focuses on inflows of foreign capital pushing up domestic demand and causing a real appreciation, followed by collapse when the capital flows reverse, perhaps in response to declining confidence. This model is put into question because of its supposed inability to explain the subsequent sharp collapse of output and surge in inflation. The alternative explanation, which the authors illustrate using a stylized model, focuses on the role of wage and price indexation and inertial components of inflation. In this explanation, the fixed exchange rate leads to a two-stage disinflation. In the first stage, lower real and nominal interest rates lead to a boom in domestic output, but inflation comes down slowly. Then, as the real appreciation grows, output growth slows, turning negative in the second stage. A key point of the model is that a prolonged recession and a period of high unemployment are necessary to achieve a sustained reduction in inflation.

I would like to make two points about this section of the paper. The first is that I find surprising the authors' view that inertia can explain the experience while capital inflows and outflows cannot. My impression is that a full explanation of the developments would rely on both channels for an initial boom followed by a collapse. The two are reinforcing, not contradictory, and I see no reason to reject one in favor of the other. Instead, the two components should be merged to provide a more complete picture.

A related issue is the behavior of real interest rates. The paper mentions that real interest rates came down at the beginning of the episode, but the authors do not provide a complete series. The data suggest that real interest rates were high by international standards at the beginning of the period and rose during 1979–81. Surely these developments are consistent with large speculative capital inflows through 1981 that were reversed as the expectation that the regime would collapse grew with the extent of the real appreciation. It would be useful to incorporate the interest rate developments more fully into the story.

The paper presents a model of disinflation through fixing the nominal exchange rate. This model tells a very different story from the one often discussed in the context of nominal anchors. In my view, the authors have this point right, while many often-heard claims about the benefits of nominal anchors are simply wrong. The nominal anchor proponents assume that announcing a fixed exchange rate enables a country to avoid the unemployment and recession phase of disinflation by increasing the credibility of the anti-inflation policy and thereby changing the behavior of wage and price setters. But these programs have worked quite differently in practice—particularly those aimed at bringing down moderate inflations. My reading of the evidence suggests that the output costs of disinflation have been at least as large for programs with nominal anchors as for those without them. (There is a stronger rationale for introducing a temporary fixed exchange rate as part of a program for stopping a hyperinflation.)

Does the Chilean experience suggest any lessons about the effectiveness of nominal anchors in disinflation? Although the authors do not address this question, it seems to me well worth asking. In Chile, the period of the fixed exchange rate saw a gradual reduction in inflation, but with slowing growth in output. The experiment collapsed before we could see the second phase of the model—the collapse of output and the surge in unemployment in 1982 occurred in the midst of a balance of payments crisis and a steep devaluation, which were not the result of further real appreciation. I inferred from the paper that the authors believe that the decline in growth would have continued if the balance of payments crisis had been postponed. They did not expect the fixed nominal exchange rate to allow Chile to avoid a recession during the disinflation because they believe that wage- and price-setting behavior responds sluggishly and that announcing a fixed exchange rate does not immediately lend credibility to an anti-inflation program. Further, Chile was able to carry out a large and sustained devaluation of the exchange rate between 1982 and 1989 while containing inflation at about 20 percent to 25 percent. Edwards and Cox-Edwards make the point that Chile was able to avoid reigniting inflation during this period because of its tight control on fiscal policies.[21] Those points would make useful contributions to this paper as well. More generally, it seems to me that the paper should try to draw lessons about the role of exchange rate policy in controlling inflation in Chile.

The paper then discusses the period after the crisis, with its return to aggressive management of the exchange rate and reinstatement (at first) of trade and exchange controls. During 1983–86, however, growth revived and unemployment came down substantially, while inflation was kept below 30 percent. Dur-

21. Edwards and Cox-Edwards (1987).

ing 1986–89, as strong growth continued, Chile's trade policy turned back toward liberalization.

I have three questions about the developments in this period. First, how much of the recovery, during both 1983–86 and 1987–89, can be attributed to the real depreciation? The paper claims that increased international competitiveness caused an export boom, but it gives little information about export performance. The paper also states that much of the export growth was concentrated in the agricultural and natural resource sectors, but it gives no information about the composition of exports. If agriculture is most of the export story, how much of the surge should we attribute to exchange rate policy rather than to other measures—perhaps programs targeted at teaching farmers how to increase their crop yields?

I also note in this context that the real exchange rate provided appears to be a relative price of manufactured products, and it is not clear that this would be the relevant exchange rate for explaining developments in these sectors. Further, I wonder whether there is a puzzle that the substantial decline in the relative price of Chilean manufactures does not appear to have sparked a surge in manufactured exports.

A second set of questions relates to the effectiveness of trade liberalization in increasing factor productivity. The paper argues that productivity has grown dramatically in Chile in recent years, and it gives a figure for the difference in total growth in factor productivity from 1972–78 to 1978–82. But it is not clear how to interpret this figure. Some trade reforms were undertaken prior to 1978, but the figures for 1972–78 include a sharp drop in output, and some of the subsequent growth is simply recovery. Furthermore, one of the main periods of interest—the return to liberalization after 1985—is not included. Another paper for this conference, that by Bosworth and Marfán, appears to reach a very different conclusion—that the lack of growth in labor productivity in Chile over long periods is puzzling. I find myself persuaded by the approach of Bosworth and Marfán and skeptical of the claims made by Dornbusch and Edwards. The two views are based on different periods and different methodologies, and it seems important to try to reconcile them. This paper would benefit from a fuller discussion of the links between liberalization and productivity that contrasted the initial period, 1973–79, with the more recent phase, 1983–89, and beyond.

Third, the authors place their discussion of Chile's return to trade liberalization provocatively after a discussion of Chile's relatively early return to world capital markets in the mid-1980s. The placement suggested to me that the ability to borrow to help smooth the structural adjustments that accompany a liberalization might have been one factor in the ability to liberalize again. Does the Chilean experience suggest that breathing space of this type was important? I believe that breathing space was important in other countries, such as South Korea during its restructuring in the early 1980s. Perhaps this is a lesson from Chile as well.

Finally, the paper turns to the period since 1989, which has been characterized by a move toward democracy and further liberalization and market reforms. One issue of current concern is the recent appreciation of the real exchange rate in the face of large capital inflows. The authors argue that this period has been managed relatively well and that there is little reason for concern, unless substantial further real appreciation occurs. Let me close my remarks with a question that has a somewhat less positive implication. Might the real appreciation caused by capital inflows and primary product exports afflict Chile with the Dutch disease, decreasing the competitiveness of its industrial sectors? Given that Chile does not appear to have a strong base in manufactured output and exports and that shifting labor into manufactures may be the path toward sustainable, long-term increases in living standards, it seems important to discuss this set of issues before reaching a sanguine conclusion about the current level of Chile's real exchange rate.

Comment by Nicolás Eyzaguirre

I agree with most of the analysis and policy implications of the paper, but I would like to concentrate on two issues that are not, in my view, supported by our recent economic experience. Those points are the effect on a small, open, and financially integrated economy of an increase in the amount (or decrease in the cost) of capital inflows and the inertial feature of inflation in Chile under an accommodating exchange rate policy.

Comparisons between the 1979–82 and 1989–92 periods, which have many features in common, will be a helpful prelude to this discussion. Inflation was in the range of 30 percent at the beginning of both periods (21.4 percent in 1989, but the annual rate was 30 percent in the fourth quarter of that year, and accelerating), and it decreased sharply in a short time. The economy was hit by a massive inflow of foreign financing at the beginning of both periods and by a sharp drop in the terms of trade at the end. Expenditures and output grew rapidly within those periods, expenditures growing more than output, despite a surplus in the fiscal accounts. The first period ended in a dramatic recession and debt crisis; economic results were outstanding in 1992, and output is expected to grow 6 percent in 1993. The current account deficit, which registered a record 14 percent of GDP in 1981, was only 1.5 percent of GDP in 1992, and in 1993, with an expected deterioration in the terms of trade of nearly 2.5 percent of GDP, it probably will not exceed 5 percentage points of output. I will argue that the different policy actions that were undertaken, both in monetary policy and in the disinflation strategy, at least partially account for the difference.

The first issue I will address concerns capital inflows and monetary policy. The authors suggest that under a fixed (or not perfectly flexible) nominal exchange rate, domestic monetary policy has no effect on absorption (equation 2-3). When analyzing the reasons for the debt crisis of the early 1980s, they model domestic absorption as being determined by world interest rates. Within that framework, the Chilean economy of the late 1970s, benefiting from large capital inflows, increased its absorption levels dramatically. Pressure on the real exchange rate led to its appreciation, a process that was not inflationary since the nominal exchange rate was fixed. To put it in a different way, a small, open economy hit by a large-scale capital inflow has no choice but to accept either an appreciation of its exchange rate or more inflation. If the outcome is an appreciation of the exchange rate, the current account will deteriorate and the economy will eventually cool off when the tradable sector is hurt enough. Subsequent unemployment will allow the relative price of tradable goods to recover.

Action can be taken to make the process less painful, however. First, fiscal policy can help dampen the increase in absorption. Second, domestic monetary policy can be strengthened by levying taxes on capital inflows, creating some nominal flexibility in the exchange rate (the nominal exchange rate was fixed between 1979 and 1982, and since nominal interest rates and domestic inflation were well above international levels, capital inflows and absorption were encouraged), and sterilizing capital inflows. Third, as the exchange rate appreciates, devaluation expectations will develop and the power of domestic monetary policy will increase. Therefore, the extent of the currency appreciation, and thus the stability of growth, can be influenced by policy. Besides, if excess capital inflows are not discouraged, and the currency therefore appreciates, leading finally to a recession, some flexibility in the labor market will allow competitiveness eventually to surge. With the improvement in competitiveness, output and employment will recover. Then, as the labor market tightens, a different policy mix will be needed to sustain the new equilibrium value of the currency. Since the accumulated foreign debt must be served and the nontradable market equilibrium will have to be reached at a lower relative price, domestic absorption will have to be smaller vis-à-vis output, compared with the situation at the beginning of the capital inflow shock. Not surprisingly, it will call for less government expenditure, usually a politically unstable solution.

In the 1979–82 period, the nominal exchange rate was completely fixed, and the authorities invested all their credibility in maintaining the fixed parity. Little sterilization was done, and capital inflows were not only tax free but encouraged. If one feature is to be singled out as the most important cause of overindebtedness, however, it is undoubtedly financial policy. It can be argued that neither international nor domestic interest rates were rationing absorption at the time. The absence of efficient financial supervision and regulation, coupled with numerous signs from authorities of an implicit state insurance scheme for financial creditors, resulted in a generalized distressed borrowing practice. It is fair to say that, for a large portion of debtors, interest rates were little more than an accounting price—economically meaningless. The extremely large Central Bank losses, arising from debtor rescue programs launched after the crisis, proved those agents' expectations were somewhat rational.

Finally, the government dramatically cut funds for public goods until 1990, and the resulting deficit in public health, education, and infrastructure is a difficult macroeconomic problem nowadays.

By contrast, after the new wave of capital inflows that began in 1990, the government and the Central Bank devoted much effort to avoiding an overappreciation of the currency. They implemented a reserve requirement scheme (Labán and Larraín present evidence supporting the effectiveness of this measure); they allowed and even encouraged short-run nominal exchange rate volatility (within a range); they pegged the evolution of the peso to a basket of currencies rather than to the U.S. dollar, a policy that amounted to an increase in the cost of borrowing abroad; and the Central Bank engaged in a massive sterilization effort. Although some real appreciation was allowed, it was on the basis of the new medium- to long-term structural features of the economy (namely, its better debt ratios and the higher sustainable amount of foreign financing available with the better economic performance and new political stability), rather than as an effort to allow higher absorption without inflation. Rather than encouraging short-term foreign financing, authorities were constantly warning economic agents against the risk of overappreciation and providing medium-term prospects of the current account to highlight the lags coming from the J-curve type of evolution. Finally, since 1986 the financial system has been subject to a new supervision and regulation scheme, designed to prevent excessive indebtedness and risk taking on the part of financial institutions. Thus, the economy is proving healthy enough to absorb the sharp deterioration in the terms of trade that has occurred this year without suffering major disturbances in output.

The second issue has to do with inflationary inertia. An economy with wage indexation and an accommodating exchange rate policy is not necessarily condemned to live with double-digit inflation (the authors do not say that, but it is implicit in the model and somewhat apparent in the reasoning). First, although in the presence of those institutional features inflation will exhibit a great deal of inertia, policymakers can take advantage of beneficial cost shocks and lock them in at a smaller inflation rate, if they can resist additional expansions of absorption under those circumstances. That was true of the currency appreciation of 1991–92 and of the reduction in tariffs during 1991. Second, efforts can be developed to move indexation gradually from a backward to a forward scheme. For that purpose, in the last years both minimum and public wages have been set according to a forward rule. Third, in an environment of productivity gains, workers will normally ask for a nominal wage increase in an amount that is greater than past inflation. However, if they believe inflation is likely to decrease and authorities avoid excessively tight labor markets, those increases can be smaller than productivity gains, allowing unit labor costs and inflation to fall. Credibility in the authorities' anti-inflationary commitment is a fundamental precondition for the adoption of forward indexing practices. One could argue that this is the case in the 1990–92 period, when inflation dropped from 27 percent to 12.7 percent; it is expected to be in the 10 percent to 12 percent range in 1993.

This strategy will require much persistence and acceptance of the idea that converging toward the inflation levels of developed countries will take time. Nevertheless, it has the advantage of avoiding major recessions as a means of cutting inflation levels—usually a big source of political instability and a road toward populist practices—and of protecting the competitiveness of the tradable sector during the transition period. Stability of the real exchange rate has proved to be one of the necessary conditions for sustained growth in small, open economies such as that of Chile.

Appendix

Table 2A-1. Macroeconomic Data, 1970–92
Percent

Year	Growth of GDP	Inflation[a]	Unemployment (1)	(2)[b]	Investment[c]
1970	2.1	34.9	6.9	...	20.4
1971	9.0	22.1	5.8	...	18.3
1972	−1.2	163.4	3.7	...	14.8
1973	−5.6	508.1	4.3	...	14.7
1974	1.0	375.9	9.4	...	17.4
1975	−12.9	340.7	15.4	16.8	15.4
1976	3.5	174.3	17.2	20.1	12.7
1977	9.9	63.5	13.3	16.2	13.3
1978	8.2	30.3	13.8	16.1	14.5
1979	8.3	38.9	13.7	15.3	15.6
1980	7.8	31.2	11.8	13.9	17.6
1981	5.5	9.5	11.1	12.5	19.5
1982	−14.1	20.7	22.1	24.3	15.0
1983	−0.7	23.1	22.2	34.7	12.9
1984	6.3	23.0	19.3	27.8	13.2
1985	2.4	26.4	16.3	...	14.8
1986	5.7	17.4	13.5	...	15.0
1987	5.7	21.5	12.2	...	16.4
1988	7.4	12.7	10.9	...	17.0
1989	10.0	21.4	9.1	...	18.6
1990	2.1	27.3	9.6	...	19.5
1991	6.0	18.7	7.4	...	18.2
1992	10.4	12.7	6.0	...	23.0

SOURCE: Central Bank of Chile (1989).
a. December to December.
b. Including public works programs.
c. Percent of GDP, in constant pesos.

Table 2A-2. External Sector Data, 1970–92

Year	Terms of trade[a]	External debt[b]	Current account[b]	Trade balance[b]	Financial services[b]	Real exchange rate[c]
1970	216	2.8	−0.1	0.2	...	69.2
1971	158	3.0	−0.2	−0.0	...	71.6
1972	150	3.3	−0.4	−0.3	...	68.6
1973	191	4.0	−0.3	−0.1	...	69.9
1974	187	4.3	−0.2	0.1	...	74.0
1975	103	4.3	−0.5	−0.1	...	63.0
1976	114	4.5	−0.1	0.5	...	70.7
1977	100	5.9	−0.6	0.2	...	76.5
1978	115	7.5	−1.1	−0.8	...	69.3
1979	115	9.4	−1.2	−0.9	...	77.2
1980	118	13.8	−2.0	−0.8	...	94.3
1981	104	14.8	−4.7	−2.7	...	108.0
1982	90	17.0	−2.3	0.0	...	97.7
1983	99	17.4	−1.1	1.0	−1.7	100.5
1984	92	18.9	−2.1	0.4	−2.0	90.0
1985	86	19.4	−1.4	0.9	−2.0	79.7
1986	93	19.5	−1.2	1.1	−1.9	68.7
1987	97	19.2	−0.8	1.2	−1.7	65.5
1988	119	17.6	−0.2	2.2	−1.9	60.7
1989	118	16.3	−0.8	1.6	−1.9	62.2
1990	107	17.4	−0.6	1.3	−1.8	59.9
1991	106	16.4	0.1	1.6	−1.8	65.2
1992	...	18.2	...	...	...	70.0

SOURCE: Central Bank of Chile (1989), Repetto (1992), and J. P. Morgan, unpublished data.
a. Index: 1977=100.
b. Billion U.S.$.
c. 1980–82=100.

Table 2A-3. Trade Indexes, 1980–91
Index: 1986=100

Year	Exports		Imports		Terms of trade
	Price	Quantity	Price	Quantity	
1980	156.3	70.7	134.0	131.1	116.6
1981	135.4	68.3	137.7	158.6	98.3
1982	113.0	77.7	120.8	100.2	93.6
1983	110.9	81.9	109.0	86.7	101.7
1984	105.9	81.8	109.2	100.2	96.9
1985	97.6	92.8	108.4	88.8	90.0
1986	100.0	100.0	100.0	100.0	100.0
1987	114.6	105.4	109.9	118.4	104.3
1988	147.5	113.8	116.7	139.1	126.4
1989	153.7	126.2	123.3	180.8	124.7
1990	144.4	140.7	129.2	186.6	111.8
1991	142.3	150.5	128.0	199.8	111.2

SOURCE: Central Bank of Chile (1989).

Table 2A-4. Composition of Trade, 1980, 1991
Percent of total

	Exports			Imports	
Category	1980	1991	Category	1980	1991
Agriculture	7.3	13.5	Consumption	23.9	14.8
Mining	59.4	48.3	Capital goods	19.2	23.9
Industry	33.4	38.1	Intermediates	56.8	57.9

Source: Central Bank of Chile (1993).

References

Agacino, R., G. Rivas, and E. Roman. 1991. "Apertura y Eficiencia Productiva: La Experiencia Chilena 1975–89." Working Paper 18. InterAmerican Development Bank, Washington, D.C.

Bianchi, A. 1992. "Overabundance of Foreign Exchange, Inflation, and Exchange Rate Policy: The Chilean Experience." In *Mobilizing International Investment in Latin America,* edited by C. Bradford, 155–74. Paris: Development Centre of the Organization for Economic Cooperation and Development.

Boeninger, E. 1991. "Governance and Development: Issues and Constraints." Proceedings of the World Bank Conference on Development Economics. Washington, D.C.

Calvo, G., L. Leiderman, and C. Reinhardt. 1993. "Capital Inflows to Latin America: The 1970s and the 1990s." International Monetary Fund.

de Gregorio, J. 1986. "Principales Aspectos de la Politica Cambiaria en Chile: 1974–85." *Notas Tecnicas* 81 (May). CIEPLAN.

de la Cuadra, S., and D. Hachette. 1990. "Chile." In *Liberalizing Foreign Trade,* edited by D. Papageorgiou, M. Michaely, and A. Choksi. Oxford: Blackwell.

Dornbusch, R. 1985. "Overborrowing: Three Case Studies." In *Dollars, Debts, and Deficits,* R. Dornbusch, 97–130. MIT Press.

———. 1986. "Stabilization Policies in Developing Countries: What Have We Learned?" In *Dollars, Debts and Deficits,* R. Dornbusch, 151–67. MIT Press.

———. 1993. "Mexico: How to Recover Stability and Growth." In *Stabilization, Debt, and Reform: Policy Analysis for Developing Countries,* edited by R. Dornbusch, 367–81. Prentice-Hall.

Dornbusch, R., and S. Edwards, eds. 1992. *Macroeconomic Populism in Latin America.* MIT Press.

Dornbusch, R., and S. Fischer. 1993. "Moderate Inflation." *The World Bank Economic Review* (January): 1–44.

Edwards, S. 1985. "Stabilization with Liberalization: An Evaluation of Ten Years of Chile's Experiment with Free Market Policies, 1973-1983." *Economic Development and Cultural Change* 33 (January): 223–54.

———. 1989. *Real Exchange Rates, Devaluation and Adjustment.* MIT Press.

———. 1993a. "Exchange Rates as Nominal Anchors." Working Paper 4246. Cambridge, Mass.: National Bureau of Economic Research.

————. 1993b. *The Sequencing of Structural Adjustment and Stabilization.* Occasional Paper 34. San Francisco: International Center for Economic Growth.

Edwards, S., and A. Cox-Edwards. 1987. *Monetarism and Liberalization: The Chilean Experience.* Cambridge, Mass.: Ballinger.

Fontaine, J. 1989. "The Chilean Economy in the Eighties: Adjustment and Recovery." In *Debt, Adjustment and Recovery,* edited by S. Edwards and F. Larraín, 208–33. Blackwell.

Foxley, A. 1983. *Latin American Experiments in Neo-Conservative Economics.* University of California Press.

Ffrench-Davis, R. 1979. "Las Experiencias Cambiarias en Chile: 1965–79." *Colección Estudios CIEPLAN* 2 (December).

Fuentes, R. 1992. "Economic Policies, Human Capital, and Their Importance in the Process of Growth." Ph.D. dissertation UCLA.

Hachette, D. 1991. "Chile: Trade Liberalization Since 1974." In *Trade Reform: Lessons from Eight Countries,* edited by G. Shepherd and C. Langoni 41–54. San Francisco: International Center for Economic Growth.

Jadresic, E. 1992. "Dinamica de Salarios y Contratos en Chile." *Colección Estudios CIEPLAN* 34 (June): 31–59.

Marfán, M., and P. Artiagoitia. 1989. "Estimacion del PGB Potencial: Chile 1960–1988." *Coleccion Estudios CIEPLAN* 27 (December): 49–62.

Martin, R. 1992. "Sources of Growth in Latin America." World Bank, Latin America and the Caribbean Region Division.

Repetto, A. 1992. "Determinantes de Largo Plazo del Tipo de Cambio Real: Aplicacion al Caso Chileno 1960-90." *Colección Estudios CIEPLAN* 36 (December): 67–98.

Taussig, F. 1928. *International Trade.* New York: Macmillan.

3 The Chilean Experience with Capital Mobility

Raúl Labán and Felipe Larraín B.

LIBERALIZATION of the capital market is a broad topic because it covers the liberalization of domestic markets and the opening of the capital account to allow for international financial transactions. The Chilean experience of the past twenty years provides useful lessons on both aspects. In this paper we concentrate on international capital movements between Chile and the rest of the world. We discuss issues related to domestic financial markets only if they have significant implications for international capital flows.

We also focus on the behavior of capital flows in the period after the 1982–83 economic crisis. The experience of the 1970s and early 1980s has been studied in great detail elsewhere. Many explanations for Chile's economic crisis of the early 1980s have been explored; developments in local financial markets and the capital account have figured prominently.[1] For example, an interesting literature emerged from the experience of Chile and other countries in the Southern Cone during this period on the issue of the optimal sequencing in the liberalization of the current and capital accounts.[2]

We are more concerned, however, with the factors behind Chile's renewed access to international capital markets in the late 1980s and early 1990s. Both internal and external factors account for this successful transition. Because Chile lives in an increasingly integrated world, it cannot escape some major global trends, even if some local authorities should wish to do so. Increasing financial integration at the world level is a result of many forces, including the rise in world trade, technological and financial innovation, and deregulation.

This paper stresses the fact that increased capital mobility has brought Chile new opportunities, but also new challenges. We show how and why capital inflows to Chile increased in the late 1980s, compare the current experience

We thank Pablo García and Marcelo Tokman for efficient research assistance.

1. See, for example, Edwards and Cox-Edwards (1987); Corbo, De Melo, and Tybout (1986); Morandé (1991); and Valdés (1992).

2. Seminal contributions to this debate are McKinnon (1982) and Edwards (1984).

with that of the late 1970s and early 1980s, evaluate the policy challenges posed by this increased capital inflow, and analyze the reactions of Chilean authorities to this new reality. Econometric evidence documents the capital inflows. An appendix presents a brief overview of the main regulations affecting capital mobility in Chile over the past two decades.

The Increase in Capital Inflows in the Late 1980s

Private capital began to return to Chile in the late 1980s. Total net capital inflows (measured by the capital account surplus plus errors and omissions) went from an average of $1 billion for 1985–87 to $3 billion in 1990 and to an average of $2.4 billion for 1990–92. Capital returned to Chile in many different forms. Foreign investment, short-term credits, long-term loans, and even repatriation of capital held by Chileans abroad all increased significantly during this period.

This happened as the Chilean economy was in a recovery that merged into one of the most successful growth periods in the country's history. Major macroeconomic indicators improved sharply after 1985. Growth of GDP went from 2.4 percent in 1985 to an average of more than 6 percent in 1986–92. This acceleration in the growth rate coincided with a sharp reduction in the unemployment rate—from more than 22 percent on average for 1980–85 to only 4.4 percent at the end of 1992—and a deceleration in the inflation rate—from over 27 percent in 1990 to 12.7 percent in 1992. The strength in the country's external position is shown by the accumulation of foreign exchange reserves, which by the end of 1992 had reached almost $10 billion, or around twelve months of imports, and by a moderate deficit in the current account, which declined from 7.8 percent of GDP in 1985 to a surplus of −0.2 percent in 1991, slipping to a deficit of 1.3 percent in 1992.

The growth of capital inflows to Chile has resulted from a combination of external and internal factors. Among the external factors are low world interest rates, a poor economic performance in the industrial countries, and a greater availability of international capital. Internal political and economic developments have been reflected in a reduction of the risk premium that investors require to hold Chilean securities.

External Factors

Culpeper and Griffith-Jones have presented evidence on net private capital flows to developing economies for the period 1982–91. They show that capital inflows have grown relatively steadily in Asia, have been poor in Africa, and have fluctuated sharply in Latin America, with a major increase since 1989.[3] According to the United Nations' Economic Commission for Latin America and the Caribbean (ECLAC), net private capital inflows to Latin America were almost seven times larger in 1991 than in 1988. External developments have increased the flow of private financial resources to Latin America in general, and to Chile in particular, since the late 1980s. Some of these external factors are common to Latin America as a whole, others are specific to Chile.

The weak macroeconomic performance of several industrialized countries since the late 1980s has coincided with a decline in world interest rates, most notably in the United States, where political cycles are another reason for the excessively low level of short-term rates. This has made short-term Latin American financial instruments, with their far higher yields, a more attractive portfolio investment opportunity.[4]

Another condition common to the region has been the increase in the world supply of capital. This is partially explained by factors that have contributed to the rapid growth and globalization of world capital markets, such as widespread liberalizations in trade and capital account and innovations in financial instruments. These innovations imply that financial markets are becoming more and more integrated even without the help of deregulation. Toward the end of the 1980s, industrial countries had reached almost complete financial integration, which has certainly reduced the capacity of the authorities to impose capital controls. Even countries like Japan, Spain, Germany, France, and Italy, which lacked a strong willingness to open the capital account, were "victims" of financial integration.[5] This is the same process that a number of developing economies are starting to experience.

These external factors certainly help to explain the increase in cross-border flows of private capital to Latin America. Even countries with significant macroeconomic and political instability, such as Brazil, Peru, and Venezuela, have been able to attract capital inflows. Nevertheless, external factors do not ex-

3. Culpeper and Griffith-Jones (1992).
4. According to Calvo and others (1992), external factors are the explanation for a significant part of the recent inflow of private capital to several Latin American economies that are pursuing different mixes of macroeconomic policies and have had different economic performances.
5. See, for example, Viñals (1990) and *The Economist* (1992).

plain the variations in the magnitude, composition, and conditions of inflows among the countries of the region. Clearly, common external factors are not the full explanation.

Internal Factors

Increased resources flowing to Latin America reflect in part the expectations of better economic prospects for the region during the 1990s. These expectations are based on the structural reforms carried out in several countries of the region, most notably in Chile, in Mexico, and in Argentina. The fact that Chile's reforms were carried out much before the rest of the region, and thus were on a solid base by the late 1980s, explains why capital flowed into Chile before it returned to other countries in Latin America. It also helps to explain why the flows into Chile have been larger relative to the size of its economy than those into other Latin American countries.

Among the five larger economies of the region, Chile received the highest private capital inflow as a percentage of GDP in 1989 and 1990 (4.3 percent and 7.2 percent, respectively) and accounted for 22 percent (1989) and 14.9 percent (1990) of total private capital flows to the region. In 1990, Chile and Mexico—which had attained macroeconomic stability and reduced their external debt burden—accounted for 77.6 percent of total private flows to Latin America. By 1991, Brazil and Mexico contributed 69 percent of total private flows to Latin America.[6]

Additional economic factors contributing to the return of private capital have been the sharp reduction in Chile's external debt burden since 1986; the solid macroeconomic performance recorded since the mid-1980s, particularly in expansion of output and trade; and the reduction or elimination of a number of capital and exchange controls.

At the political level, the legitimization of free-market policies, the renewed commitment to sound macroeconomic management with the return of democracy in 1990, and the central role the country has given to consensus in shaping its economic policy and reforms are also important. Strong signals in this direction were provided in 1990 with the approval, almost by consensus, of both a tax reform and a labor reform and by the implementation of a contractionary monetary policy.[7]

Finally a successful policy of promoting exports, together with an able man-

6. Salomon Brothers (1992).
7. 1990 was the year in which private capital flows and capital repatriation reached their highest levels. Labán and Larraín (forthcoming).

agement of foreign debt, sharply reduced Chile's external debt burden. The stock of total external debt fell from $19.5 billion in 1986 to $18.2 billion in 1992 (in nominal dollars), while the ratio of debt to GDP declined from 115.9 percent to 48 percent.[8] Furthermore, lower global interest rates and a strong expansion of exports reduced the ratio of foreign interest service to exports from 36.5 percent in 1986 to approximately 10 percent in 1992. During 1985–92, Chile reduced its existing foreign debt by $11.3 billion through several debt conversion programs. In September 1990, Chile reached an agreement to restructure almost all of its remaining commercial bank debt. Chile's much improved external solvency has been internalized in the secondary market for Chilean debt, where its discount has declined sharply, from 34 percent in June 1990 to 14 percent in March 1991 and to 9 percent in early 1993.

The international financial community's regained confidence in Chile's economic and political prospects translated into a reduction of the risk premium that foreigners need to invest in Chilean securities. Thus Chile was removed in 1991 from the list of nonperforming economies, those for which U.S. banks are required to make loss provisions on any additional lending. Standard & Poor's gave Chile a triple-B rating in 1992, the best risk rating of any Latin American country and the only one with investment grade.

A Tale of Two Periods: 1978–81 and 1989–92

In the past two decades, Chile has experienced two sharp increases in capital inflows. In the late 1970s and early 1980s, Chile received extensive foreign credit, mostly in the form of syndicated loans from commercial banks. After the beginning of the debt crisis in 1982, voluntary foreign capital dried up for most of the decade. At the end of the 1980s, however, Chile regained access to voluntary foreign capital markets, and capital inflows have risen sharply.

These two experiences have other broad similarities. Both periods were characterized by strong economic expansion, by a deterioration in the terms of trade, and by significant appreciation in the real exchange rate. A closer examination of the two periods points to major differences, however.

Capital Inflows

Figure 3-1 shows that the current levels of total net capital inflows are significantly smaller than those of the earlier period, both as an absolute value

8. This ratio averaged 81 percent during the 1980s.

Figure 3-1. Capital Inflows to Chile, Selected Years, 1978–92

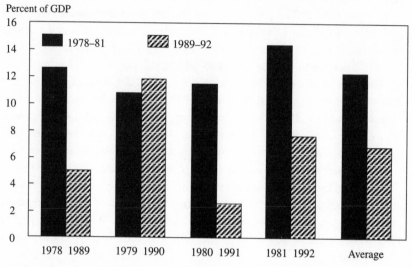

Percent of GDP

SOURCE: Central Bank of Chile.

and as a share of GDP. The average capital account surplus for 1978–81 was slightly more than $3.1 billion, or 12.3 percent of current GDP. At its highest point in 1981, capital inflows to Chile represented 14.4 percent of GDP. In contrast the average total net inflow of capital for 1989–92 has been less than $1.5 billion, or only 6.8 percent of GDP.

The difference in magnitudes between 1978–81 and 1989–92 is even more striking if we do not consider 1990. With that year excluded, the average capital account surplus during the recent period was around 5 percent of GDP. Only in 1990 did total net capital inflows reach a relative size (11.8 percent of GDP) equivalent to that observed during 1978–81.

Major changes have also occurred in the composition of capital inflows. Within the category of foreign credits, loans from commercial banks to support the general balance of payments were the central form of credit in the earlier episode, but they almost disappeared in the late 1980s and early 1990s. Currently, there are more trade loans, and a large part of medium- and long-term private capital flows is now in the form of foreign investment and project loans. It is clear, then, that Chile's return to voluntary credit markets must be understood in a different way.

The proportion of equity to debt is much higher in the later period. Figure 3-2 shows that total net foreign investment was much higher in 1989–92 than it was in 1978–81. During 1978–81, it averaged U.S.$248.8 million a year, or

Figure 3-2. Composition of Capital Inflows, Selected Years, 1978–92

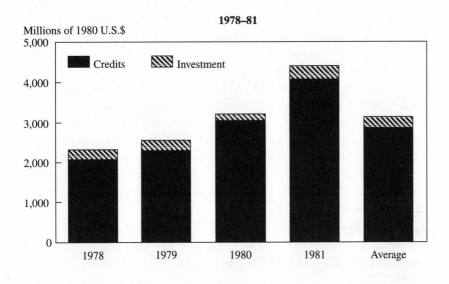

1978–81

Millions of 1980 U.S.$

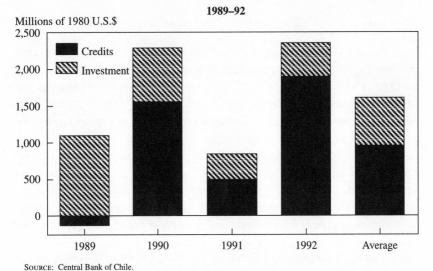

1989–92

Millions of 1980 U.S.$

SOURCE: Central Bank of Chile.

just about 8 percent of total net capital inflows (including errors and omissions). The equivalent figures for 1989–92 are U.S.$657.4 million, or 41 percent of total capital inflows. In particular, total net foreign investment in 1990 was about 3.6 percent of GDP, the highest rate in Latin America.

From 1985 to 1990, much of the foreign investment was raised using debt conversion mechanisms started in 1985. Now that the secondary market discount on Chilean debt is low, debt swaps have ended and foreign investment involves fresh money. On average during 1985–89, 66 percent of total net foreign investment came through debt conversion mechanisms. This declined to 25 percent by 1990 and was almost nil in 1991; no new debt-swap operations have been registered since 1992.

The distinction between debt and equity is not a matter of indifference for a country. Foreign investment flows tend to have a more desirable cyclical pattern than foreign credit. Based on the Latin American experience of the past fifteen years, Hanson argues that credit flows tend to be extremely procyclical.[9] Furthermore, Larraín and Velasco have shown that profit remittances on foreign investment in Chile tend to be more procyclical than interest payments; thus, remittances tend to be higher—relative to interest service—in good periods.[10]

Capital inflows in the form of debt (ΔD) or equity (*FDI*) could be used basically for three purposes: reserve accumulation (ΔR), the financing of a current account deficit (*CAD*), and capital flight (*KF*) according to the following identity:[11]

$$(3\text{-}1) \qquad\qquad (\Delta D + FDI) = CAD + \Delta R + KF.$$

In the late 1970s and early 1980s, Chile's foreign borrowing went mainly to cover large current account deficits, which had reached unsustainable proportions (15 percent of GDP in 1981); a smaller fraction went to finance the country's reserve accumulation, and a minor portion went to capital flight (measured here as errors and omissions in the balance of payments). For the period 1978–81, about 73 percent of the capital account surplus went to finance current account deficits and only 27 percent to accumulate foreign reserves ($850 million on average), as shown in figure 3-3. During the more recent episode (1989–92), 79 percent of net total capital inflows financed the accumulation of foreign reserves—$1.1 billion on average—and only 21 percent to finance current account deficits.[12] Reserve accumulation has increased sharply since mid-1990. At that time the exchange rate reached the lower limit of its crawling band, forcing the Central Bank to accumulate large amounts of reserves to prevent appreciation of the exchange rate.

The way a country uses an inflow of foreign capital has interesting implica-

---

9. Hanson (1992).
10. Larraín and Velasco (1990).
11. See Sachs and Larraín (1993, chapter 22, pp. 703–05).
12. In 1991, Chile even had a current account surplus in addition to a capital account surplus.

Figure 3-3. Uses of Capital Inflows, Selected Years, 1978–92

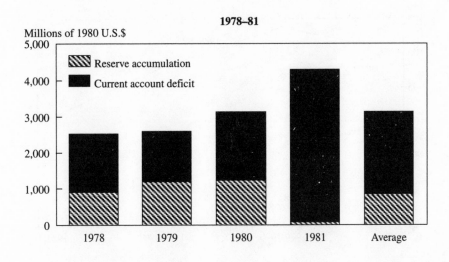

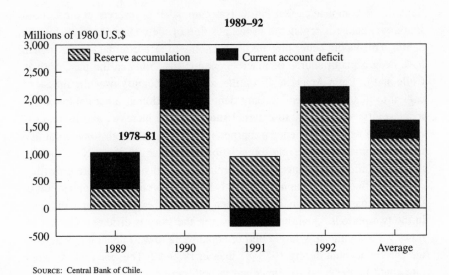

SOURCE: Central Bank of Chile.

Figure 3-4. Chile's Real Exchange Rate, Selected Years, 1978–92

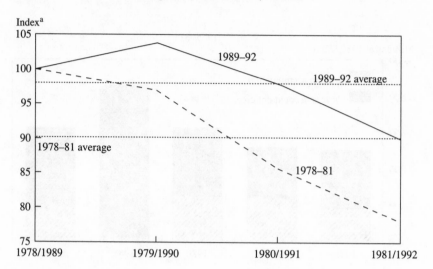

Index[a]

Source: Central Bank of Chile.
a. 1978 and 1989 = 100.

tions. If the complete capital inflow is accumulated as reserves at the Central
Bank, no change is registered in the position of the country as a net foreign
debtor. This would better prepare the economy to face external shocks, which
have been a major source of macroeconomic instability in the past, both in
Chile and in Latin America. If, on the contrary, a country uses the inflow of
capital to finance a current account deficit, its position as a net debtor would
increase, its vulnerability to external shocks would increase, and its real exchange rate would experience a sharper appreciation (through some combination of nominal exchange rate appreciation and higher inflation). Nevertheless,
the use of inflows to finance capital formation would support future growth.

A sharp increase in capital inflows is bound to produce an appreciation of
the real exchange rate. Qualitatively, then, we should expect the same outcome
in the two periods. Quantitatively, however, the story is different. Capital inflows were significantly larger and oriented more toward financing deficits in
the current account during 1978–81 than in 1989–92. Thus the real exchange
rate could be expected to appreciate in both periods, but the strength of the
appreciation should have been larger in the earlier episode.

This is supported by the evidence, as figure 3-4 shows. For purposes of
comparison, both periods start with an index of 100 for the real exchange rate.
During 1978–81, the appreciation is a full 22 percent. In 1989–92, the appreci-

ation is only 10 percent. In the more recent period the exchange rate reached its peak in 1990; but even if the appreciation is measured from that year, it only reaches 13 percent.

Of course the effect of capital inflows on the real exchange rate depends on the reaction of the authorities. In both periods, import tariffs were reduced, limiting the real appreciation.[13] Fiscal policy was responsible in both periods, which also helped to prevent a larger appreciation.[14] Private spending, however, was much more expansionary during the first episode, thus putting downward pressure on the real exchange rate. In both periods, the authorities allowed a decline in interest rates through a more expansionary monetary policy. Sterilization, preventing the expansionary effects of reserve accumulation, was also an important feature of both episodes.

In 1980 the authorities moved toward almost full liberalization of the capital account, eased foreign exchange controls, and exerted downward pressures on the real exchange rate. In contrast, the reforms to the capital account and to foreign exchange controls during the most recent episode were carried out with care to help prevent a sharper appreciation. The authorities removed controls on capital outflows faster than those on capital inflows, introduced a reserve requirement on foreign credits, implemented direct measures to substitute domestic for foreign sources of project financing, and changed restrictions on foreign exchange operations to increase the demand for foreign currency relative to its supply.

During the first episode Chile had a fixed nominal exchange rate; during the later period, it had a band of fluctuation, which was set to achieve a stable real exchange rate. The band was initially defined for the dollar-peso parity. In 1992, however, it was changed to one defined for a basket of foreign currencies; this effectively increased the relevant foreign cost of funding. The difference in exchange rate systems suggests that the appreciation of the real exchange rate should have been larger in the earlier period.

Thus as a result of the magnitude and use of the foreign resources and as a result of the policy reactions, one should have expected, as actually happened, a much larger real appreciation of the real exchange rate in 1978–81 than during 1989–92.

13. In Chile, primary goods (most notably copper) represent a large fraction of exports. This suggests that imports are closer substitutes, both in supply and demand, for nontradables than for exports; thus, a reduction of import tariffs is likely to lead to a higher equilibrium real exchange rate, as compared with an export base less concentrated on primary goods (Dornbusch 1980).

14. For a discussion of fiscal policy in Chile during the early 1990s, see Labán and Larraín (forthcoming).

External Conditions

External factors have also been an important part of the story in the two experiences. Increased availability of funds in international capital markets played a part in the recent experience, the recycling of petrodollars in the earlier experience.

The behavior of nominal interest rates in international markets, however, was widely divergent in the two periods. As figure 3-5 shows, the 180-day London Interbank Offer Rate (LIBOR) in U.S. dollars increased from 9.5 percent in 1978 to 16.7 percent in 1981. In contrast, during the 1989–92 period, it declined from 9.3 percent to 3.9 percent, sustaining an average of just 6.9 percent during the period.

Real interest rates, however, behaved differently, as figure 3-6 illustrates. During 1978–80, they were very low (even negative in 1979), and then surged in 1981 and 1982. In 1989–92 real rates have been slightly more than 4 percent and quite stable; they increased to 5.8 percent in 1991, and dropped sharply— by more than 2 full percentage points—in 1992.

What matters to investors, though, is the gap between local and foreign rates. A wide differential developed in the two cases, as shown in figure 3-7, because rates fell abroad and because they increased in Chile. The interest rate gap was much higher, however, in the earlier period, when it was between 15 and 20 percentage points in 1978 and the first half of 1979. In the most recent episode, a wide gap developed only in the first three quarters of 1990 (almost 8 percentage points on average). After the government introduced reserve requirements and a stamp tax on foreign credits in mid-1991, the "corrected" gap fell to less than 2 percentage points. The larger gap in the first episode helps to explain why the real appreciation was stronger.

External Vulnerability and Capital Inflows

A widely used indicator to measure a country's debt burden is the debt-to-export ratio. Between 1979 and 1981, as Chile was attracting foreign capital, this ratio increased steadily, and a major jump occurred in 1981. Thus starting at between two and three times exports, the country's foreign debt jumped to more than 400 percent of exports in 1981. Figure 3-8 shows a different situation for 1989–92, when the debt-export ratio followed a downward trend, by the end of 1992 standing at about 180 percent of exports.

Reserve accumulation occurred in both periods. The country's stock of foreign exchange reserves increased substantially between 1978 and 1980, from

Figure 3-5. The International Nominal Interest Rate, Selected Years, 1978–92[a]

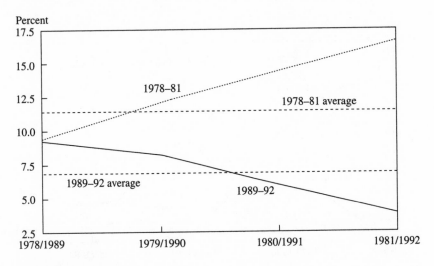

Percent

SOURCE: Central Bank of Chile.
a. 180-day LIBOR, U.S.$.

Figure 3-6. The International Real Interest Rate, Selected Years, 1978–92[a]

Percent

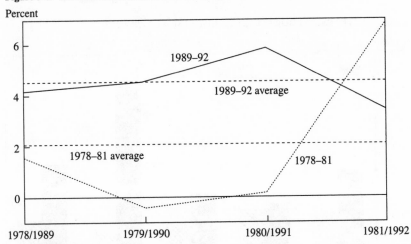

SOURCE: Central Bank of Chile.
a. 180-day LIBOR, U.S.$, deflated by U.S. wholesale prices.

**Figure 3-7. The Real Interest Rate Differential between Chile and Abroad,
Selected Years, 1978–92**[a]

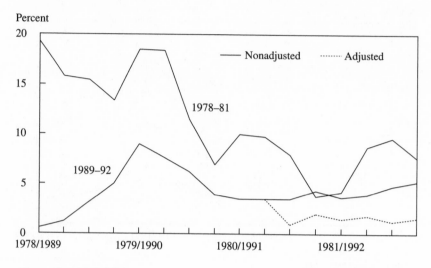

SOURCE: Central Bank of Chile.
a. Local Chilean rate vs. LIBOR.

Figure 3-8. The Ratio of Debt to Exports, Selected Years, 1978–92

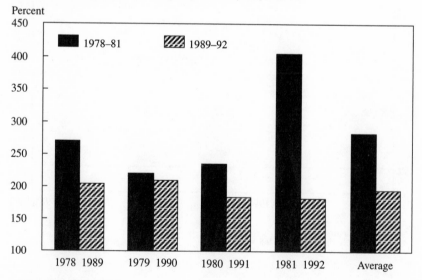

SOURCE: Central Bank of Chile.

Figure 3-9. The Ratio of International Reserves to Imports, Selected Years, 1978–92

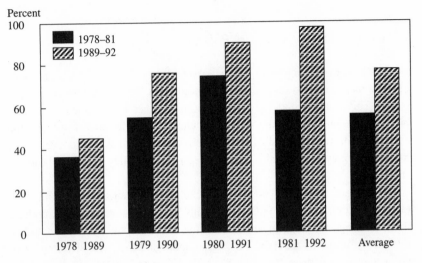

SOURCE: Central Bank of Chile.

37 percent to 75 percent of annual imports. Then in 1981, the country lost reserves, and the ratio fell to 58 percent, as shown in figure 3-9.

In the more recent period, there have been no detours from a steadily upward trend. Reserves have climbed year after year, from 45 percent of imports in 1989 to almost 100 percent in 1992. The current level of reserves in Chile is clearly above what could be considered a reasonable buffer stock.

Nowadays the financing of Chilean investment is less dependent on the availability of foreign saving. While in the 1980s foreign resources financed on average more than 40 percent of total investment, it accounted for only 1.3 percent of total saving in the period 1990–92. Chile's vulnerability to external shocks has been further reduced by the significant increase in the diversification of exports, both of goods and of destination markets. Shipments of products other than copper represented 37 percent and 54 percent of total exports in the 1970s and 1980s, respectively; in 1992, they accounted for 62 percent of total exports.

Policy Challenges

What are the consequences for the country of increased inflows of capital? In a small and financially integrated economy like that of Chile, capital mobility may reduce the effectiveness of monetary policy if the authorities wish to avoid large fluctuations in the exchange rate.

Losing Control of Monetary Policy

With a fixed exchange rate, perfect asset substitution, and free capital mobility, domestic authorities in a small economy lose total control over monetary policy. This is the Mundell-Fleming result. In other words, such a scenario prevents the authorities from setting simultaneously the interest rate and the exchange rate (unless binding capital controls exist). The ineffectiveness of monetary policy is especially complicated if fiscal policy is inflexible in the short run.

If assets are not perfect substitutes or capital movements are not totally free (as in practice), monetary policy maintains some of its effectiveness under a fixed exchange rate regime. In a well-known work Kouri and Porter studied this issue for Australia, Italy, the Netherlands, and the Federal Republic of Germany in the 1960s, at a time when they were operating under fixed exchange rates; they found that the monetary policy had a surprisingly high degree of effectiveness.[15]

Appreciation of the Real Exchange Rate

Chile has decided to follow a development strategy based on the expansion of exports and efficient import substitution. The maintenance of a stable and competitive real exchange rate path is an intermediate objective, which has received central priority in achieving this goal. But the exchange rate is both the price of an asset, which is subject to the volatility that is common to financial markets, and a variable that plays a central role in medium-term resource allocation. A stable path for the real exchange rate means an evolution for this variable that is more related to medium-term fundamentals than to short-run financial instability but at the same time allows monetary policy to have some effectiveness and for the exchange rate to help accommodate short-run shocks.

A growing body of theoretical and empirical evidence suggests that excessive instability of the real exchange rate has a depressive effect on exports and on private real investment.[16] Others have suggested protecting the tradable sector from short-run stabilization policy and other transitory shocks because they

15. Kouri and Porter (1974).
16. Caballero and Corbo (1990) and Larraín and Vergara (1993).

can have more durable effects on the tradable than on the domestic sector.[17] In the same direction, excessive instability of the real exchange rate or of real interest rates caused by short-run speculative capital flows can have a negative effect on productive irreversible investment and, thus, on economic growth.[18]

Both economic theory and international evidence indicate that the process of economic development may bring a strengthening of the domestic currency and, thus, a sustainable increase in welfare.[19] Thus it may be too costly to try to sustain the real exchange rate over its long-run equilibrium for a long period of time and not allow it to reflect these structural changes.[20] Also by trying to sustain a real exchange rate above its equilibrium value, the country ends with an inflation rate for nontradables that is higher than it would otherwise have been.

Policy Response to Increased Capital Mobility in the 1990s

Chilean economic authorities faced a major policy dilemma.[21] On the one hand, defending export competitiveness required that the domestic interest rate not be allowed to deviate too far from the world rate so as to prevent a significant capital inflow that would cause an appreciation of the peso. On the other hand, the aim of preserving macroeconomic stability required a domestic real interest rate consistent with a path for aggregate demand that would allow for a gradual reduction in inflation.[22] In a context of increasingly integrated financial markets, as we have seen, reconciling these two objectives is not easy.

In the presence of high capital mobility, there may be an optimal government intervention in the exchange market that could provide some effectiveness to the monetary instrument and simultaneously prevent excessive volatility in the real exchange rate. Microeconomic foundations for this intervention are the presence of sticky prices and of dynamic comparative advantages in the tradable sector and the absence of a market in which to price the "option

---

17. Krugman (1987).

18. Tornell (1990). See also Bernanke (1983), Dixit (1990), and Pindyck (1991).

19. Dornbusch (1989) and Dornbusch, Fischer, and Samuelson (1977).

20. According to Krugman (1987), in the presence of dynamic comparative advantages, the real exchange rate, relative wages, and the trade specialization path are all endogenous. Therefore, transitory shocks (for example, transitory undervaluation of the domestic currency) can have permanent effects on them. Thus, this path dependence should be taken into account in an evaluation of the costs and benefits of maintaining the real exchange rate on a transitory basis over its long-run equilibrium value.

21. Central Bank of Chile (1992).

22. In Chile, the principal monetary policy tool is the real interest rate (ex-ante) on short-term (ninety days) Central Bank bonds.

to-wait-and-see" in the presence of irreversibility.[23] An example of such an intervention may be an optimal band of fluctuation for the exchange rate, dirty floating, or a suboptimal band combined with dirty floating. To cope with increased capital inflows, the Chilean authorities took actions affecting exchange rate policy, sterilized capital inflows, reduced domestic interest rates, selectively liberalized capital outflows, and restricted capital inflows.

Exchange Rate Policy

Since 1983 the exchange rate has been tied to the dollar in a narrow band whose amplitude was of ±5 percent in June 1989 and whose central rate was (generally) adjusted monthly to the difference between domestic inflation and an estimate of international inflation. In essence this policy aimed to maintain the real exchange rate, while allowing a small area of breathing room for monetary policy (inside the band).

The combination of a macroeconomic adjustment in January 1990, when ex-ante real rates on long-term Central Bank bonds reached 9.7 percent, and increased capital mobility due to a lower perception of country risk prompted massive capital inflows that quickly moved the exchange rate to the bottom of the band.[24] At that point, and with downward pressure continuing on the exchange rate, the country operated de facto under a pegged exchange rate regime, and the band was sustained only by Central Bank intervention. After a significant increase of reserves in 1991, the Central Bank widened the band to ±10 percent in January 1992. Again, in spite of the bank's efforts, the exchange rate quickly converged with the lower point of the band.

Part of the pressure on the real exchange rate was attributed by the authorities to transitory factors (as discussed below), but another part was thought to come from permanent (structural) factors such as the consolidation of the export sector, the reduced burden of foreign debt, and the increase in net foreign investment. In other words, some of the capital flows were attracted by a reduction in Chile's perceived country risk.

Hoping to add market uncertainty to capital movements, the bank finally changed the peg of the central rate to a basket of currencies with weights of 50 percent for the dollar, 30 percent for the deutsche mark, and 20 percent for

23. Suppose the government of a small, financially integrated economy dislikes excessive variability of the real exchange rate and of output. Thus it tries to minimize a loss function that depends on these two objectives but has only one short-run stabilization instrument—monetary policy. In this case, an optimal flotation band for the exchange rate may exist.

24. As a result of both improved economic indicators and a smooth transition to democracy.

the yen. This policy makes the relevant international interest rate for arbitrage operations a combination of the German, Japanese, and U.S. rates rather than the U.S. rate alone, as it had been. This reduces the vulnerability of the Chilean economy to fluctuations in U.S. interest rates, which had reached record lows in the early 1990s.

Monetary Policy and Sterilization

Through open market operations, the Central Bank has sterilized the monetary effects of its purchases of foreign exchange reserves (necessary to avoid a sharper appreciation of the peso) in order to control inflation. This policy started after the Central Bank increased long-term real interest rates on its bonds from 6.9 percent to 9.7 percent in January 1990, at a time when the exchange rate was at the upper limit of the band. A few months and several hundred million dollars of capital inflows later, in July 1990, the exchange rate touched the bottom of the band and intervention began.

As a result of sterilization, the composition of the bank's balance sheet has changed, with more reserves on the asset side and more issues of domestic bonds on the liability side. Because the interest rate on Central Bank bonds has been substantially above the rate that could be earned on foreign exchange reserves, the bank's financial position has worsened. The operating loss from sterilization amounted to an estimated 0.5 percent of 1990 GDP during the period 1990–93. In fact, Chile has not been alone in Latin America in following this policy. Colombia has heavily pursued sterilization, and Rodriguez has estimated the 1991 loss stemming from these operations at 0.5 percent of GDP.[25]

Sterilization is, clearly, no panacea on other grounds, too. It tends to maintain the differential between domestic and foreign rates, thereby perpetuating the capital inflows. Calvo and others report that in Latin America, the reduction of local interest rates has been much slower in countries that have sterilized vis-à-vis those that have not, and the case of Chile confirms this trend.[26] Theoretical analyses have also shown that sterilization may reduce social welfare.[27]

Chilean authorities were willing to pay the costs of sterilization because they were sure that a number of transitory elements were behind the downward pressure on the exchange rate. Among them were unsustainably high real interest rates that prevailed in Chile during 1990 and record low nominal interest

25. Rodriguez (1991).
26. Calvo and others (1992).
27. See Calvo (1991).

rates in the United States since 1991, possibly related to the U.S. political cycle. Figure 3-7 presents evidence on the interest rate, which highlights the widening gap between U.S. and Chilean interest rates, a gap that reached its peak in early 1990.

Capital Controls

Several economists have argued in favor of some sort of capital controls. Tobin argued that it was necessary "to put some sand in the wheels" of the extremely efficient international capital markets because financial flows—especially short-term—provoke wide fluctuations in the exchange rate that adversely affect the real sector.[28] Thus Tobin favored taxing short-term capital flows. Krugman has recommended the use of capital controls aimed at protecting the tradable sector from short-run instabilities.[29] Summers suggests that taxes of various kinds are justified in the presence of speculation.[30] Tornell has shown that, in the presence of irreversible investment, Tobin taxes on short-term international capital movements can improve welfare, as compared with a situation without the tax. Tornell's model, however, assumes that the only source of instability is external.[31] Calvo and others, discussing different policy reactions to capital inflows, conclude that the least damaging option may be some form of capital control.[32] An evaluation of the arguments and conditions under which capital controls may be justified and the reasons why capital controls are increasingly harder to enforce can be found in Hanson, Viñals, and Williamson.[33]

Some specialists have argued that capital controls should not be implemented simply because they are ineffective. As the economy of a nation becomes more integrated into the world economy (in goods and services as well as in its finances), the capacity of regulators to enforce capital controls in the medium run is sharply reduced.[34] Thus in spite of controls, the capital account may be de facto opened.

Control of outflows naturally has some leaks, such as the overinvoicing of

28. Tobin (1978).
29. Krugman (1987).
30. Summers (1988).
31. Tornell (1990).
32. Calvo and others (1992).
33. See Hanson (1992), Viñals (1990), and Williamson (1991).
34. See, for example, *The Economist* (1992). Williamson (1991), however, argues that the supposed ineffectiveness of capital controls is "vastly exaggerated."

imports, the underinvoicing of exports, and the use of the parallel market.[35] In Chile, however, what has mattered more in the 1990s is the control of inflows, which has different leakages.

Between 1988 and the first quarter of 1991, Chile experienced a massive short-term inflow of private capital. The economic authorities imposed a 20 percent nonremunerated reserve requirement, aimed at preventing a sharper appreciation of the real exchange rate, on foreign credits. They extended the stamp tax of 1.2 percent per year—previously paid by local currency credits only—to foreign loans as well in June 1991. An attempt to avoid leakages while at the same time targeting short-term credits, this measure applied to all credits (except trade loans) during their first year. In January 1992, this reserve requirement was extended to foreign currency deposits, and it was raised to 30 percent in May 1992, when U.S. interest rates reached record lows and the Chilean authorities had little room to maneuver in reducing local interest rates.

Data on short-term capital inflows show an important change in their pattern after the second quarter of 1991. Short-term capital inflows had averaged around $110 million each quarter from 1989 to the first quarter of 1991, but they dropped to an average of only about $40 million thereafter. This change coincided with the introduction of the reserve requirement, but it is uncertain whether these capital controls—and further adjustments—contributed significantly to the reversion in the speculative flows of capital.

We attempted to measure the effect of several policies on the inflow of short-term capital. The policies were: the introduction of reserve requirements in Chile in June 1991 and their modification in May 1992, the extension of the stamp tax to foreign credits in June 1991, and the change from a dollar-peso band to a basket of currencies. Thus we run the following regression, with quarterly data for the Chilean economy for the period from January 1984 to April 1992.[36]

$$(3\text{-}2) \quad SRCF_t = a_0 + a_1\, iGAP_t + a_2\, FD_t^*/GDP_t,$$

where $SRCF$ are short-term capital inflows, $iGAP$ is the real interest rate gap, and FD^*/GDP is the ratio of foreign debt to GDP. The $iGAP$ variable was measured with and without the effects of the controls mentioned above and the change in the exchange rate regime.

35. Calvo and others (1992). In Chile, however, the overinvoicing of imports is a rather expensive way to send capital abroad, since it requires the payment of a 31 percent tax (18 percent VAT in addition to 11 percent duty).

36. Later in the chapter, we study the factors explaining the increase in short-term capital inflows to Chile after the debt crisis and justify the use of this equation to evaluate the effect of these policies.

Table 3-1. Econometric Results for the Determinants of Short-Term Capital Inflows to Chile, January 1984–April 1992

Factors	SRCF	SRCF[a]
Constant	3,797.5	4,010.9
	(4.1)	(4.9)
iGAP (nonadjusted)	14.3	. . .
	(1.01)	
iGAP (adjusted)	. . .	16.6
		(3.27)
FD*/GDP	−2,805.4	−3,198.1
	(−0.79)	(−3.41)
$\bar{R}^2$ adjusted	0.31	0.64
Durbin-Watson	0.71	1.34

SOURCE: Authors' calculations. The numbers in parentheses are t-statistics.
a. Corrected.

The main result of this exercise is that the explanatory power of the regression increases substantially when the corrected measure is used. The adjusted $\bar{R}^2$ goes from 0.33 to 0.64 when the real interest gap is measured properly, and both *iGAP* and *FD*/GDP* become statistically significant with the correction (see table 3-1).

Selective Opening of the Capital Account

In Chile, many economists have opposed the use of controls on capital inflows, suggesting that the authorities should have relied only on a more aggressive and widespread elimination of controls on capital outflows. As a result of the significant influx of private capital, the Chilean authorities have followed an asymmetrical policy regarding the opening of the capital account. While additional obstacles have been imposed on capital inflows, the authorities have relaxed a number of restrictions on capital outflows.

Taking advantage of the strong external position of the country (international reserves on the order of twelve months of imports and growing, a large surplus in the capital account, and a low, perfectly manageable deficit in the current account), the authorities liberalized capital outflows (see the appendix).

Those who favor a faster liberalization of capital outflows (and who criticize the use of capital controls) base their argument on the presumption that free capital mobility is optimal and that the capacity of regulators to impose controls on capital inflows is low in an economy that is increasingly integrated to the rest of the world in goods, services, and finance.

Williamson has pointed out that the removal of controls on capital outflow can stimulate a net inflow of capital, as actually happened in Britain in 1979 and Yugoslavia in 1990.[37] This apparent paradox may be the result of a decline in the perception that the decision to invest in a given country is irreversible or in the credibility of a country's commitment to a nondistortional taxation policy, both conditions resulting from a more open capital account.[38]

Labán and Larraín investigate formally whether an asymmetrical opening of the capital account, more liberal on outflows than on inflows, could be an effective way to promote a net capital outflow from the country.[39] Their main conclusion is that a liberalization of capital outflows, understood as a reduction in the minimum period for repatriation of foreign investment capital, makes the decision to invest in domestic assets less irreversible. This may induce an increase in net capital inflow by making it less attractive to wait to invest until the uncertainty is resolved.

Thus according to these empirical and theoretical findings, liberalizing outflows may not be an appropriate policy to defend the real exchange rate in the presence of massive capital inflows. Nevertheless, the relaxation of some specific controls on capital outflows is bound to lead to an increase in net capital outflows. Among the controls that might be lifted are the restriction for institutional investors, most notably pension funds, on investing abroad and allowing repatriation of profits and capital on debt equity swaps ahead of schedule. Both of these policies were applied in Chile during 1992. The reduction from three years to one year of the repatriation period for foreign investment, approved in March 1993, is likely to encourage inflows more than outflows of capital.

Fiscal Policy, Commercial Policy, and Reforms in Domestic Capital Markets

A more restrictive fiscal policy could help to cool down the economy and thus could avoid (or mitigate) an appreciation in the real exchange rate. If this policy has the additional effect of reducing local interest rates, it could help to dampen capital inflows. Whether this policy is accomplished through increased taxation or through a reduction in spending will make a difference.

Chile used a significant tax increase (about 2 percent of GDP per year) to finance social spending in 1990. This, together with a large increase in fiscal

37. Williamson (1991).
38. Nevertheless, as Sargent (1983) and Hanson (1992) suggest, investors should be aware that a country has substantial incentives to deviate from a regime of flexible exchange rates and capital mobility to extract an inflation tax from its residents. The capacity of overcoming this time-inconsistency problem is one of the most important benefits that countries such as Chile and Mexico can expect of a free-trade agreement with the United States.
39. Labán and Larraín (1993).

revenue as a result of economic growth, trade expansion, and a reduction in tax evasion, has allowed for a substantial increase of government spending (in excess of 13 percent in 1991 and of 8 percent in 1992) coupled with increased public saving (from 5 percent of GDP in 1990 to 5.9 percent in 1991). On the whole, fiscal policy has been responsible (no deficit spending), although fiscal spending has increased significantly.

Commercial policy has also been used to support the real exchange rate. In order to avoid a real revaluation of the exchange rate as a response to increased capital inflows, the Chilean authorities reduced import tariffs from 15 percent to 11 percent in June 1991. It is clear by now that this measure was insufficient to prevent an appreciation of the real exchange rate by 9 percent in 1991 and another 9 percent in 1992.

Reforms have also been carried out in domestic capital markets. One of these has allowed domestic investment projects with no history to be eligible for financing by the Chilean privately managed pension funds (AFPs), which previously had resorted as a rule to external financing, thus prompting capital inflows. The reform allowed them to substitute foreign credit for domestic credit and thus to dampen the capital inflows. Strict quantitative limits on the financing of AFPs for these projects, however, imply that the maximum funding is on the order of $200 million at present.

Capital Mobility and Effectiveness of the Monetary Policy

Kouri and Porter developed a model in which capital movements are a consequence of disequilibrium in the domestic monetary market.[40] The usual Mundell-Fleming result applies, in that an excess supply of domestic currency, under a fixed exchange rate and perfect capital mobility, provokes an equivalent loss of reserves.

(3-3) $FCAP_t = \beta_0 + \beta_1 \Delta r_t^* + \beta_2 \Delta Y_t + \beta_3 \Delta W_t + \beta_4 CAB_t + \beta_5 \Delta DCCB_t,$

where $FCAP$ are capital inflows, r^* is the foreign interest rate, Y is GDP, W is domestic wealth, CAB is the current account balance, and $DCCB$ is the domestic credit of the Central Bank. β_5 is known as the offset coefficient (OC), which measures the loss (gain) of foreign exchange reserves resulting from an expansion (contraction) of domestic credit by the central bank. Thus the OC should fluctuate between -1 (basic Mundell-Fleming) and 0 (no capital mobility) under fixed exchange rates.

This model helps to determine whether or not the government has control

40. Kouri and Porter (1974).

over monetary policy. If the country is operating under perfect capital mobility and a fixed (or pegged) exchange rate regime, the government has no control over monetary policy.[41] In this case, $ß_5 = -1$. If, on the contrary, $ß_1 = 0$ and $ß_5 = 0$, monetary policy is completely independent. And if $-1 < ß_5 < 0$, as should be expected in general, the effectiveness of monetary policy is diminished. This may be the result of imperfect capital mobility (because of legal or other restrictions on capital flows), of imperfect substitutability between domestic and foreign assets, or of the use of a floating exchange rate.

Earlier Empirical Findings for Chile

Corbo and Matte used quarterly real data for the period January 1975 to January 1982 to find an offset coefficient of -0.244 and a coefficient of -0.55 for the CAB.[42] When a dummy for the period February 1980 to January 1982 was included, $β_5$ changed to -0.32 and $β_4$ to -0.31. (The inclusion of this dummy variable responds to the liberalization of international financial operations for commercial banks in April 1980.) The first quarter of 1983 was excluded since new coefficient instability was detected at that moment. Based on these results, the authors concluded that—contrary to what policymakers believed at that moment—the Central Bank had some degree of control over monetary policy during this period. Chile had a fixed exchange rate regime for a significant part of the sample period (March 1979 to February 1982).

McNelis, recognizing the changing degree of openness of Chile's capital account, estimated the Kouri-Porter model for the same period using the Kalman filter technique.[43] This allows for coefficients that vary with time, in particular for a compensation coefficient that is dependent on time. As expected, McNelis found large instability of the estimated coefficients during this period. He reported, as expected, that $ß_1$ increases with the degree of financial integration. Nonetheless, he found that the large shift in $β_1$ occurred in 1976, when trade reform was under way, rather than in 1978, when the process of financial liberalization began. $ß_4$ was high on average (0.88), but with a declining time path. This finding is consistent with the idea that as financial liberalization proceeded, the flow of foreign capital was increasingly less dependent on developments in the current account. Finally, $ß_5$ had a positive sign for 1974–80 and was negative (the expected sign) only in 1981–82; during this period, however, it was much smaller (around -0.07) than that found by Corbo and Matte.

41. In this world, fiscal policy will be extremely effective. See Mundell (1968).
42. Corbo and Matte (1984). Real data were used because of the presence of high inflation.
43. McNelis (1991).

Based on these findings, McNelis concluded that the large capital inflow into Chile was more a result of external (supply-side) exogenous factors than of internal considerations, and that toward the end of the period, capital flows were practically unrelated to current account and did not significantly offset monetary policy.

Morandé, using a VAR technique for the period 1977–82, finds that capital inflows partially compensated for changes in both domestic credit and the trade balance.[44] He also argues that the large private capital inflows into Chile were the result of exogenous external factors and changes in domestic credit. The latter were especially important between the end of 1979 and the beginning of 1981, when domestic credit policy was strongly restrictive. After this period, capital movements were largely explained by their own innovations.

The Results

We ran a similar regression for the period January 1975 to February 1992, extending by about ten years the period covered by earlier analyses and including new variables. The results of this regression are:

$$(3\text{-}4) \qquad FCAP_t = 4749.1 - 11.49\ \Delta r_t^* + 0.12\ \Delta Y_t - 0.38\ CAB_t$$
$$\phantom{(3\text{-}4) \qquad FCAP_t =}\ (2.09)(-0.15) \qquad (1.83) \qquad (-6.57)$$

$$- 0.07\ \Delta DCCB_t - 8517.8\ D^*/GDP + 1652.2\ D_1 - 14457\ D_2,$$
$$(-2.75) \qquad\qquad (-6.941) \qquad\qquad\quad (2.29)\ (-6.431)$$

$$T = 70;\ R^2 = 0.75;\ \text{Durbin-Watson} = 1.66;$$

where D^*/GDP represents the ratio of foreign debt to GDP; D_1 is a dummy variable that takes a value of 1 for the period February 1980 to February 1992 and 0 otherwise (it intends to capture the liberalization of the capital account); and D_2 is a dummy for January 1983.

Results from this regression have some similarities to those of the earlier studies. The offset coefficient is -0.07, much smaller than that of Corbo and Matte but similar to that of McNelis. The coefficient for the current account deficit (-0.38) is equivalent to that of Corbo and Matte.

The ratio of external debt to GDP (not included in previous work) has the expected sign—foreign capital inflows are inversely related to the country's debt burden—and is highly significant: Although the capital account remained

44. Morandé (1991).

largely open to inflows during 1983–87, the debt overhang prevented large capital flows to Chile. This result suggests that renewed inflows into Chile since the late 1980s owe much to the solution of the debt overhang. The change in output has a positive effect on capital inflows, highlighting their pro-cyclical nature.

The fact that the coefficient of Δr^*_t is not significantly different from 0 suggests that—in contrast to what some other economists have suggested—the increase in capital inflows into Chile since the late 1980s is related more to internal than to external factors, represented here by the change in the international interest rate.[45] As we will see later, considering only short-term inflows of private capital inflows allows more room for external factors.

We then examined how the coefficients of this regression changed over time. We first divided the sample period into four periods: the first is a time when the capital account was less liberalized (January 1975–January 1980), although as some have suggested, trade liberalization should have allowed for some degree of de facto financial integration.[46] The second period (February 1980–February 1982) is one of almost complete liberalization of financial transactions; the third (March 1982–April 1987) is the period of external debt crisis; and the last (January 1988–April 1992) is when Chile regained access to private foreign capital.

We introduced a number of dummy variables to allow for this division. These dummies (with the exception of D_1 and D_2 of equation 3-4) interact in a multiplicative way with CAB_t and $\Delta DCCB_t$ for the second and third period. The final regression is:

$$(3\text{-}5) \quad FCAP_t = 4590.\ 7 - 3.87\ \Delta r^*_r + 0.09\ \Delta Y_t - 0.23\ CAB_t$$
$$(21.8)\ (-0.19) \qquad (1.51) \qquad (-3.84)$$

$$- 0.09\ \Delta DCCB_t - 7341.5\ D^*/GDP + 1695.7\ D_1 - 14645\ D_2$$
$$(-3.13) \qquad\qquad (-5.377) \qquad\qquad (2.45)\ (-7.581)$$

$$- 0.243\ CAB_t\ D_3 + 0.083\ \Delta DCCB_t\ D_4.$$
$$(-2.93) \qquad\qquad (2.40)$$

$$T = 70;\ R^2 = 0.82;\ \text{Durbin-Watson} = 1.67$$

Our results indicate that during the period 1988–92, the current account coefficient was not statistically different from its average value over the full period. The opposite is true for the period 1980–82, when this coefficient was

45. Calvo and others (1992).
46. Valdés (1992) and McNelis (1991).

larger (in absolute terms) than that for the rest of the sample. Surprisingly, the offset coefficient was even smaller than the average coefficient during 1988–92.

Finally we applied the Kalman filter technique for the period February 1983 to February 1992. The results show that the offset coefficient increases (in absolute terms) from 1988 to 1990, reducing the effectiveness of monetary policy. Since February 1991 this coefficient has declined and has even taken positive numbers. This suggests that starting from mid-1991, authorities have recovered partial control over monetary policy. We believe that this result is consistent with policies, as discussed earlier. The coefficient of Δr^*_t fluctuated substantially during this period, but without a clear pattern, suggesting that aggregate capital inflows have been quite inelastic to changes in international interest rates. The results also suggest that the current account has had little to do with the capital inflows of the late 1980s.

Short-Term versus Long-Term Capital Inflows: 1984–92

We now study the main factors explaining the inflow, both short-term and long-term, of capital to Chile after the foreign debt crisis of the early 1980s.

The Behavior of Short-Term Capital Inflows

We run a regression using quarterly data for the Chilean economy for the period January 1984–April 1992, in which short-term capital inflows to Chile (*SRCF*) are assumed to be explained by the interest rate differential, adjusted for the policy measures described earlier (*iGAP*); the ratio of foreign debt to GDP (*FD*/GDP*); the current account deficit (*CAD*); the rate of growth in GDP (g_{GDP}); and the ratio of domestic investment to GDP (*I/GDP*).

The coefficient of the *iGAP* is supposed to capture the sensitivity of short-term capital inflows to interest rate arbitrage opportunities and is expected to have a positive sign. The coefficient of the ratio of foreign debt to GDP, which is supposed to capture changes in country risk, is expected to have a negative sign. The coefficients of the current account deficit, of growth in GDP, and of the ratio of investment to GDP are expected to have a positive sign.

As we can see from table 3-2, only the coefficients of the interest rate differential and of the ratio of foreign debt to GDP turned out to be statistically significant, with t-statistics of 4.45 and -2.27, respectively, and to have the correct signs. The coefficient of the current account deficit was statistically insignificant, with a t-statistic of 0.25, but it had the correct sign; but those

Table 3-2. Explaining Capital Inflows to Chile, 1984–92

Factors	SRCF	LTCF
Constant	4,107.0	3,323.6
	(4.9)	(2.6)
iGAP	16.4	0.56
adjusted	(4.45)	(0.22)
FD*/GDP	−3,207.4	−4.045.0
	(−2.27)	(−1.84)
CAD	40.8	−25.8
	(0.25)	(−1.3)
gGDP	−0.18	9.61
	(−0.01)	(0.45)
I/GDP	−0.93	12.3
	(−0.04)	(3.23)
DD	. . .	1,201
		(5.68)
$\bar{R}^2$ adjusted	0.71	0.91
Durbin-Watson	1.62	1.71

SOURCE: Authors' calculations. The numbers in parentheses are t-statistics.

on the growth rate of GDP and on the investment rate are both statistically insignificant and have the wrong sign. The adjusted $\bar{R}^2$ is 0.71 and the D-W statistic is 1.62.

Based on these results, we can conclude that the sharp increase in short-term capital inflows to Chile since the late 1980s is a result of the increase in opportunities for interest rate arbitrage and the decline in the foreign debt overhang. The increase in opportunities for arbitrage is a result of both external forces (for instance, the decline in U. S. interest rates) and internal factors (such as the macroeconomic adjustment program of 1990). The decline in short-term capital inflows in mid-1991 is well explained by a reduction in the interest rate differential, which occurred as a response to the decline in domestic interest rates and to several policies that increased the cost of foreign funding, as already discussed.

Explaining Long-Term Capital Inflows

Using quarterly data for the Chilean economy over the period January 1984 to April 1992, we analyze in this section the factors behind the inflow of long-term capital to Chile (LTCF). This variable is constructed by totaling medium-and long-term foreign credits to the domestic private sector and direct foreign investment. We assume LTCF to be explained by the interest rate differential, adjusted for the policy measures described earlier in the paper (iGAP); the ratio of foreign debt to GDP ($FD*/GDP$); the current account deficit (CAD); the rate of growth of GDP (g_{GDP}); and the ratio of domestic investment to GDP (i/GDP). We also introduce a dummy variable (DD), which takes a value of one after the return to democracy in early 1990 and zero otherwise.

The results of this regression, shown in table 3-2, are the following: the interest rate differential is statistically insignificant but with the correct sign; the ratio of foreign debt to GDP and the investment rate are both statistically significant (t-statistics of 1.84 and 3.23, respectively) and have the expected signs. The current rate of growth of output is statistically insignificant but has the correct sign, while the current account deficit is both statistically insignificant and has the wrong sign. Finally, the dummy variable for the change in political regime is highly significant (t-statistic of 5.68) and has the correct sign. The adjusted $\bar{R}^2$ of the equation is 0.91 and the D-W statistic is 1.71.

Thus we can conclude based on this information that the increase observed in medium- and long-term capital inflows to Chile after 1989 has been a result of domestic factors such as the reduction of the debt overhang and better prospects for economic growth, captured here by a higher investment rate, and for the return to democracy. Shorter-term considerations, such as the prospect of opportunities for interest rate arbitrage and the current rate of growth of GDP, were not significant, and neither was the financing of the current account deficit. In fact, the adjustment of the equation for medium- and long-term flows was similar to and without the corrections we introduced to the interest rate differential to capture the several policy measures introduced since mid-1991.

Conclusions

This paper has analyzed the experience of Chile with capital flows over the past two decades. In contrasting the two periods with heavy capital inflows, 1978–81 and 1989–92, we have argued that important differences exist. In 1978–81, the magnitudes were higher, credit (as opposed to foreign investment) was much more important, and the inflows were used mainly to finance current account deficits; not surprisingly, the appreciation of the real exchange rate was stronger, too.

Increased capital inflows provide important opportunities, but they also pose some major challenges. The main challenges are how to prevent a significant appreciation of the real exchange rate and how to maintain some control over monetary policy. Chilean authorities have responded to the problem mainly through accumulating and sterilizing reserves, increasing controls on capital inflows through reserve requirements, and liberalizing capital outflows.

This combination of policies has failed to prevent an appreciation in the real exchange rate on the order of 9 percent a year during 1991 and 1992.

Our empirical analysis is specially centered on the period after the debt crisis. The Kalman filter technique used to estimate the offset coefficient suggests that capital mobility increased (and so the effectiveness of monetary policy declined in a semi-fixed exchange rate regime) after 1988 and then has been reduced since mid-1991, when reserve requirements were introduced. Thus the authorities seem to have regained some control over monetary policy since that date.

Another important empirical result is that the factors explaining the evolution of short-term capital inflows in the Chilean economy since 1984 are different from those relevant to understanding the behavior of medium- and long-term capital inflows.

Short-term private capital inflows have responded to opportunities for interest rate arbitrage—that are a mix of internal and external factors—and to the decline in the country risk, associated here with the reduction of the ratio of foreign debt to GDP. In fact, the introduction of a reserve requirement in June 1991 and its successive modifications and the extension of the stamp tax to foreign credits effectively reduced the interest rate gap between Chile and abroad, and short-term capital inflows declined significantly.

On the other hand, the sharp increase in medium- and long-term private capital inflows since the late 1980s has been mainly a result of favorable domestic political and economic changes such as the reduction of the debt overhang and better prospects for economic growth (captured here by a higher investment rate) and for the return to democracy. These have been translated into a reduction of the premium required of foreign investors who want to buy Chilean long-term securities. Our results also show that medium- and long-term capital has not been sensitive to the interest rate differential.

Comment by Ronald I. McKinnon

The paper by Labán and Larraín covers an important aspect of Chile's successful struggle, now almost twenty years old, to sustain an open market economy. From 1978 through 1981, a deluge of foreign capital contributed to a severely overvalued real exchange rate. The subsequent financial crash almost undermined the first wave of reforms. Despite the resulting huge debt overhang, the country engineered a remarkable recovery in the late 1980s with a controlled depreciation of the real exchange rate and modest net flows of capital.

In the early 1990s, however, the Chilean government is once again struggling to prevent exchange overvaluation in the face of "excessive" capital inflows. Learning from its earlier unfortunate experiences, the government is now restricting inflows of foreign capital more severely, as Labán and Larraín document. Fortunately the domestic economy is now more robust financially. It is no longer so dependent on foreign saving, and the banking system is under better supervision and control.

First I will critically review the empirical results presented by Labán and Larraín. What have been the main factors determining flows of foreign capital into and out of Chile since 1975? Then I will speculate on what should be the link between domestic interest rate policy and efforts to avoid the destabilizing flows of international capital Chile has experienced over the past twenty years.

Chile and the International Capital Market

Using a modified Kouri and Porter model, Labán and Larraín claim that changing domestic financial and regulatory variables dominate the ebb and flow of financial capital into the Chilean economy.[47] In their regression, changes in foreign interest rates per se turned out not to be statistically significant in explaining external capital flows.

Of those domestic factors that can be quantitatively represented in time series in the authors' regression, the ratio of external debt to GNP was most important in determining the willingness of foreigners to lend to Chile. (Incidentally, the authors should define this foreign debt overhang more precisely. I suspect they are referring just to "old" government-guaranteed debt rather than to "new" private debt.) Somewhat paradoxically, the debt overhang arising from the 1982–84 crash frightened foreign investors so that capital inflows in the late 1980s were manageable; the authorities could manipulate the rate of crawl of the nominal exchange rate to secure a real devaluation.

Once the ratio of debt to GNP was worked down and Chile's foreign trade and domestic financial policies appeared to be successful, however, a shift in portfolio preferences led to rather massive gross inflows of private capital from 1989 to 1992. But this time the controls on capital inflows and a program of monetary sterilization held the exchange appreciation to about 10 percent in real terms—in contrast to the 22 percent real appreciation in 1978–91. In

47. Kouri and Porter (1974).

1991–92, the Chileans imposed fairly heavy reserve requirements and stamp taxes on foreign credits—except for those obtained by exporters.

In their regression, the authors also found that the current account was significantly negatively related to capital inflows. But because the capital and current account are jointly determined, the current account is not truly exogenous; it is not a legitimate exogenous right-hand-side variable.

Also significant in their Kouri-Porter regression was the offset coefficient for domestic credit expansion, but which was only about -0.07 or -0.09 depending on which version of the regression was used. This offset coefficient was sufficiently small numerically—perhaps because of their capital restrictions—to allow the Chilean authorities to retain some control over the domestic monetary base. They could sell domestic bonds to mop up the domestic liquidity that would otherwise be created by the huge buildup of exchange reserves. Dollar reserves rose from about 3.6 billion at the end of 1989 to 9.9 billion by April 1993 or eleven months of the annualized flow of imports. With the bulk of the private foreign capital inflow now going into exchange reserves, no wonder the Chilean officials once again feel under siege by the world's capital markets!

The exchange-rate-adjusted rate of interest on peso deposits within Chile exceeded the London Interbank Offer Rate (LIBOR) by almost 20 percentage points in the 1978–81 period. Sadder and wiser, we know that interest rates within Chile in this period were falsely high and reflected adverse risk selection and a high degree of moral hazard in bank lending. This interest differential briefly approached 10 percentage points in early 1990, but by 1991–92 was closer to five percentage points. If adjustment is made for the extra costs of foreign borrowing associated with reserve requirements and stamp taxes, then Labán and Larraín show that this differential was reduced to two or three percentage points from late 1991 through 1992. In summary, the effective interest rate gap was more modest in the 1989–92 episode in comparison with the earlier one.

Interest Rate Policy

Surprisingly Labán and Larraín do not give a lot of attention to domestic interest policy, although it is a critical factor in determining the pressure for capital inflows (and outflows). Yet in retrospect at least, the huge interest rate gap in 1978–81 would have overwhelmed any attempted controls on capital inflows so that severe exchange rate overvaluation became inevitable. In the 1989–92 period, the reserve requirements and stamp taxes on foreign credits seemed to be sufficient to give the authorities some room to tighten domestic monetary policy on the one hand, while avoiding severe appreciation of the real exchange rate on the other. But the huge buildup of exchange reserves in the first half of 1993 suggests that this room for maneuver may soon vanish.

Would Labán and Larraín agree that the Chilean Central Bank, with the advantage of 20–20 hindsight, should have intervened in 1978–81 to scale down domestic nominal interest rates in line with the exchange rate *tablita* so that the interest differential with LIBOR remained modest?[48] Such a scaling down would have mitigated the problem of excess capital inflows and could also have limited the adverse risk selection and moral hazard in bank lending that had become so extravagant.

The answer to this question is important in its own right both as a historical exercise and as a response to the general problem of jointly managing domestic monetary policy and the capital account in the foreign exchanges in any liberalizing economy. If in the 1990s there is another run from dollars into Chilean pesos, the Chilean authorities might soon have to rethink their policy on the domestic interest rate and the exchange rate. One or the other might have to go.

The authors have confined their comprehensive empirical analysis to Chile's experience over the past twenty years. Nevertheless, the problem they have identified is more general. Other developing economies have found that, as they liberalize and appear to be successful, a fairly sudden change in foreign portfolio preferences begins to swamp the domestic economy with unmanageable inflows of foreign capital.[49]

Comment by Felipe G. Morandé

This paper concentrates on capital inflows rather than on capital movements more generally, perhaps because Chile is a net recipient of funds. But we must not forget that there is a supply of and a demand for foreign funds, and the paper almost exclusively focuses on supply aspects. My own empirical research apparently supports this concentration on supply aspects in one respect for the 1978–82 period: inflows of foreign capital were almost the only driving force behind the fluctuations in the real exchange rate.[50] But those inflows were insensitive to interest rate differentials and were determined by the demand for

48. McKinnon (1993, chapter 6).
49. McKinnon (1993).
50. Morandé (1988).

funds, effectively but decreasingly constrained by capital and exchange controls. So this raises the question of what was pushing demand.

What was the role of domestic financial market deregulation? The authors compare this period with 1988–93, noting that capital inflows are lower and have a completely different composition. How has the change in financial regulation that was implemented after the 1983 crisis influenced this situation? I am afraid that the authors' reluctance to talk about the effect of financial deregulation and about the problems caused by insufficient and inefficient supervision of financial operations on the foreign indebtedness process will leave the picture incomplete.

Why did Chileans embark in 1978–82 on a kind of crazy process of indebtedness at home and abroad? Was it because they thought their permanent income was higher than their actual income? And if so, is this phenomenon recurring now? Why or why not?

The authors favor controlling capital inflows based on macroeconomic considerations (real exchange rate stability and control of the money supply). Opening capital outflows is not an effective way to curtail capital inflows (on the contrary, the inflows could even increase). How much of the "harm" that a volatile exchange rate can cause to the real exchange rate and the real sector could be mitigated by allowing the private sector to develop appropriate financial instruments? If these instruments do not exist today, is it because their role is being played by the Central Bank?

Concerning the model itself, why, if the investment is irreversible in one alternative (in the sense that foreign investors will never have the possibility of getting their funds back in their home countries), would investors want to invest their funds in the first place? This could be a consequence of working with objective functions, which only indirectly reflect people's preferences, or of the assumption that economies last just two periods.

In general, it seems intuitive that liberalization of short-run capital outflows will attract more short-run capital inflows, but what is important from a macro point of view is whether net capital will increase or decrease. In cases where funds that were previously brought in by foreigners or funds belonging to domestic residents can flow out (legal capital flight), foreign capital outflows can increase more than capital inflows, at least for a while. A different question is whether more in-and-out flexibility will cause more instability of capital flows and so potentially greater instability of the real exchange rate. But this is not taken up by the model (to illustrate such a question, the model should consider first differences of variables and variances).

The case for controlling capital inflows is weakened sometimes because of the ineffectiveness of controls. Indeed, short-term capital inflows, after declining in the second part of 1991 because of the first impact of the reserve requirement, increased significantly in 1992, reaching more than U.S.$1.6 billion, not much less than in 1990 before the imposition of the reserve requirement. Of course this phenomenon could be the result of expectations that the exchange rate would be revalued, but in any case it demonstrates how weak the capital controls can be as a tool to protect the exchange rate.

Labán and Larraín mention welfare-decreasing effects of capital controls, such as higher domestic interest rates, as arguments against the case for such controls. These negative effects could be larger now because the world is more financially integrated, and well-administered economies like Chile's have access to financial opportunities that did not exist ten or fifteen years ago. In other words, until recently there was a naturally high spread between domestic and foreign interest rates because domestic financial instruments were imperfect substitutes for financial instruments of firms or governments of industrial countries. But today private firms even have direct access to well-developed financial centers (like Chile's telephone and electric companies, which have been placing stock shares in New York).

The authors allude to the role of fiscal policy in supporting the real exchange rate and affirm that in the past three years the expansion of fiscal spending has not contributed to that role. This is true, but not very important from an empirical point of view. Indeed, a recent study by Arrau, Quiroz, and Chumacero indicates that to get an increase of 1 percent in the real exchange rate, fiscal spending should be reduced by 10 percent.[51]

In the econometric section, I would like to see more statistics about the series and the regressions. Are the series stationary? (It is hard to believe capital inflows are.) What is the evidence on autocorrelation of residuals? And homoscedasticity? I also would like to see more information on the sources used to construct the data and the units in which the series are expressed (dollars, pesos, real terms).

The paper's finding that the Kouri-Porter offset coefficient is very low for the whole sample is interesting, but without more knowledge about the data, one cannot be sure whether the estimation is robust.

Other studies (not cited in this paper) have tried to separate the effect of capital controls from other aspects that affect the offset coefficient and that make domestic financial instruments imperfect substitutes for foreign instruments.[52]

It does not make sense that the offset coefficient is lower in 1988–92 than in

51. Arrau, Quiroz, and Chumacero (1992).
52. Among those papers are McNelis and Schmidt-Hebbel (1991) and Charoenwattana and Isaac (1992), which construct an ad hoc index to account for the restrictiveness of capital controls.

any earlier period because the former coincides with Chile's return to voluntary lending after several years of "punishment." The authors recognize this, calling the finding "puzzling." Using the Kalman filter technique seems to yield a more reasonable result because according to the authors the compensation co-efficient increases up to 1990 and then decreases starting in February of 1991, with the imposition of reserve requirements on capital inflows.

Finally the paper would benefit greatly from some analysis concerning the significant resources that Chilean firms and individuals are investing in neighboring countries, such as Argentina and Peru, as these countries go through liberalizing reforms. Indeed in 1992 Chile was among the first five foreign countries originating foreign investment in Argentina and the second (after the United States) in Peru. At the same time resources from Chile are going to the stock exchanges of those countries. This is a topic that from both a micro and a macro perspective should be included in a paper about capital movements (as this paper claims to be) rather than capital inflows (as this paper really is).

Appendix: Regulations Affecting International Capital Flows, 1974–92

Fully free capital mobility across a country's borders is a rare phenomenon. A more realistic yardstick measures the extent of restrictions that nations impose on international capital flows. Regulations sometimes allow only (or mainly) the central bank or other public entities to move capital across national borders. Such an environment of repressed international capital mobility can be expressed by imposing quotas, taxes, or reserve requirements on capital flows; by prohibiting some types of financial transactions; or by requiring certain cross-border operations to be approved on a case-by-case basis. Often restrictions on capital mobility take the form of limited access to the official foreign exchange market for particular transactions.

A milder—but still significant—form of international financial repression occurs when the nonfinancial private sector has the right to engage in cross-border capital transactions, while domestic financial intermediaries are excluded. Under a regime of free capital mobility, domestic intermediaries such as banks or securities firms are allowed to engage in unhindered international financial operations.

Over the past two decades, the Chilean economy has evolved toward increasing freedom for capital movements. But the path has not been steady. From a highly restrictive situation at the end of 1973, Chile moved toward increasing liberalization. This process accelerated sharply in 1980, but after the 1982–83 economic crisis the liberalizing reforms were partially reversed.

Liberalization started once again after 1985 and continued into the current decade. By early 1993, Chile's capital account was quite open, but some restrictions still applied. The rest of this section reviews the Chilean experience with regulation on capital flows over the past two decades.

The Early 1970s

Financial repression and exchange controls have been increasingly applied in the Chilean economy since the early 1930s. They were intensified from 1970 to 1973, as the Unidad Popular government attempted to implement in Chile a centrally planned economy.[53] Immediately after taking office, the government nationalized more than half of the private commercial banks.

Thus at the moment of the military coup in 1973, the government had almost complete control over foreign exchange operations, for both current and capital account transactions. In addition the state controlled most of the banking sector. Overall about 85 percent of Chile's financial system was in the hands of the state in 1973. With controls on nominal interest rates and an inflation rate that was more than 600 percent in 1973, financial repression was rampant.

After the coup in September 1973, the military regime implemented major economic and institutional reforms aimed at stabilizing the economy and permitting the transition from central planning to markets. Among these reforms were the privatization of state owned and controlled firms (including banks) and the liberalization and deregulation of domestic markets and international transactions for goods, services, and finance.

The Reforms of the Mid-1970s

In 1974 many firms expropriated by the previous government were returned to their original owners. The domestic financial market began to be liberalized with the authorization of new, unregulated financial intermediaries called *financieras*. Domestic interest rates were liberalized, and the government attempted to follow a free banking policy in the domestic market.[54] Inflation came down to 300 percent in 1974.

Among the measures the government adopted to cope with the shortfall of foreign exchange during the 1974–76 period was a holiday for tax and exchange controls adopted in early 1974, which allowed those funds registered

53. Larraín and Meller (1991).
54. de la Cuadra and Valdés (1990).

at the Central Bank under the holiday scheme to be claimed as a legitimate source of income before the tax authority. In 1975, this regime was replaced by window purchases, which allowed individuals to sell foreign currency without the need of identification, but the proceeds of this operation were not acceptable as a source of funds for the tax authority.

In December of 1974, the government introduced Decree Law 600, which significantly liberalized foreign direct investment. Aimed at reducing the risks associated with foreign direct investment, the DL600 was based on the principle of nondiscrimination between local and foreign investors. It offered foreign investors protection such as:

—the ability to sign a contract with the state of Chile, with the power of law, that could only be affected by a constitutional reform;

—the ability to choose between a fixed tax regime or the same tax treatment as local companies; and

—guaranteed access to the official foreign exchange market for dividend and capital repatriation.

This contract required the incoming funds to use the official market, case-by-case approval by the government, and a minimum residence period of three years for capital, though profits could be remitted from the first year. These guarantees were also extended to credit inflows associated with the same investment.

The foreign investment law was incompatible with the country's membership in the Andean Pact, and thus Chile decided to abandon the pact. With this decision, Chile was able to allow foreign banks to open subsidiaries and branches and to allow direct foreign investment in commercial banks. Both conditions were banned by the Andean Pact.

The Access of Banks and Nonbanks to Foreign Loans, 1974–80

In 1974, the government reformed the Foreign Exchange Control Law.[55] Article 14 of this law allowed nonfinancial firms to borrow from abroad, and the capital account became widely open for these agents. Banks, however, faced severe limitations on foreign borrowing up until April 1980. Restrictions on external borrowing by the nonbanking sector were less binding during 1975–80, so the liberalization of international financial transactions in March 1980 played a less important role in the increase of private nonfinancial foreign

55. Decree Law 326.

borrowing (which had been increasing sharply since 1978) than is usually believed.

Article 14 of DL326 also allowed domestic banks to guarantee the foreign borrowing of nonbanks. They ended up guaranteeing around 40 percent of this borrowing, thus opening a broad channel for capital inflows.

Nonbanks also had wide access to international trade credit during 1975–79. The liberalization of international trade implied a higher degree of capital mobility. Authorization of external trade credits for exports and the use of article 1 of DL326 for import credits formalized the access of Chilean nonfinancial firms to trade credits in banks abroad.

Between 1977 and 1980, there was an explosion of international loans to nonfinancial firms under article 14. Valdés suggests that most of these funds were the return of capital flight that had occurred during the Allende government.[56] Reasons for lenders to prefer this channel were the nondiscrimination guarantee provided by article 14 and the ability it afforded lenders to claim an acceptable source of funds to Chilean tax authorities. In April 1979, the Central Bank imposed a reserve requirement for nonbanks on article 14 inflows that had an average maturity of less than sixty-six months. Operations of average maturity below twenty-four months were prohibited, those between twenty-four and thirty-six months were subject to a 25 percent reserve requirement, and those over thirty-six months required a 15 percent reserve.

Window purchases for nonbanks were allowed after 1975. Operations under this regime did not require documentation to justify the purchases to the tax authorities and did not provide guaranteed access to a formal exchange market for repatriation, but they had lower transaction costs than those accomplished under article 14. Window sales were allowed in the second quarter of 1979 when the nominal exchange rate was fixed. The opening of both windows allowed for the almost complete disappearance of the illegal parallel exchange market after mid-1979.

According to Valdés, if we account for DL600, the reform of the Foreign Exchange Control Law (especially article 14), and the window purchases, by 1975 Chile's capital account was almost completely open for nonresidents, including both investment and repatriation.[57] Since 1975, short-term portfolio investment by nonresidents has been allowed under article 14 of DL326. The fact that these capital movements were almost negligible between 1975 and 1977 was not the result of legal restrictions. Rather, it was due to an extremely

56. Valdés (1992).
57. Valdés (1992).

high premium required for this kind of operation at a time when Chile did not have adequate access to international capital markets.

A Turning Point: 1980

Until April 1980, most capital inflows to Chile were associated with nonfinancial firms and individuals. Valdés argues that most of the increase in capital inflows during this period was caused by a reduction in the premium required by both domestic and foreign investors rather than by explicit policies directed toward opening the capital account to nonbanks.[58] This argument is based on the fact that the legislation on both article 14 and window purchases had been in place since 1975 and that trade liberalization was carried out without direct concern about its effects on the trade credit market.

Until April 1980, restrictions, including quotas and reserve requirements, on international transactions by domestic financial institutions were many and also very complex. Commercial banks were first authorized to obtain loans using article 14 in September 1977, but under very restrictive limits on stocks and on monthly inflows. In April 1978, banks were granted an increase in quotas, and new quotas were imposed on short-term foreign credits. In April 1979, in addition to the quotas, nonremunerated reserve requirements were imposed on foreign loans that had been effected through article 14 that had average amortization periods of less than sixty-six months. By June 1979, the quotas on the stock of foreign credit and on article 14 foreign debt had been eliminated.

In April 1980, the most binding restriction on foreign credit was eliminated: the quota on article 14 monthly inflows of loans. This led to a substantial increase in capital inflows even though the reserve requirements and the quota for short-term loans remained.

Until April 1980, domestic banks were for the most part left out of the international financial intermediation business. Loans were obtained directly by nonbanks. The April 1980 reform of article 14 effectively ended the discrimination against domestic financial intermediaries. Eliminating the monthly quota on inflows of individual banks provoked a sharp increase in the volume of capital inflows intermediated by private commercial banks without reducing inflows by nonbanks.

The liberalization of capital inflows in April 1980, however, was not total. Banks continued to be prevented from taking a net position in foreign exchange. They were allowed to lend their dollar funds only as dollar-indexed

58. Valdés (1992).

peso loans. This restriction did not prevent nonfinancial firms from carrying out arbitrage operations. Also, foreign credits with an average term of less than twenty-four months were not allowed, and those between twenty-four and sixty-six months were subject to reserve requirements.

The limit on investment by domestic banks and *financieras* in bank equity abroad was also raised in 1980. During 1981, further restrictions on international financial intermediation that discriminated against domestic banks were eliminated. In August of that year, domestic banks were allowed to open branches abroad.

In short, the capital account was wide open for nonbanks after 1975. Reserve requirements on article 14 were not binding given the large interest differential. Nonbanks could also engage in arbitrage through window purchases and sales of dollars. In contrast, domestic banks were largely repressed regarding international financial intermediation and the possibility to engage in arbitrage operations prior to April 1980. Although financial repression was quickly reduced after that date, the capital account for banks was not fully liberalized.[59]

The Crisis and Its Aftermath: 1982–85

During 1982, the Central Bank further liberalized the capital account. In June of that year, the government abandoned the fixed exchange regime that had been in place since 1979. A month later, reserve requirements on short-term capital inflows through article 14 were reduced from 20 percent to 5 percent, and banks were allowed to take positions in foreign exchange with a maximum exposure of 50 percent of their capital and reserves. In September, the Central Bank announced the payment of interest (LIBOR) on reserve requirements held on article 14 loans with average maturity of more than four years. In August, the authorities moved toward a floating exchange rate system. They also introduced a preferential dollar scheme to help local debtors of the banking system that held dollar-denominated or dollar-indexed liabilities and debtors with registered debts abroad.

In September 1982, the government sharply reduced the maximum monthly sales of foreign currency through the open window, abandoned the floating exchange rate system in favor of a crawling peg, and reinstated exchange controls. It introduced foreign currency quotas for those traveling abroad and reduced the maximum share of export revenues that exporters could keep abroad. Borrowers through article 14 and DL600 were allowed to anticipate the purchase of foreign currency needed to pay their debts, under the condition that

59. Valdés (1992).

they would not prepay abroad. In November, the Central Bank introduced the swap, a foreign exchange guarantee.

In February 1983, the Central Bank intervened in private contracts, decreeing a suspension of ninety days in the payment of foreign debt obligations for all residents. By the end of 1983, the minimum term to repay imports, eliminated in mid-1982, was reintroduced, requiring a minimum of 120 days between importation and payment. In early 1984, the preferential dollar scheme was eliminated for exporters (who did in fact benefit from devaluation) and for public enterprises.[60] Only in mid-1985 was the preferential dollar subsidy fully eliminated. In that same year, two debt-equity conversion mechanisms were created: chapter XVIII, for residents, and chapter XIX, for nonresidents.

The Second Half of the 1980s

Regulations on international capital flows and foreign exchange operations did not suffer significant changes between 1986 and 1988. In December 1989, however, with the creation of an autonomous Central Bank, the organizing principle for the regulation of foreign exchange operations suffered a major change. From a system in which all operations were prohibited unless explicitly authorized, Chile moved to one in which all operations were allowed—under the norms dictated by the Central Bank—unless explicitly banned.[61] Nonetheless, the Central Bank kept the power to determine which agents would be approved and which transactions could be accomplished through the formal foreign exchange market, and which through the informal or parallel market. The Central Bank also maintained the right to intervene in the foreign exchange market and to set the exchange rate regime.

The Reforms after the Return to Democracy, 1990–93

Since 1990 the opening of the capital account and the reduction of foreign exchange controls have continued. There is still, however, much that can be done to improve the integration of the Chilean economy into world capital markets and the functioning of the foreign exchange market.

The progress achieved in reducing capital controls has been greatly influenced by the sharp increase in the availability of both long-term and short-term

60. This allowed a better focalization of this subsidy. Nevertheless, import-substituting industries continued to have access to the subsidy.
61. Fontaine (1989).

foreign capital. Thus the opening of the capital account has been gradual and asymmetrical: progress has been quicker in reducing and eliminating controls on outflows than on inflows. In fact, a reserve requirement on short-term capital inflows was introduced in June 1991.

Regarding capital outflows, in 1990 the Central Bank allowed residents to use the informal foreign exchange market for investment in foreign countries. In February 1991, Chilean commercial banks were authorized to invest abroad up to 25 percent of their foreign exchange deposits. In April of that year, capital repatriation on foreign investments made through debt-equity swaps (chapter XIX) was allowed ahead of schedule after payment of a fee to the Central Bank. Capital repatriation was further liberalized in October 1991, and again in May 1992.

In June 1991, domestic commercial banks were authorized to grant trade credits in other Latin American countries under the terms of the ALADI agreement. In May 1992, pension funds (AFPs) were authorized to invest abroad up to 1.5 percent of the value of their fund; this limit was raised to 3 percent in August of that year. In August 1992, the Central Bank eliminated the minimum required period before the repatriation of capital and profits on chapter XIX investments. And in March 1993, the capital repatriation period for regular foreign investment under DL600 was reduced from three years to only one year.

Other measures have also been adopted to substitute domestic financing for foreign funding, in an attempt to limit the net inflow of foreign exchange. For example, in 1991 the Central Bank increased the limit on domestic bank trade credits from 30 percent to 40 percent of their long-term deposits. In 1992, pension funds were allowed to participate in the funding of new projects, which had previously been banned. Shortly after the implementation of this mechanism, the government estimated that some important mining and infrastructure projects, which used to be financed with external borrowing, would be able to place around U.S.$200 million in bonds among local pension funds.

In June 1991, the economic authorities extended the stamp tax to foreign credits except on those granted to exporters; this tax applied previously only to domestic credits. In the same month, the authorities introduced a nonremunerated reserve requirement of 20 percent on all foreign credits except those granted to exporters; this was extended to foreign currency deposits in January 1992 and was increased to 30 percent in August 1992.[62]

Until April 1991, exporters were required to surrender all proceeds to the Central Bank at the official exchange rate. After this date, they were allowed

---

62. The maximum reserve requirement allowed by law is 40 percent.

to keep 5 percent of their export proceeds, an amount that was increased to 10 percent in March 1992. Also in 1992, the Central Bank gave more flexibility to the arbitrage norms in the spot and forward markets for foreign exchange. This measure gave better access to the foreign exchange market and to the coverage of exchange rate risk to both banks and nonbanks.

Thus the evolution of restrictions on the mobility of international capital and on exchange controls in Chile points to an interesting comparison between the two periods of large capital inflows. During 1978–81, changes in the regulatory framework were consistent with the objective of permitting a greater integration of Chile into the world economy, and no special attention was placed on preventing a larger inflow of capital or a major buildup of foreign debt. In contrast, during 1990–93, deregulation has moved faster in reducing controls on capital outflows than on inflows, and some restrictions on short-term inflows have even been introduced. Regulatory reforms concerning capital flows in the 1990s have therefore been consistent, to a large extent, with the objective of preventing a large appreciation in the real exchange rate.

References

Arrau, P., J. Quiroz, and R. Chumacero. 1992. "Ahorro fiscal y tipo de cambio real." ILADES/Georgetown University Working Paper 44 (May).

Bernanke, B. 1983. "Irreversibility, Uncertainty and Cyclical Investment." *Quarterly Journal of Economics* 98 (February): 85–106.

Calvo, G. A. 1991. "The Perils of Sterilization." IMF Staff Papers 38 (December): 921–26.

Calvo, G. A., L. Leiderman, and C. Reinhart. 1992. "Capital Inflows and Real Exchange Rate Appreciation in Latin America: The Role of External Factors." IMF Working Paper WP/92/62.

Caballero, R., and V. Corbo. 1990. "The Effect of Real Exchange Rate Uncertainty on Exports: Empirical Evidence." *The World Bank Economic Review* 3(2): 263–78.

Central Bank of Chile. 1992. "Evolucion de la Economia en 1992 y Perspectivas para 1993." September. Santiago.

Charoenwattana, J., and A. Isaac. 1992. "Private Capital Inflow in Chile: 1975–85." American University, Department of Economics.

Corbo, V., and R. Matte. 1984. "Capital Flows and the Role of Monetary Policy: The Case of Chile." Working Paper 92. Catholic University of Chile, Department of Economics. Santiago.

Corbo, V., J. De Melo, and J. Tybout. 1986. "What Went Wrong with the Recent Reforms in the Southern Cone?" *Economic Development and Cultural Change* 34 (April): 607–40.

Culpeper, J., and S. Griffith-Jones. 1992. "Rapid Return of Private Flows to Latin America: New Trends and New Policy Issues." ECLAC.

de la Cuadra, S., and S. Valdés. 1990. "Myths and Facts about Financial Liberalization in Chile: 1974–82." Working Paper 128. Catholic University of Chile, Department of Economics. Santiago.

Dixit, A. 1990. "Investment and Hysteresis." Princeton University, Department of Economics.

Dornbusch, R. 1980. *Open Economy Macroeconomics.* Basic Books.

Dornbusch, R. 1989. "Real Exchange Rates and Macroeconomics: A Selective Survey." *Scandinavian Journal of Economics* 91 (2): 401–32.

Dornbusch, R., S. Fischer, and P. Samuelson. 1977. "Comparative Advantage, Trade, and Payments in a Ricardian Model with a Continuum of Goods." *American Economic Review* 67 (December): 823–39.

The Economist. 1992. "The Fear of Finance." September 19.

Edwards, S. 1984. "The Order of Liberalization of the External Sector in Developing Countries." Essays in International Finance. 156 (December). Princeton University.

Edwards, S., and A. Cox-Edwards. 1987. *Monetarism and Liberalization: The Chilean Experiment.* Cambridge, Mass.: Ballinger.

Fontaine, J. A. 1989. "The Chilean Economy in the Eighties: Adjustment and Recovery." In *Debt, Adjustment and Recovery: Latin America's Prospects for Growth and Development,* edited by S. Edwards and F. Larraín, 208–33. Blackwell.

Hanson, J. 1992. "Opening the Capital Account: A Survey of Issues and Results." World Bank Working Paper. May.

Kouri, P., and M. Porter. 1974. "International Capital Flows and Portfolio Equilibrium." *Journal of Political Economy* 86 (May/June): 443–67.

Krugman, P. 1987. "The Narrow Moving Band, the Dutch Disease, and the Competitive Consequences of Mrs. Thatcher." *Journal of Development Economics* 27 (October): 41–55.

Labán, R., and F. Larraín. 1993. "Can a Liberalization of Capital Outflows Increase Net Capital Inflows?" Working Paper 155. Catholic University of Chile, Department of Economics.

———. Forthcoming. "Continuity, Change and the Political Economy of Transition in Chile." Forthcoming in *The Macroeconomics of Populism in Latin America,* edited by S. Edwards and R. Dornbusch. University of Chicago Press.

Larraín, F., and P. Meller. 1991. "The Socialist-Populist Chilean Experience: 1970–73." In *The Macroeconomics of Populism in Latin America,* edited by R. Dornbusch and S. Edwards. University of Chicago Press.

Larraín, F., and A. Velasco (1990). "Can Swaps Solve the Debt Crisis? Lessons from the Chilean Experience." *Princeton Studies in International Finance* 69 (November).

Larraín, F., and R. Vergara. 1993. "Private Investment and Macroeconomic Adjustment: the Case of East Asia." In *From Adjustment to Sustainable Growth: The Role of Capital Formation,* edited by L. Servén and A. Solimano (forthcoming). World Bank.

McKinnon, R. 1982. "The Order of Economic Liberalization: Lessons from Chile and Argentina." In *Economic Policy in a World of Change,* edited by K. Brunner and A. Metzler, 159–86. Amsterdam: North Holland.

———. 1993. *The Order of Economic Liberalization: Financial Control in the Transition to a Market Economy.* Baltimore: Johns Hopkins University Press (forthcoming).

McNelis, P. 1991. "Flujos de Capital y Política Monetaria: Se Compensan en Chile y Venezuela?" In *Movimientos de Capitales y Crisis Financiera: Los Casos de Chile y Venezuela,* edited by F. Morandé, 31–49. ILADES.

McNelis, P., and K. Schmidt-Hebbel. 1991. "Tipo de cambio real, saldo comercial y ajuste monetario en Chile (1975–1982): Una interpretacion real-financiera del boom." In *Movimientos de Capitales y Crisis Economica,* edited by F. Morandé, 75–106. ILADES/Georgetown University and IIMC, Santiago.

Morandé, F. 1988. "Domestic Currency Appreciation and Foreign Capital Inflows. What Comes First? (Chile, 1978–1982)." *Journal of International Money and Finance* 7 (December): 447–66.

———. 1991. "Flujos de Capitales Hacia Chile, 1977–1872." In *Movimientos de Capitales y Crisis Financiera: Los Casos de Chile y Venezuela,* edited by F. Morandé, 107–33. Instituto Latinoamericano de Doctrino y Estudios Sociales (ILADES).

Mundell, R. 1968. *International Economics.* Macmillan.

Pindyck, R. 1991. "Irreversibility, Uncertainty, and Investment." *Journal of Economic Literature* 29 (September): 1110–48.

Rodriguez, C. 1991. "Situación Monetaria y cambiaria en Colombia." November.

Sachs, J., and F. Larraín. 1993. *Macroeconomics in the Global Economy.* Prentice-Hall.

Salomon Brothers. 1992. "Private Capital Flows to Latin America." Sovereign Assessment Group. February. New York.

Sargent, T. 1983. Comment on G. Ortiz, "Dollarization in Mexico: Causes and Consequences." In *Financial Problems of the World Capital Market: The Problem of Latin American Countries,* edited by P. Aspe and others, 71–106. University of Chicago Press.

Summers, L. M. 1988. "Tax Policy and International Competitiveness." In *International Aspects of Fiscal Policies,* edited by J. Frankel, 349–75. University of Chicago Press.

Tobin, J. 1978. "A Proposal for International Monetary Reform." *Eastern Economic Journal* 4: 153–59.

Tornell, A. 1990. "Real vs. Financial Investment: Can Tobin Taxes Eliminate the Irreversibility Distortion?" *Journal of Development Economics* 32 (April): 419–44.

Valdés, S. 1992. "Financial Liberalization and the Capital Account: Chile, 1974–84." Catholic University of Chile, Department of Economics.

Viñals, J. 1990. "Spain's Capital Account Shock." CEPR.

Williamson, J. 1991. "On Liberalizing the Capital Account." *AMEX Bank Review.* Oxford University Press.

4 Saving, Investment, and Economic Growth

Manuel Marfán and Barry P. Bosworth

THE RAPID growth of the Chilean economy in a context of macroeconomic stability has attracted international attention. Chile stands out almost as a laboratory for the economic liberalization measures—such as privatization, open trade policies, and financial market deregulation—that have become a cornerstone of the current orthodox view of economic development policies. The purpose of this paper is to review the growth performance of the Chilean economy over the past two decades and to evaluate the effect of the reforms on growth and on Chile's ability to sustain rapid growth in the future.

This review leads us to mixed and sometimes unanticipated conclusions. Recent trends in output growth and rates of saving and investment have been highly favorable, but they come on the heels of a disastrous performance during the 1970s and early 1980s. To a great extent, the growth of the Chilean economy during the 1980s should be viewed as a recovery from an extreme depression, fueled by high levels of surplus labor. It is surprising that the benefits of economic liberalization are not more evident in an improved efficiency of resource use as measured by either the level of labor productivity or the joint productivity of capital and labor. Over the past two decades, the growth rates of labor productivity in Chile have been below those of comparable economies and below the rate Chile had achieved in the 1960s. Thus conclusions about the effectiveness of the economic reforms on economic growth are critically dependent on whether the focus is on recent rates of economic growth, discounting past output losses, or on a comparison of levels of output per worker and rates of saving and investment between the pre-1973 period and the present.

Similar conflicts of interpretation are evident in trends in saving and investment. The national saving rate has increased dramatically over the past decade, reflecting rising rates of private saving and a strong government fiscal position. Chile has also done much to strengthen incentives for both private saving and investment. The rise in the rate of saving began, however, from disastrously

165

low rates brought on by a severe recession in 1981–83. Today the share of GDP devoted to capital formation remains low relative to international norms, and it is adequate to finance growth of about 4 percent annually.[1]

What does emerge—particularly in the evaluation of the economic events of the past ten years—is the clear benefit of pragmatic, conventional macro-economic policies that emphasize stable prices, stable growth in demand, and a concern for the contribution of the public and private sectors to national saving.

In evaluating future policy options, there is little debate about the merits of an open economic strategy. Chile displays increasing investment opportunities, and its main challenges are to attain a rate of national saving sufficient to provide for a sound financing of those opportunities and to generate larger increases in productivity in response to a reduction of its labor surplus.

Economic Growth

Chile has long had a low rate of economic growth. Even in the first half of the twentieth century, a comparatively prosperous period for Latin America as a whole, Chilean GDP per capita rose at an annual rate of only 1.4 percent.[2] In the 1950s and 1960s, annual per capita growth averaged 1.1 and 2 percent respectively. In international rankings, Chile's relative standard of living has been sliding down for many decades.

Major objectives of the program of economic stabilization and liberalization carried out in the years after 1973 were to reverse Chile's relative income decline and to raise the rate of long-term economic growth. The liberalization of domestic financial markets, the privatization of state-owned enterprises, and the near elimination of restrictions on foreign trade were all advocated as means of promoting the more efficient use of resources in production. Furthermore, reforms of the tax system, the strong effort to shift the public sector budget balance from deficit to surplus, and the establishment of a funded social insurance fund were seen as means of increasing domestic saving and capital formation.

For many years the violent cyclical fluctuations of the Chilean economy made it difficult to evaluate those programs from the perspective of their effect on economic growth. GDP per capita plummeted by 23 percent in 1971–75, expanded by 38 percent in 1975–81, and suffered another severe decline of 18 percent in 1981–83.

1. This paper was prepared prior to the recent revisions of the Chilean National Accounts. Those revisions raised the rates of national saving and investment in the 1980s. The revisions would slightly increase the estimate of sustainable future growth.

2. Hofman (1993).

Chile has, however, managed to sustain the current economic expansion for a decade with a strong average annual growth in per capita GDP of 4.5 percent. In addition, unemployment has been reduced to 5 percent of the labor force, a rate comparable to the low levels of the early 1970s. The full recovery from the recession suggests that it should be possible to evaluate the effects on total incomes of the reform programs of the past twenty years in a context that is largely free from cyclical distortions.

The pattern of GDP growth in 1960–92 is shown in figure 4-1. The sustained rise in output since 1983 is impressive, but it is also evident that much of the expansion should be interpreted as part of a cyclical recovery from the depressed levels of 1983. Rates of unemployment (panel 2) have varied over a wide range, rising from an estimated 3.9 percent of the work force in 1972 to 19 percent in 1982, before declining to 4.9 percent in 1992.[3]

Furthermore, as shown in the third panel, the output gains are less impressive when measured per capita or per worker. In fact, output per worker never exceeded 1980–81 levels until 1991.[4] Instead, the strong growth of output has been supported by extremely large increases in employment—4.2 percent annually since 1983. The employment gains have been made possible through both a reduction in unemployment and a rapid growth of the labor force: the economically active population grew at an annual rate of 2.5 percent in the 1980s compared with 1.6 percent for the total population.

The most surprising feature of Chile's economic growth performance is the lack of more substantial gains in output per worker—particularly within the context of the standard argument that programs of economic liberalization will translate into significant gains in economic efficiency. It is also of concern for future Chilean economic policy. With unemployment now below 5 percent of the work force, Chile can no longer rely on a redundant labor supply to support future growth without running a serious risk of reigniting inflation pressures.

It may be premature, however, to conclude that the economic liberalization did not translate into gains in economic efficiency. The Chilean economy has been extremely unstable over the past twenty years. It has had two severe economic downturns, and the instability in turn depressed domestic investment. Thus it is possible that lower rates of capital formation offset all, or a portion of, the efficiency gains that emerged from the liberalization programs.

3. This measure of unemployment treats participants in the special employment programs between 1975 and 1988 as being employed. If they are included among the unemployed, the unemployment rate peaked in 1983 at 31 percent of the labor force.

4. The implication of little or no growth in labor productivity during the 1980s is fully supported by the measures of the real wage, which showed no gain in 1980–90.

Figure 4-1. Aggregate Trends in the Chilean Economy, 1960–92

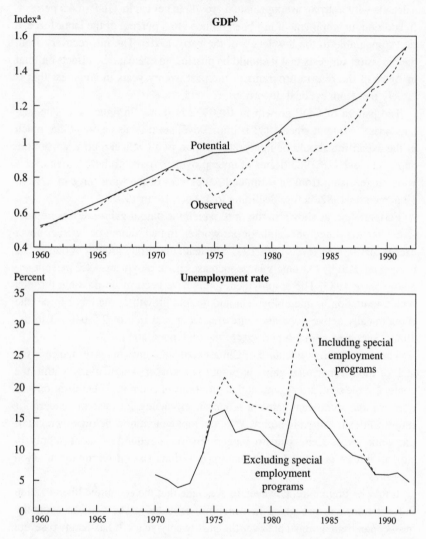

In the following section we examine the sources of growth in Chile in greater detail.

Growth Accounting

A recent study by André Hofman provides the basis for a review of aggregate economic growth in Chile and a comparison of its performance with the

Figure 4-1. (*continued*)

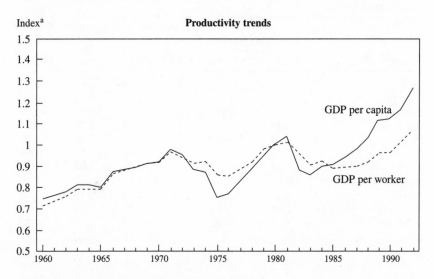

Index[a]   **Productivity trends**

SOURCES: Central Bank of Chile and authors' estimates.
a. 1980 = 1.
b. 1977 prices.

economies of other countries. The Hofman study provides internationally comparable data on output, employment, educational levels of the work force, and
the stock of physical capital over the period from 1950 to 1989 for six Latin
American countries, eight OECD (Organization for Economic Cooperation
and Development) countries (including Spain and Portugal), and three Asian
economies.[5] Hofman uses these data in a standard growth accounting exercise
in which the growth in output (*Y*) is allocated to increases in the quantity and
quality of the inputs of capital (*K*) and labor (*L*) and a residual of growth in
joint factor productivity.

(4-1) $$Y = Ae^{\delta t}K^{\alpha}(LQ)^{\beta}.$$

We have ignored his adjustment for the quality of capital, but we do include
Hofman's measure of labor quality (*Q*). Our calculations are based on an assumed elasticity of output with respect to physical capital of 0.4 for the developing countries of Latin America and Asia, 0.35 for the Iberian countries, and
0.3 for the OECD. The sum of the elasticities for physical capital and quality-
adjusted labor is in all cases equal to 1.0.

In table 4-1 the data are organized to allocate the change in output per

5. Hofman (1993). The capital stock data are available on a computer diskette that accompanied Hofman (1992).

Table 4-1. Sources of Growth in Output per Worker, Seventeen Countries, 1950–89
Annual rate of change

Country	Output per worker		Capital-labor substitution		Joint factor productivity	
	1950–73	1973–89	1950–73	1973–89	1950–73	1973–89
Chile	2.87	0.63	1.81	0.42	1.05	0.21
Argentina	2.21	−0.35	1.75	1.50	0.45	−1.82
Brazil	3.91	0.69	3.32	2.74	0.57	−2.00
Colombia	3.16	1.60	1.13	1.49	2.01	0.10
Mexico	4.20	0.23	2.83	1.81	1.32	−1.55
Venezuela	3.59	−1.74	2.38	1.27	1.18	−2.98
Average Latin America	3.32	0.17	2.21	1.55	1.09	−1.35
Korea	4.25	5.34	2.06	5.66	2.14	−0.30
Taiwan	4.86	5.33	1.57	4.39	3.25	0.90
Thailand	3.61	4.60	1.68	2.30	1.90	2.24
Average Asia	4.24	5.09	1.77	4.13	2.43	0.92
Portugal	5.73	1.99	2.96	2.61	2.69	−0.61
Spain	5.77	3.52	2.57	2.99	3.12	0.52
Average Iberia	5.75	2.75	2.76	2.80	2.90	−0.05
France	5.05	3.01	1.72	1.95	3.27	1.03
Germany	5.97	2.53	2.40	1.32	3.49	1.20
Japan	7.88	2.87	2.55	2.22	5.19	0.63
Netherlands	4.35	1.71	1.98	1.36	2.33	0.34
United Kingdom	2.87	2.01	1.61	1.38	1.23	0.62
United States	2.40	1.25	0.94	1.11	1.45	0.14
Average OECD	4.82	2.23	1.89	1.53	2.88	0.69

SOURCES: Table 4A-1 and authors' calculations as explained in text.

worker between its two components—the contribution of changes in capital per worker and the change in joint factor productivity—for two periods, 1950–73 and 1973–89. In the table capital is defined in a broad sense to include both physical capital and "human capital," with the latter measured by increases in the average educational level of the economically active population.[6] The choice of 1973 as a year of transition tends to understate slightly the rate of growth before 1973 and to overstate growth in subsequent years because while it marks the beginning of a recession, it corresponds with the initiation of the Chilean economic reforms. For the other countries of Latin America the choice of 1989 as a terminal year introduces a strong negative cyclical element into

6. The calculation of labor quality follows a procedure developed by Maddison (1989) in which an index of educational attainment is constructed using weights of 1.0 (primary), 1.4 (secondary), and 2.0 (university). Maddison then assumed a 0.5 elasticity of labor quality with respect to educational attainment on the basis that some of the increase in income by educational level is associated with basic intelligence rather than education. Support for the assumption of a large contribution of education to growth is available in Mankiw, Romer, and Weil (1990).

the calculations of productivity growth, but that is not true for Chile. In the Hofman study the quantity of labor inputs is generally measured by the labor force (the economically active population) rather than by actual employment, which we used in figure 4-1, but with an adjustment for secular changes in hours of work.

As shown by the first line of the table, Chile's relatively low rate of economic growth is due to both a low rate of capital accumulation per worker and consistently small improvements in joint factor productivity. This pattern is even more evident after 1973 than before. In the 1950–73 period, Chile ranked near the bottom of all the surveyed countries, with an annual rate of growth in output per worker of 2.9 percent. Of that growth, 1.8 percentage points is attributed to increased capital per worker and only 1.1 percent to improvements in the efficiency with which inputs were used.

In the period after 1973, the performance of output per worker is even worse, falling off to only 0.6 percent a year. A substantial part of the falloff can be attributed to a lower rate of capital accumulation per worker, 0.4 percent annually; but there is an even larger slowdown in the residual of joint factor productivity, from 1.1 to 0.2 percent annually. This result seems surprising given the emphasis on economic liberalization as a means of increasing levels of labor productivity and real wages. To an unusual degree, Chile's recent economic growth has been heavily labor-using. While that has been advantageous for the short-run goal of reducing unemployment, it is not encouraging with respect to the desire to raise productivity and real wages.

It is possible that the poor performance of productivity in the overall period of 1973 to the present is largely concentrated in the chaotic years of the 1970s and early 1980s, and insufficient emphasis is given to the sustained expansion of output since 1983. We addressed this issue by computing indexes of the growth in capital per worker and joint factor productivity on an annual basis for the period 1960 to 1992. The results are shown in figure 4-2. The calculations differ from those of Hofman only in that we use actual employment, rather than the labor force, to compute output per worker. This formulation has no effect on the secular measures, but it does reduce the magnitude of cyclical change in productivity.[7]

First, it is evident that a significant portion of the slowdown in labor productivity growth can be attributed to a falloff in the rate of accumulation of capital per worker—a not-unexpected result given the chaotic behavior of the economy over the 1973–83 period. If capital per worker had continued to grow at

7. The employment series includes the special employment programs between 1975 and 1988. Their exclusion would further increase the cyclical fluctuation in output per worker without altering the long-run trend.

Figure 4-2. Sources of Growth in Output per Worker, 1960–92

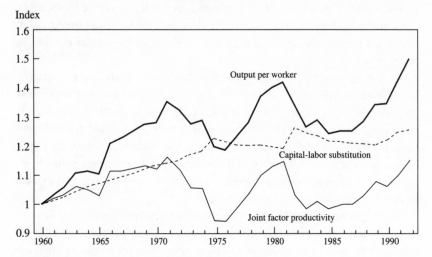

SOURCE: Authors' calculations as explained in text.

the same rate as in 1960–72, output per worker would have been 18 percent higher in 1992.

More striking, joint factor productivity shows no evidence of a sustained upward trend after 1970. Although the acceleration of growth in total factor productivity after 1983 is suggestive of an improvement, it is necessary to distinguish between cyclical and secular influences.[8] We know from studies of other countries that changes in labor productivity and joint factor productivity have very large cyclical components. Using the unemployment rate as an index of the cyclical component, it is possible to obtain a rough estimate of the underlying trend by regression:

$$(4\text{-}2) \qquad fac = 0.110 + 0.0023 \cdot t - 0.8 \cdot RU;$$
$$\qquad\qquad (5.5) \qquad (1.3) \qquad\qquad (4.3)$$
$$\qquad\qquad R^2 = .35$$

where *fac* represents the logarithm of joint factor productivity, *t* is a simple time trend, and *RU* is the unemployment rate.

It is also possible to test for a potential break in the trend during the 1980s by including a second time trend beginning in some year during the reform

---

8. This is the fundamental issue accounting for the difference between our conclusion and that of Dornbusch and Edwards in this volume. They attribute the gain in factor productivity after 1983 to the reforms, and they argue that it will persist, while we conclude that it is largely due to cyclical factors.

period. Equation 4-3 shows a typical result based on assuming a trend break in 1983.

$$(4\text{-}3) \quad fac = 0.092 + 0.009 \cdot t - 1.4 \cdot RU - 0.013 \cdot t83 - 0.069 \cdot d83.$$
$$\phantom{(4\text{-}3) \quad fac =} (5.4) \quad (5.7) \quad\quad (5.7) \quad\quad (2.1) \quad\quad\quad (2.3)$$
$$R^2 = .58$$

Surprisingly, the regression implies that the underlying trend has deteriorated still further.[9] The reasons for this result are quite evident. Earlier changes in total factor productivity have a large cyclical component, and the 10 percentage points of decline in the unemployment rate between 1982 and 1992 are more than sufficient to account for the observed gains in total factor productivity. Even as late as 1992, given that unemployment fell by 1.5 percentage points during the year, it is difficult to discount the possibility that the gains in productivity are largely short-run in nature.[10]

Jadresic and Sanhueza have obtained analogous results in a recent study. Using similar data for the 1960–90 period, they undertook to estimate by regression a production function of the form shown in equation 4-1.[11] They included the unemployment rate as a measure of cyclical influences—the equivalent of an estimate of Okun's Law for Chile. In their preferred equation, Jadresic and Sanhueza obtained a capital coefficient of 0.3, which is in close agreement with other international studies (but below the value of 0.4 used in our calculations), a coefficient of −1.6 on the unemployment rate, and an estimated trend for the rate of growth in total factor productivity of −0.4 percent annually. Rather than finding any evidence of an acceleration of trend growth in the 1980s, they found it necessary to include a dummy variable with a positive coefficient for the years 1979–82. Our tests with their data could detect no evidence of a positive shift in the trend of the rate of growth in the years after 1983. Serious problems of colinearity among the variables suggest that the estimates of trend growth should not be taken too seriously, but the study is useful in rejecting any evidence of a sharp break in the underlying growth rate.

9. Delaying the introduction of the second trend term to a later year of the 1980s still did not produce positive coefficients.

10. The unemployment rate was below its previous cyclical low in the years after 1987, which might be interpreted as a return to full capacity and the absence of further cyclical effects. Any subsequent gains in productivity would be assumed to be indicative of a more favorable long-run trend. Equation 4-3, on the other hand, assigns equal weight to both positive and negative deviations of the unemployment rate from its mean, implying a continuing disequilibrium explanation. The data are insufficient to resolve these two interpretations: holding the unemployment rate constant after 1987 produces a larger positive trend, but a much worse standard error of the regression.

11. Jadresic and Sanhueza (1992). In contrast, we imposed values on the parameters in computing our indexes.

It is tempting to dismiss these results with an argument that the Chilean national accounts have underestimated growth during the 1980s. But an independent indicator of output per worker, based on adjusting survey estimates of the average wage for changes in the price level, yields similar results: large fluctuations in the real wage, but very little secular growth.

Sources of Labor-Intensive Growth

The Chilean experience is puzzling both for the apparent labor bias in its economic growth after 1973 and for the absence of a link between economic liberalization and gains in the efficiency of resource use. It is possible, of course, to argue that the gains of liberalization have been overshadowed by the costs of stabilizing the economy after its experience with extreme inflation in the early 1970s. If true, however, that would still be a discouraging answer because it suggests that the costs of stabilization alone are both larger and more durable than normally argued. Thus we have examined some other arguments.

Embodiment of Technology

A potential explanation for the failure to observe greater improvements in economic efficiency grows out of a more general criticism of growth accounting exercises: that they usually treat the process of technical change as independent of the rate of capital accumulation. If technical change and other sources of improvements in joint factor productivity are linked to rates of investment, the growth accounts outlined in table 4-1 may assign too small a weight to capital accumulation. This would be the case, for example, if technological and other improvements were embodied in new capital. Since Chile did suffer a sharp deceleration of growth of capital, the accounting may understate the potential for improvement in joint factor productivity growth through higher future rates of investment.

One response to this criticism is to examine the performance of the accounting framework in explaining the observed differences in growth rates across the sample of seventeen countries shown in table 4-1. It is an interesting and diverse set of countries because it includes several of the high-performing Asian economies as well as the Iberian countries, which experienced considerable economic liberalization with their entry into the European Community.

Scatter diagrams of the relationship between growth in labor productivity and the individual contributions of growth in total factor productivity and capital per worker are shown in figure 4-3 for two periods, 1950–73 and 1973–89.

Figure 4-3. Cross-National Comparison of Labor and Joint Factor Productivity, Seventeen Countries, 1950–89[a]

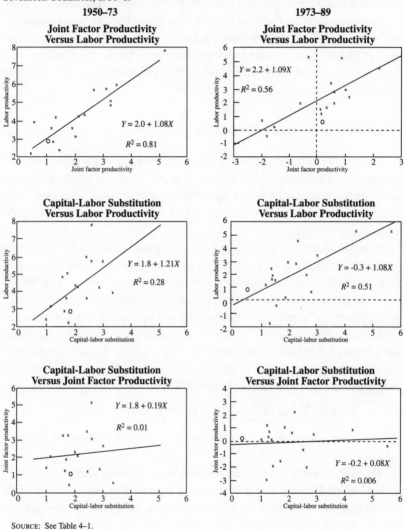

SOURCE: See Table 4–1.
a. The circular point denotes Chile.

First, there is a strong correlation between changes in labor productivity and joint factor productivity about the expected 45-degree line. And, somewhat surprisingly, there is a stronger correlation between the growth in the contribution of capital per worker and labor productivity in the second period than in the first. It is also worth noting that a regression relating labor productivity growth to the separate components of education and physical capital per worker produced positive coefficients near their hypothesized values, but only the coefficient on physical capital was of high statistical significance.

More important for the issue of embodied technology, there is no evidence in the third panel of any systematic correlation between changes in capital per worker and changes in joint factor productivity. That is, the countries with high rates of capital accumulation have not experienced gains in total factor productivity that were larger than expected.[12]

Changes in the Industrial Mix

A program of economic liberalization could result in major realignments of output among industries. But since the changes in relative prices that would drive such a reallocation reflect more than just the cost of labor inputs, the program would not necessarily imply an increase in labor productivity for the economy as a whole.

A methodology outlined by Nordhaus can be used to examine the influence of changes in the shares of employment and output using data for seven industries provided by Esteban Jadresic.[13] The change in aggregate labor productivity, π (based on actual employment, not the economically active), is allocated to a component based on productivity growth in the individual sectors (π_i) with fixed output weights (w_i), plus a term that is positive if output shares are growing for industries with above-average productivity growth rates, plus another term that is positive if the labor shares (S_i) are growing in industries with above-average levels of productivity (P_i):

$$(4\text{-}4) \qquad \bar{\pi} = \sum \bar{w}_i \pi_i + \sum (w_i - \bar{w}_i)\pi_i + \sum (P_i/P - 1)\partial S_i/\partial t.$$

That decomposition for the two periods 1970–80 and 1980–91 is shown in table 4-2.

The shift in output and employment among sectors is clearly a relatively minor part of the story. Labor productivity expanded steadily over the whole period in agriculture and in the utilities, but it has been relatively flat in trade, while manufacturing and the other sectors showed some increase in the 1970s,

---

12. This same conclusion was obtained in Mankiw, Romer, and Weil (1990), using a much larger sample of countries. They found that the inclusion of measures of human capital accumulation eliminated the excessively strong influence of physical capital accumulation on economic growth rates that they had previously observed. We also tested the correlation between joint factor productivity and capital per worker excluding education with no appreciable effect on the results.

13. The specific sectors are: (1) agriculture, forestry, and fisheries; (2) mining; (3) manufacturing; (4) construction; (5) public utilities and transportation; (6) trade; and (7) other. Employment is defined to exclude workers in the special programs between 1975 and 1988. See Jadresic (1986) and Nordhaus (1972).

Table 4-2. Decomposition of Changes in Labor Productivity, 1970–91
Percent

Period	Actual change	Fixed weights	Differences in growth rates	Differences in levels
1970–80	15.2	14.1	−1.5	2.5
1980–91	−6.0	−8.5	1.3	1.2

SOURCE: Authors' calculations.

but declined substantially during the 1980s.[14] The extent of the evidence of a decline in productivity across many sectors also argues against an interpretation of the decline in overall productivity as misreporting.[15]

Labor Redundancy

The most reasonable explanation for the behavior of labor productivity in Chile is the existence of large amounts of excess labor, which encourages labor-intensive methods of production. Cheap labor, however, is not enough to account for the lack of growth in joint factor productivity. Instead, we would need to hypothesize a persistent shift toward more labor-intensive growth, such as would follow a decline in the relative price of labor, that covered up the underlying improvements in efficiency of overall resource use. As illustrated in table 4-1, growth in other countries that started out with large labor surpluses—particularly the high-growth Asian economies—has not shown a similar lack of gains in general efficiency.

Certainly the price of labor relative to capital did decline in Chile after 1973. Because of extraordinarily high real interest rates in the late 1970s and early 1980s, the cost of capital rose sharply. But such a shift in the relative price of labor versus capital would not distort the measurement of change in joint factor productivity unless the elasticity of substitution between capital and labor were substantially greater than the assumed value of unity.[16]

14. As noted by Marfán (1992b), this pattern of productivity change at the sectoral level also implies a sharp narrowing of the differences in the level of productivity among these sectors after 1982, since the declines are concentrated in high-productivity industries, while the low-productivity sectors show steady improvement. There is also no apparent relationship between the industry-level changes in productivity and whether the sector produces tradable or nontradable output.

15. It is worth noting that, at least during the 1980s, indexes of changes in real wages correspond very closely to the changes in aggregate labor productivity.

16. The issue of substitution between labor and other productivity factors is not fully dealt with in the construction of the joint productivity index because the income share weights were assumed to be constant over the full period 1960–92. At present the income share data required to compute a more adequate index are not available for the period after 1982.

Alternatively, the issue can be examined from the perspective of a more complex production process that includes inputs other than capital and labor, such as energy and raw materials. It is often difficult to adjust accurately for price changes in the calculation of real output when relative prices and production technologies are changing rapidly. Shifts in the input mix have greater potential to affect measures of output per worker. The relative price of these other inputs undoubtedly rose relative to the price of labor during the period under consideration, both because of the sharp rise in energy prices worldwide and because of a significant devaluation of the real exchange rate.[17] Since Chile imports much of its machinery and equipment, and because raw materials are sold in open auction-type international markets, a devaluation reduces the relative price of Chilean labor. Even if the elasticity of substitution between labor and the other factors was quite limited, relative price changes of this magnitude could generate substitutions of labor for other factors sufficient to offset or to camouflage improvements in the underlying performance of labor productivity. For example, using a constant-elasticity of substitution (*CES*) production function to relate output to labor and a nested basket of capital and other inputs, the first-order conditions would suggest that average labor productivity (*Y/L*) would be related to the real wage (*w/p*) as follows:

$$(4\text{-}5) \qquad\qquad Y/L = \{(w/p)(1/\beta)\}^{\sigma},$$

where β is the distributional parameter for labor and σ equals the elasticity of substitution.

With σ equal to unity, a 10 percent change in the relative price of labor would induce a 10 percent change in observed output per worker. The effect is rapidly damped, however, for lower values of σ. It would also be reasonable to assume that such a response would stretch over many years. By using domestic value added and a two-factor framework, the presentation in figure 4-2 may not provide an accurate decomposition of the observed change in labor productivity—improperly attributing the decline to joint factor productivity instead of factor substitution.

A recent attempt to construct a measure of potential GDP for Chile based on the assumption that labor was redundant and capital was the limiting factor is provided in a paper by Marfán and Artiagoitía.[18] Their measure of productive

17. It is difficult to obtain precise measures of the change in the real exchange rate during the early 1970s because of the extreme nature of the domestic inflation and the fact that it appears to have been understated in official indexes. Estimates based on a corrected version of the CPI, however, suggest a real devaluation of about 50 percent between 1970 and 1975, a gradual recovery to the 1970 level by 1981, a second devaluation in excess of 50 percent over the 1981–88 period, and a modest appreciation in recent years.

18. Marfán and Artiagoitía (1989) and Marfán (1992b).

capacity, based on the accumulation of annual vintages of capital, performed well in predicting the onset of excess demand pressures in 1971, 1981, and 1989 (see figure 4-1). It is of less relevance for the future, however, now that unemployment has declined to low levels.

Future Growth Prospects

The issue of accurately assessing the sources of growth in Chile takes on added importance when we turn to questions of the potential for noninflationary growth in the future. Having used up a reserve of unemployed labor, Chile is faced with an abrupt reduction in the magnitude of feasible growth in the future. An assumption of no improvement in joint factor productivity would suggest that growth will be limited by future expansion of the labor force plus increases in capital per worker. Alternatively, beginning from the hypothesis that improvements in joint factor productivity have been camouflaged by a substitution of labor for capital and other inputs, the basic prospects seem more optimistic; but the importance of increasing capital formation takes on added importance: deficiencies in saving and capital accumulation can no longer be covered by the substitution of labor for capital. Between 1983 and 1992 Chile achieved an average annual rate of growth of output of 6.2 percent with only a 3 percent rate of increase in the capital stock. That cannot continue.

A possible scenario would begin with a growth in the basic labor force of 1.5 percent and with educational improvements in labor quality at the assumed average annual rate of 1 percent of the past decade. The projection of future growth in joint factor productivity is more problematic. It has averaged 1 percent annually over the past ten years, but it was 3 percent a year in the 1987–92 period. The previous analysis suggested that many of the most recent gains resulted from cyclical factors. Thus a conservative projection of future prospects should be based on the longer-term trend of 1 percent annually. If the capital stock expands in line with output, maintaining a constant return to capital, the sustainable growth rate would approximate 4.2 percent annually $(1.0 / .6 + (1.5 + 1.0))$.[19]

The specific capital stock that we are using implies a capital-output ratio of 2.2 and an implicit annual depreciation rate of 5 percent.[20] Thus the gross rate of investment needed for sustained growth would be 20.2 percent of GDP

19. This result assumes a Cobb-Douglas production function with a labor share of 0.6.

20. The capital-output ratio, valued in prices of 1992, averaged 2.2 in both the 1960s and the full period of 1960–92. The ratio declined substantially during the 1980s, in part because of excess capacity at the beginning of the period.

$((.042 + .05) \cdot 2.2)$. That compares with an actual rate of fixed investment of 18.9 percent in 1990–92.[21]

Higher estimates of the underlying rate of growth in the labor force or joint factor productivity would yield more optimistic projections of the potential for future growth, but in that case capital formation would emerge as a major constraining influence. For example, an optimistic projection of 3 percent annual growth in joint factor productivity would yield a 7.5 percent annual growth in output, but it would require an increase in the rate of gross capital formation to 27.5 percent of GDP—far above any rate of saving or investment that Chile has been able to achieve in the past.[22]

It is sometimes tempting to make reference to the performance of the high-growth Asian economies in speaking of future growth prospects for Chile. Yet the above analysis suggests the dangers of such a comparison: the composition of past growth has been so dramatically different. The Asian economies have experienced sustained growth in joint factor productivity in excess of 2 percent annually and rates of capital-labor substitution far above those of Chile. Physical capital accumulation per worker averaged 6.9 percent annually in the 1973–89 period, compared with 0.4 percent in Chile. Furthermore, those investment rates were achievable, without depressing the rate of return, because of the concurrent large increases in joint factor productivity and labor quality. The Asian countries, for example, started out far behind Chile in years of education per capita, but some have now moved substantially ahead. Similar high rates of growth in Chile will require rates of investment in physical capital and education significantly above those of the past decade and the generation of savings sufficient to finance them, a subject of the following section.

Saving and Investment Trends

Rates of saving and investment have obvious significance as determinants of long-run growth. In the case of Chile, however, the behavior of saving and investment is equally important in explaining the instability of the overall economy during the 1970s and early 1980s and the sharp variation in key relative prices such as interest rates and exchange rates. A brief summary: the economic reforms of the 1970s—particularly commercial reforms—expanded private investment opportunities without a concomitant increase in national

21. The recent national income account revisions raised the investment rate to 23.3 in 1990–92.

22. The incremental investment requirements are lower in Chile than in most industrialized countries because its capital-output ratio is well below the average of about three, which has been observed in the OECD countries.

saving. The excess demand for saving during the last half of the 1970s introduced pressures on domestic interest rates and an increasing current account deficit as a source of foreign borrowing. The debt crisis of 1982 interrupted that inflow of foreign financing and brought on a severe recession. Today Chile continues to be troubled with a rate of private saving that is inadequate to finance domestic investment.

An Overview

A summary view of aggregate saving and investment trends is provided in figure 4-4. It is based on the accounting identity in which gross domestic investment is equal to national plus foreign saving. Domestic investment includes both public and private fixed capital (plant and equipment plus residential investment) and inventory accumulation. National saving is the sum of saving in both the public and private sector, and foreign saving is equal to the current account deficit. The most interesting features of the figure are the magnitude of variation in both saving and investment and the importance of foreign saving in the period 1976–88.

A more detailed breakdown of saving and investment is severely constrained by some deficiencies in the available data. First, in the Chilean national accounts, inventory accumulation is a residual measure that includes the statistical discrepancy between the expenditure and income measures of GDP. The statistical discrepancy appears to introduce an excessive degree of short-run volatility in total investment, so that in what follows we focus on the behavior of fixed investment, largely ignoring inventory. Second, the Chilean national accounts do not provide any sectoral disaggregation of national saving, such as between the public and private sectors. Such estimates must be constructed on the basis of very incomplete information.

Gross fixed capital formation is shown in figure 4-5 as a percent of GDP in both current and constant prices of 1977. With the exclusion of inventory accumulation, the overall volatility is somewhat reduced, but the figure reveals another important feature: the sharp divergence of the trend in investment rates when measured in nominal and constant prices. In nominal prices, the average rate of investment held up amazingly well through the turmoil of the 1970s and early 1980s, and it appears to be moving above its historical rate in recent years. The constant price data reveal a far more substantial decline in real capital accumulation during the 1970s and a current rate that is equal to or below that of the 1960s. These differences reflect a large increase in the relative price of imported capital goods. These products were subject to relatively low tariffs in the 1960s and thus benefited less from the trade liberalization of the 1970s.

Figure 4-4. Domestic Investment and Its Financing, 1960–92

Percent of GDP

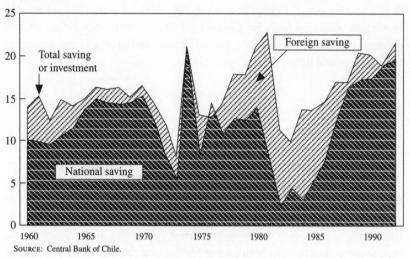

SOURCE: Central Bank of Chile.

Figure 4-5. Gross Fixed Capital Formation, 1960–92

Percent of GDP

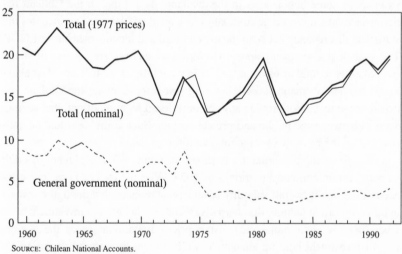

SOURCE: Chilean National Accounts.

The share of nominal GDP devoted to investment would, at today's relative prices, need to rise by 30 percent simply to offset the effect of the change in relative prices. That is an important factor in accounting for the reduced rate of capital formation discussed in the previous section. The nominal data are most relevant for examining saving behavior, but it is real investment that matters for physical capital formation and economic growth.

The figure also highlights the strongly pro-cyclical behavior of the investment rate, linking short-run macroeconomic events with long-run growth. Finally, it includes a measure of investment by general government (excluding public enterprises). The general government component declined significantly during the Pinochet regime, but it is responsible for very little of the observed volatility.

Figure 4-6 provides an estimated division of national saving between its public and private sector components. The most reliable information for the public sector is current account saving of the government, including public enterprises and the Central Bank, with a separate accounting for the Copper Stabilization Fund. The data are severely distorted, however, by the extreme nature of the inflation in the early and mid-1970s: public sector disssaving is estimated to have exceeded 17 percent in 1973 with an offsetting rise in private saving. The 1971–75 period is excluded from the figure to allow for greater detail on the changes in other years. This focus on a broad definition of government is most useful to illustrate the shift back toward substantial public saving during 1976–80, the sharp decline in 1981–86, and the recovery in later years. Although the public sector is largely responsible for the cyclical changes in national saving, private saving was severely depressed during 1975–83. The private saving rate has steadily increased over the past decade. It is also noteworthy that saving within the pension fund system has grown to represent a significant share of total private saving.

The inclusion of government enterprises in the measure of government saving, however, creates a problem of interpreting the trend in the private saving rate. The Chilean privatization program resulted in a large reclassification of firms from the public to the private sector. Part of the reported rise in the private saving rate simply reflects the reclassification. We have constructed estimates of general government saving and investment, allocating government enterprises to the private sector.[23] Those data are shown in table 4A-2. The general government balance was less volatile in the early 1970s because a large proportion of the decline of public saving in those years was the result of losses in the public enterprises.[24] The residual estimate of private saving shows a

23. These estimates are drawn from Larraín (1991) and recent publications of the International Monetary Fund (IMF). We chose to rely primarily on the IMF data because they cover the more recent period. Both sources provide nearly identical estimates of general government investment, but there are significant differences on the saving side.

24. Larraín (1991, pp. 90–106).

Figure 4-6. Public and Private Saving, 1960–91

Percent of GDP

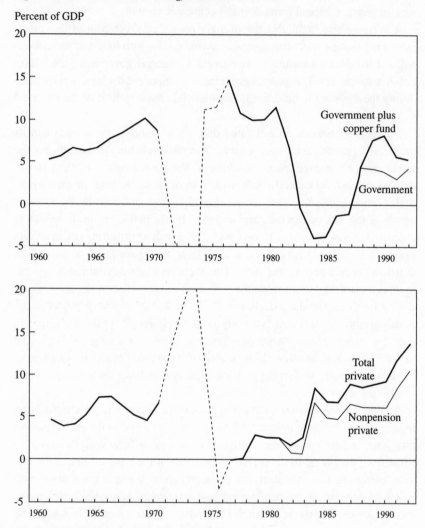

smaller decline in the late 1970s, and thus less of a rise during the 1980s. The alternative measures of private saving are very similar today because there are few remaining state-owned enterprises.

A main feature of the Chilean economy is the enormous instability of the macroeconomic aggregates: the magnitude of the shocks, both internal and external, that affected the economy over the past twenty years. That instability

has had a dominant effect on rates of saving and investment and makes it difficult to evaluate the impact of the policy reforms on rates of capital accumulation. Perhaps the sole variable that has behaved in a stable way is real exports
of goods and services, which steadily increased their share of GDP during
seventeen of the eighteen years considered. Real exports have grown at an average rate of 8.8 percent throughout the period, more than doubling their share
in GDP and becoming the driving force for growth of output.

To analyze these events, we consider different macroeconomic regimes and
varying transmission mechanisms from economic policy and foreign shocks
to aggregate demand and prices. For analytical purposes, we identify four periods:

—1974–78: a focus of policy on efforts to stabilize and reduce inflation
under an adverse external economic scenario;

—1979–81: an effort to restore growth on the basis of heavy reliance on
inflows of foreign capital;

—1982–89: a period of deep crisis followed by rapid recovery, with economic policy constrained by an acute foreign exchange shortage and a domestic financial crisis (for some purposes we differentiate the period of crisis and
recession (1982–85) and recovery (1986–89);

—1990–92: a period of stabilization and democratization, with economic
policy efforts aimed at attaining a viable path for saving, investment, and long-
run growth.

Table 4-3 provides information on average rates of saving and investment,
and their components, for each of these periods.

The 1974–78 Period

This was a period of enormous institutional changes. The commercial reform was initiated during this period, along with the first round of privatization
of public firms, and a rapid deregulation of the domestic financial system and
interest rates. Two additional main reforms were liberalized rules for direct
foreign investment and the modification of the tax system, which introduced a
value added tax, expanded the indexation of the tax system, and reformed and
simplified income taxes. Explicit tax incentives for dividend payments were
introduced to encourage the development of a domestic capital market, nonexistent at the time.

In 1975 the government engaged in a strict stabilization program aimed at
reducing a triple-digit rate of inflation. The program gave high priority to fiscal
consolidation, with drastic cuts in expenditures and expansion of revenues.
The overkill of the fiscal program was more than apparent: saving of the overall

Table 4-3. Components of Saving and Investment, Selected Periods, 1974–92

Item	1974–78	1979–81	1982–85	1986–89	1990–92[a]
Components of investment[b]					
Change in inventories	2.2	6.1	−1.6	1.4	2.1
Fixed capital formation	14.6	17.6	14.0	16.8	19.2
Nonresidential	10.8	13.3	10.6	13.0	15.0
Residential	3.9	4.3	3.4	3.7	4.2
Total investment	16.8	23.7	12.4	18.2	21.3
Components of saving[c]					
Foreign[d]	2.6	9.0	8.6	3.7	1.3
National	13.3	11.5	3.6	13.6	18.3
Public sector[e]	11.5	9.3	−2.4	2.8	3.6
Copper and oil funds	0.0	0.0	0.0	1.9	1.9
Private pension funds	0.0	0.3	1.9	2.6	3.3
Private[f]	1.8	1.9	4.2	6.3	9.6
Total saving	15.9	20.5	12.2	17.2	19.6

SOURCES: Marfán (1992b), Gonzáles and Marfán (1992), and the Chilean National Accounts.
a. Saving data cover 1990–91 period.
b. Percent of GDP, 1977 prices.
c. Percent of GDP, current prices.
d. Equals the current account deficit (SNA).
e. Equals the general government, public firms, and Central Bank, net of the copper and oil funds.
f. Calculated as a residual.

public sector (financial and nonfinancial public sector, including public firms) rose from negative values in 1973 to a historic peak of 14.6 percent of GDP in 1976.[25]

The intensity and length of the resulting recession was related primarily to the lack of credibility on the stabilization effort, evident in the enormous real interest rates of the financial system. Net foreign saving also grew during the period, as an adverse external economic situation and the initiation of the commercial reforms resulted in a current account deficit averaging 2.6 percent of GDP, with a local peak of 5.2 percent in 1975.

Private saving, on the other hand, proved to be more sensitive to the recession than to the reforms, averaging a modest 1.8 percent of GDP, down from almost 10 percent in 1974 and an average of 5.4 percent in the 1960s. Private production firms were facing simultaneous challenges from the financial sector with overwhelming interest rates, higher taxes—especially on retained earnings—and profound changes in relative prices induced by the commercial reform. Few honest economic activities could compete with the prevailing interest rates, and firms started to accumulate increasing debts, which were to explode a few years later. Labor income was severely depressed in the face of the steep decline in employment and real wages, further lowering saving rates.

25. González and Marfán (1992).

The recession, the rise in the price of capital goods due to depreciation, higher taxes, and real interest rates, and the emphasis on the purchase of existing assets (privatizations and takeovers) are the main explanations for the significant fall in investment (GFCF). The ratio of GFCF to GDP averaged 14.6 percent of GDP (at constant prices of 1977), which compares poorly with the 20 percent average of the 1960s. Most of the decline in the overall investment rate was the result of lower rates of public capital formation (see figure 4-5).

The 1979–81 Period

The main novelty of 1979–81 was the large inflow of financial capital from abroad, resulting from capital account liberalization and the adoption of a fixed exchange rate. Previously, macroeconomic overheating would be signaled by either an acceleration of inflation or shortages of international reserves, linked to current account deficits. With an open capital account, any current account deficit could be covered by voluntary capital inflows, and the normal symptoms would be absent.

As part of an effort to reduce inflation to international standards, the economic authorities moved in 1979 to a fixed nominal exchange rate, which lasted until 1982. But, with an open capital account, the exchange rate became an important price not only in the goods market, but also for financial decisions. Deregulation of the financial system had allowed owners of financial firms to get involved in the takeover and management of nonfinancial enterprises while they retained their traditional role as financial intermediaries. Banks were borrowing from abroad not just to lend domestically, but also to finance takeovers of other firms and the formation of large conglomerates (the *grupos*). Bank comptrollers valued domestic assets on the basis of international interest rates, while asset sellers valued them according to the much higher domestic interest rate.[26] Convergence of the domestic and foreign interest rates in the context of a fixed exchange rate would only occur after a significant volume of takeovers. In fact, interest rate convergence was never achieved, despite the steep rise in private foreign debt.

These events had important consequences for saving and investment. On the saving side, the inflow of foreign funds to finance purchases of existing assets drove up the prices of assets, generating wealth effects that influenced decisions on saving.[27] Despite the large gains in income during this period (7.2

26. For a formal model of the dynamics of this behavior, see Arellano (1983).

27. Share prices more than doubled between 1978 and 1980 in real terms. In 1981, at the eve of the crisis, prices fell by 20 percent.

percent a year on average), private consumption expanded at an even more rapid pace (8 percent) and private saving remained very low.[28] National saving averaged 11.5 percent of GDP. Meanwhile, under the impetus of strong output growth and much lower real costs of financing, investment surged to a peak of 19.5 percent of real GDP by 1981. In nominal prices, foreign saving, as measured by the current account deficit, was equivalent to half of fixed investment during 1978–81, with a peak of 14.5 percent of GDP in 1981.[29] This dissociation between investment and national saving behavior was the natural consequence of the rising foreign debt. Another natural consequence was real currency appreciation (see figure 4-7).

The 1979–81 period was marked by a "laissez-faire" approach to the design and implementation of macroeconomic policy. The authorities assumed that improvements in resource allocation and productivity induced by the reforms would promote growth, underestimating the role of more conventional elements such as national saving and investment efforts. They believed the overall surplus of the public sector implied that the current account deficit was a reflection of private sector decisions, and thus not a cause of concern in a market economy.[30] Relative price distortions—especially the real exchange rate and interest rates—and inflation above international standards would also be corrected by automatic market mechanisms.

In 1981 the first symptoms of a recession started to appear, initiated by a drop in the terms of trade and an increase in international interest rates. Near the end of 1981 the government began to expand its regulation of the financial system and to reduce the concentration of the banking system's liabilities, but it was too late, and the financial system began to collapse.[31]

The 1982–89 period

Voluntary lending came to an end in 1982 with the Mexican debt crisis. The shift to an adverse external scenario, with rising international interest rates and

28. Voluntary private saving averaged 1.9 percent of GDP. Private expenditure on consumer durable goods was expanding very rapidly during this period as a consequence of the reduction in tariffs and nontariff barriers. From the perspective of households, these purchases had an aspect of saving.

29. This ratio underestimates the real effects of the current account deficit, since it is valued with an appreciated currency.

30. Díaz-Alejandro (1984).

31. See Barandiarán (1983), Arellano (1984), and Arellano and Marfán (1986) for more details on this period.

Figure 4-7. Selected Economic Indicators, 1975–92

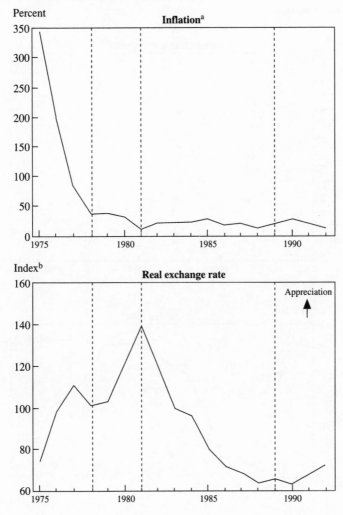

deteriorating terms of trade, found the Chilean economy in a risky situation: an overheating level of output, a double-digit deficit in the current account as a percentage of GDP, distorted relative prices, and a huge foreign currency liability in the private sector. In addition, private firms were generally overindebted in local currency, both because debts had been rolled over during the previous period of high interest rates and because the largest conglomerates had financed their takeovers with domestic and foreign loans.

Figure 4-7. (*continued*)

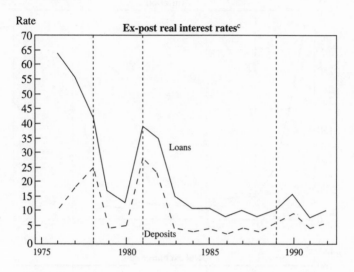

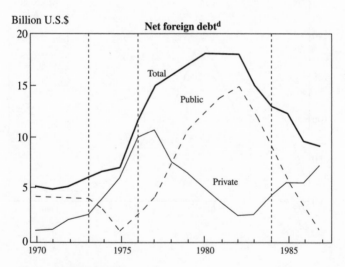

SOURCE: Central Bank of Chile.
a. Corrected CPI, December to December, annual percent change.
b. 1983 = 100.
c. Nominal rates for 30-80 days of the banking system minus actual inflation.
d. Net foreign debt = gross debt – reserves. End-of-year balance.

In 1982 real GDP fell by 14.1 percent, unemployment rose to 25.7 percent of the labor force (including government special employment programs), gross fixed capital formation dropped by 33.9 percent and overall investment by 65.3 percent in real terms, and national saving fell to only 1.7 percent of nominal GDP. The fiscal surplus of 1981 was rapidly consumed by the cost of the pension system reform, the drop in the price of copper, and the effects on government income of the domestic recession. The fixed nominal exchange rate policy introduced in 1979 collapsed in 1982, and the real exchange rate began a steady depreciation that was to continue until 1988.

A distinguishing aspect of Chile's debt crisis was that Chile's foreign debt was initially private. The capital loss associated with currency depreciation was enormous, and massive bankruptcies started to appear. In January 1983, the economic authorities intervened with five banks—including the two largest ones of the private sector—liquidated three other banks, and directly supervised the management of two others.[32] Except for a reduction of 30 percent in the value of deposits in the liquidated banks, the state guaranteed the liabilities of the other banks involved.[33] These banks, in turn, were seizing firms with nonperforming loans, so the state took control of those firms as well.

The Central Bank was the primary institution charged with providing a solution to the financial turmoil, and the actions that it took had important implications for national saving. It made exchange rate subsidies, asset transfers, soft loans, and asset swaps with the private sector, through which it accumulated, by the end of 1985, liabilities equal to 85 percent of GDP. To avoid the bankruptcy of the Central Bank, the government, in turn, transferred treasury bonds issued for this purpose to the monetary authorities. The worsening of the Central Bank balance started to appear clearly in its current account cash balance, which showed increasing deficits (dissaving) until 1986.[34]

Additional actions by the Central Bank were motivated by the recognition that the high real interest rates were expropriatory and distorted resource

32. These ten banks represented almost two-thirds of the capital and reserves of the private banking system.

33. The nonperforming domestic loans of the main banks in which the government intervened represented 20 percent of their assets and four times their capital and reserves. See Arellano (1984) for further details. This situation cannot be blamed on the difficult macroeconomic situation. The Central Bank and foreign banks operating in Chile whose management did not engage in extensive speculation displayed a normal situation (Arellano and Marfán, 1986).

34. The quasi-fiscal deficit of the Central Bank—measured as the current account cash balance—averaged 3.9 percent of GDP between 1983 and 1989, with a peak of 5.8 percent in 1986 (González and Marfán, 1992). The cost of the Central Bank operations during this period is still being paid at present. The debt of the Treasury with the Central Bank is U.S.$8.1 billion, and the debt of banks related to the crisis is U.S.$4 billion. In total they represent more than 30 percent of GDP, and the servicing is subtracted from domestic saving.

allocation. The bank was successful in bringing interest rates down during this period (see figure 4-7), initially through a coercive policy of publishing a "suggested" interest rate and later by following a monetary policy of interest rate targets.[35] It reversed the deregulation process of the 1970s and introduced severe controls in the exchange rate market and the financial system.[36]

The main determinant of policy, however, was the acute foreign exchange shortage, especially until 1985, which explains the deep underutilization of domestic resources during this period. For analytical purposes, we will differentiate the period of severe external constraint (1982–85) from that of recovery (1986–89).

The abrupt termination of foreign lending forced a large devaluation to reduce the current account deficit. The devaluation and rising international interest rates pushed net income payments to foreigners from 4.2 percent of GDP in 1981 to 11.1 percent in 1985.[37] The only relaxations of the external constraint in the first period were the initially feeble short-run switching effects of real depreciation and higher import tariffs and foreign borrowing of the public sector (see figure 4-7). The rest had to be accommodated by recession. In fact, until the late 1980s most of the forecasts for short-run output growth were based on balance of payments models that projected the capacity to import as the relevant constraint on output. The ratio of real imports to real GDP fell steadily until 1984.

The recovery of 1986–89 followed from the gradual relaxation of the foreign exchange constraint. Export growth was promoted by the real depreciation, begun in 1982. The debt burden was reduced by agreements allowing the postponement of payments and debt rescues, which at present total U.S.$11.3 billion. The terms of trade improved after 1985, and a decline in international interest rates after 1985 permitted a steady reduction in foreign income payments from 11.1 percent of GDP in 1985 to 6.7 percent in 1989.

These events had a dramatic effect on the behavior of saving and investment. National saving fell from 11.5 percent of nominal GDP in 1979–81 to 3.6 percent in 1982–85 and recovered to 13.6 percent in 1986–89 (table 4-3). The decline was due exclusively to reduced saving in the public sector, which

35. It is worth noting that the mix of exchange rate policy and interest rate targets was designed to obtain arbitrage conditions to prevent incentives for capital flight. Also the informal exchange rate was never allowed to exceed the limit at which it could fuel capital flight.

36. Foreign exchange market regulations followed the principle that everything was forbidden except what was explicitly allowed. Regulations on the financial system, in turn, were finally put in order by a severe banking law in 1986.

37. Foreign income is defined as the difference between nominal GDP and Available Gross National Income. It represents the sum of net interest payments and other factor payments, less current transfers from abroad. Nominal figures do not include the effect of terms of trade.

was faced with the costs of rescuing the financial sector, a decline in the price of copper, the effects of the recession on tax collections, and the costs of the pension system reform. Severe actions were taken to reduce current expenditures and to raise revenues, aggravating the social costs of the recession and fueling massive protests until 1986.

The authorities initiated a set of policies aimed at increasing private saving. Of these, the most important were the efforts to ease domestic debt burdens and a tax reform passed in January 1984. The overindebtedness of the private sector was tackled by introducing several new programs.[38] They included partial write-offs in cases of insolvency and debt rescheduling with favorable interest rates in cases of illiquidity. They imposed a heavy cost on the public sector, but they were successful in inducing firms to contribute additional resources to debt reduction. The efforts made by productive firms to reduce their debt may have been a significant factor in the rise in private saving during this period. Private saving rose from 1.9 percent of nominal GDP in 1979–81 to 4.2 percent in 1982–85 and 6.3 percent in 1986–89.

The tax reform of 1984 lowered personal income and corporate taxes, broadened income brackets to reduce progressivity, and introduced incentives for retaining profits at the firm level. The latter action represented a reversal of the incentives for dividend payments enacted during the 1970s.[39]

National saving was also strongly influenced by two important elements of forced saving introduced at the beginning of the decade. The first of these, the new pension system, contributed 1.9 percent of GDP to national saving in 1982–85 and 2.6 percent in 1986–89. The extent to which that saving may have been offset by reduced saving in the private or public sectors makes uncertain its net effect on saving. The other element was the Copper Stabilization Fund (CSF), introduced in 1981, which became important with the rise of copper prices in 1988. The CSF is designed to avoid the effects of volatility in international copper prices. That volatility has been an important historical source of macroeconomic instability in Chile. Since the state is the main exporter of copper in Chile, high copper prices relax both external and fiscal

38. Debt relief programs for personal debts, especially mortgages for housing purchases, were much weaker, and a solution in this area is still pending today.

39. An additional element considered in the initial draft project was the introduction of a consumption tax at the personal level, with an annual statement of wealth. This idea did not pass, and it was replaced by an incentive for tenure of a restricted list of assets. From the standpoint of the implicit incentives involved, this amendment was a simple subsidy on wealth, which has no theoretical or empirical foundations to promote private savings. This reform had its justification in providing tax incentives for the privatization of firms seized during the financial crisis. For owners with high incomes, the incentive was such that the tax reduction justified the purchase of shares of these firms regardless of the path of future profits or losses.

Table 4-4. Gross Fixed Capital Formation, 1981–89
Percent of GDP, 1977 prices

Year	Total	Residential investment	Nonresidential investment		
			Subtotal	Public	Private
1981	19.5	5.2	14.3	5.1	9.2
1982	15.0	3.9	11.1	4.7	6.5
1983	12.9	3.2	9.6	4.8	4.9
1984	13.2	3.0	10.2	6.0	4.2
1985	14.8	3.5	11.3	7.1	4.2
1986	15.0	3.4	11.5	7.3	4.3
1987	16.5	3.8	12.7	6.7	6.0
1988	17.0	3.8	13.2	6.1	7.1
1989	18.6	3.8	14.8	6.3	8.5

SOURCES: Estimation from data published by Marfán and Artiagoitía (1989), Larraín (1991), and Lehmann (1991).

constraints and in the past led to excessively expansionary policies.[40] Declining copper prices forced drastic adjustments.

The CSF is a mechanism by which the public sector is forced to save a part or all of its extra income during periods in which international prices exceed a reference price constructed according to historical information. Thus with high prices the foreign constraint is still relaxed, but the fiscal constraint is not, and conversely with a price decline. The reference price of the CSF started to be binding in 1988, and its contribution to national saving was 3.8 percent of GDP in 1988–89 and 1.3 percent in 1990–92.[41]

Investment followed a path quite different from that of national saving. With the loss of foreign saving as a source of financing, domestic investment was forced back into balance with domestic saving (see table 4-4). Private nonresidential investment was particularly hard hit by the cyclical contraction, falling from 9.2 percent of GDP in 1981 to a modest 4.2 percent in 1984–85 before recovering to 7.8 percent in 1988–89.

An additional explanation for the continued low rate of investment is that the economic and political upheaval of the period introduced large political risks for longer-term investment decisions. Except for export activities, the investors of the 1960s up to the early 1980s had lost their productive assets

40. The fact that the state is the main exporter is an important reason why a real depreciation in Chile improves fiscal accounts. As a counterpart, the private sector is a net importer and faces negative short-run income effects in a depreciation. In a balance of payments crisis, real depreciation helps fiscal policy, contrary to other countries such as Argentina and Brazil, where a depreciation worsens the fiscal accounts.

41. The accumulation of a large fund by the public sector may be a temptation to use it for other purposes. To avoid this, the fund has been used for prepayment of government debt, especially with the Central Bank. It also funded the creation of an Oil Stabilization Fund in 1991 to protect the economy from fluctuations in international oil prices.

through expropriations, through takeovers at low prices, or through bank-ruptcy.[42]

Political risks did not subside along with recovery during the second half of the 1980s. A large proportion of the population had the feeling of an intolerable social unfairness. The welfare benefits of the boom of the late 1970s had accrued mainly to speculative financial conglomerates, but the costs of the resulting recession and financial crisis, although inevitable, were felt by the general population, especially the fiscal adjustment. This social mood continued during the recovery, when the fiscal accounts started to improve. Instead of compensating the losers, the government used the improved fiscal situation to reduce taxes. Between 1985 and 1989 almost all taxes were reduced, especially direct taxes.[43]

The 1990–92 Period

The presidential election of December 1989 was won by a center-left coalition. The foremost economic task for the new administration was to establish its commitment to macroeconomic stability. It initiated a new adjustment program, led by the Central Bank, to reduce inflation.[44] It also introduced a tax proposal that raised corporate and personal income taxes and the rate of the VAT; reduced the special tax treatment for agriculture, mining, and transportation; and closed a number of important loopholes.[45] The net result of the new

42. It is striking, for instance, that the deregulation of direct foreign investment during the 1970s did not expand foreign investment even though the DL600 was perceived as very permissive. Only during the late 1980s, when there was a larger social acceptability of these norms, did foreign investment start to boom.

43. There is no comparable tax burden for this period, given the important changes in accounting definitions. For instance, until the mid-1980s, tax devolutions were considered expenditures, while today they are considered negative tax income. In spite of these differences, gross figures still provide a broad idea of the changes in the tax burden. In 1981 the tax collection net of taxes on copper was 25.0 percent of nominal GDP and 22.6 percent in 1985 (Larraín 1991). In 1990 the tax burden was 15.8 percent (from unpublished Budget Office data). Direct taxes for the same years represented 5.8 percent, 3.7 percent, and 2.8 percent, respectively.

44. The Central Bank drastically raised its interest rate targets, especially long-term interest rates. A second policy target was to enlarge the term structure of the Central Bank domestic debt. After a few months, when this second goal had been attained, long-term interest rates were reduced, and the adjustment program concentrated mainly on high short-term rates.

45. The rationale for this reform was to provide sound financing for the social program. The main tax increases were designed so that the final level would be located halfway between those of 1983 and 1989. The reform maintained relative incentives for retaining profits at the firm level and introduced a tax rebate of up to 2 percent of taxable profits for new investments. The overall target was to rapidly increase tax collection by 2 percent of GDP, as compared with the budget law inherited from the previous administration. The actual level of tax collection attained was that

Table 4-5. General Government Statistics, 1989–92
Percent of GDP

Item	1989	1990	1991	1992
Current income[a]	23.7	22.4	24.5	25.4
Tax revenues	16.3	15.8	18.3	19.1
Net copper income[a]	2.2	17.6	1.2	1.4
Other	5.2	4.9	5.0	5.0
Current expenditures	19.7	19.7	20.7	19.8
(Excluding interest payments)	17.8	17.6	n.a.	n.a.
Government saving[a]	4.0	2.7	3.9	5.6
Capital income	2.0	1.5	1.3	1.2
Capital expenditure[a]	4.0	3.4	3.6	4.3
Overall surplus	2.1	0.9	1.5	2.5
Deposits in copper fund	4.2	2.5	0.7	0.3

SOURCE: Chilean Ministry of Finance.
a. Net of deposits in the copper fund.

government's policies (see table 4-5) has been a rise in general government saving from 2.7 percent of GDP in 1990 to 5.6 percent in 1992 and an expansion of the overall budget surplus.

These actions were effective in reducing inflation, but the high domestic interest rates initiated an increased inflow of short-term capital seeking to profit from favorable arbitrage conditions. The success of the new government in rescheduling foreign debt repayments on favorable long terms, ending the main problem of the 1980s, also enhanced Chile's attractiveness to international investors.

The foreign capital inflows, both short-term and long-term, created pressures for currency appreciation and problems for a Central Bank policy based on targets for both domestic interest rates and the real exchange rate. Given the experience with excessive capital inflows in the late 1970s, the government has been reluctant to allow net capital inflows to expand beyond 3 percent to 4 percent of GDP. An easing of monetary policy raises the risk of excessive inflation pressures, however, and there is resistance to the alternative of an exchange rate appreciation, which is seen as reducing the competitiveness of exports. This puts substantial pressures on fiscal policy to relieve the pressures on the current account through even larger budget surpluses.

The continuing pressures for currency appreciation in the presence of substantial fiscal surpluses reflect a structural problem within the Chilean economy in that private saving consistently falls short of the demands for new in-

targeted, but the increase that resulted was higher because it corrected an overestimation of the tax collection of the budget law.

vestment. In the short run the government has tried to relieve the pressures by taxing capital inflows, but that does not constitute an effective long-run response. Private saving has increased dramatically relative to the depressed levels of the early 1980s.[46] Much of the gain has been offset, however, by the reduction in foreign saving. A low rate of private saving continues to a major problem for the Chilean economy both because of its implication for financing future economic growth and because of the pressures that it places on the real exchange rate and net capital inflows.

Chile has also had substantial success in promoting the growth of a private financial system to encourage the efficient allocation of saving. Private financial saving, defined as the annual change in M7 adjusted for inflation, has grown from less than 10 percent of GDP prior to 1980 to more than 20 percent in 1990–92.[47] While financial saving includes a much wider range of transactions than private saving of the national accounts, its growth is indicative of an improvement in financial intermediation.

In the aggregate, the 1990–92 period was highly positive. Growth averaged 6 percent annually, inflation declined, and external and fiscal accounts were within viable limits. Furthermore, gross fixed investment grew at an annual rate of 8.4 percent, reaching 19.8 percent of GDP in 1992. That level approaches the level of the 1960s, but in the more recent period there was a much larger concentration in nonresidential investment. There is increasing evidence, however, that the growth in exports and investment is straining domestic resources, as reflected in upward pressures on interest rates and the exchange rate.

Empirical Studies

Despite the instability of the underlying economic regime, several attempts have been made to account for the behavior of saving and investment in Chile using statistical models. In general, they yield few surprises: the results seem similar to those obtained in other countries. For example, rates of saving appear to be positively correlated with the level and rate of growth of income.[48]

46. See table 4-2 and appendix table 4A-2. Saving with the private pension system accounted for about one-fourth of private saving in the 1990s.

47. M7 is the widest definition of money of the nonfinancial private sector. It includes M1 plus time deposits, savings accounts, Central Bank and treasury bonds, mortgage bonds, and deposits in foreign currency in the domestic financial system. It does not include firms' property rights, and it considers mutual funds, insurance companies, and pension funds as part of the nonfinancial private sector.

48. Estimates for the Chilean case may be found in Caballero and Corbo (1986), Foxley (1986), González and Marfán (1992), Lehmann (1992), and Schmidt-Hebbel (1984). Of these only

The studies have not been able to find a significant role for interest rates or stock prices, despite the wide range of fluctuation in the value of these hypothesized determinants in Chile over the past twenty years. The puzzle about private saving is not in its cyclical behavior, but in the consistently low rate, which has extended over many decades.

A rough evaluation of Chilean saving relative to that of other countries can be provided by estimating a simple regression on cross-national data that relates national saving rates (percent of GNP) to the level of GNP per capita (Y/P) and the rate of income growth (dY), the two primary determinants of saving rates from the time-series analysis. We used data averaged over 1971–90 for twenty-five countries that seemed most relevant to the Chilean situation. They include the ten largest economies of Latin America, six middle-income East Asian countries, and the G-7 economies plus Spain and Portugal. These countries were selected to provide a wide range of variation in the relevant variables. Income per capita was measured in U. S. dollars for each year and averaged over the full period. Income growth and the saving rate are averages over the period. The resulting equation was:

(4-6) $S/Y = 0.61 *(Y/P) + 1.48 *dY + 13.52.$
                    (2.1)   (3.4)
                            $R^2 = .38$

As would be expected, Chile's average saving rate for the full 1971–90 period was far below the norm for its level and rate of income growth—an actual rate of 11 percent compared with a predicted rate of 18.8 percent. It was also below the norm in 1986–90, when higher rates of income growth would have led to a predicted rate of 23.7 percent of GNP versus an actual rate of 15.5 percent. This was less true by 1992, when the national saving rate had reached 20.5 percent of GNP. In recent years the national saving rate has risen above the average of the other Latin American countries, but it remains nearly 10 percentage points of GNP below that of the East Asian economies.

Private investment behavior has also been studied empirically by Zucker (1988), Solimano (1989), and Lehmann (1991), all of whom have used Q-theory models of the investment decision. They conclude that investment is most strongly affected by changes in expected output growth, but that there is also a significant role for the interest rate, credit availability, and the exchange rate. Some studies also include tax policy. Again, Chile does not seem to differ from other countries in the behavior of investment, but it has differed dramatically in the range of events that have affected investment decisions.

González and Marfán (1992) and Lehmann (1992) use measures of private disposable income instead of GDP or GNP.

Implications for the Future

We have argued that much of the growth in the Chilean economy over the past decade should be interpreted as a cyclical recovery from a deep recession. The use of the recent historical trend provides an unduly optimistic projection of Chile's long-term growth prospects. For the past thirty years Chile has been faced with a redundant supply of labor, and it has not needed to generate increases in capital per worker or joint factor productivity to achieve growth. Instead, the limits to growth have been defined by the propensity to import during periods of foreign exchange shortage and by the availability of capital to expand productive capacity during periods with no external constraints.

That situation is now changing. With dramatically lower unemployment, future gains in output will require larger increments of capital, and improvements in management skills and in the underlying technology of production processes will become more important. Rates of saving and investment and improvements in economic efficiency will have a more controlling effect on future growth.

There is little indication that Chile faces any difficulty in generating adequate incentives for additional investment. In recent years a strong growth of domestic investment has placed consistent upward pressures on interest rates and the exchange rate. Instead, the problem is a lack of saving to finance the full range of viable investment projects. Efforts to fill the gap through inflows of foreign saving have in the past led to severe financial instability and crisis. Thus the major task for the future is to find a means of raising the rate of national saving.

The Chilean government has already taken most of the obvious actions to strengthen incentives for private saving. The creation of a stable and expanding economy, large improvements in financial intermediation, highly positive real interest rates, a fully funded pension system, and relatively light taxation of income from capital are all factors that should promote saving. And private saving rates have recovered from the severely depressed levels of the early 1980s. Given the extreme losses of real incomes, however, it is not surprising that strong pressures on consumption limit expectations of further large increases in the private saving rate. The empirical evidence also suggests that, while changes in taxes and interest rates have substantial effects on the composition of savings, their effect on net saving is small.

Furthermore, Chile is already benefiting from substantial net increases of foreign capital. And, while much of the current inflow is in the form of more stable long-term and equity investments, there are risks, as Chile learned in the early 1980s, to allowing net inflows to exceed 3 percent or 4 percent of GDP.

Thus the major option for further expansion of the national saving rate is likely to lie with efforts to generate larger saving in the public sector. Again, Chile has already taken major steps in this direction. Privatization of enterprises and the elimination of most subsidies did in the past contribute to public saving, and the government has had substantial surpluses in recent years (table 4-4). At the same time, a democratic government will be under strong pressures to improve public services—particularly in areas such as education and the infrastructure that are likely to make positive contributions to future growth. Consequently, it will be difficult to reduce expenditures, and any further increase in public sector saving is likely to take the form of higher taxes.

Policies of increasing government saving were criticized in the 1980s on the grounds that higher public sector saving would be offset by reduced private saving. That has been examined in numerous empirical studies and specifically for developing economies by Corbo and Schmidt-Hebbel.[49] They conclude that about one-fourth of a rise in public saving achieved through a permanent tax increase would be offset by reduced private saving. This suggests that increases in government saving remain the most certain means by which policy can increase the national saving rate.

Comment by José de Gregorio

The authors of this paper pursue a very challenging task, asking one of the most important questions about the Chilean economy: How much can it grow? After reading the paper, I was reminded of two intense debates among Chilean economists during the 1980s. By 1980 there was heated discussion about whether the Chilean economy would be able to sustain growth at 8 or 10 percent a year indefinitely. The 1982 recession, which caused a 15 percent decline in output, answered the question. In the mid-1980s, as a result of massive unemployment, many economists asked how long it would take to reduce unemployment to historical levels (around 6 percent). The answer at that time was that this objective could be achieved between 1995 and 2000. The impressive record of the past few years—the unemployment rate reached 6.3 percent in 1989—reveals that those predictions were too pessimistic.

The important lesson I want to draw from these examples is that it is extremely difficult to make an accurate forecast of the future path of the Chilean

49. Corbo and Schmidt-Hebbel (1991).

economy, which has been subject to so many structural changes. Perhaps the best evaluation of this paper can be done in ten more years, but its analysis is a warning for those tempted to forecast again permanent growth of 8 percent or more a year.

The paper is divided into two major parts, and so are my comments. The first part of the paper uses a Solow growth decomposition to analyze the determinants of economic growth in Chile since 1950. That part closes with a discussion of future growth prospects, concluding that a reasonable estimate is about 4 percent a year. I believe that a rate of growth of about 5 percent is feasible, and I agree with the authors that a substantially higher rate of growth is unlikely.

The second part of the paper discusses the evolution of saving and investment in Chile since 1960 and concludes that private saving must be increased. This part of the paper is unnecessarily long, containing many details that are inconsequential for saving and investment.[50] For this reason, I prefer to focus on a topic not sufficiently elaborated in the paper but essential to understanding the behavior of saving and the prospects for growth: the role of financial markets.

Prospects for Growth

The main evidence provided in this paper is that since the 1982–83 crisis growth in output has been the result of growth in employment in an economy in which labor has been a redundant factor, with little growth in total factor productivity (TFP).

The first issue one needs to address is the usefulness of traditional measures of total factor productivity, over a period as diverse as 1950–90, to predict the future performance of productivity. Are the traditional measures of total factor productivity good estimates of the technological parameter envisioned in the Solow growth paradigm, or are they contaminated with so many other factors—for example, policy and external shocks—that it is virtually impossible to estimate reliably the true state of technology? In the Chilean case I am inclined to answer that such an estimate is unreliable. To illustrate how misleading it may be to attribute all unexplained fluctuations to total factor productivity, consider figure 4-4, which shows a very high correlation between total factor productivity and output per worker, consistent with the real business cycle theory, which in its extreme version argues that output fluctuations are

50. For example, I do not see the relationship between the flaws in computing the CPI in 1973–74 and 1976–78 and savings and investment.

mainly the result of technological shocks. Specifically, according to that figure, the 1982 recession would have been caused mainly by a negative technological shock—that is, bad luck rather than, as I think most of the participants in this conference and observers of the Chilean economy would agree, bad policies.[51] Thus traditional measures of total factor productivity include other factors, in addition to technology, that may obscure the real gains in efficiency.

To amend measures of total factor productivity it is necessary to take into account labor hoarding and capital utilization. Omission of these factors would overestimate the contribution of technology to fluctuations in output. More fundamentally, there are many channels through which economic policy and the environment in which it takes place can influence total factor productivity that are ignored in the analysis. Since Barro there has been an explosion of empirical work on growth determinants.[52] Some of that evidence has shown, relatively convincingly, that openness, well-functioning capital markets, and macroeconomic and political stability are good for growth because they can increase the rate of investment and its efficiency.

Since Chile is an open market economy, with a fluent capital market, and is macroeconomically and politically stable, I am a bit more optimistic than the authors about the prospects for growth of total factor productivity. I would argue that Chile satisfies the conditions to achieve relatively high growth. Perhaps during the recovery of the late 1980s the efficiency gains did not show up because, given the existence of redundant and cheap labor, the first step was to grow in labor-intensive activities.

As labor becomes scarce, new activities will orient themselves toward more capital-intensive sectors or techniques. The experience of Southeast Asia shows how countries go through product cycles, moving on to more sophisticated sectors. For example, Hong Kong and Singapore moved from textiles to electronics and more recently to banking. This evidence also shows that total factor productivity can evolve in different ways even in countries with similar per capita growth records (about 6 percent a year). In Hong Kong, with investment rates at about 20 percent, total factor productivity accounted for about 60 percent of growth. In Singapore, in contrast, where investment went from 10 percent in 1960 to 40 percent in 1982, there was apparently no growth in total factor productivity.[53]

Another aspect that is important to consider is that the efficiency of investment may increase because the composition of investment becomes more con-

51. Of course bad policies were combined with bad luck in the crisis, but the source of the bad luck was an unfavorable external environment rather than a negative technology shock.

52. Barro (1991).

53. See Young (1992) for further details.

Table 4-6. Growth Decomposition, 1990–93
Percent

Year	GDP growth	Investment rate	Employment growth	TFP growth
1990	2.1	20.2	2.0	−1.4
1991	6.0	18.8	0.7	3.6
1992	10.4	21.3	4.1	5.5
1993[a]	5.8	21.5	2.5	1.8
Average	6.1	20.5	2.3	2.4

SOURCE: Central Bank of Chile and author's calculations.
a. Estimated.

ducive to promoting growth. For example, imports of capital goods and machinery and equipment and foreign investment appear to have greater spillover effects than investment in infrastructure. A cursory look at the recent evidence suggests that Chile has been doing well in these areas.[54]

To quantify growth prospects one could consider recent regressions on growth across countries and estimate the implied rate of growth for Chile, and I would suggest that Bosworth and Marfán follow this route. Alternatively, one could extrapolate the time series evidence for Chile, with the precautions mentioned above. For example, the focus could be on 1990 onward, under the assumption that it represents a better description of what the future will look like. Table 4-6 shows growth decompositions, which, for comparability, use equation 4-1 of the paper, where labor is adjusted by quality. The computations in the table assume a capital-output ratio of 2.2, depreciation of 5 percent, labor share of 0.6, and annual growth of labor quality of 1 percent. Data for 1993 are close to most of the current forecasts, with the economy growing at 6.5 percent without being overheated, and employment growth consistent with the 2 percent growth in the labor force and a reduction in unemployment from 4.9 percent to 4.4 percent.[55]

Contrary to the estimations obtained by Bosworth and Marfán, the 1990s, as table 4-6 shows, experienced much higher growth in total factor productivity than previous decades. Although a 2.6 percent average growth in total factor productivity could be somewhat high, especially because growth in total factor productivity was high in 1992 and because this period corresponds to the expansionary phase of the cycle, there are good grounds to consider 2 percent

54. For example, during the peak, 1980–81, foreign direct investment and imports of capital goods represented 0.6 and 3.9 percent of GDP, respectively. In contrast, during 1991–92, foreign direct investment and imports of capital goods reached 2.2 and 6.6 percent of GDP, respectively.

55. Recent national accounts data based on 1986 prices show much higher investment rates than those of table 4-6, which are based on prices of 1977.

Table 4-7. Savings Rates across Countries
Percent of GDP

Countries	Number of countries	National savings	Private savings	Period
G-7[a]	7	23.0	22.9	1960–88
Other OECD[a]	16	22.5	20.0	1960–88
Latin America[b]	6	15.9	12.6	1980–87
East Asia[c]	5	24.5	n.a.	1973–85
Africa[c]	15	10.4	n.a.	1973–85

a. Elmerskov, Shafer, and Tease (1991).
b. Blejer and Ize (1989). Six largest Latin American economies.
c. World Bank (1987; table A.11). East Asia excludes Papua Nueva Guinea.

growth in total factor productivity feasible.[56] Assuming that the investment rate remains at 20 percent and the quality of labor continues to grow at 1 percent a year, the economy could achieve a rate of growth of 5.1 percent.[57] For the same rate of growth of total factor productivity, higher growth of output could be achieved with higher investment rates. For example, a rate of investment of 25 percent would lead to 6 percent growth. Additionally, higher growth of output could be achieved with higher growth of the quality of the labor force. For example, 2 percent growth of the quality of the labor force would lead to 5.7 percent growth of output.[58] Finally, faster growth of total factor productivity could also lead to faster growth of output. For an investment rate of 20 percent and rates of growth of total factor productivity of 1.5 or 2.5 percent, the rates of growth of output could be 4.6 or 5.6 percent a year.

Financial Markets, Growth, and Savings

An important message of the second part of the paper is that a rate of private savings of 14 percent, such as that achieved in 1992 (although high given the low savings that have characterized Chile), is still low to finance high investment and to sustain growth. Table 4-7 presents some evidence on national and private savings rates for several groups of countries. Despite measurement problems that make it difficult to compare data across countries, Chile's perfor-

56. This 2 percent is equivalent to 2.6 percent if labor quality grows at 1 percent and is included in the residual instead of employment growth.

57. Jadresic and Sanhueza (1992) conclude that Chile can grow between 5 and 6 percent in the future. Their estimations assume that the quality of the labor force grows at 1.7 percent, which is consistent with their historical estimates based on the evolution of wages for different levels of education.

58. With an investment rate of 20 percent, the capital-output ratio would decline toward 1.8 since the rate of growth of output would be higher than that of capital. If the rate of investment were 25 percent, the capital-output ratio would be 2.3.

mance appears to be low, being similar to the average of Latin America and above that of Africa. Chile has made tremendous progress in increasing savings, but it may need to make additional efforts to boost savings and investment.[59]

To understand the evolution of savings in Chile, in particular the poor performance of national savings after the financial liberalization of the 1970s, it is very important to analyze the role of financial markets in promoting savings and growth, and this paper does not sufficiently emphasize its role. A financial liberalization is unlikely, at least in the first few years, to increase private savings, for two reasons. First, the sensitivity of savings to interest rates is low, and hence the increase in interest rates that comes after financial markets are liberalized does not have important effects on the level of savings. Second, and more important, the removal of borrowing constraints will, as the life cycle theory of consumption predicts, reduce savings.[60] Borrowing constraints constitute a form of forced savings, and once they are eliminated, the incentive for the private sector to accumulate financial wealth to finance consumption is reduced. In Chile this phenomenon was reinforced by the abundance of external credit.[61]

The unregulated framework in which the financial market operated before the 1982 crisis also hindered its potential to improve growth performance. The fragility of the financial market may have induced expectations that the government would actually bail out failing firms and banks in the event of a systemic crisis. This was what actually happened, and it may have contributed to reduced corporate savings. Furthermore, it may also have encouraged careless behavior in the financial system that resulted in a reduction in the efficiency with which savings were allocated.[62] Now the operation of the Chilean financial system is quite different, with adequate prudential supervision and better prospects for the future, so the current levels of savings can be maintained and efficiency can continue to increase.

What financial markets can do effectively is to increase the efficiency of investment, allocating credit to its best use. In addition, the process of growth itself induces increased and better financial intermediation. The current reform

59. However, a more definite picture would require examining the potential for foreign savings. In particular, the growing trend of foreign investment may provide some sustainable source of financing, which would allow less domestic effort.

60. Modigliani (1986).

61. Note that although forced savings, in the form of borrowing constraints, could increase capital accumulation, they are likely to reduce welfare by distorting the intertemporal allocation of consumption. Moreover, borrowing constraints could reduce growth by reducing the incentives for savings in human capital. See de Gregorio (1992).

62. de Gregorio and Guidotti (1992).

of the Chilean financial sector, encouraged by the good performance of recent years, should help to improve its role in allocating credit and consequently provide more room for high growth of total factor productivity. I would have liked the paper to examine these issues.

Comment by Joaquín Vial

The paper by Marfán and Bosworth raises one of the key issues concerning economic reforms: Have the structural changes of the 1970s and 1980s produced such a transformation that Chile will be able to maintain its recent growth performance in the future? The authors mention two facts to support the idea that an affirmative answer to that question cannot be taken for granted. First, they note the extremely low rates of productivity growth in recent decades. Second, they argue that investment and especially domestic savings are still too low to sustain high rates of growth.

Even though I fully agree with their conclusions regarding the importance of raising domestic savings and the rates of productivity growth as a precondition to achieving high and stable growth, I am less pessimistic about the recent performance of productivity and savings. We can find explanations for the unusual combination of high growth, low savings, and low rates of labor productivity growth in the past decade. But explanations of past performance do not guarantee that the situation will improve in the future. This is why I think the findings of this paper are timely and perceptive and should have a preeminent place on the policy agenda for the next decade in Chile.

I will focus on alternative explanations for the authors' findings, and I will group them in three categories: the first concerns data; the second concentrates on sectoral differences, the role of relative prices, and the reallocation of resources; and the third concerns the role of natural resources in Chile's recent growth performance.

The Data

First I would like to point out the difficulty of using data on the Chilean economy to find medium- and long-term trends, especially during the 1970s and 1980s. The economy experienced two severe depressions in less than ten years, when GDP fell by 12.9 percent in 1975 and 16 percent between 1981 and 1983. At the same time the Chilean economy had to suffer the adjustment

Table 4-8. **Average Labor Productivity per Month**
1992 U.S. dollars

	Shares in 1992		Average productivity		
	Labor		Level		Annual rate of
Sector	force	GDP	1986	1992	growth
Agriculture	18.0	8.2	272.8	311.7	2.2
Manufacturing	16.7	20.8	861.9	853.9	−0.2
Construction	7.2	6.0	716.3	573.6	−3.6
Commerce	17.6	19.1	538.7	745.2	5.6
Services	30.9	29.0	461.6	644.8	5.7
Other[a]	9.6	16.9	1,027.8	1,200.5	2.6
Total	...	...	552.2	685.5	3.7

SOURCES: National Institute of Statistics and Central Bank of Chile.
a. Includes mining, electricity, water and gas, and transportation.

costs of moving from a chaotic socialist experiment in the early 1970s to a free market achieved in just a few years by the rigid imposition of reforms.

These deep economic crises make it extremely difficult to find and analyze medium- and long-term trends. This is particularly true for labor productivity and investment ratios, since there have been methodological changes in the computation of the national accounts and in employment surveys that have direct effects on the variables being studied. The authors try to correct for some of these problems, but I think the data are still rather unsatisfactory. In particular, I would like to call attention to the 1986 input-output matrix just released by the Central Bank. It shows that the national accounts calculated on the basis of the 1977 I-O matrix severely underestimate investment and national savings for the year 1986. In fact gross fixed investment in 1986 would have been 24 percent higher than previously estimated in the national accounts.

Sectoral Differences

One of the characteristics of developing countries is the diversity in productivity. If the economy is growing and the incentives are right, however, these differences should decrease over time. The exploitation of differences in productivity among sectors is one of the ways to achieve faster growth with comparatively low investment ratios, as pointed out by Lewis and other contributors to the literature of economic development. One way to check if the development process is taking advantage of this source of efficiency gains is to compare average productivity among sectors. This is done in table 4-8.

The results are clear: with the exception of the construction sector, there is a trend toward equalization of average productivity among sectors. Even the traditionally slower agricultural sector shows an average rate of increase in productivity close to 2 percent a year, which is lower than the average, but still enough to reduce the gap between agriculture and manufacturing.

One striking feature of the Chilean economy during the 1980s—when the reform process was finally showing its positive effects on growth—is that the largest gains in productivity are concentrated in nontradable sectors (commerce and services). Before jumping to the wrong conclusions, let us remember that in the first half of the 1980s the economy suffered its worst crisis since the Great Depression, and open unemployment jumped to almost 30 percent. Commerce and services were the two main sectors in which informal activities flourished during the crisis, absorbing part of the surplus labor. As the rest of the economy recovered and created new and more permanent jobs, informal employment and jobs with very low productivity were gradually eliminated in these two sectors.

It is harder to explain the decrease in labor productivity in the manufacturing and construction sectors. Some of the reasons may be found in the incentives to increase the use of labor, especially in the first half of this period: (1) a very low value of the peso, which reduced the cost of labor and made capital goods more expensive; (2) specific employment incentives (subsidies and evaluation criteria for the assignment of public investment projects, including the construction of public housing); and (3) limited access to credit to finance investment projects. After the real appreciation of the peso in 1991–92, both investment and labor productivity in the manufacturing sector increased significantly. Reasons frequently cited among business people to explain this renewed investment effort are a more competitive environment and the resulting need to reduce labor costs.

The Role of Natural Resources

One of the problems in the Chilean national accounts is that they do not take due consideration of the increase or depletion of the stock of natural resources in capital accumulation.[63] If we examine the main forces behind the growth of the past decade, we will recognize the increased use of natural resources as an explanation for growth. Between 1980 and 1992, GDP grew by 54.5 percent in real terms. In the same period, real exports of goods and services rose by 119 percent. The composition of exports (see table 4-9) shows that natural resource-based exports are predominant, composing about 72 percent of total exports in 1992. In the past decade they have been growing at

63. This is not done in the 1986 I-O matrix, either.

Table 4-9. Composition of Chilean Exports, 1992

Exports	Percent of total exports	Exports	Percent of total exports
Mining products	47.3	Pulp and paper	6.8
Copper	38.9	Fishmeal	5.4
Farm products	12.3	Other	28.1

SOURCE: Central Bank of Chile.

almost the same rate as overall exports, and even more than agricultural products.

If we look at the investment figures we will find severe underestimation of investment in these sectors. Just to give an example: in the case of forestry, which constitutes the basis for about 10 percent of total exports and has more than doubled in the past decade, only the cost of the plantation is imputed as investment. The increase in value of the trees as they grow is not accounted for. The same is true for the plantation of fruit trees. These measurement errors are specific to renewable natural resources and imply a downward bias in investment which, in the particular case of Chile in this period, could be very significant.

Conclusion

Earlier I commented on the apparent paradox of having high growth with low investment in Chile during the 1970s and 1980s. My conclusion is that most likely investment and consequently domestic savings have been severely underestimated for this period. Does this mean that we should not worry about the future prospects for growth of the Chilean economy? I agree with the authors on the need to give special attention to savings, investment, and productivity in the near future.

Evidence is mounting that the country is reaching a limit in the rate at which it is using its natural resources. In some cases the limit has to do with the size of the final markets: fresh fruits and, perhaps, copper. Expansion of these activities will be possible only if production costs are reduced and translated into lower prices. In other cases the limit has to do with the physical capacity of the environment to sustain the current rate of exploitation of natural resources; this is clearly the case of the fishing sector, where there is evidence of overfishing and depletion of the biomass in some activities.[64] Forestry and its derived products is the only area in which there is still potential for growth

64. Gómez-Lobo (1991).

among the traditional sectors based on natural resources. There have been sizable increases in the total area of artificial plantations in the past two and a half decades, and further increases are projected well into the next century. This will not compensate, however, for the loss of dynamism in the other sectors.

As we move closer to the end of the first half of the current decade, we will find that growth of potential output is increasingly linked to the development of competitive advantages in manufacturing and services. This process will require a higher intensity of traditionally measured investment and savings, as we move away from natural resources. This is one of the biggest challenges for the Chilean economy in the next few years.

If recent years can be considered indicative of emerging trends, then we have reason to be moderately optimistic: the rate of fixed investment with respect to GDP will be about 19.5 percent for 1990–93, the highest average for any period of the same length in the past two decades. The average rate of domestic savings for the period will be close to 19 percent, also the highest in a long time.

We have also witnessed increases in productivity growth at a rate of 3.7 percent a year during the past six years. The figures for average productivity in the different sectors of the economy show that there is ample room for additional gains through sectoral reallocation of resources. This is not an easy process, however: a significant effort must be made to transfer the required skills to the workers who have been expelled from declining sectors such as traditional agriculture, coal mining, or the textile industry. At the same time, the educational system must be restructured to respond better to the requirements of a much more dynamic economy.

None of these initiatives will come easily or will be provided automatically by market mechanisms. A substantial policy effort must be made to reduce the social costs of the reallocation of resources and to increase the flexibility of the economy to facilitate that process. There are obvious trade-offs between increasing flexibility and protecting jobs, and they should be addressed in the right manner; otherwise opposition from the labor movement could jeopardize the process. It might be necessary to provide some measure of income protection to the unemployed, and perhaps subsidies for retraining, as conditions of maintaining an open economy, free from protectionist barriers. These are costly instruments, and financing them would require additional savings.

Table 4A-1. GDP and Labor and Capital Inputs, 1950–89
Average annual compound growth rates

Country	GDP				Labor quantity			
	1950–73	1973–80	1980–89	1973–89	1950–73	1973–80	1980–89	1973–89
Chile	3.42	3.39	2.90	3.11	0.53	1.88	2.93	2.47
Argentina	3.59	2.29	-1.15	0.34	1.35	0.77	0.63	0.69
Brazil	6.91	7.04	2.21	4.30	2.89	3.21	3.87	3.58
Colombia	5.12	4.97	3.26	4.00	1.90	2.13	2.56	2.37
Mexico	6.50	6.43	1.31	3.52	2.21	4.01	2.71	3.28
Venezuela	6.56	4.10	0.37	1.99	2.87	5.10	2.79	3.79
Average Latin America	5.35	4.70	1.48	2.88	1.96	2.85	2.58	2.70
Korea	7.49	7.07	8.68	7.97	3.11	3.74	1.54	2.50
Taiwan	9.32	8.28	7.41	7.79	4.25	3.31	1.58	2.33
Thailand	6.39	7.19	6.83	6.99	2.68	2.59	2.05	2.29
Average Asia	7.73	7.51	7.64	7.58	3.35	3.21	1.72	2.37
Portugal	5.50	3.22	2.55	2.84	-0.22	1.06	0.66	0.83
Spain	6.12	2.08	2.85	2.51	0.33	-2.36	0.12	-0.97
Average Iberia	5.81	2.65	2.70	2.68	0.06	-0.65	0.39	-0.07
France	5.13	2.83	2.03	2.38	0.08	-0.40	-0.77	-0.61
Germany	5.92	2.18	1.92	2.03	-0.05	-1.19	0.06	-0.49
Japan	9.55	2.90	4.06	3.55	1.55	0.30	0.95	0.67
Netherlands	4.74	2.42	1.72	2.03	0.37	-0.32	0.81	0.31
United Kingdom	3.02	0.95	2.50	1.82	0.15	-1.11	0.54	-0.19
United States	3.65	2.09	3.15	2.68	1.22	1.41	1.43	1.42
Average OECD	5.34	2.23	2.56	2.42	0.50	-0.22	0.50	0.18

Table 4A-1. *(continued)*

Country	Physical capital				Labor quality			
	1950–73	*1973–80*	*1980–89*	*1973–89*	*1950–73*	*1973–80*	*1980–89*	*1973–89*
Chile	4.21	2.34	1.88	2.08	0.59	0.94	0.96	0.95
Argentina	4.53	4.50	1.08	2.56	0.84	1.25	1.28	1.27
Brazil	9.44	11.17	5.29	7.82	1.33	1.38	2.22	1.85
Colombia	3.79	5.14	4.80	4.95	0.65	0.79	0.83	0.81
Mexico	7.14	7.38	4.20	5.58	1.53	0.80	2.11	1.53
Venezuela	7.59	8.08	3.23	5.32	0.94	1.11	1.16	1.14
Average Latin America	6.12	6.44	3.41	4.72	0.98	1.05	1.43	1.26
Korea	6.04	15.50	11.83	13.42	1.55	1.94	2.85	2.45
Taiwan	5.91	12.42	7.58	9.67	1.55	2.05	3.00	2.58
Thailand	4.60	4.44	5.59	5.09	1.55	2.05	1.99	2.02
Average Asia	5.52	10.79	8.33	9.40	1.55	2.01	2.61	2.35
Portugal	5.52	5.44	4.48	4.90	1.49	1.49	2.15	1.86
Spain	6.30	6.74	3.91	5.14	0.79	0.79	1.72	1.31
Average Iberia	5.91	6.09	4.20	5.02	1.14	1.14	1.94	1.59
France	4.89	5.43	3.44	4.31	0.43	0.53	0.83	0.70
Germany	7.67	4.07	3.14	3.55	0.20	0.20	0.14	0.17
Japan	8.87	8.04	6.19	7.00	0.62	0.51	0.54	0.53
Netherlands	5.87	4.11	2.70	3.31	0.51	0.62	0.70	0.66
United Kingdom	5.05	3.38	3.69	3.55	0.24	0.37	0.39	0.38
United States	3.26	3.84	3.06	3.40	0.48	0.18	1.19	0.75
Average OECD	5.94	4.81	3.54	4.09	0.41	0.40	0.63	0.53

SOURCE: Hofman (1993).

Table 4A-2. Components of National Saving, 1970–92
Percent of GDP

Year	National saving	General government saving[a]	Private saving	Addenda Copper stabilization	Addenda Pension fund saving
1970	15.2	6.3	8.9	...	...
1971	12.4	0.6	11.8	...	...
1972	8.3	−3.9	12.2	...	...
1973	5.2	−2.9	7.7	...	...
1974	20.7	3.9	16.8	...	...
1975	7.9	5.1	2.8	...	...
1976	14.5	4.5	10.0	...	...
1977	10.7	1.5	6.4	...	...
1978	12.6	2.6	6.9	...	...
1979	12.4	6.0	4.3	...	...
1980	13.9	6.9	4.8	...	...
1981	8.2	3.9	6.1	...	0.9
1982	2.1	−2.7	3.5	...	1.9
1983	4.4	−1.8	4.3	...	1.7
1984	2.9	−0.6	4.8	...	1.9
1985	5.4	1.1	6.1	...	2.0
1986	7.7	2.0	3.5	...	2.2
1987	12.6	3.6	4.3	...	2.3
1988	16.3	6.1	5.7	3.4	2.7
1989	17.2	8.2	10.1	4.2	3.1
1990	17.5	5.2	9.0	2.5	3.3
1991	19.0	4.6	14.4	0.7	3.3
1992	19.6	5.9	13.7	0.3	n.a.

SOURCE: Authors' estimates as explained in text.
a. General government includes Copper Stabilization Fund.

References

Arellano, J. P. 1983. "De la liberalisation a la intervention. El mercado de capital en Chile 1974–83." *Colección Estudios CIEPLAN* 11 (December): 5–49.

———. 1984. "La dificil salida al problema del endeudamiento interno." *Colección Estudios CIEPLAN* 13 (June): 5–25.

———. 1985. "Politicas sociales y desarrollo: Chile 1924–1984." Santiago: *Ediciones CIEPLAN*.

Arellano, J. P., and M. Marfán. 1986. "Ahorro-inversion y relaciones financieras en la actual crisis economica chilena." *Colección Estudios CIEPLAN* 20 (December): 61–93.

Barandiarán, E. 1983. "Nuestra crisis financiera." *Revista de Estudios Publicos* 12 (Spring).

Barro, R. 1991. "Economic Growth in a Cross Section of Countries." *Quarterly Journal of Economics* 106 (May): 407–33.

Blejer, M., and A. Ize. 1989. "Adjustment Uncertainty, Confidence, and Growth: Latin America After the Debt Crisis." IMF Working Paper WP/89/105.

Caballero, R., and V. Corbo. 1986. "Analisis de la balansa comercial: Un enfoque de equilibrio general." *Cuadernos de Economia* 23 (December): 285–313.

Corbo, V., and K. Schmidt-Hebbel. 1991. "Public Policies and Saving in Developing Countries." *Journal of Development Economics* 36 (July): 89–115.

de Gregorio, J. 1992a. "Economic Growth in Latin America." *Journal of Development Economics* 39 (July): 59–84.

———. 1992b. "Liquidity Constraints, Human Capital Accumulation and Economic Growth." International Monetary Fund.

de Gregorio, J., and P. Guidotti. 1992. "Financial Development and Economic Growth." IMF Working Paper WP/92/101.

Díaz-Alejandro, C. 1984. "De la represion al colapso financiero." In *La politicas economica en la encrucijada,* edited by J. A. Ocampo, 13–36. Bogota, Colombia: Centro de Estudios sobre Desarrollo Economico, University of Los Andes.

Elmerskov, J., J. Shafer, and W. Tease. 1991. "Savings Trends and Measurement Issues." OECD, Economics and Statistics Department, Working Paper 105.

Foxley, J. 1986. "Determinantes del ahorro nacional: Chile 1963–1983." *Cuadernos de Economía* 23 (April): 119–127.

Gómez-Lobo (1991). "Desarrollo sustentable del sector pesquero chileno en los años 80." In *Desarrollo y Medio ambiente. Hacia un enforque integrador,* edited by J. Vial. CIEPLAN.

González, P., and M. Marfán. 1992. "Determinantes fiscales del consumo privato en Chile." CIEPLAN.

Hofman, André. 1992. "Capital Accumulation in Latin America: A Six-Country Comparison for 1959–89." *Review of Income and Wealth* 38 (December): 365–401.

———. 1993. "Economic Development in Latin America in the 20th Century: A Comparative Prespective." In *Explaining Economic Growth,* edited by A. Szirmai, B. van Ark, and D. Pilat, 241–66. New York: North Holland.

Jadresic, E. 1986. "Evolución del empleo y desempleo en Chile, 1970–85. Series anuales y trimestrales." *Colección Estudios CIPELAN* 20 (December): 147–93.

———. 1992. "Dinamica de salarios y contratos en Chile." *Colección Estudios CIEPLAN* 34 (June): 5–30.

Jadresic, E., and G. Sanhueza. 1992. "Producto y Crecimiento Potencial de la Economía Chilena." Banco Central de Chile.

Larraín, Felipe. 1991. "Public Sector Behavior in a Highly Indebted Country: The Contrasting Chilean Experience." In *The Public Sector and the Latin American Crisis,* edited by F. Larraín and M. Selowsky, 89–136. San Francisco: International Center for Economic Growth.

Lehmann, S. 1991. "Determinantes de la inversion productiva privada en Chile (1981–89)." *Colección Estudios CIEPLAN* 33 (December): 19–58.

————. 1992. "Determinantes del gasto privado en bienes de consumo durable y habitual en Chile (1981–89)." *Colección Estudios CIEPLAN* 34 (June): 61–99.

Maddison, Angus. 1989. *The World Economy in the 20th Century.* Paris: Organization for Economic Co-operation and Development.

Mankiw, N. Gregory, D. Romer, and D. Weil. 1990. "A Contribution to the Empirics of Growth." Working Paper 3541. Cambridge, Mass.: National Bureau of Economic Research.

Marfán, M. 1992a. "Protección de salarios reales." CIEPLAN's Workshop on Economic Situation.

————. 1992b. "Reestimation del PGB potencial en Chile: Implicancias para el crecimiento." *Cuadernos de Economía* 29 (August 87): 187–206.

Marfán, M., and P. Artiagoitía. 1989. "Estimación del PGB Potential: Chile 1960–88." *Colección Estudios CIEPLAN* 27 (December): 49–62.

Modigliani, F. 1986. "Life Cycle, Individual Thrift, and the Wealth of Nations." *American Economic Review* 76 (June): 297–313.

Nordhaus, William. 1972. "The Recent Productivity Slowdown." *Brookings Papers on Economic Activity 3:* 493–536.

Schmidt-Hebbel, K. 1984. "Consumo e inversion en Chile: 1974–1982." In *Del auge a la crisis de 1982,* edited by F. Morandé and K. Schmidt-Hebbel, 147–90. Santiago: ILADES.

World Bank. 1987. *World Development Report.* Oxford University Press for the World Bank.

Young, A. 1992. "A Tale of Two Cities: Factor Accumulation and Technical Change in Hong Kong and Singapore." *NBER Macroeconomics Annual* 7: 13–54.

5 The Distribution of Income and Economic Adjustment

Mario Marcel and Andrés Solimano

THE ECONOMIC history of Chile of the past three decades is one of the more fascinating (albeit dramatic) cases of radical changes in development strategies and political regimes in Latin America. Central to those shifts in policy is the role attached to income distribution by the different actors who led the political and economic changes in Chile during that period. The explicit quest for redistribution started in the mid-1960s, when a centrist government led by President Eduardo Frei took power under the banner of a "revolution in freedom." That government introduced gradual changes in the patterns of wealth and income distribution in Chile, through agrarian reform and expanded social services, within the framework of a developmentalist economic strategy. In 1970 a democratically elected Marxist president, Salvador Allende, came into office promising a radical redistribution of wealth and income in favor of the urban working class and the peasantry.

Redistributing income and wealth and establishing the foundations for Chilean-tailored socialism ("the Chilean way to socialism") were the top priorities of the Unidad Popular government. After an initial bonanza followed by a few years of economic destabilization and acute political conflict, the military took power, deposed Allende, and installed an authoritarian regime. The new regime once again sought to reshape the economic landscape of Chile, this time along free-market lines. It proposed to tackle hyperinflation and large macroeconomic imbalances first, as a precondition for the success of its program of trade liberalization, privatization, financial sector reform, and labor demobilization. Income distribution was a lower priority than adjustment and liberalization.

After the military regime, a civilian government led by President Aylwin took office in early 1990. The economic program of the new administration

We acknowledge the comments by Eliana Cardoso and Carol Graham and other participants at the Brookings conference. Efficient assistance and comments by Raimundo Soto and Jaime Crispi are appreciated.

preserved most of the structural reforms instituted by the Pinochet regime. This government had a more progressive distributive twist, however, to redress a forgotten dimension of the liberalization program initiated by the military regime. The plan envisioned a significant increase in social spending, supported by sustained growth of GDP and changes in labor legislation and in the tax system.

The experience of Chile is interesting for addressing a broad set of questions related to economic reform, income distribution, and public policies. Do macroeconomic adjustment and its sequels in the labor market—such as protracted unemployment and decline in real wages—affect the distributive position of low income groups? What is the effect of inflation on income distribution? Is economic growth inequalizing or equalizing? Is a more liberal policy regime compatible with social equity? Does inequality initially worsen and then improve in the process of economic reform? To what extent can social policy, through the public provision of education, health, housing, and transfers, correct the distributional outcomes of pure market processes?

This paper gives an overview of the different economic policies adopted in the period 1960–92 and of the distributive and macroeconomic outcomes associated with it, discussing the nature and effect of the social policies implemented in that period. It uses a simple econometric model to determine the distribution of personal income in Chile, using time-series information on income shares by quintile for the period 1960–91. The analysis seeks to gauge the relative importance of labor market variables (unemployment and real minimum wages), macroeconomic variables (GDP growth, inflation, rate of capacity utilization), and structural factors (education, type of economic policy regime). The model is estimated under alternative closures. A decomposition exercise is carried out to evaluate the relative contribution of the explanatory variables and to explain the actual changes in the share of both the bottom 40 percent and the top 20 percent income groups for relevant periods.

An Overview

Income distribution in Chile is very unequal. While the bottom 40 percent of the population receives around 10 percent of national income, the top 20 percent receives 60 percent. The situation is even more dramatic if we consider that the income share of the bottom 20 percent of the population is around 4 percent. The ratio of the income shares of the top and bottom 20 percent of the population has fluctuated between 18 and 23 in the past three decades in

Table 5-1. Income Distribution in Chile, 1959–92
Income shares per quintile, in percent

Group	Alessandri government, 1959–64	Frei government, 1965–70	Allende government, 1971–73	Pinochet regime, 1974–89	Aylwin government, 1990–93
1st quintile	3.2	3.2	3.1	2.7	3.4
2d quintile	7.5	7.1	7.5	6.4	6.7
Bottom 40 percent	10.7	10.3	10.6	9.1	10.1
3d quintile	11.9	11.4	12.5	10.6	10.5
4th quintile	20.1	19.7	21.5	18.3	17.9
Middle 40 percent	32.0	31.1	34.0	28.9	28.4
5th quintile	57.9	58.6	55.4	62.0	61.5
Ratio of 5th quintile over 1st quintile	18.1	19.5	17.9	23.0	18.1

SOURCE: "Survey of Household Incomes," Department of Economics, University of Chile.

Chile.[1] This pattern of income distribution is more unequal than in East Asia and in the OECD. In Latin America, however, income distribution is more unequal than in Chile in countries such as Brazil and Peru, though in Argentina and in Uruguay income distribution is less unequal than in Chile.[2]

Table 5-1 and figure 5-1 provide information on the evolution of income distribution (shares in national income by quintiles) during the past five governments in Chile, from 1959 to 1992. The figures correspond to the shares of income recipients per capita from a homogeneous sample of around 3,000 households in greater Santiago, as compiled by the University of Chile.[3]

The picture emerging from table 5-1 is that of a relatively stable income share of the bottom 40 percent of the population during the 1960s with some increase during the Allende government. During the Pinochet regime (1974–89), however, the income share of the bottom 40 percent declined, on average, by 1.5 percentage points compared with the 1960–73 period. This represents a

1. Survey data may tend to *underestimate* the degree of income inequality in the country for two reasons. On the one hand, nonwage incomes (in particular capital incomes, rents, and interests earnings) tend to be underreported by survey respondents. On the other hand, the survey covers the metropolitan area of Santiago and not rural areas, where income distribution tends to be more skewed.

2. See Larraín and Vergara (1992) and Cardoso and Helwege (1992).

3. Studies on income distribution and its relation to economic policies in Chile in that period include Pollack and Uthoff (1986), Rodriguez (1985), Torche (1987), Oyarzo (1990), Meller (1991), Raczynski and Romaguera (1992), Solimano (1992), and Solimano (1993). For a discussion of other sources of information and for selected years on income distribution in Chile, see the appendix.

Figure 5-1. Income Distribution in Chile, 1958–92

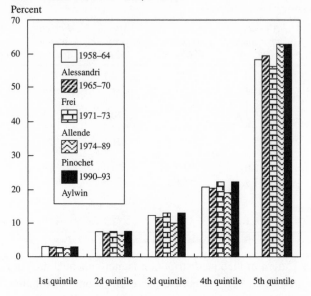

Percent

☐	1958–64
	Alessandri
▨	1965–70
	Frei
⊞	1971–73
	Allende
⧖	1974–89
	Pinochet
■	1990–93
	Aylwin

1st quintile   2d quintile   3d quintile   4th quintile   5th quintile

SOURCE: "Survey of Household Incomes," Department of Economics, University of Chile.

drop of nearly 14 percent in the income share of that group. The Aylwin government has partly reversed that trend; the share of the bottom 40 percent during its first two years in office increased by 1 percentage point over the years of the Pinochet regime.

The story for the top 20 percent is the opposite; its income share increased modestly in the 1960s, declined by nearly 3 percentage points under Allende, and increased by 4.7 percentage points during the Pinochet regime. In the Aylwin administration, the share of the top 20 percent declined by 0.5 percent.

A major part of the redistribution of income during the Pinochet period took place from the middle class (third and fourth quintiles), whose income share declined by more than 3 percentage points in 1960–73, to the top 20 percent. During the Aylwin government the share of the middle 40 percent and the top 20 percent declined by 0.5 percentage points; that share was redistributed to the bottom 40 percent.

Structural Reform

Economic policies and politics in Chile have experienced major swings in the past three decades. The Alessandri government of 1958–64 was a conservative administration that focused most of its energies on reducing inflation and consolidating macroeconomic stability. Economic liberalization was not a major part of the economic agenda of the Alessandri government at that time.[4] The Frei administration, starting in early 1965, implemented a program of economic modernization with moderate redistribution. That program included an agrarian reform; the quasi nationalization of foreign-owned copper mining, the main source of foreign exchange at the time; and an aggressive expansion of education, public health, and physical infrastructure. Labor union affiliation expanded significantly. In macroeconomic terms, the Frei administration was relatively orthodox, giving high priority to moderating inflation and controlling potential fiscal and balance of payments disequilibriums.

The Allende government—strongly influenced by the rise of the political left in Chile (and elsewhere) in the late 1960s—felt empowered to attempt a radical redistribution of income toward the urban working class and the peasantry.[5] The economic program of the Allende government, which had strong Marxian roots, included nationalizing most medium- to large-scale industrial firms, the banking system, and the main natural resources and accelerating the agrarian reform. The stated goal was to lay the foundations for transforming the Chilean economy into a socialist one. It pursued expansive monetary and fiscal policies along with generous increases in minimum and public sector wages supported by price controls and tight foreign exchange rationing. This expansionary stance also extended to social spending.

A military coup ousted the Allende government in September 1973. The economic policies of the military regime (amply documented elsewhere) included a vast program of economic liberalization and reform to be carried out in an authoritarian context.[6] The liberalization program included opening up trade; rationalizing the public sector, including privatizing most state-owned enterprises; and reforming the financial sector and social security. Labor unions were at first demobilized and repressed, but then allowed to operate under a new labor law that precluded nationwide and sectoral negotiation over wages and other working conditions. The main macroeconomic objectives were to reduce and stabilize inflation (very high after Allende; see table 5-2), to correct a large fiscal deficit, and to ensure a sustainable balance of payments

4. A very complete discussion of the economic policies of the Alessandri and the Frei administrations is in Ffrench-Davis (1973).

5. An insider view of that period is provided by Bitar (1979). See also Larraín and Meller (1991).

6. See Edwards and Cox-Edwards (1987), Fontaine (1989), Meller (1990), Corbo (1993), and Corbo and Solimano (1991).

Table 5-2. Main Economic and Social Indicators, 1960–92
Percent unless otherwise indicated

Indicator	Alessandri government, 1959–64	Frei government, 1965–70	Allende government, 1971–73	Pinochet regime, 1974–89	Aylwin government, 1990–93
GDP growth[a]	3.9	4.1	0.7	3.4	5.9
Rate of inflation[b]	26.6	26.3	285.7	79.9	19.6
Public sector deficit[c]	4.7[d]	2.1	16.1	0.5	−0.3
Unemployment rate[e]	5.2[d]	5.9	4.8	17.1	6.5
Average real wage[f]	62.2[d]	84.2	90.0	81.4	94.7
Minimum real wage[f]	116.8[d]	101.8	134.0	83.0	83.0
Public sector real wage[f]	...	81.4	87.9	75.3	78.3[g]
Social expenditure[c]	...	...	...	4.5	3.6
Price of copper[h]	32.4[d]	61.0	59.6	78.7	110.2

SOURCES: For growth of GDP and social expenditure, Central Bank of Chile, *Indicadores Económicos y Sociales*. For rate of inflation, Central Bank, Cortázar and Marshall (1980), and Yañez (1979). For public sector deficit, Corbo (1993). For unemployment rate, Universidad de Chile, Encuesta de Ocupación Gran-Santiago. It includes emergency employment programs. For average real wage and minimum real wage, Jadresic (1990). For public sector real wage, Cabezas (1989) and Dirección de Presupuestos, Ministerio de Hacienda, Chile.
a. Annual average.
b. December–December.
c. Percent of GDP.
d. 1960–64.
e. Percent of labor force.
f. 1970=100.
g. 1990–91.
h. U.S.$ per pound.

position. Left-wing parties were banned for most of the period, and centrist political parties were considerably restricted in their activities. The parliament remained closed for sixteen years.

Aylwin, elected in the first open presidential election since 1970, preserved most of the structural reforms implemented during the previous administration that had yielded high growth in the late 1980s. The tax system was reformed. Corporate and personal income taxes were raised, and a value added tax was implemented to finance increased social expenditure for low-income families. The minimum wage was raised, and the parliament passed changes in labor legislation to redress the imbalance in the relative bargaining power between labor and capital that it had inherited from the military regime. Moderate redistribution was framed in policies of fiscal and monetary restraint aimed at maintaining macroeconomic stability.

Table 5-2 summarizes the main indicators of economic performance in the period 1960–92, for the five presidential periods. The 1960s were a period of moderate growth—about 4 percent a year—with an annual inflation rate of 26 percent. Unemployment hovered around 5 or 6 percent, and real wages increased steadily. The Allende years, the early 1970s, caused great macroeconomic dislocation, as fiscal deficits soared (reaching nearly 25 percent of GDP in 1973) and inflation climbed to three-digit levels. The redistributive impulse of the Unidad Popular government was in part reflected in massive increases in minimum and public sector wages. The acceleration of inflation in 1972 and 1973 eroded part of the initial increase in wages, though wages still increased, on average, in real terms during the 1971–73 period. The minimum wage hike along with the decline in unemployment is likely to account for much of the increase in the income share of the bottom 40 percent of the population.

The Pinochet period led, in a stop-and-go fashion, to a resumption of output growth, a slow decline in inflation, and a rapid elimination of fiscal deficits. On average, however, growth performance for the whole period does not look very impressive. Of course, averages conceal considerable intraperiod variation in the data. Growth performance was very strong in 1976–81 and in 1985–89, though the economy experienced two big recessions in 1975 and 1982–83. Inflation ran at an annual average rate of 248.7 percent between 1974 and 1978 and declined slowly to an average annual rate of 23.6 percent a year between 1978 and 1989.

Labor market performance was bleak during most of the period, an important factor behind the deterioration of income distribution for low-income groups detected during the Pinochet regime. On average, for metropolitan Santiago, the *effective* unemployment rate was 17.1 percent during 1974–89, triple the average rate of the 1960–73 period.[7] In addition, average real wages during 1974–89 were close to the level of the early 1960s and nearly 9 percentage points below that of the Allende period. The minimum wage declined by 26 percent in real terms in 1974–89 from the level of 1960–73 and almost 40 percent from the Allende years. The fall in the income share of the middle class (third and fourth quintiles) can be associated with a decline in salaries (and employment) in the public sector (the single most important employer of middle-income groups). In fact, on average the index of real wages in the public sector declined nearly 13 percentage points in 1974–89 compared with the average under Allende and 6 points compared with the level under Frei. Moreover, after 1974–75 the real price of goods and services intensive in the consumption basket of the middle class went up. In fact, before the military gov-

7. These figures include emergency employment programs that paid less than the national minimum wage (see appendix).

ernment, public education from primary school to university, public health, and housing were provided either free of charge or highly subsidized to the middle class. With the fiscal reform of the mid-1970s, most of these subsidies were either eliminated or reduced for middle-income groups. A large part of the resources taken away from the third and fourth quintiles went, in the end, to the top 20 percent (in other words, a regressive distributional shift).

During its first three years, the Aylwin administration consolidated the strong performance the Chilean economy had registered in the second half of the 1980s, and it has generated impressive momentum in investment and growth since 1991. Inflation declined (now in the annual range of 10–13 percent) in a context of fiscal balance and a strong balance of payments. Unemployment declined to historic lows (the unemployment rate was 4.4 percent in 1992). In 1990–92 the average real wage was 7.2 percent higher than in 1980–89 (the average real wage in 1992 was 10.4 percent higher than in 1980–89). The real minimum wage in 1990–92 is on average the same as that of 1974–89, but the real minimum wage is around 5 percentage points higher in 1990–92 than in 1980–89. In 1992 the real minimum wage was nearly 15 percentage points higher than the average of 1980–89. Clearly the combination of lower unemployment and higher minimum and average real wages in 1990–92 coincides with the improvement of nearly 1.0 percentage point in the income share of the bottom 40 percent of the population.

Social Policies

Chile began to provide social services in the early 1920s, enacting basic legislation concerning primary education, public health, labor regulations, and social security.[8] The development of trade unions and rapid urbanization put pressure on the state to expand social services. Financing for the newly created social services and for the expansion of public employment came mainly from the nitrate and copper industries, which provided an important source of revenues to the government.

1960–73: "EXTENSIVE" SOCIAL AND REDISTRIBUTIVE POLICIES. The governments of Frei and later of Allende expanded social expenditure for education, health, and housing as part of their plan for redistributing income. The "welfare state" expanded to satisfy the demands of traditionally well-organized groups of white- and blue-collar workers. Entitlement grew substantially in areas such as housing, higher education, and health insurance.

8. See Arellano (1985).

Figure 5-2. Social Expenditure, Selected Years, 1955–92

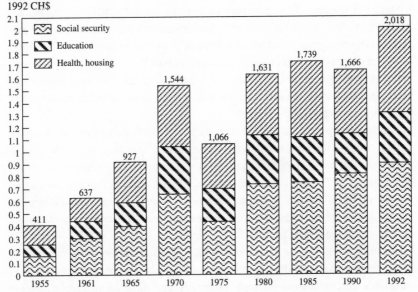

Billions of
1992 CH$

SOURCES: Arellano (1985), Contraloría General de la República, and Dirección de Presupuestos, Chile.

Emerging groups of the rural and urban poor were included as recipients of these policies.

Despite the fact that benefits were extended well beyond the most vulnerable groups of the population into the middle and even higher income groups, efforts to target social expenditure were limited. The government was reluctant to engage in any major confrontation with the middle class. Between 1961 and 1970, social expenditure nearly doubled in real terms, demanding a growing share of GDP and of total government expenditure. Education and social security were the most important items, accounting for nearly two-thirds of social spending (see figure 5-2). Nearly half the growth in these sectors was due to an increase in school enrollment, which grew at an annual rate of 5.5 percent, and in the number of pensioners (10.3 percent). This was a phase of extensive development of social services.

This trend of the 1960s was accentuated by the Allende government, but its actual effectiveness was increasingly constrained by the fiscal crisis generated at the time and by the fact that the operative capacity of the public sector was increasingly burdened by the demands of newly nationalized enterprises, banks, farms, and mining.

1974–89: FISCAL AUSTERITY, TARGETING, AND REDEFINITION OF SOCIAL POLICIES. After the military coup of 1973, government priorities changed. The goals of macroeconomic adjustment and structural reforms and state retrenchment had taken their toll on social policies. Existing social programs not only represented a large share of government expenditure, but also were subject to the inertia of the status quo caused by the expansion of entitlement over the previous thirty years. As a result of changes in priorities and macroeconomic fluctuations, social expenditure followed a rather unstable pattern during this period.

Initially, during the stabilization program of 1975, part of the reduction in public expenditure concentrated on cutting social spending. In fact social expenditure fell more than GDP and total government expenditure during the recession of 1975. This made the macroeconomic crisis of the mid-1970s particularly painful for low- and middle-income groups, as social expenditure declined at the same time as unemployment increased. No wonder income distribution worsened at that time.

In contrast, during the recession of 1982–83, an effort was made to maintain and extend social spending, particularly to support the unemployed through subsidies, emergency employment programs, and money transfers targeted at low-income groups.[9]

In the late 1970s important institutional reforms were initiated in social security, education, and the primary health system. The basic principles of these reforms were: decentralizing the management of social programs that were transferred from the central government to local governments (municipalities); converting social spending from a program of broad coverage to one targeted toward vulnerable groups; changing the financing of social services from direct provision of the service to subsidy on demand by users; and encouraging the private sector to participate in the provision of social services.[10]

Social security was transformed from a pay-as-you-go scheme into a private capitalization system; public schools were transferred to municipalities and funded by a standard grant-per-student scheme, paving the way for further private provision of education; a two-tier system was created for health and nutri-

---

9. Meller (1991) documents that the cost of the unemployment subsidy programs of 1982–83 represented about 1.5 percent of GDP and benefited some 600,000 unemployed; the program of subsidies to debtors in dollars, around 2,000 people, cost nearly 3 percentage points of GDP.

10. See Raczynski and Romaguera (1992). The decentralization-cum-privatization scheme had a convenient political side effect for the military government in the sense that it transferred to municipalities the responsibility for dealing with nearly 120,000 employees, teachers, doctors, and other health and education workers. This group was very active in the past, both in wage demands and in political mobilization.

Table 5-3. Government Expenditure in Three Major Social Programs, 1980–91
Annual average rates of growth

Years	Overall expenditure[a]	Expenditure per capita[b]	Expenditure per beneficiary[c]
1980–85	2.5	0.8	−0.5
1985–89	0.5	−1.2	−0.4
1989–91	2.8	1.2	4.2

SOURCE: Authors' estimates, based on official figures.
a. Includes primary and secondary education, health insurance, and pensions.
b. Overall expenditure/total population.
c. Overall expenditure/beneficiaries of government programs.

tion in which privately provided health services coexisted with health insurance companies (ISAPRES) and a public health service for low-income groups that could not afford to pay for health care.[11]

Despite progress in some areas, the overall trend of social expenditure during the period was one of restraint. Social expenditure fell by 16 percent in 1975–76 and by 12.7 percent between 1983 and 1987, never recovering its 1970 level, either as a share of GDP or in real per capita terms (figure 5-2). The fall in social expenditure was particularly sharp in health, housing, and nontargeted transfers. These changes especially affected the middle class. When these figures are contrasted with the growing number of beneficiaries of broad social programs during this period, the effects of financial restraint look stronger, as illustrated in table 5-3, for the 1980s.

The restraint of social expenditure impaired other major developments in social policy during the military government. On the one hand progress in targeting did not necessarily improve the situation of lower-income groups. In 1990 the poorer 40 percent of the population captured nearly two-thirds of government expenditure in health and half of the expenditure in public education (see table 5-4). As both sectors were subject to deep budgetary cuts during the 1980s, however, most of the proceeds of lower expenditure in middle- and higher-income groups went to improve the financial position of the government rather than to increase direct benefits for the poor.

On the other hand financial pressure on social programs also threatened the success of structural reforms in those areas. By the end of the 1980s the reduction in the real value of government transfers to decentralized schools and to health centers had resulted in a scarcely sustainable system, rejected by important segments of the population. This situation in the social sectors influenced the public mood toward bringing back to power in 1990 the parties of

11. See Raczynski and Romaguera (1992) for a detailed discussion of the reforms in that area. See also Castañeda (1990).

Table 5-4. Distribution of Government Social Expenditure, 1990

	Share of national income	Social expenditure			
Group		Monetary subsidies	Education	Health	Housing
Lower 40 percent	13	52	46	67	48
Middle 40 percent	32	38	36	27	40
Upper 20 percent	55	10	18	6	12
Total	100	100	100	100	100

SOURCE: Mujica and Larrañaga (1992), based on a CASEN survey.

the center left, which had platforms that emphasized social and redistributive policies.

1990–92: SOCIAL DEBT AND SOCIAL INVESTMENT. The Aylwin government took office in 1990 with two main commitments in social policy: the restoration of benefits for low- and middle-income groups that had been curtailed in the last years of the authoritarian government; and the development of new social programs targeted at high-risk groups in urban areas and programs that would improve the quality of basic social services. The former was labeled as servicing the "social debt" and the latter, "social investment." Accomplishing these objectives required a substantial amount of resources that would be funded by higher taxes, by then at a historic low relative to GDP.

The broad political consensus that emerged in Chile during the transition to democracy on the need to increase the social effort facilitated an early agreement on these issues, and a tax reform was enacted in record time by mid-1990. In a first stage, extending from mid-1990 through 1991, social debt policies had priority: pensions and social subsidies were raised, and debt-relief schemes (for debt of low-middle income groups on housing, for example) were launched. By the end of this period, however, government policy started moving toward social investment. At the end of 1991 some major programs in basic education, health infrastructure, youth training, and project funding for the poor were already in place, and they doubled their share of social expenditure in the next two years.

The Aylwin government did not reverse the institutional changes in the social area that had been made in the 1980s. Social security remains a private capitalization system, and the government endorsed decentralization of education and health. In fact, these institutions may have gained more legitimacy as further resources and democratic control softened the hard stance of teachers, medical staff, organized workers, and the public, who at different times have questioned the rationality of the new institutions and their lack of resources. However, pressures to increase salaries of health and education workers in the state sector remain.

The tax reform of 1990 increased fiscal revenues associated with rapid growth, and the reallocation of government resources allowed social expenditure to experience a growth rate of 10 percent a year in 1991 and 1992 without undermining fiscal equilibrium.[12] Particularly important was the increase in funding for health, housing, and social investment programs, as the latter replaced social assistance as the third most important area of social policy after the funding of social security and basic social services.

This effort at improving equity through social policies has been particularly fruitful because the inertial forces in social expenditure have finally eased as a result of a reversal of demographic trends and structural reforms that diverted the demand of high- and middle-income groups for social services toward the private sector. In the case of the broad-based programs depicted in table 5-3, the growth of expenditure per beneficiary nearly doubled the rate of increase in overall public expenditure. The data in table 5-3 show a decline of 10–12 percentage points (from 45 percent to 33–35 percent) between 1988 and 1992 in the percentage of the population below the poverty line.[13]

Econometric Analysis

Modeling the determinants of income distribution is a complex issue that involves the interaction between factor markets (primarily the labor market), macroeconomic variables, and structural factors such as education and ownership of assets, all this taking place in a historical context influenced by political developments.[14]

The model to be estimated econometrically identifies four sets of factors that are expected to affect income distribution in Chile in the period under

12. A similar increase is planned for 1993.

13. See MIDEPLAN (1992).

14. The empirical analysis is based on the Survey of Household Incomes of the University of Chile for Greater Santiago from 1960 to 1992. Early literature on the topic harks back to David Ricardo (1817); later a neat formalization of different theories of distribution was provided by Kaldor (1956). More recent contributions include several strands. The effects of macroeconomic fluctuations and inflation on income distribution are studied in Blinder and Esaki (1978), Cardoso, Paes de Barros, and Urani (1992), and Galor and Zeira (1993). The effect of structural adjustment policies on income distribution is developed in Bourgingnon, de Melo, and Suwa (1991) and in the empirical papers in that volume. The interaction between growth and income distribution (and history) is surveyed by Lindert and Williamson (1985) and reexamined in Taylor (1991) and in Person and Tabellini (1991). The interaction between politics and income distribution is developed, along relatively neoclassical lines, in Alesina and Rodrik (1991) and in Peroti (1990).

study: (1) labor market variables, such as the unemployment rate and the real minimum wage; (2) macroeconomic variables including the rate of growth of GDP, the rate of capacity utilization, and the inflation rate; (3) the ability to generate earnings, for example, education; and (4) some indicators of changes in the economic structure resulting from structural reforms and from changes in the political regime under which the distributive process takes place.

The general specification of the model can be written as:

$$(5\text{-}1) \qquad S_i(t) = a_i + b_i Z(t) + c_i MINWAGE(t) + d_i INF(t)$$
$$+ e_i EDUC(t) + f_i DUMMY + \varepsilon(t),$$

where $S_i(t)$ is the income share of the quintile i ($i = 1, 2..., 5$) in total income in year t. The variable $Z(t)$ is a generic indicator of the level of economic activity (as reflected in the goods or labor markets) in year t. We explore three alternative specifications for variable $Z(t)$: (1) The aggregate rate of unemployment; (2) the rate of capacity utilization; and (3) the rate of growth of real GDP. Only one of these $Z(t)$ variables is included in each regression at a time, to avoid problems of multicollinearity.[15]

The variable $MINWAGE(t)$ is the real minimum wage in year t[16]; $INF(t)$ is the rate of change in the CPI (end of year) in period t; $EDUC(t)$ is the share of the population over fourteen years with more than primary schooling in year t. The DUMMY variable assumes the value 0 between 1960 and 1973 and 1 between 1974 and 1992. It intends to capture changes in the economic structure of Chile associated with the reforms implemented after 1974. A dummy variable denoting the political regime, for example democracy and authoritarianism, could not be included in the estimation, since it would be very collinear with the dummy post-1974 denoting change in economic structure.[17]

The model is estimated by OLS, a technique that imposes the following cross-equations restrictions to the coefficients of the model.[18]

---

15. An alternative specification would be to use a Gini coefficient or a Theil index as dependent variables in the regressions. However, the specification with income shares by quintile allows more information on changes in the relative income position of each group than an aggregative index.

16. The average wage index in Chile comprises wages paid in national (private and public) and foreign-owned firms employing more than fifty workers. In that respect, the average wage index is not a very good proxy of the income of low-income groups (say first and second quintiles) that are often employed in small-scale enterprises (fewer than fifty workers), in the informal sector (self-employment), and in traditional agriculture. See Solimano (1988a and 1988b).

17. Such political dummies would take values 0 in 1960–73 and 1990–92 (periods of democracy) and 1 in 1974–89 (the period of authoritarianism).

18. Blinder and Esaki (1978).

(5-2) $$\Sigma_i\, a_i = 1$$

(5-3) $$\Sigma_i\, b_i = \Sigma_i\, c_i = \Sigma_i d_i = \Sigma_i e_i = \Sigma_i f_i = 0$$

(5-4) $$\Sigma_i\, \varepsilon_i = 0,$$

for all t.

Given that all right-hand side variables are the same across equations, estimating each equation by OLS is equivalent to estimating the complete system by SUR (seemingly unrelated regressions).[19]

Table 5-5 presents the results of the estimation for the period 1960–91 using the (aggregate) rate of unemployment as the $Z(t)$ variable (model 1) for each of the five quintiles separately and then for the bottom 40 percent (first and second quintiles) and for the middle 40 percent (third and fourth quintiles). The estimates show that the unemployment rate has a negative coefficient in all quintiles except the fifth quintile (top 20 percent). The coefficient is significant at 95 percent confidence for the bottom 20 percent and 40 percent. This lends support to the hypothesis that aggregate unemployment hits more low-income groups and so has a regressive effect on income distribution.[20]

The minimum real wage (lagged one period) has a positive and significant effect (at 90 percent significance) on the share of low-income groups (first and second quintiles). It is interesting to note that a reduction in the minimum real wage redistributes income toward the top 20 percent; its coefficient is negative in the equation of the fifth quintile.

The inflation variable fails to be significant for low-income groups (except in the second quintile) and has a significantly negative effect on the income share of the fifth quintile (top 20 percent).[21] This variable has an insignificant effect on the bottom 40 percent. The education variable has no positive effect on the income share—though it may have on the income levels—of all quintiles, except the top 20 percent. This suggests that education levels above primary school in Chile have tended, on average, to benefit primarily high-income groups (though Chile is a country in which a high percentage of the population is educated). Finally, the post-1974 dummy is insignificant across all quintiles in the specification with unemployment rates. Using a capacity utilization variable (model 2; table 5-6) instead of the unemployment rate, the regression gives slightly better fits (higher R^2s) for all quintiles.[22] Table 5-6

19. See Rao and Mitra (1971).

20. This result also appears in Oyarzo (1990). His model explains the income share with aggregate unemployment, inflation, and a time trend.

21. Oyarzo (1990) also obtains a similar result for the inflation rate.

22. This variable was constructed using the estimates of potential GDP of Marfán (1992).

Table 5-5. Model 1: Income Distribution, 1960–91

Category	Dependent variables						
	Income share, 1st quintile	Income share, 2d quintile	Income share, bottom 40 percent	Income share, 3d quintile	Income share, 4th quintile	Income share, middle 40 percent	Income share, 5th quintile
Explanatory variables							
Constant (C)	2.31	6.83	9.14	11.29	18.10	29.40	61.45
	(2.73)	(6.73)	(5.10)	(9.25)	(11.50)	(11.20)	(15.80)
Unemployment rate (UNEMP)	−0.044[b]	−0.027	−0.071[b]	−0.022	−0.008	−0.031	0.10
	(−3.12)	(−1.58)	(−2.37)	(−1.098)	(−0.33)	(−0.71)	(1.57)
Real minimum wage, lagged (SALMIN-1)	0.007[c]	0.009[c]	0.017[c]	0.013[c]	0.027[b]	0.040[b]	−0.058[b]
	(1.64)	(1.66)	(1.72)	(1.86)	(3.06)	(2.70)	(−2.61)
Inflation rate (INF)	−0.0002	0.001[b]	0.0015	0.003[b]	0.002[b]	0.005[b]	−0.007[b]
	(−0.30)	(2.33)	(1.183)	(3.42)	(2.15)	(2.88)	(−2.49)
Education (EDUC)	0.006	−0.013	−0.007	−0.024	−0.025	−0.049	0.057
	(0.43)	(−0.81)	(−0.26)	(−1.25)	(−1.01)	(−1.19)	(0.92)
Dummy post 1974 (DUMMY)	0.137	−0.22	−0.087	−0.37	−0.795	−1.17	1.25
	(0.36)	(−0.49)	(−0.108)	(−0.67)	(−1.12)	(−0.98)	(0.714)
Statistics							
R^2	0.48	0.68	0.59	0.76	0.79	0.79	0.77
Number of observations	31	31	31	31	31	31	31
Durbin-Watson	1.85	2.23	2.06	2.33	2.04	2.15	2.16

SOURCE: Authors' calculations. The numbers in parentheses are *t*-statistics.
a. Significant at 95 percent.
b. Significant at 90 percent.

Table 5-6. Model 2: Income Distribution, 1960–91

Category	Dependent variables						
	Income share, 1st quintile	Income share, 2d quintile	Income share, bottom 40 percent	Income share, 3d quintile	Income share, 4th quintile	Income share, middle 40 percent	Income share, 5th quintile
Explanatory variables							
Constant (C)	-2.34	3.54	1.19	8.30	16.50	24.80	74.00
	(-1.70)	(2.08)	(0.40)	(3.99)	(6.02)	(5.48)	(11.34)
Unemployment rate (UNEMP)	5.71[a]	4.07[a]	9.77[a]	3.71[b]	2.02	5.74	-15.51[a]
	(3.90)	(2.24)	(3.12)	(1.68)	(0.69)	(1.19)	(-2.23)
Real minimum wage, lagged (SALMIN-1)	0.002	0.006	0.008	0.010	0.026[a]	0.036[a]	-0.045[a]
	(0.57)	(1.14)	(0.92)	(1.52)	(3.01)	(2.52)	(-2.16)
Inflation rate (INF)	0.001[a]	0.003[a]	0.004[a]	0.004[a]	0.003[a]	0.007[a]	-0.011[a]
	(2.06)	(3.25)	(2.83)	(3.76)	(2.11)	(3.01)	(-3.37)
Education (EDUC)	-0.009	-0.025	-0.035	-0.036	-0.032	-0.068	0.104
	(-0.71)	(-1.48)	(-1.186)	(-1.72)	(-1.18)	(-1.50)	(1.58)
Dummy post 1974 (DUMMY)	0.27	-0.048	0.22	-0.173	-0.62	-0.79	0.57
	(0.76)	(-0.11)	(0.29)	(-0.32)	(-0.88)	(-0.68)	(0.34)
Statistics							
R^2	0.54	0.71	0.64	0.77	0.79	0.80	0.79
Number of observations	31	31	31	31	31	31	31
Durbin-Watson	2.01	2.38	2.23	2.37	2.04	2.15	2.23

SOURCE: Authors' calculations. The numbers in parentheses are *t*-statistics.
a. Significant at 95 percent.
b. Significant at 90 percent.

shows that the variable of capacity utilization (ratio of current GDP to potential GDP) has a significantly positive effect on the income shares of the first, second, and third quintiles. This suggests that recessions (a decline in the rate of capacity utilization) affect the poor and middle-income groups more than they affect the rich. In this specification, the coefficient of the real minimum wage loses its significance for the share of low-income groups.

Inflation is significant but positive for low-income groups. This result might challenge conventional wisdom, though several observations are in order here. First, the relationship between inflation and income distribution may depend on the level of inflation—for example, the relationship might be nonlinear. To explore this possibility we estimated the model adding an additional variable, the rate of inflation above 40 percent a year. The coefficient of this high inflation variable turned negative for the first to the fourth quintiles but was statistically insignificant.

Second, there may be indirect effects of inflation on income distribution. In a full structural model, inflation and the rate of capacity utilization are related through aggregate supply and aggregate demand. In our sample, the coefficient of correlation between the two variables for the whole sample period (1960–91) is -0.62. This negative correlation may reflect the dominance of supply shocks in the period. In this case, we should expect a negative indirect effect of inflation on the shares of low-income groups through the capacity utilization variable.

Third, the inflation tax is a source of revenue for the government that could have financed subsidies to low-income families. In that case there would be a positive relationship between inflation and the share of the low quintiles.

Fourth, the period under consideration includes the Allende years, when a redistribution of income toward low-income groups coincided with an acceleration of inflation, and the Pinochet years, in which a deterioration in income distribution coincided with a period of disinflation. Then income shares of the first and second quintiles did move in the same direction as the inflation rate.

Fifth, both the first and the fifth quintiles correspond to groups whose income tends to be positively tied to the price level because it comes from self-employment in the informal sector or from profits and high-salary groups.

Summing up, the relationship between the level of inflation and the income share of low-income groups reflects several competing effects at work, and thus it need not be negative.

The third specification (model 3; table 5-7) includes the rate of growth of real GDP as an explanatory variable. This variable has a positive and significant coefficient for the bottom (first) quintile and the bottom 40 percent, a smaller but still positive coefficient for the third and fourth quintiles, and a negative coefficient for the fifth quintile. Table 5-7 suggests that growth of GDP, on average, was equalizing in Chile—that is, it narrowed down income differentials by benefiting low-income groups. Given that the rate of growth of GDP is (negatively) correlated with the rate of unemployment and (positively) associated with the rate of capacity utilization—variables that have a greater effect on the low quintiles—this result is in line with the findings of model 1 (table 5-5) and model 2 (table 5-6). The dummy variable that appeared as insignificant in the previous specifications with unemployment and capacity utilization becomes negative and significant for all quintiles except the fifth. This suggests that after 1974 a shift occurred in the Chilean economy that tilted income distribution in favor of the top 20 percent of the population, thereby offsetting the equalizing effect of growth, which on average was not very high either. In the other specifications, that regressive shift was largely captured through the increase in the average unemployment rate after 1974 or the lower average rates of capacity utilization observed in that period. That shift, however, is not captured by the rate of GDP growth.

Finally, table 5-8 reports the estimates of model 4 (specification with the rate of unemployment) for the period 1974–91, including the ratio of social expenditure to GDP (unfortunately a comparable series for that variable is not available, continuously, for the period 1960–73). The ratio of social expenditure to GDP has a positive and significant effect on all quintiles except the fifth. This suggests that social expenditure benefited both the relative income position of the middle class and the bottom 40 percent in the period 1974–91 vis-à-vis the top 20 percent.[23] In addition, the coefficients of the unemployment variable and the real minimum wage are higher, in absolute value, in this sample than in the sample for the whole period.

The estimates of the models may be used to explain actual changes in income shares in Chile during some key periods. Table 5-9 shows the actual changes in income shares of both the bottom 40 percent and the top 20 percent in the period 1974–89 compared with 1960–73 and 1990–92 compared with 1974–89, as explained by changes in the explanatory variables of model 1 (table 5-5; unemployment specification) and model 3 (table 5-7; growth specification). The decline of 1.4 percentage points for the bottom 40 percent in 1974–89 compared with 1960–73 is explained in model 1, mainly by the average increase in the rate of unemployment (−0.83 percentage point) and by the decline in the real minimum wage (−0.44 percentage point). The contribution of changes in inflation and education over the relevant periods is of secondary

23. It is worth considering that social expenditure includes public spending in health, housing, and subsidies to low-income groups besides education.

Table 5-7. Model 3: Regressions Income Distribution, 1961–91

				Dependent variables			
Category	Income share, 1st quintile	Income share, 2d quintile	Income share, bottom 40 percent	Income share, 3d quintile	Income share, 4th quintile	Income share, middle 40 percent	Income share, 5th quintile
Explanatory variables							
Constant (C)	1.766	6.511	8.278	11.05	18.03	29.08	62.63
	(1.92)	(6.21)	(4.37)	(8.84)	(11.34)	(10.91)	(15.56)
Unemployment rate (UNEMP)	0.036[a]	0.020	0.056[b]	0.015	0.003	0.018	−0.074
	(2.21)	(1.11)	(1.69)	(0.68)	(0.11)	(0.38)	(−1.05)
Real minimum wage, lagged (SALMIN-1)	0.0053	0.008	0.013	0.011[b]	0.027[a]	0.038[a]	−0.052[a]
	(1.05)	(1.39)	(1.28)	(1.68)	(3.06)	(2.61)	(−2.33)
Inflation rate (INF)	0.0004	0.002[a]	0.002[b]	0.003[a]	0.002[b]	0.005[a]	−0.008[a]
	(0.63)	(2.47)	(1.67)	(3.26)	(1.95)	(2.69)	(−2.57)
Education (EDUC)	0.015	−0.007	0.008	−0.019	−0.023	−0.043	0.035
	(1.08)	(−0.454)	(0.275)	(−1.014)	(−0.96)	(−1.04)	(0.56)
Dummy post 1974 (DUMMY)	−0.587[b]	−0.668[b]	−1.25[b]	−0.74[b]	−0.94[b]	−1.69[b]	2.947[a]
	(−1.90)	(−1.899)	(−1.97)	(−1.78)	(−1.76)	(−1.88)	(2.18)
Statistics							
R^2	0.39	0.67	0.55	0.75	0.78	0.79	0.76
Number of observations	31	31	31	31	31	31	31
Durbin–Watson	1.64	2.12	1.88	2.32	2.05	2.17	2.13

SOURCE: Authors' calculations. The numbers in parentheses are *t*-statistics.
a. Significant at 95 percent.
b. Significant at 90 percent.

Table 5-8. Model 4: Regressions Income Distribution, 1974-91

Category	Dependent variables						
	Income share, 1st quintile	Income share, 2d quintile	Income share, bottom 40 percent	Income share, 3d quintile	Income share, 4th quintile	Income share, middle 40 percent	Income share, 5th quintile
Explanatory variables							
Constant (*C*)	−3.560	−3.540	−7.10	−3.150	−1.410	−4.570	111.67
	(−1.82)	(−0.89)	(−1.23)	(−0.48)	(−0.16)	(−0.31)	(5.70)
Unemployment rate (*UNEMP*)	−0.101[a]	−0.113[a]	−0.214[a]	−0.137	−0.173[a]	−0.311[a]	0.525[a]
	(−6.02)	(−3.28)	(−4.32)	(−2.46)	(−2.37)	(−2.48)	(3.11)
Real minimum wage, lagged (*SALMIN*-1)	0.023[a]	0.037[a]	0.060[a]	0.050	0.077[a]	0.127[a]	−0.188[a]
	(3.97)	(3.19)	(3.56)	(2.62)	(3.11)	(2.98)	(−3.26)
Inflation rate (*INF*)	0.0017	0.007	0.008	0.011	0.014	0.026	−0.034[a]
	(1.34)	(2.55)	(2.22)	(2.649)	(2.59)	(2.69)	(−2.65)
Education (*EDUC*)	0.042[a]	0.055	0.098	0.071	0.094	0.165	−0.263
	(2.61)	(1.69)	(2.06)	(1.32)	(1.33)	(1.37)	(−1.62)
Dummy post 1974 (*DUMMY*)	0.766[a]	1.086[a]	1.852[a]	1.504[a]	2.112[a]	3.617[a]	−5.469[a]
	(3.71)	(2.59)	(3.055)	(2.20)	(2.36)	(2.36)	(−2.65)
Statistics							
R^2	0.88	0.58	0.69	0.57	0.63	0.62	0.595
Number of observations	17	17	17	17	17	17	17
Durbin-Watson	2.35	2.38	2.35	2.59	2.80	2.72	2.59

SOURCE: Authors' calculations. The numbers in parentheses are *t*-statistics.
a. Significant at 95 percent.

Table 5-9. Explaining Changes in Income Shares of Bottom 40 Percent and Top 20 Percent
Percent

Factors	Bottom 40 percent				Top 20 percent			
	1974–89 with respect to 1960–73		1990–92 with respect to 1974–89		1974–89 with respect to 1960–73		1990–92 with respect to 1974–89	
	Model 1	Model 3	Model 1	Model 3	Model 1	Model 3	Model 1	Model 3
Actual change in income share	−1.4	−1.4	1.0	1.0	4.7	4.7	−0.5	−0.5
Explained by change in:								
Unemployment rate	−0.83	...	0.75	...	1.20	...	−1.06	...
GDP growth	...	−0.006	...	0.14	...	0.007	...	−0.18
Real minimum wage	−0.44	−0.341	−0.024	−0.019	1.52	1.36	0.08	0.07
Inflation	−0.003	−0.003	−0.09	−0.12	0.01	0.014	0.42	0.48
Education	−0.113	0.129	−0.113	0.10	0.92	0.56	0.72	0.44
Dummy	−0.087	−1.25	−0.087	−1.25	−1.25	2.95	1.25	2.95
Residual	−0.07	−0.07	0.56	2.1	−0.2	−0.19	1.19	4.3

SOURCE: Authors' calculations.

importance. In contrast, the change in the rate of growth of GDP (which was of small magnitude in 1974–89 and 1960–73; see table 5-1) has little power to account for the decline in the share of the bottom 40 percent in the period 1974–89. The dummy variable accounts for most of the decline in the share of the bottom 40 percent between the two periods.

The increase of 4.7 percentage points in the share of the top 20 percent in the period 1974–89 is explained at around 60 percent (2.72) by the increase in unemployment and the decline in the real minimum wage, which squeezed the relative share of the bottom 40 percent (and also part of the income share of the middle 40 percent). The beneficiary of that redistributive shift was the top 20 percent. Once again, the model with the rate of growth of GDP did not give a strong accounting of the reason for the shift in income distribution toward the top 20 percent.[24]

Finally, the improvement in the income share of the bottom 40 percent by 1 percentage point during 1990–92 is explained to a large extent by the improvement in labor market performance as reflected by the decline in unemployment and the increase in minimum wages during this period.

Conclusions

After a relatively stable period of income distribution throughout the 1960s and a redistribution toward low-income groups during the Allende government, income distribution worsened for the lowest 40 percent during the Pinochet regime. The top 20 percent was the great beneficiary of the Pinochet government's redistribution policies, which discriminated against low-income groups and the middle class. The Aylwin administration restored most of the income share of the bottom 40 percent, but those in the top 20 percent still capture a greater percentage of national income than the historical average before 1973.

Our empirical analysis shows that an important factor in the deterioration of income distribution for the poor in Chile in the initial years of the market-oriented reform process is the weak performance of the labor market after 1974, which resulted in high and persistent unemployment and a squeeze on the real minimum wage and other wage categories. Inflation and education cannot account for the post-1974 deterioration in income distribution for low-income groups.

24. Other factors that probably explain the regressive shift in income distribution during the Pinochet years are the decline in public-sector wages in real terms that affected, mainly, the middle class and the assets redistributions associated with the privatization and the rescue operations of the main financial intermediaries after the crisis of 1982–83 (see Meller, 1991).

The share of national income held by the middle class (third and fourth quintiles) declined by nearly 3 percentage points, on average, during 1974–89. The reform of the public sector, through reduction of employment and a prolonged decline in public-sector wages, seems to account for an important part of the decline in the share of this group (see table 5-9). A post-1974 dummy is important in explaining the increase in the share of the top 20 percent; it suggests a sort of permanent regressive shift in income distribution against the middle class in Chile for the reforms.

The empirical analysis shows that recessions entailing high unemployment are socially regressive, concentrating a disproportionate burden of the adjustment on the poor, whose share of income declines.[25] Growth is rather weak as an equalizing force unless it is accompanied by a major effect on labor markets.[26] This might explain why trickle-down was so sluggish during 1976–81. Only when the Chilean economy approached full capacity, when real wages increased, and when unemployment dropped to a historical low in the early 1990s did income distribution start to improve.

This process justifies some moderate optimism about the prospects for income distribution in Chile in the next few years. If the economy keeps growing and investment grows even faster—as in the past two years—the labor market will remain tighter than in any period in the past thirty years, and distribution of income may well improve.

Further progress in the welfare of lower-income groups can be sought through social policies. Social programs demand a high share of government resources in Chile, and they are directed in a fairly large proportion toward the poorest 40 percent of the population. The scope for improving the quality of social services is greater today than in the past, as most of the pressures on social expenditure coming from entitlement and demographic pressures have eased during the late 1980s and early 1990s.

Further targeting, on the other hand, should be studied cautiously, to avoid the risk of a poverty trap in which incentives are weaker for self-empowerment to operate and pull the poor out of poverty by its own means after a critical threshold of basic needs are met. Also social policies should not alienate middle-income groups already affected by adverse distributive trends in the past.

The analysis indicates that the effects of inflation and income distribution are complex, subject to potential nonlinearities and several effects of opposite sign.

25. A drop in the rate of capacity utilization reduces relatively more the income share of low-income groups.

26. GDP growth appears as "equalizing" if its coefficient is greater for the lower quintiles.

We posed at the beginning the question to what extent a liberal policy regime (an open, market economy) is compatible with social equity. The experience of Chile indicates that income distribution deteriorated, on average, during the program of reforms. Important contributing factors were the macroeconomic crises and their sequels of high unemployment and depressed real wages. In fact, it is not clear that more structural reforms, such as trade liberalization and deregulation, are socially regressive. However, our conclusion from the Chilean experience is that market outcomes, which dominate in a liberalized economy, may generate regressive results through, for example, high and persistent unemployment and other market failures. In this case, social policy can correct regressive shifts in income distribution caused by market processes.

Finally a sort of Kuznets relationship between economic reform and income distribution seems to be at work. In this case income distribution would tend to worsen in the initial phase of a process of reform when real wages fall and unemployment increases, and then improve later on as medium-term growth takes off and labor market conditions improve. Of course, more empirical analysis of the evolution of income distribution in other reforming economies is needed to explore this relationship more fully.

Comment by Eliana Cardoso

This paper raises important questions, not only for Chile but for all Latin American economies. Does macroeconomics matter for distribution? What about inflation, minimum wage legislation, and economic reform? Insufficient observations, not surprisingly, produce unstable results and give ambiguous answers.

I differ with the authors on a few minor points. First, the authors are interested in the effect of different macroeconomic variables on distribution, but they, like most of us, also expect education to play an important role in explaining inequality in earnings. Nonetheless, the methodology the authors use is unusual. The well-established procedure is to enter years of schooling as an explanatory variable for income at a given point in time. But if one is trying to understand how the business cycle affects distribution, the cross-section observations of incomes in a single year obviously do not solve the authors' problem. The best solution is to decompose inequality. The purpose of the decomposition is to isolate the effect of changes associated with education from the effects of all other sources of change in inequality. One can divide the population into subgroups with the same level of education according to the number of completed years of schooling and, based on this division, compute a measure of the average income inequality within groups.[27] One could then measure the effect of the evolution of different macro variables on the inequality within groups with the same education level.[28]

My second point refers to the use of yearly data in a study of the effect of the variation of unemployment and inflation on the variation of inequality. The data for income distribution come from household surveys collected during a given month of the year. The unemployment rate and the real minimum wage at that point are not necessarily the same as the average annual unemployment rate and the real minimum wage. If one does believe that these variables affect distribution, then their measurement should coincide with the period for which the survey data were collected. I want to establish that the countries characterized by macroeconomic instability are those in which distribution can change dramatically with the business cycle and with inflation. This is not a minor point, as Brazilian experience illustrates: the Gini coefficients in figure 5-3 oscillate widely within the space of a few months in Brazil, during a period marked by macroeconomic instability. It is also curious that the authors use the minimum wage of the previous year to explain income shares of the current year.

Let me leave econometrics aside and turn my attention to more exciting issues. Recent social policies in Chile and their effect on poverty are controversial. The questions surround two issues. One is the interpretation of a range of social indicators. The other is how to understand the change in indicators: were they driven by macroeconomic developments or by social policies?

The democratic opposition to the military regime charged severe neglect on the social front. Figure 5-4 shows stylized Lorenz curves for 1969 and 1987. The Lorenz curve for 1987 lies completely outside the 1969 curve and indicates a clear and sharp increase in inequality. Moreover, between 1970 and

27. The average income inequality within groups, I, is defined as:

$$(5) \qquad I = \sum_{i=1}^{5} \alpha_i \, TW_i,$$

where TW_i is the inequality within subgroup i as measured by the Theil index; $\{\alpha_i\}$ is a system of weights, $\alpha_i \geq 0$ and $\Sigma \alpha_i = 1$. The measure of inequality within groups, I, can change either because the inequality within groups, $\{TW_i\}$, has changed or because the weights, $\{\alpha_i\}$, have changed. Because one does not want the measure I to be affected by changes in the distribution of the population by educational level, one can define the weight of each subgroup i as the average of the period shares in total population. Therefore, the weights would be constant, and only variations in $\{TW_i\}$ would affect the measure of inequality within groups, I.

28. Cardoso and others (1992) and Cardoso (1993) use this methodology to study the cyclical variation of earnings in Brazil between 1982 and 1991.

Figure 5-3. Gini Coefficient, Brazil, 1981–91[a]

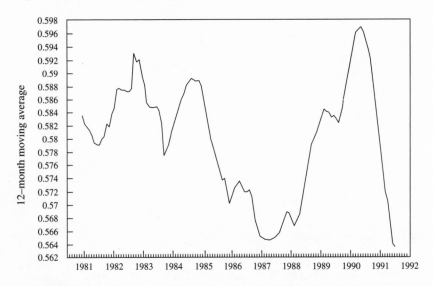

SOURCE: Cardoso (1993), p. 114.
a. Metropolitan areas average.

1987, the percentage of Chilean households in poverty more than doubled, from 6 percent to 13.5 percent (table 5-10).

Proponents of the military regime, in contrast, show evidence of improvement in living standards, measured by social indicators (see table 5-11). Reduction of infant mortality is extraordinary in comparison with other countries in Latin America, even if such achievement represents the continuation of a long-term trend (figure 5-5). The debate remains open.

Between 1974 and 1989, social policies targeted the poor, avoiding spillovers to the middle class. Moreover, the private sector was assigned an enhanced role in providing social services, and an effort was made to use market mechanisms in the distribution of services. Castañeda, a strong supporter of these reforms, provides a careful explanation of the decentralization measures undertaken in education, health, and housing.[29] Chile also privatized its national pension fund in 1981. Castañeda believes that overall the reforms were very successful; they were able to protect the poorest during a time of severe economic crisis. Castañeda claims that despite overall reductions in per capita social welfare expenditures, total spending for the poorest decile increased. He

29. Castañeda (1991).

Figure 5-4. Lorenz Curves, 1969 and 1987

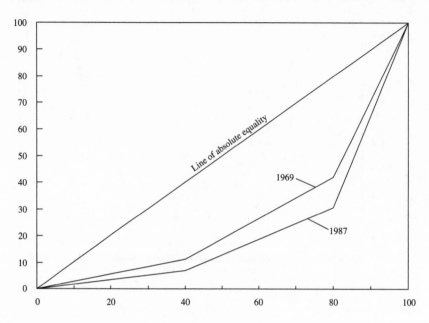

SOURCE: "Survey of Household Incomes," Department of Economics, University of Chile.

Table 5-10. Households in Poverty in Chile, 1970–87[a]
Percent

	1970	1987
Urban	3	13.0
Rural	11	15.7
Total	6	13.5

SOURCE: Economic Commission for Latin America (CEPAL) (1991).

a. The poverty line is approximately $1,000 (1987) a year for a household of four members. This poverty line corresponds to the cost of a food basket estimated at $21.71 a person a month in urban areas and $16.73 a person a month in rural areas.

uses broad social indicators (such as the decline in infant mortality) to support this view.

Estudios CIEPLAN and MIDEPLAN disagree with this interpretation.[30] They observe that government expenditures were cut. Even though the share of social expenditures in total expenditures increased significantly, the share of social expenditures in GDP barely remained constant (table 5-12). The increase of this share in the mid-1980s is due to changes in the pension system. With the reform of the pension fund, the government remained in charge of

30. Estudios CIEPLAN (1991) and MIDEPLAN (August 1991).

Table 5-11. Social Indicators, 1955–90

Year	Infant mortality[a]	Life expectancy[b]
1955–60	115	...
1960–65	106	58
1965–70	88	61
1970–75	67	64
1975–80	44	67
1980–85	24	71
1985–90	19	71

SOURCE: MIDEPLAN (1991).
a. Per 1,000 live births.
b. At birth, in years.

Figure 5-5. Infant Mortality in Chile, 1940–90[a]

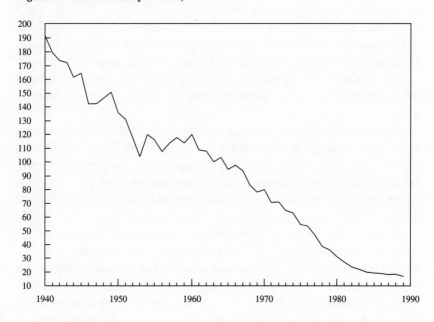

SOURCE: MIDEPLAN (1991).
a. Per 1,000 live births.

the retirees of the old system. Payments to retirees caused a fourfold increase of expenditures in this area, which was included in total social spending. This explains most of the increase in real social expenditures per capita during the 1980s after the severe cuts between 1974 and 1979.

Meller argues that the adjustment measures of the 1980s were regressive even though the government was successful in targeting social expenditures

5-12. Social Expenditures, Selected Years, 1955–90

Year	Percent of GDP	Percent of total government expenditures
1955	6.0	31.7
1960	8.6	39.6
1965	10.0	45.2
1970	10.5	42.5
1975	10.3	36.0
1980	10.3	37.1
1985	15.1	57.0
1990	11.7	65.2

Source: MIDEPLAN (1991).

toward the very poor.[31] The authorities provided generous subsidies to dollar debtors while reducing subsidies to the unemployed.

Graham states that in practice no decentralization occurred, that the efforts of the Pinochet regime to overcome the costs of the economic progress constituted the "dismantling of one of the most progressive and comprehensive social welfare systems in the continent."[32] A large number of beneficiaries of the pre-1973 social welfare system either had their benefits cut or lost them completely.

Poverty in Chile undoubtedly increased during the military regime because of the deep recessions of 1974 and 1983. In the early 1980s, as unemployment reached crisis proportions, the social programs were broadened to include large-scale emergency programs, such as the minimum employment program (PEM) and the occupational program for heads of households (POJH). These programs have been criticized for not giving the poor the potential to help themselves in the future, but they did reach a great number of people and did mobilize resources quickly. By 1989 all employment programs had been phased out, but until 1988 the economic recovery had not been strong enough to improve the lot of the low-income groups. Social expenditures became better targeted, and in this sense they became more efficient. But social programs remained too modest to counteract the effects of unemployment, which remained high until 1988. On assuming power in 1990, the new democratic government significantly increased the social effort.

The Gini coefficients in table 5-13 show that the trend in inequality in Chile is similar to the trend observed in most Latin American countries in the 1980s, with the exception of Colombia and Costa Rica. Nonreforming countries, such as Argentina and Guatemala, did even worse than Chile. Moreover, those broad

31. Meller (1991).
32. Graham (1991), p. 2.

Table 5-13. Gini Coefficients, Latin American Countries, Selected Periods, 1979–89

Country	1979–81	1987–89
Chile	0.52	0.53
Argentina	0.41	0.44
Brazil	0.59	0.60
Colombia	0.58	0.53
Costa Rica	0.48	0.42
Guatemala	0.48	0.59
Panama	0.49	0.56
Uruguay	0.44	0.45
Venezuela	0.43	0.44

SOURCE: Psacharopoulos, Lee, and Wood (1992).

trends hide dismal details. Studies for Argentina and Brazil have shown that during the 1980s inequality and poverty increased not because the poor became poorer, but because their numbers increased: the middle classes disappeared.[33] In most of Latin America today we see two groups, the very rich and the very poor. Yet this has not been fertile ground for social and political unrest, in part because the socialism debacle destroyed the 1950s utopia. But the growing opposition of the middle class to inequality and targeted programs may help explain the fall of Pinochet at the end of the decade. As politicians turn their attention to the middle class once again, will the very poor sink back into oblivion?

Comment by Carol Graham

The paper provides a very good and up-to-date description of income distribution and poverty trends in Chile and of the specific causes of the regressive distributive effects of the Pinochet regime's economic model, with a focus on the labor market and wage levels. It also notes positive trends in targeting social welfare expenditures to the poorest 40 percent of the population. The paper also emphasizes the critical role of social policy in addition to growth in correcting regressive distributional outcomes.

As the distributive effects of changing policies are clearly spelled out in the paper, I will focus my comments on an issue that is raised in the paper but is much less explicitly spelled out: social policy and its role in alleviating poverty. Specifically, I would also like to comment on the positive aspects as well as

33. See Morley and Alvarez (1991) and Ravallion and Datt (1991).

the limitations of the Pinochet regime's restructuring and targeting of Chile's social welfare system, particularly because the authors conclude by warning of the dangers of excessive targeting in Chile.

The Pinochet regime's concept of targeting social expenditure developed by Miguel Kast was in part ideological, based on a limited view of the government's role in providing social services. The government should provide services only to those who cannot meet their most basic needs, and the rest of society should rely on the private sector. After 1980 a variety of social sectors, such as health, education, and social security, were restructured along these lines, offering private care for those who could afford it and public care for those who could not. While social spending per capita during the Pinochet years did not reach the same level it had attained during the 1970s, it actually increased for the poorest deciles. This was in part due to the role of monetary subsidies. The economic crisis was so severe that the regime's emergency employment programs had to be kept in place for more than a decade, and at their height in 1983 they employed 13 percent of the nation's labor force.

The targeting of social welfare policies had divergent effects, both positive and negative. First and foremost, targeted social welfare expenditures and emergency employment programs were critical to protecting the welfare of the poorest sectors, many of whom had been previously marginalized from the social welfare system because of its bias toward formal and sector-specific employment. Indicators such as infant mortality not only continued to improve during the crisis years, but accelerated in their rate of decline. This is accentuated during the crisis of the 1980s by the record of Chile's neighbors, where the poorest sectors were affected regressively by both poor macroeconomic performance and regression if not total withdrawal of state services. Those countries clearly had no improvement in social welfare indicators, as did Chile. Some countries even experienced deteriorations.

Second, the military regime's effective targeting and restructuring of social welfare policy would not have been possible without the extensive preexisting social welfare system, which was among the most extensive on the continent, and without Chile's relatively efficient institutional structure. Unlike neighboring countries such as Brazil, Peru, and Venezuela, Chile's ministries functioned relatively efficiently. Therefore, in many cases the regime's policies only required reorienting existing programs, such as school meal and mother and child nutrition programs, rather than introducing new programs.

Third, while the poor in the lowest quintiles, who were previously marginalized from benefits, gained access, many at the margin in the middle deciles either lost access or were left with public systems of deteriorating quality as capital went to the newly created private systems. And considering the replicability of the experience, it is unlikely that a democratic regime could have reoriented benefits for the poorest at the expense of the middle sectors, who tend to have far more political weight. This is an additional issue to consider when trying to answer Patricio Meller's question of how to replicate the Chilean experience without Pinochet. It is no surprise that with the transition to democracy the Aylwin government is balancing its efforts between targeted programs for the poorest groups and increasing equity more generally.

The flaws of the military's targeting strategy stem more from the regime's approach than from the nature of its policies. It is difficult to argue that extending services to the poorest sectors and focusing the balance of social expenditure on the poorest 40 percent of society is a bad thing. What was negative is the top-down manner in which the regime did so. The regime stigmatized users of public services, such as recipients of free lunches in schools, and built special low-income housing complexes far away from city centers and with poor access to public transport. Subsidies were implemented in a manner that created dependency. Examples of this are the excessively low wages paid in the emergency employment programs—while wages in safety-net programs clearly should have been below the minimum, the one-half to one-quarter that was paid clearly was insufficient to raise anyone above the bare subsistence level, and only in the final few years were the programs complemented with training programs and linkages to the private sector. Another example was restricting the use of day-care facilities to mothers with malnourished children. The result was that mothers with well children who wanted to work had a difficult time finding public child care.

As the paper notes, the Aylwin government is maintaining the structural reforms in the social sector, with a new emphasis on government investment in improving the quality of public-sector services, to narrow the gap between public and private services and to increase social spending more generally. Indeed, the paper makes the point that democratization and the extension of resources to the reformed institutions were essential to legitimizing the reforms among important groups such as public-sector workers and unions. The regime has attempted to restore some benefits to low- and middle-income groups on the one hand and has created new programs for high-risk groups, such as unemployed youth, on the other hand. It has also put a new emphasis on encouraging the participation of the poor by implementing a demand-based social fund, the FOSIS. This change in approach is essential to making the shift from a strategy that leaves many people in a "poverty trap," as it is referred to in the paper, to one that emphasizes self-empowerment.

The current regime's social policies are to be commended and serve as an example for other countries. One caveat, however. In the same way that the military's targeting successes would not have been possible without the preexisting social welfare system, the Aylwin regime's broader poverty alleviation and social welfare policies would not be possible without the strong economy that it inherited or without safety nets to protect the poorest during the restructuring process. This stands in sharp contrast to the broad immiserization that occurred during the 1980s in neighboring countries like Peru and Brazil.

The paper ends by noting that while the recessions associated with liberal reforms have regressive distributive effects, it is not clear that structural reforms such as trade liberalization and deregulation do. It would certainly be useful to know more about the distributive effects of the structural reforms in the social welfare sectors, an aspect on which the authors might elaborate a bit more.

An additional point of emphasis, however, is that while the regressive distributive effects of the Chilean model are notable, Chile's position vis-à-vis neighboring countries is also important. The underlying economic conditions in Chile create the conditions for social policy to improve social equity, while in most neighboring countries, where heterodox or populist experiments have been pursued, the effects of economic collapse were even more regressive, and underlying economic conditions make the implementation of an adequate social welfare policy virtually impossible. In Peru, for example, from 1985 to 1990, while all sectors suffered a consumption drop of 53 percent, the poorest two deciles suffered drops of more than 60 percent. The only groups that were able to protect themselves from severe drops in household income were those with links to foreign transfer networks or those in which people were highly educated, those in the highest income deciles; more than 50 percent of the population has fallen below the poverty line. While optimally it is possible to implement liberal policies without such regressive distributive effects as occurred in Chile, avoiding such policies for fear of their distributive effects will result in far worse outcomes for the poor in the long run. And as we are attempting to draw lessons for other countries, we should give more attention to strategies that will reduce the regressive distributive costs on the one hand and will legitimate the concept of orthodox economic reform in the political arena on the other.

Appendix

The basic data for this paper come from various official sources.

INCOME DISTRIBUTION. The series used in this paper come from the University of Chile Employment and Income Surveys for Greater Santiago. These surveys have been carried out continuously on a quarterly basis since

Table 5A-1. Alternative Estimates of Income Distribution, Selected Years, 1969–91
Percent

| Group and year | University of Chile | INE | | CASEN National |
		EPF greater Santiago	ENE national	
Lower 40 percent				
1969	11.7	19.4	...	...
1978	9.7	14.5	14.1	...
1987	7.5	...	...	12.3
1988	8.9	12.6	11.8	...
1989	9.5	...	12.6	...
1990	9.0	...	13.3	13.6
1991	9.6	...	14.7	...
Middle 40 percent				
1969	31.3	36.2	...	...
1978	29.5	34.6	34.0	...
1987	24.0	...	...	31.2
1988	26.4	32.8	27.8	...
1989	27.7	...	27.9	...
1990	26.7	...	28.7	32.1
1991	28.2	...	30.6	...
Upper 20 percent				
1969	57.0	44.4	...	...
1978	60.8	50.9	51.9	...
1987	68.5	...	...	56.5
1988	64.7	54.6	60.4	...
1989	62.8	...	59.5	...
1990	64.3	...	58.0	54.3
1991	62.2	...	54.7	...

SOURCES: University of Chile, Employment Survey for Greater Santiago. Households Budget Survey, INE. Distribution of Spending. National Employment Survey, INE. CASEN Survey, MIDEPLAN.

1956; the June survey includes an earnings block. The collected data have been classified by quintiles of income earners (instead of households).

The University of Chile data on income distribution were subject to some controversy in the early 1980s, after the publication of Heskia's study, which produced the first annual series of income distribution over a relatively long period (up to 1978).[34] The basic criticism of these surveys was that they underestimated actual incomes, but they were also criticized on the grounds that they varied the degree of underestimation over income groups and time.[35] This criticism is valid, though it is also applicable to other income surveys.

Table 5A-1 compares the series used in this paper with data on income

34. Heskia (1979).
35. See Cortázar (1982), Riveros and Labbe (1986), and ECLA (1987).

distribution from three other sources for the years in which information is available. These alternative sources are: (1) household budget surveys for Santiago, carried out by the National Institute of Statistics (INE); (2) the Caracterización Socioeconómica Nacional (CASEN) national survey, commissioned by the Ministerio de Planificación Nacional (MIDEPLAN), and (3) INE's National Employment Survey, which once a year collects earnings data at a national level very much as the University of Chile does in Santiago. From this table it appears that although there are differences in the levels of income shares for the different groups in some years, the changes in the available periods are broadly consistent among the different sources (see table 5A-1).[36]

UNEMPLOYMENT. Unemployment rates are obtained from the University of Chile quarterly surveys for greater Santiago. The basic data have been adjusted to include workers enrolled in emergency employment programs as unemployed. This procedure was customarily used in the 1980s in Chile to keep closer track of the actual conditions of the labor market. Such an adjustment is also relevant for our analysis in this paper because these workers were paid a subsidy that used to be only a fraction of the national minimum wage.

CAPACITY UTILIZATION. Capacity utilization ratios are taken from Marfán (1992), updated for 1992. These ratios are calculated on national account figures, which also provide the figures for growth of GDP.

INFLATION AND REAL WAGES. Inflation rates are calculated as the annual rates of change in the Consumer Price Index, published by INE. This index has been reestimated for the high inflation periods of 1970–73 and 1970–78 by Yañez (1984) and Cortázar and Marshall (1980) with substantially different results. For 1970–78, therefore, annual inflation rates have been taken from these sources.

The adjusted CPI is also applied to deflate the annual change in money wages. The latter is obtained from the National Wages Index, published by INE.

EDUCATION. An indicator for education is also included in the equations estimated above. This is given by the share of adult population with complete basic education or more; the information is provided by employment surveys.

---

36. This difference may well arise from the fact that the alternative series are based on income data for households rather than for income earners, and poorer households tend to be larger than richer ones.

References

Alesina, A., and D. Rodrik. 1991. "Distributive Politics and Economic Growth." Working Paper 3668. Cambridge, Mass.: National Bureau of Economic Research (March).

Arellano, J. P. 1985. *Políticas Sociales y Desarrollo. Chile 1924–1984.* CIEPLAN (Corporación de Investigaciones Económicas para Latinoamerica). Santiago.

Bitar, S. 1979. *Transición, Socialismo y Democracia.* Mexico City: Siglo XXI.

Blinder, A., and H. Esaki. 1978. "Macroeconomic Activity and Income Distribution in the Postwar United States." *The Review of Economics and Statistics* 60 (November): 604–09.

Bourgingnon, F., J. de Melo, and A. Suwa. 1991. "Modeling the Effects of Adjustment Programs on Income Distribution." *World Development* 19 (11): 1527–44.

Cabezas, M. 1989. Revisión Metodológica y Estadística del Gasto Social en Chile 1970–86. *Notas Técnicas* 114. CIEPLAN.

Cardoso, E. 1993. "Cyclical Variations of Earnings Inequality in Brazil." *Revista de Economia Política* 13 (December).

Cardoso, E., and A. Helwege. 1992. *Latin America's Economy. Diversity, Trends, and Conflicts.* MIT Press.

Cardoso, E., R. Paes de Barros, and A. Urani. 1992. "Inflation and Unemployment as Determinants of Inequality in Brazil: The 1980s." Paper presented at the NBER-IDB Conference "Stabilization, Economic Reform and Growth," December 17–18, 1992.

Castañeda, T. 1990. *Para Combatir la Pobreza. Política Social y Descentralización en Chile durante los '80.* Santiago: Centro de Estudios Públicos.

Central Bank of Chile. 1990. *Indicadores Económico y Sociales, 1960–1989.* Santiago.

———. *Boletín Mensual.* Various issues.

Corbo, V. 1993. "Economic Reforms in Chile: An Overview." Paper presented at the annual meeting of the Eastern Economic Association. Washington, D. C., March 19, 1993.

Corbo, V., and A. Solimano. 1991. "Chile's Experience with Stabilization Revisited." In *Lessons of Economic Stabilization and Its Aftermath,* edited by M. Bruno and others, 57–91. MIT Press.

Cortázar, R. 1982. Desempleo, Pobreza y Distribución: Chile 1970–81. *Apuntes CIEPLAN* 34. Santiago: CIEPLAN.

Cortázar, R., and J. Marshall. 1980. "Indice de Precios al Consumidor en Chile: 1970–1978." *Colección Estudios CIEPLAN* 4 (Noviembre).

ECLA. 1987. Antecedentes Estadísticos de la Distribución del Ingreso. Chile, 1940–1982. *Serie Distribución del Ingreso,* 3. Santiago.

Economic Commission for Latin America (CEPAL). 1991. "Una Estimacion de la Magnitud de la Pobreza en Chile." *Coleccion Estudios CIEPLAN* 31 (March) 107–29.4.

Edwards, S., and A. Cox-Edwards. 1987. *Monetarism and Liberalization: The Chilean Experiment*. Ballinger.

Estudios CIEPLAN. 1991. "Estado, Politica Social y Equilibiro Macroeconomico." *Estudios CIEPLAN* Numero especial 31 (March).

Ffrench-Davis, R. 1973. *Políticas Económicas en Chile: 1952–1970*. CEPLAN. Ediciones Nueva Universidad.

Fontaine, J. A. 1989. "The Chilean Economy in the 1980s: Adjustment and Recovery." In *Debt, Adjustment and Recovery. Latin America's Prospects for Growth and Development*, edited by S. Edwards and F. Larraín, 208–33. Blackwell.

Galor, O., and J. Zeira 1993. "Income Distribution and Macroeconomics." *The Review of Economic Studies* 60 (January): 35–52.

Graham, C. 1991. "From Emergency Employment to Social Investment." Brookings.

Heskia, I. 1979. Distribución del Ingreso en el Gran Santiago. *Documento de Investigación* 41. Departamento de Economia, Universidad de Chile.

Jadresic, E. 1990. "Salarios en el Largo Plazo: Chile 1960–1989." *Colección Estudios CIEPLAN* 29 (Septiembre): 9–34.

Kaldor, N. 1956. "Alternative Theories of Distribution." *Review of Economic Studies* 23: 83–100.

Larraín, F., and P. Meller. 1991. "The Socialist-Populist Chilean Experience: 1970–1973." In *The Macroeconomics of Populism in Latin America,* edited by R. Dornbusch and S. Edwards, 175–222. National Bureau of Economic Resesarch. University of Chicago Press.

Larraín, F., and R. Vergara. 1992. "Distribución del Ingreso, Inversión y Crecimiento." *Cuadernos de Economia* 87 (August): 207–28.

Lindert, P., and J. Williamson. 1985. "Growth, Equality and History." *Explorations in Economic History* 22 (October): 341–77.

Marfán, M. 1992. "Reestimacién Del Crecimiento Potencial en Chile: Implicancias para el Crecimiento." *Cuadernos de Economia* 87 (August): 187–206.

Meller, P. 1990. "Chile." In *Latin American Adjustment: How Much Has Happaned?* edited by J. Williamson, 54–85. Institute of International Economics.

———. 1991. "Adjustment and Social Costs in Chile During the 1980s." Special Issue: Adjustment with Growth and Equity. *World Development* 19 (11): 1545–62.

MIDEPLAN (Ministerio de Planificacion y Cooperacion de Chile), Departamento de Planificación y Estudios Sociales. (1991). *Evolución de las Politicas Sociales en Chile, 1920–1991.* August.

———. 1992. *Población, Educación, Vivienda, Salud, Empleo y Pobreza.*

Morley, S., and C. Alvarez. 1991. "Recession and the Growth of Poverty in Argentina." InterAmerican Development Bank: Preliminary, November.

Mujica, P., and O. Larrañaga. 1992. "Políticas sociales y de distribucion del ingreso en Chile." *Documentos de Trabajo* 106. Washington, D.C.: InterAmerican Development Bank.

Oyarzo, C. 1990. "Ciclo Económico y Distribución Del Ingreso: Chile, 1960–90." *Serie de Investigación* 28. ILADES-Georgetown.

Peroti, R. 1990. "Political Equilibrium, Income Distribution and Growth." Massachusetts Institute of Technology, Department of Economics.

Person, T., and G. Tabellini. 1991. "Is Inequality Harmful for Growth? Theory and Evidence." Working Paper 3599. National Bureau of Economic Research. January.

Pollack, M., and A. Uthoff. 1986. "Pobreza y Mercado del Trabajo: Aspectos Conceptuales y Metodologia." *Documento de Trabajo.* Programa de Empleo para Latinoamerica y el Caribe (PREALC). Santiago.

Psacharopoulos, G., H. Lee, and W. Wood. 1992. "Poverty and Income Distribution in Latin America and the Caribbean: an Update." LATHR. The World Bank.

Raczynski, D., and P. Romaguera. 1992. "Chile: Poverty, Adjustment and Social Policies in the 1980s." Paper prepared for the conference "Confronting the Challenges of Poverty and Inequality in Latin America." The Brookings Institution and the Interamerican Dialogue, July 16–17.

Rao, C., and S. Mitra. 1971. *Generalized Inverse of Matrices.* John Wiley.

Ravallion, M., and G. Datt. 1991. *Growth and Redistribution Components of Changes in Poverty Measures.* LSMS Working Paper 83. Washington, D.C.: The World Bank.

Ricardo, D. 1817. *Principles of Political Economy and Taxation.* Penguin Books (1971).

Riveros, L., and F. J. Labbe. 1986. Situación Distributiva y el Impacto del Desempleo: un Análisis de Largo Plazo. *Revista Economia y Administracion.* Universidad de Chile.

Rodríguez, J. 1985. *La Distribución del Ingreso y el Gasto Social en Chile.* Santiago, ILADES.

Solimano, A. 1988a. "El Impacto Macroeconómico de los Salarios Mínimos en Chile." *Revista de Análisis Económico* 3 (June).

———. 1988b. "Política de Remuneraciones en Chile: Experiencia Pasada, Instrumentos y Opciones a Futuro." *Colección Estudios CIEPLAN* 25 (Diciembre): 159–90.

———. 1992. "Economic Growth and Income Distribution in Chile: Macroeconomic Trade-Offs Revisited." *Revista de Análisis Económico* 7 (November): 43–68.

———. 1993. "Growth, Equity and Stability: The Chilean Economy in the 1990s." In *The Rocky Road to Reform. Income Distribution, Economy Growth and Politics in the Third World,* edited by L. Taylor. MIT Press.

Taylor, L. 1991. *Income Distribution, Inflation and Growth: Lectures on Structuralist Macroeconomic Theory.* MIT Press.

Torche, A. 1987. "Distribuir el Ingreso Para satisfacer las necesidades Básicas." In *Desarrollo Económico en Democracia,* edited by F. Larraín, 167–214. Ediciones Universidad Católica de Chile.

Yañez, J. 1979. "Una Corrección al Indice de Precios al Consumidor durante el Período 1971–1973." Universidad de Chile, Departamento de Economia.

———. 1984. *El Gasto Público en los Sectores Sociales* 1970–1980. Determinacion y Análisis. Universidad de Chile, Facultad de Ciencias Economicas y Administrativas.

6 Social Security Reforms

Peter Diamond and
Salvador Valdés-Prieto

THE CHILEAN privatization of social security has received a great deal of attention from countries contemplating a similar reform and from international institutions that advise and lend to third world countries. This privatization has dramatically altered the politics of the provision of earnings-related retirement income, insulating benefits and assets from the political process. At the same time, the private providers of social security have been closely regulated; there has not been reliance on unregulated market forces. A second gain from privatization is its enormous contribution to the development of capital markets in Chile. Offsetting these gains is cost—privatized annuities have noticeably higher administrative costs than a more traditional defined benefit social security system.

Reformers elsewhere should take special note of three specific aspects of the reform as it has been carried out in Chile. One is that Chile chose to retire the pension debt associated with the preexisting pension system, which requires a large primary fiscal surplus for forty or more years. The surplus has been used to finance the pensions of the old pension system and the promises associated with the transition. This fiscal sacrifice has allowed the flow of payroll tax revenue into privatized mandatory savings accounts to be genuine new savings, available to finance investments by the private sector and some debt issues by the government. Such a fiscal effort can be avoided, but then there is no increase in national saving; there can even be a fall in national saving if high interest rates imply a larger pension after privatization and the government simply increases its debt to accommodate.

Second, in Chile the conversion of accumulated wealth to annuities occurs at one age only (retirement). This choice implies that there are missing insurance markets relative to earlier time frames and that workers are exposed to

The authors are grateful to many people for discussions about the history and workings of the social security reform; they are particularly grateful for the invaluable assistance of Juan Carlos Méndez.

257

the risk that their funds have low value just when they are used to purchase an annuity.

Third, the system relies on individual annuity purchase at retirement, which occurs with incomplete information about individual life expectancies. Thus there is a selection problem as individual life insurance companies try to attract the better risks. Since annuity purchase is not mandatory, there is the further selection problem of some individuals' choosing phased withdrawal rather than annuity purchase.

These issues raise three questions. One question is which countries will find the benefits of similar reforms outweighing the costs. A second question, for a country with an existing pay-as-you-go system that wishes to proceed with precisely the Chilean reform, is the timing of such a reform (relative to the fiscal soundness of the general budget). The third question is the possibility of alternative institutional designs that might have lower administrative costs and generate an annuities market that functioned better than in Chile.

Overview

Chile began its social insurance system in 1924. By the 1970s it had developed a pattern that is not uncommon in many countries; it had separate defined-benefit systems for different industries and occupations. These were not unified, so benefit structure and levels were different in different sectors. Having multiple bureaucracies was inefficient. The political determination of benefit levels had resulted in very high contribution rates, which (including health) were in the range of 51 to 59 percent in 1975. Government financial support to health and pensions plus contributions for government employees cost 20.5 percent of total government expenditure. A major problem was the political tendency to raise benefit promises when short-run financing was available because of the immaturity of different systems. There was little reason to think that the complementary problem of benefit levels' being vulnerable to short-run fiscal difficulties would not be serious. That is, pensions were excessively dependent on the state of public finance relative to a reasonable standard.

In the light of these problems, planning on social security reform was begun in the 1970s under the Pinochet government. After a significant fiscal surplus had been built up, implementation of the program began in 1981.

The heart of the reform is a privatized mandatory savings plan together with a market for indexed annuities that allows conversion of accumulations into retirement income streams. All covered or dependent workers must place 10 percent of their monthly earnings in a savings account with an approved (regulated) intermediary, an *Administradora de Fondos de Pensiones,* referred to as an AFP. Each AFP manages a single fund, with the complete return on the fund allocated to the individual accounts. The AFP also provides survivors and disability insurance. Workers must pay a commission charge to the AFP, in addition to the 10 percent, to finance insurance and to cover costs and profits. Workers are free to select any AFP and to switch.

On becoming eligible to receive pension benefits, a worker can choose between a sequence of phased withdrawals or a real annuity. In Chile, this second option involves a switch of financial intermediary, as the annuity must be purchased from an insurance company. The fact that Chile has a long history of using indexed debt has made it easy for the annuity option to be restricted to indexed annuities. In addition, there is a sizable guaranteed minimum pension. The minimum pension is not indexed, but it is adjusted by the government from time to time.

Four visible effects of the reform are important—effects on worker confidence in future provision of pensions, effects on capital accumulation and investment in the private economy, effects on the level of administrative costs associated with the provision of pensions, and effects on the government budget.

By the late 1970s, workers had little confidence that the social security institutions would provide them with significant pensions in the future. Thus there was limited opposition to the reform from workers. Having individual privatized accounts gave the workers some confidence that they would receive benefits in the future. When the new democratic government chose to keep the pension reform, this confidence increased.

The combination of a steady flow of contributions and very high real rates of return (an average of 14.5 percent from July, 1981, to July, 1992) has meant a large accumulation of funds invested in the Chilean economy. As of June, 1992, the total accumulations were U.S.$12.44 billion, equal to 35 percent of 1992 GDP; equity holdings by pension funds were 9.6 percent of the value of the Santiago Stock Exchange (with life insurance companies holding another 1 percent); and 61.1 percent of registered corporate bond issues outstanding were held by pension funds, with life insurance companies holding close to an additional 30 percent. This growth has been accompanied by an evolution of regulation of the markets in which these funds are invested, which has caused capital markets to function far better than they did before the reform. At present, close to 40 percent of the assets of pension funds are in public debt.

Administrative costs of the new system include both those of the AFPs that manage mandatory accumulation and those of the insurance companies that produce disability insurance, life insurance, and annuities. We present estimates that the average administrative charges per effective affiliate while active include: U.S.$51.6 a year for collection, account management, and fund management; U.S.$30.8 a year if the annuity option is chosen, not available if the phased withdrawal option is chosen; and U.S.$6.7 a year for disability and survivors insurance. The total is U.S.$89.1 a year (for 1991), which is 2.94 percent of average taxable earnings. The cost per person is not far from costs observed in other privately managed pension systems, such as defined-benefit private pensions in the United States, where reported average costs per active worker are U.S.$187.3 a year. Chilean costs compare unfavorably with reported administrative costs in the well-run unified government-managed systems for which there is appropriate information. For example, for services while working, the Employees' Provident Fund in Malaysia costs U.S.$10 a year on the same basis as the U.S.$51.6 a year reported above. As a share of covered earnings, the cost figures are 0.32 percent and 1.70 percent for Malaysia and Chile. We are not aware of a suitable figure for the United States for services while working, because the Internal Revenue Service (IRS) charges only a small sum to the Social Security Administration (SSA) for collection.[1] In the annuity portion of costs, the SSA of the United States, which appears to be the cheapest, produces them at a cost estimated at U.S.$15.1 a year on the same basis as the U.S.$30.6 a year reported above. As a share of covered earnings, these cost figures are 0.08 percent and 1.01 percent for the United States and Chile.

Chilean costs are close to those of very expensive government-managed systems. For example, the Zambia Provident Fund costs $U.S.46.8 a year, compared with the U.S.$51.6 a year for Chile. As a share of covered earnings, these cost figures are 2.34 percent for Zambia and 1.70 percent for Chile. At the same time, Chilean costs are close to those of privately run systems. For example, reported administrative costs per worker in occupational pension plans in the United States, of the defined-contribution variety, are U.S.$46.7 a year.

Mandatory savings flow into new individual accounts rather than directly to pay pensions owed by the existing, mature social insurance system. With the Chilean decision to unwind outstanding pension debt, there has been little issue of new (explicit) public debt to finance the benefits paid under the old system. This financing decision has implied an increase in fiscal saving. In addition, active workers who switched to the new system have received explicit government debt on account of past contributions. The decision to avoid debt financing has meant that the government chose to improve the primary fiscal balance by 3.5 to 4 percent of GDP each year in the 1980s. The level of fiscal saving is anticipated to remain at about this level for another decade, with a

---

1. We thank Olivia Mitchell and Annika Sunden for this information.

gradual decrease thereafter. Before the start of the pension reform, the government built a primary surplus of 5.5 percent of GDP with a view to avoiding financing the reform with debt. Thus most of the measured transition deficit—the deficit in the old pension system—was financed out of a primary surplus. In addition, an increase in the age of retirement under the old system decreased the implicit liabilities of the government. Over the business cycle, minor portions of this deficit were financed by the issue of debt and by the sale of shares in formerly state-owned utilities, with pension funds purchasing some of these shares.

Social Insurance and Voluntary Saving and Insurance

The centerpiece of attention of the Chilean social security reform is the privatized mandatory savings system. Two aspects of the context in which it operates seem important. One is the institutions used to redistribute income to the elderly poor (since the mandatory savings program itself has no intended redistribution). The second refers to private savings outside the mandatory system.

Chile has two programs that redistribute income explicitly toward the elderly, the Assistance Pension and the Minimum Pension. The Assistance Pension was created in 1961. Since 1975, a flat Assistance Pension has been paid to individuals over age sixty-five and to the disabled over age eighteen who meet two tests. The first test is that they do not receive another pension and the second is a needs test based on an interview at home with a social worker from their municipality (with a reinterview required after three years). In 1987, 9.8 percent of all residents above sixty-five years of age received this pension. Although in theory the assistance pension is lost if a worker receives one peso a month in pensions from the earnings-related pensions, it is not known whether this condition is enforced.

A survey conducted in 1987 found that 65 percent of recipients of the Assistance Pension were women, 82 percent of recipients had never contributed to any pension system, and the rest did not meet the minimum requirement regarding the number of years of contribution of the pension system to which they had contributed. According to the CASEN 87 survey, the benefits from the expenditure of this program were divided among income classes as follows: lowest decile, 35.2 percent; lowest quintile, 50.4 percent; lowest 40 percent, 73.8 percent.[2]

2. Haindl, Budinich, and Irarrázabal (1989, pp. 71, 75).

Table 6-1. The Assistance Pension in Chile, 1987–90

Year	Number of pensions paid[a]	New pensions issued[b]	Percent of salary[c]	Cost[d]
1987	318,715	19,039	16.4	76.1
1988	290,966	33,391	10.2	80.6
1989	292,321	40,198	7.7	81.6
1990	293,199	50,321	10.5	96.0

SOURCES: *Estadísticas Seguridad Social 1990*, pp. 39, 62–63; percent of average reported salary after contributions from Superintendencia de AFP, *Boletín Estadístico*, various numbers.

a. Monthly average.

b. Number issued each year.

c. Percent of average reported salary after contribution. The average reported salary after contributions is for those who contributed to the earnings-related pension system AFP in November of each year. For 1990 it was estimated on the basis of the methodology used by the Superintendency of AFP for September 1990, plus the wage index variation until November 1990. For the previous years, a preliminary average reported salary was obtained by dividing the flow of contribuitons to AFPs for November by the total number of contributors. Then this figure was adjusted so that the November 1989 number would equal the number produced by the Superintencency of AFP methodology minus the change in the wage index. Finally, the series was put on an after-contribution basis by subtracting the 10 percent contribution rate of the AFP system. Those with salaries at the average level reported here do not pay personal income taxes.

d. Millions of U.S.$.

The recent history of the assistance pension is summarized in table 6-1. The pension level is small relative to the average earnings of people covered by the mandatory savings program. The assistance pension is entirely financed from general revenue. The administrative cost of assessment is paid by the munici-palities, and the cost of delivery is paid by INP, a government agency. The amount of this pension is fixed in nominal terms without automatic adjustment for inflation. In 1987–89, the government pursued a policy of reducing the real value of the assistance pension by neglecting adjustments for inflation. In June 1990 the assistance pension was raised 82 percent in nominal terms.

A minimum pension has been paid since 1952 to those who have contrib-uted to the pension system. This practice was continued in the reform that created the new pension system. The minimum pension is considerably more generous than the assistance pension and cannot be claimed together with the assistance pension. For example, the level observed in June 1992 was 25.2 percent of the average taxable income after contributions for that month, con-siderably higher than the amounts shown in table 6-1.

Although minimum pensions exist both in the old pension system and in the new AFP system, we will consider only the latter. The minimum pension covers old age, disability, and survivorship. For old age, it is paid to men over sixty-five and to women over sixty if the pensioner has completed at least twenty years of contributions and does not receive other income that totals more than the minimum pension. The disabled are also eligible for the mini-mum pension provided they have ten years of contributions, two years of con-tributions out of the last five years, or, in the case of disability caused by an accident, continuous contributions up to the date of the accident.

Table 6-2. Projected Fiscal Cost of the Minimum Pension
Millions of dollars a year unless otherwise specified[a]

	Men	Women	Total	Percent of GDP[b]
Real rate of return of pension funds is 3.5 percent	39.2	103.7	142.9	0.45
Real rate of return of pension funds is 5.0 percent	4.9	33.8	38.8	0.12

SOURCE: Wagner (1991), table 25, demographic alternative EEF, which considers the fall in fertility and increase in life expectancy.
a. The exchange rate was 22.1 Unidades de Fomento per U.S. dollar for December 1991.
b. GDP for 1991 was U.S.$32 billion.

A minimum pension is also available for widows (but not widowers) and for surviving children under age eighteen. The rules for eligibility of the family are the same as those for eligibility for a disability pension. The means test also applies to these pensions. Up to now there has been no administrative implementation of this means test with regard to income sources different from mandatory earnings-related pensions. The minimum pension for a surviving widow is 60 percent of the standard amount, and for each child under eighteen, 15 percent of the standard amount.[3]

In the new system, the minimum pension is financed out of general revenue. The treasury pays for the minimum pension only after the funds in the individual account have been exhausted. Thus the financing is "pay-as-you-go" (PAYG), with no accumulation put aside for future obligations. The present value of outstanding commitments to pay minimum pensions is substantial. In the tradition of conventional pension systems, the commitment to pay the minimum pension is not contractual, but legislated. Because it is defined in nominal terms and adjustment for inflation requires specific legislation, the real value of the minimum pension varies.

Wagner (1991) has estimated the fiscal cost of the minimum pension in the AFP system using a microeconomic simulation model for a steady state in terms of demographics and maturity of the pension system, but with the same per capita capital stock and education levels present in the late 1980s.[4] In the simulation, the level of the minimum pension is set at the historical average for the last thirty-five years in real terms. The results of the simulation are shown in table 6-2. Since the minimum pension tops up the earnings-related pension, its cost is sensitive to the level of earnings-related pensions and so to the real rate of return.

The fiscal cost of the minimum pension is low in Chile, relative to that observed in Australia (4 percent of GDP) and New Zealand (8 percent of

3. Torche and Wagner (1992, p. 26).
4. Wagner (1991, pp. 35–91).

Table 6-3. Contributors and Pensions in the New System, 1987–90

	1987	1988	1989	1990
Contributors[a]	1,675,615	1,772,371	1,917,629	1,961,547
Old age, disability, and				
survivorship pensions[b]	45,915	56,366	69,435	87,061
Early pensions	0	772	2,824	5,790
Administrative personnel[c]	5,864	6,552	6,921	8,005

SOURCE: Habitat (1991, pp. 39, 175, and 333).

a. The number of contributors is the number for just the month of November. The number that contributes at least once a year is much larger.

b. The number of pensions refers to those paid in December of each year.

c. Personnel also corresponds to December.

GDP), which have minimum pensions at a similar level in relation to average wages but do not have an offset for benefits from a mandatory system.

Wagner's study also projects that the proportion of each cohort receiving the minimum pension will vary between 10.7 percent and 33.7 percent as the assumed real rate of return varies from 5 percent to 3.5 percent. The number of minimum pensions is large because the minimum pension is a high proportion of the average reported taxable income, and many workers spend only part of their careers in covered employment. The uncovered sector is large, and there is a high degree of movement between covered and uncovered sectors.

Mandatory savings through AFPs are meant to be "nonredistributive." We put nonredistributive in quotation marks because a mandatory system will typically affect the distribution of utilities in ways that depend on the regulations governing the mandatory system. Moreover, the distributional consequences of different ways of allocating administrative costs are controversial.

Contributions are mandatory only for dependent workers in the formal sector. Each month every covered worker is required to pay 10 percent of earnings into an individual account held by the AFP of the worker's choice. Table 6-3 reports the numbers of contributors in recent years. The AFP chosen for fund accumulation is also the source of disability and survivors insurance. The mandatory contribution includes a commission in addition to the 10 percent for retirement to cover this insurance and to provide income to the AFP. Thus the mandatory contribution rate to the new system is in the range of 13 to 14 percent. The maximum taxable income is indexed to the CPI and is close to U.S.$17,000 at current exchange rates, in annual terms. In June 1992 only 3.8 percent of dependent contributors earned more than the maximum taxable wage. The minimum taxable income is the minimum salary for one day of work.

Chilean statistics report both "affiliates"—those who have contributed at least once in their lifetime and "contributors"—those who contributed last month. The large volume of rotation in the Chilean labor market can be inferred from the following facts: (1) in June 1992, 40.5 percent of the affiliates did not contribute in the previous month; (2) as of June 1992, 74 percent of the affiliates registered at least one contribution in the previous twelve months, so on international definitions they were "covered"; and (3) as of June 1992, 77 to 80 percent of those gainfully employed had contributed to either the new or the old earnings-related government-sponsored pension system for at least one month out of the previous twelve.[5]

Affiliates are free to select any AFP and to switch at any time after a minimum of four months with an AFP. The AFPs provide fund management services, do the record-keeping of individual accounts, purchase a group insurance policy for invalidity and death, perform collection and payment functions, and answer questions and provide information about the workings of the system. The affiliates own the funds, with the resources of the AFP kept separate. By law, each AFP manages a single fund, with the complete return on the fund allocated to the individual accounts. The funds in the individual accounts cannot be given in guarantee for loans.

An individual becomes eligible to start receiving a pension by reaching age 65 for men, 60 for women, whether or not the individual continues to work. Early pensions are allowed if the accumulation is large enough relative to both the minimum pension and indexed earnings over the last ten years.

On becoming eligible to receive pension benefits, a worker is able to choose between a sequence of phased withdrawals (with maximum size limited by formula), the purchase of an annuity from an insurance company, or a combination of these two. In the phased withdrawal option, the worker bears longevity risk and investment risk, unless he falls to the minimum pension, where he bears inflation risk and budget risk. In the annuity option, the worker bears the risk of insolvency of the insurance company, which is regulated. The annuity market is restricted to indexed annuities.

While the accumulation has been going on since 1981, there were few pension benefits in the new system until 1988. The decision to force a switch of financial intermediary to obtain an annuity was motivated in part by the fact that the investment portfolio needed to back annuities is less heavy on equities than that of AFPs and in part by the desire to spread fund management among more entities.

Disability insurance promises to top up the individual account to a target level set by formula in order to allow purchase of an annuity in the private market. The worker retains the right to choose phased withdrawal.

---

5. Instituto Nacional de Estadísticas (1992) and Chamorro (1992).

Table 6-4. Contributors and Pensions in the Old System, 1987–90

Factors	1987	1988	1989	1990
Contributors	441,728	421,012	390,061	367,833
Pensions[a]	914,587	899,152	892,289	888,432
Administrative personnel	4,804	4,536	3,678	n.a.
Average taxable income old system/average taxable income new system (percent)[b]	71.0	62.1	58.7	54.7

SOURCES: *Estadísticas Seguridad Social 1990*, pp. 15, 39–46; and Ministry of Labor (1989, p. 41).
Note: Only civilians are reported.
a. The number of pensions is the total minus military, police, and assistance pensions.
b. The average taxable income in the new system is estimated as indicated in the section on the minimum pension.

The level of benefits depends on the contribution history of the worker. For covered workers whose first evaluation is issued while still working, the target total disability pension is 70 percent of the average of indexed taxable income over the previous ten years; the target partial disability pension is 50 percent of the same average.[6] For covered workers satisfying lesser conditions of attachment to work, including those unemployed, the total disability pension is 50 percent of the average taxable income and the partial disability pension is 35 percent of the average taxable income.

Since 1990 there have been two types of disability pensions. One is a pension for total disability, which applies when the loss of the ability to work is more than two-thirds. The second is a pension for partial disability, when the loss of the ability to work is between one-half and two-thirds. Determination of disability is made by regional medical boards. In addition, disability pensions are always evaluated twice, the second time three years after the disability was first claimed. The system does not require the invalid to retire from the labor market.

Widows, disabled widowers, dependent children, and in some cases parents of deceased workers are eligible for survivors pensions. A variety of rules determine the amount relative to the earnings of the deceased workers and the numbers of beneficiaries. Like the disability pension, this is a defined-benefit system with the formula set by the government, but operated by private providers and packaged with the other pension services.

In the 1981 reform, switching to the new system was voluntary for workers covered under the old system. Most of the younger workers chose to switch. Thus the old system was left with fewer contributors than pensioners. Table 6-4 shows the recent evolution of this system.

6. We do not report the rules for independent workers, who can participate in the system voluntarily.

In the old system there are no statistics on the number of pensioners, just on pensions, and a number of people hold two pensions.[7] The low average taxable income in the old system is explained in part by the relatively large number of independent workers in it. For example, in September 1990, 63,819 independent workers contributed to the old system, and 48,316 contributed to the new system.

The contribution rate in the old system varies by social security institution. In March 1989 it was 18.84 percent in the Servicio de Seguro Social (blue-collar workers) and 20.70 percent for the general plan in EMPART (white-collar workers). Benefits in the old system are calculated in the conventional way, considering an average income for the last three years before pensioning, the total number of years of contributions, and an accrual factor.

During the 1980s, the government merged the thirty civilian social security institutions into one, introduced computers and microfiches, and streamlined the payments and collections systems. It established for the first time a registry of employers who owed contributions, and in 1989 it set up a special collection procedure.

There is one exception to the unification of the old system: the military and the police continue to have separate social security institutions. Their pensions are calculated on the basis of the seniority rules that have been in force in these institutions for decades.

Although most employers are forced to collect contributions and pay them in full to the pension institutions, the Civil Service was an exception until very recently. Continuing a practice that originated in the 1950s, the government declares that close to half of a civil servant's compensation is wage and the rest is nontaxable for social security purposes. A civil servant who is in the old system still gets full benefits, with the treasury covering the shortfall. For the government, the effect of this trick is to delay contributions for an introductory period. For civil servants who have chosen the new system, however, this rule reduces reported taxable earnings and pension benefits without any guarantee that the government will pay late contributions—with interest—when they request a pension. A fiscal effort to redress this problem was started in 1992.

A separate program pays pensions in case of worker accidents and professional diseases (WAPD). The disability insurance provided by the AFPs pays all cases not covered by WAPD insurance, so sometimes life insurance companies litigate with WAPD providers. Recent statistics show that in the AFP system the first evaluation yielded 667 new partial invalids and 1,657 new total

7. Under some circumstances, a worker who switches industry could receive two pensions in the old system.

invalids a year. In contrast, the WAPD system issued 308 new partial disability pensions and 89 new total disability pensions a year.

Possible incentives for individual savings for retirement (and individual purchase of life insurance) include special tax treatment for savings, for voluntary life insurance purchase, and for contractual savings facilities. Chilean legislation provides three tax advantages for voluntary long-term savings and none for voluntary life insurance. These advantages are available only by saving through the AFP that is handling the worker's mandatory savings account.

Voluntary contributions added to the individual account held in an AFP are exempt from income tax at the time of contribution.[8] Interest earned in that account is free from tax as earned, but pensions received are treated as taxable income. Withdrawals from these amounts are limited to pensions, which may explain why few individuals use this option. Severance payments made by an employer can also be transferred into the worker's individual account under tax-exempt status.

Individuals may make voluntary contributions to the mandatory savings account and voluntary deposits into a second account at the same AFP holding the mandatory account. Funds in the second account may be withdrawn with a few days notice, provided the number of withdrawals in each calendar year is four or less. Currently these savings are not exempt from income taxes, but the interest earned on the accounts enjoys favorable tax treatment. If these funds are transferred into the old-age account, they enjoy the same exemption from income taxes as mandatory savings.

In contrast to this treatment of individual savings, no tax advantage is provided for pension funds developed by employers under rules devised by themselves, with or without the agreement of the unions. This implies that one of the main driving forces behind the growth of private pensions in the Organization for Economic Cooperation and Development (OECD) is absent in Chile.

A final aspect is that the system encourages contractual saving programs. Employers are mandated to collect contributions for contractual savings requested by the worker, provided they are arranged through an AFP. Out of the 1989 average of 108,730 deposits a month in the second (voluntary) account, 90.5 percent were part of contractual savings programs. The average of these monthly deposits was U.S.$12.8 a month in 1989.[9]

 HISTORY OF THE OLD SYSTEM BEFORE REFORM. To place our discussion of political economy in context, we briefly review the history of pensions in Chile. The oldest pension systems in Chile were established by the Spanish

8. This amount was limited to 10 percent of taxable income up to 1990 but is not limited now.
9. Ministry of Labor of Chile (1989, pp. 29–30).

crown. After independence, the army and navy established pensions for veterans in the 1820s. In the late nineteenth century, a pension system was established by the government for its own employees, on a pay-as-you-go basis. In the early twentieth century, the Railroad Company, fully owned by the state, created a separate pension system for its own employees, and close to thirty private companies followed its lead and the current international practice. Each employer designed a different pension regime.

In 1924, Congress legislated mandatory contributions by all private firms. It is ironic that both the creation of the old social insurance system and the reform of 1980 occurred under military rule. The new mandatory pension system allowed those firms that had preexisting plans to continue with them.

Different social security institutions (SSIs) were created for white-collar and blue-collar workers. They were designed to be fully funded, although investment in government debt was expected to be substantial. The rules were different for blue-collar and white-collar workers. Blue-collar workers would receive old-age pensions at age 55, 60, or 65 (men and women); white-collar workers would receive a pension after thirty-five years of work (general plan), regardless of age.

The contribution rate for pensions was low in the period 1924–52: 5 percent for blue-collar workers and 10 percent for white-collar workers. Total contributions rose from 1937 onward with the purpose of financing health care and, in the case of white-collar workers, severance payments also. Still, substantial surpluses accumulated and were invested in government bonds, apartment buildings, and a few haciendas. Investment performance was dismal. The environment for investors became adverse, as interest rate caps in the capital market after 1929 led to negative real interest rates in 1932 and again starting in 1939. The Great Depression, which had extreme consequences in Chile, led to a short bout of inflation in 1932, during which prices doubled and the real value of the government bond portfolio held by SSIs fell to half. Legislation establishing rent controls for dwellings eliminated another significant investment alternative for social security funds. Tariff policies that changed the internal terms of trade against the country and in favor of city factories made the investments in haciendas unprofitable, but SSIs were not allowed to hold equity in industrial firms. The result was that in the period 1947–52 investment income represented only 8.67 percent of total income for the civilian SSIs.

In the case of blue-collar workers, a substantial share of the cash surplus associated with the introduction of mandatory pensions, plus an extra 2 percent contribution introduced in 1937, was devoted to the establishment of free health services for members. In the case of white-collar workers, most of the

Table 6-5. Uses of Funds in Chilean SSIs in 1947–52
Percent of total expenditure

SSIs	Seguro obrero (blue-collar)	EMPART (white-collar)	Railroad workers	Bank employees
Pensions	8.3	18.2	29.8	29.9
Health services	75.9	3.1	7.5	8.4
Family allowances[a]	0	67.2	32.4	52.2
Other subsidies	0	3.8	0	0.7
Administrative costs	15.8	7.6	45.5	10.1

SOURCE: Wagner (1983, vol. 2, pp. 22–23).
a. The level of family allowances in EMPART was so large that it increased the income of covered employees by 21 percent on average. Ffrench-Davis (1973, p. 191).

surplus was transferred back to members in cash, in the form of large family allowances. Table 6-5 reports on the uses of funds.

By the end of the initial period, the total contribution rate for the blue-collar SSI was 7 percent to 9 percent, depending on the region of work, and the government contributed an additional 1.7 to 2.7 percent of taxable wage. The white-collar SSI was charging 23 percent of the taxable salary for pension purposes.

In 1952, a drastic reform to the pension system took place. Following a reform proposal first presented to Congress in 1941 by Salvador Allende and influenced by international trends inaugurated by the Beveridge Report in England, the existing pension system was unified and streamlined on a pay-as-you-go basis. This system operated for the next twenty-eight years. The first reform separated the health insurance system from the pension system. As the introductory surpluses had been used to establish a permanent expenditure program—free health care for blue-collar workers—and it became clear that if pensions were going to be paid a financial crunch was unavoidable, separation insulated the health system from future financial pressures.

These reforms required a massive increase in contribution rates, spread out over three years. By 1955 the total contribution rate for blue-collar workers was 15 percent, plus 5 percent of fiscal subsidy. In addition, in 1953 a new contribution was imposed on white-collar workers to finance new severance payments and family allowances. This added up to seventeen additional percentage points of wages. The tax on formal labor increased from 9 percent to 32 percent of taxable salary.

The second reform of 1952 established that blue-collar workers would get annuities as pensions starting at age 65 and calculated on the basis of a conventional benefit formula. It was defined as 100 percent of an average monthly salary, which in turn was the average of nominal salaries for the past five years, after adjusting for inflation the two earliest years. The result was a stochastic real pension, heavily dependent on the inflation rate during the past three years and the realized taxable salary over the past five years. Adjustments for subsequent inflation were legislated to occur only on January 1 of each year, if accumulated inflation since the last increase surpassed 15 percent. The large volatility of inflation in Chile resulted in significant variations in real pensions. This reform deprived blue-collar workers of the option to withdraw funds at ages 55 and 60 and reset the pension levels of many pensioners.

The law of 1952 established that at most 1.2 percent of contributions would be spent in administrative expenditure, without specifying what would happen in case this condition was not fulfilled. The actual figures in the 1960s and 1970s, excluding the cost of capital, were around 8 percent of contributions.

The third reform of 1952 changed the rules in the white-collar SSI. Pensions were established for 65 years of age, calculated as in the blue-collar SSI, but the option of a pension for thirty-five years of service was maintained, and most preferred it. Women had a younger pensioning age. One difference was that adjustments in pensions for subsequent inflation were legislated to occur when accumulated inflation since the last increase surpassed 10 percent. Another difference is that the inflation adjustment would be smaller for pensions above the minimum salary.

The 1952 reform failed to create political incentives that would make sure that all benefit increases were financed. This can be seen in the benefit increases after the reform. For example, in 1956 affiliates who did not meet the minimum requirement on contributions were allowed to "fill in" the missing contributions using the funds from a loan provided by the same SSI—and with no penalty for the delay in paying the contribution. The loan would carry a very low nominal interest rate.[10] In addition, new groups with full rights to benefits were added, even though they had not completed their contributions. These new expenditures were at first charged to the SSI, without any tax increase or explicit revenue source to finance them.

Rent-seeking behavior, coupled with the quest for a progressive image, led to substantial inequities. On the one hand, indexing of white-collar pensions above the minimum pension was below full past inflation. On the other hand, by the late 1970s, close to 40 percent of expenditure was taken by *perseguidora* pensions, which granted full indexation to the wage level to a few high-income workers.

No rules or organizations that would maximize the return and security of investments were provided to the two large SSIs. On the contrary, the legislature intervened in great detail, for example specifying how much money would

10. Wallich (1983, p. 61).

be directed to 25–30 year mortgage loans to affiliates and what interest rates would be charged. They paid a nominal interest rate of 5 percent and amortization rate of 2 percent a year, in a setting where average inflation was close to 20 percent. The result was that the two large government-controlled SSIs obtained a rate of return much lower than that of the older, privately managed SSIs. A calculation for the 1950–77 period shows that the real value of assets held increased by 804 percent for privately managed SSIs and only 57 percent for the large public SSIs.[11] The difference is assigned to the fact that privately managed SSIs were not encumbered by legislative mandates nor by the frequent use of their cash balances for monetary control.

Although the pension system fell far short of performing its insurance purpose adequately, this does not mean that its finances were out of control, because the level of benefits was quite low. The old Chilean system was close to overall cash equilibrium in 1976. In addition, it appears to have been close to maturity by 1977, with the ratio of contributors to pensioners stabilized at a number close to 2.0, typical of OECD pension systems in which the introductory period is over.

We conclude that the old system had a number of fundamental problems. The level of pensions was low, and close to 70 percent of pensions in 1979 were minimum pensions.[12]

The real value of pensions was highly variable over time—the standard deviation of the real value of minimum pensions was 29 percent of the mean for the years between 1955 and 1979.[13] In the absence of significant investment earnings, the contribution rates were high. In 1979 contribution rates for pensions alone were 22.95 percent in the blue-collar SSI and 24.91 percent in the white-collar SSI, and in 1976, total contributions ranged between 51 and 59 percent. Ignoring family allowances, the pension system was regressive. A full evaluation of the redistributive effect of all the traditional social security services including pensions, family allowances, and medical care is not available.

Some of the risk that the pension system posed to the fiscal balance had been limited by a constitutional reform in 1970, which restricted the right to initiate law in pension matters to the executive branch. The old system, however, contained no political incentives to prevent populist management by the executive, as in 1971, nor to manage efficiently the demographic transition that Chile is expected to have from 1990 to 2030.

11. Wallich (1983, p. 75).
12. Büchi (1993, p. 8), and Piñera (1991).
13. Wagner (1991, p. 60).

The 1980 Reform and the Transition

Reforms had been proposed for many years. In 1962 the Prat Commission issued a two-volume report proposing structural reforms to the pension system. In 1968 the Frei government proposed the establishment of a new funded pension system financed by additional contributions, with the funds centrally managed by a council of ministers. This proposal failed to obtain congressional approval because it would concentrate too much power in the executive branch.

In 1973, before the military coup, a group of economists circulated a diagnosis of what was wrong with the existing system and a proposal for reform contained in a larger report called the "brick." As this proposal was largely implemented, it is useful to register their diagnosis: excessive contribution rates, discrimination and injustice in benefits, and high administrative costs. They did not mention the low quality of insurance offered to the individual worker, the lack of political incentives to limit the fiscal cost of the system, nor the reduction of the stock of national savings that the introduction of the system had caused.

Key elements in their proposal included: separation of the income redistribution and insurance functions; the options of lump-sum withdrawal and annuity purchase; replacement of legislated rules by contractual rules in fund management; nonnationalized fund management organized along the lines of savings and loans associations, with investment of contributions in bonds and equities issued by the private sector; and full privatization of the selection of provider.

The first pension reform occurred during the period 1974–79, when steps were taken to prepare the ground for the reform outlined in the "brick." The most notable steps were:

—A program of fiscal tightening (shown in table 6-6) that started in 1977, as soon as the recovery from the recession of 1975 had taken hold and growth of GDP had resumed. Its main purpose was to finance the planned reform of social security. Government study groups had found in 1974 that a transition that avoided debt financing would create a substantial budget deficit, and a decision was made to build a budget surplus to finance it. The alternative— building the surplus simultaneously with a tax-financed reform—was considered fiscally risky.

This program implied efforts to reduce the growth rate of public consumption (wages plus purchases of goods and services) over a long period, and the boom in economic activity aided its political viability. The buildup of the surplus became very large only in 1979, as shown in table 6-6. It is possible that

Table 6-6. Fiscal Effort in Chile before the Reform, 1977–80
Percent of GDP, general government

Year	1977	1978	1979	1980
Tax revenue	26.6	25.5	25.7	26.3
Other revenue	12.1	7.7	6.8	6.6
Net income from capital	−0.5	−0.8	0.7	−0.3
Public consumption	15.9	14.7	12.1	11.9
Transfers to social security	7.0	6.9	7.0	7.1
Other transfers and other	8.4	3.6	4.4	4.7
Interest on the public debt	1.7	1.6	1.2	0.8
Public investment	4.2	3.5	3.2	2.6
Fiscal balance	0.9	2.2	5.2	5.5
GDP growth rate	9.9	8.2	8.3	7.8

SOURCE: Larraín (1991, pp. 97–98).

starting a fiscal saving program was feasible only because the Chile of 1979–80 was under military control, with the military accessible to radical proposals from its economists.

—Introduction of uniform indexing rules for all pensions. This was the most difficult reform politically because a large number of the *perseguidora* pensions with the best indexing rules were held by retired army and navy officers, and Chile had a military government. The agreement that led to this uniformity included some adjustment of the salaries of active officers.

—Introduction of uniform pensioning ages of 65 for men and 60 for women for civilian pensions. This eliminated the right to obtain a pension through years of service alone. The implied delay in retirement ages left the old system with a cash surplus after a short transition period.

The 1980 reform implemented the proposal in the brick. Privatization of provision was the most controversial element of the reforms. Substantial effort was devoted to limiting the risk of fraud. Pension funds (PFs) were defined as separate legal entities from fund management companies (AFPs), minimum diversification guidelines were incorporated in the law, and a strong new supervisory body was created. In the absence of a body of regulatory experience to serve as a guide, investment in equities and foreign investment were not allowed in the initial law. Investment in corporate bonds was limited to nonholding companies, defined in turn by the proportion of directly productive assets to total assets. Some unions and employer associations were goaded to start their own fund management companies, to ensure diversity.

In response to further political considerations and concern about the efficiency of existing banking supervision mechanisms, a February 1981 law prevented banks from becoming providers to the new pension system. A modernization of financial regulation started at this time, three years before the bank insolvency wave of 1983, with the introduction of prudential regulation to banking in 1980. An August 1981 law imposed a schedule of reduced bank loans to affiliated parties, and modern securities and companies laws were passed in the same year (they had been in preparation since 1978).[14] It is suggestive that the military began worrying about the solvency of banks only after the pension reform was approved and they realized that most of the funds would be invested in bank debt for the first years. Investment in equity was banned until 1985 because of fears of fraud in the local stock market.

Because individual choice of provider was not perceived to present difficulties, the law devoted little attention to it. For example, there was no attempt to offer a legal framework to potential trustee institutions that could help individual affiliates with their decisions. Groups of workers represented by trustees were implicitly discouraged by a regulation that prohibited discounts in commissions charged, even in the case of groups.

Civilian workers were left free to switch to the new system because constitutional protection of their property right to an entitlement in the old system prevented the government from forcing them to do so. Those working for the army, navy, air force, and police have not yet been allowed to switch.[15]

Those already pensioned continued receiving their pensions under the rules of the old system. For active workers, entitlements in the old system were acknowledged in a way consistent with the new, defined contribution approach. Those workers who in the previous five years had contributed for at least twelve months to a given SSI and switched to the new system were issued a recognition bond, which attempted to represent the contributions made under the old system. This bond would mature when the worker reached pensioning age and would earn 4 percent real interest between the date of switch and maturity.

The budget surplus built up in the previous years, plus the cash surplus projected for the old system, was expected to finance the transition deficit. The projected deficit did not include interest costs of new public debt issued to finance the transition because no such debt was planned. Contribution rates were reduced to close to 14 percent. Those that remained in the old system did not experience a cut in contribution rates. The response of the workers in the formal sector was a massive switch to the new system by those below age 45.

14. de la Cuadra and Valdés-Prieto (1993, p. 88).

15. Two explanations have been offered for their exclusion from the 1980 reform: that significant groups of officers feared fraud by private providers; and that the military were not prepared to overhaul their complex compensation system, which would be required if they switched to the new system.

The new pension system has been subject to many reforms that have not altered its basic structure. The three main areas of reform have been investment rules, the design of disability and survivors insurance, and the authorization of early pensioning.

In the investment area, notable reforms include the authorization of investment in domestic equities in 1985 and in foreign investment in March 1990. The Aylwin government postponed this last authorization until late 1992. More generally, the existence of growing pension funds, seeking additional investment opportunities, has been a powerful stimulus for the authorities to seek financial innovation. For example, further reforms are currently under discussion, including new regulations to reduce conflicts of interest between fund managers and affiliates.

Two reforms of disability and survivors insurance deserve mention. Initially, in the event of death or disability, the AFP guaranteed that the life insurance company it had hired would pay the real annuity defined by law. Starting in 1988, this insurance was divided in two parts. The insurance now pays a large lump sum to the individual account of those affiliates that suffer disability or death. Then the individual affiliate or survivor may purchase a real annuity.

In March 1990, coverage was extended to partial disability. In addition, rather than investigating disability once, all such pensions are granted for three years and then are reviewed. Some rules give incentives for rehabilitation of invalids, and others tend to discourage fraud.

Early pensioning was created in 1988. This reform waived the age requirement for those affiliates that could show that the funds they hold in their individual account are sufficient to purchase a real annuity or to start phased withdrawals at an adequate rate.

ASPECTS OF THE TRANSITION. Entry into the AFP market occurred in several waves. In May 1981, eleven AFPs started operations, and a twelfth followed at the end of the year. These included AFPs linked to business groups, one linked to an employers' association (Habitat), and two linked to unions or employees' associations (Magister, Cuprum). In this period suppliers made a massive effort to achieve scale and to increase their total market. The next wave started in 1986, with the appearance of the first AFP oriented to high-income workers, in this case an AFP organized by a labor union. The third wave of entry occurred in 1992, when five new AFPs started operations.

Exit of AFPs has not been traumatic. In 1983, with the deep recession that took unemployment close to 30 percent, commission income fell and AFPs suffered, some of them falling into insolvency. The pension funds did not suffer losses. Even more important, the business groups that owned some of the largest AFPs failed and were taken over by the government, even though their AFP affiliate continued operating successfully. Through both mechanisms a large number of AFPs were for sale or were liquidated. In the case of a couple that failed, the superintendency took charge of liquidation (as provided in the law), fused them, and auctioned the resulting AFP. It actually auctioned the access to affiliates enrolled in those AFPs, in the sense that no expenditure in salespeople was necessary to obtain their affiliation. In this way AFP Union was bought by American International Group (an insurance group). In the case of the AFPs whose owners were taken over, a Special Liquidation Commission auctioned controlling share packages. At this point, Bankers Trust and Aetna bought Provida and Santa María. In 1991 a French insurance company bought AFP Proteccion from the union of workers in Banco del Estado (a state-owned commercial bank). In January 1993 Bankers Trust sold its controlling package in Provida to a coalition of three local business groups of intermediate size. Banguardia, an AFP formed by a labor union, has been tightly controlled by the superintendency since 1990.

In the life insurance segment, a medium-sized company that sold real annuities went bankrupt in 1984. This was a result of large losses associated with the devaluation of August-September 1982 and high indebtedness with banks.[16] As prescribed in the law, pensioners absorbed the loss of 25 percent of the annuity value in excess of the minimum pension. Because actual losses were larger than this amount for many pensioners, the state guarantee will operate. The government will begin covering its loss when the existing funds are depleted, which had not happened until 1992. Apparently political pressures for a 100 percent guarantee were absent. It is surprising that only one life insurance company failed in a recession during which GDP fell 14.3 percent. After this experience solvency regulations on life insurance companies were tightened in 1987 and in 1989.

The annuities market also has exhibited a rapid supply response. In the four years between 1988 and 1992, close to fifteen providers entered this market, raising the total to nineteen. Solvency regulations also evolved rapidly, after initially requiring excessive cash investments from shareholders when an annuity was sold. A concept close to duration mismatch was introduced in 1989, and it significantly reduced the financial barriers to entry into this industry.

The start-up of the system was notable because of massive marketing campaigns, including TV advertisements and many salespeople, many of whom were subcontracted to marketing firms that were specially set up for this pur-

16. Frugone (1992, pp. 95–98).

pose. Many affiliates needed information to decide whether they would switch to the new system, and salespeople were available to influence them. (An alternative procedure would have been to force affiliates to decide first whether to switch or not, without allowing them to choose an AFP until six months after that decision was made.) The first selection of AFP was particularly difficult because there was no track record to distinguish among the AFPs.

In June 1982, two months after affiliates could switch into the new system, a regulation forced AFPs to hire directly all the salespeople they employed. In August 1982, the Registry of AFP Salespeople was created, and AFPs were restricted to hiring from the registry only. This registry allowed the superintendency to punish those found to deceive affiliates. In September 1983 personnel in branch offices became regulated, and AFPs were banned from sharing offices with others. Chilean AFPs are prohibited from entering into marketing agreements with other firms, including banks. The purpose is to ban joint marketing that may allow affiliates to receive services in addition to those specified in the law. However, this regulation was relaxed in January 1993 regarding the second savings account mentioned earlier.

The concern leading to this ban is natural since a primary reason for mandatory savings is a tendency of people to save too little. This suggests that many people would try to defeat the system by accepting gifts in exchange for a low rate of return on their savings.

A similar transition has occurred in the annuity markets since early pensions were authorized in 1988. This area has also experienced a proliferation of salespeople in the form of insurance brokers. Some brokers have charged commissions close to 4 percent of the accumulated balance in the individual account. But this area has not been strongly regulated up to now.

Workers who in the previous five years had contributed for at least twelve months to a given SSI and then switched to the new system were issued a "recognition bond," which was supposed to represent the contributions made under the old system. This bond would mature when the worker reached pensioning age and would earn 4 percent real interest between the date of switch and maturity.

The amount of this bond at the individual level was calculated on the basis of the average taxable income reported in the months for which contributions were paid, the number of months of contribution since affiliation to the old system, and actuarial factors that distinguished by sex and by age. It has been argued that substantial redistributions occurred with this procedure, some of which were regressive and others progressive.[17] Some of these redistributions

---

17. Arrau (1992, p. 61).

are those typically associated with the change from a conventional benefit formula that does not consider the timing of contributions and imposes a common actuarial factor. Others were due to the inability of SSIs to access personal records reliably.

Those who particularly lost out on the change from defined benefit to defined contribution were women (who have a longer life expectancy at retirement age) and those with steeper age-earnings profiles, presumably disproportionately concentrated among those with higher income. In addition, there were mistakes in the selection of actuarial factors for calculating the recognition bond.[18]

It is estimated that more than 10,000 affiliates switched to the new system even though it was financially costly for them. During the 1980s the authorities passed several laws allowing affiliates that had been in the old system to return to the old system. As other affiliates were not subject to a reduction in benefits to finance this increase, these redistributions were financed with general revenue.

Table 6-7 presents the fiscal effect of the reform with the actual experience up to 1987 and projections until 2015. The numbers exclude military and police SSIs, assistance pensions, and minimum pensions. The fiscal effect is defined as the deficit of the old system (contributions minus pension benefits) plus the value of the recognition bonds that come due in each year. The deficit in the old system is not entirely due to the transition, because substantial minimum pensions are included on the expenditure side, but they may be compensated by the slight surplus it reached after the increase in retirement ages for white-collar workers.

A major issue is the violence of the business cycle that Chile experienced in the 1980s, which led to a 14.3 percent drop of GDP in 1982 and stagnation until 1985, followed by a very fast recovery, including years when growth of GDP was 9.5 percent (1989) and 10 percent (1992). This is important because the fiscal effect of the transition is strongly procyclical. Thus table 6-7 presents data and projections relative to potential and to actual GDP. The transition deficit reached as much as 4.84 percent of actual GDP in 1987. This shows the role of the decision to build a budget surplus before the reform, as it started with a fiscal surplus of 5.5 percent of GDP in 1980.

On the other hand, if everybody had remained in the old system, the recession would have caused a substantial pension deficit because unemployment rates rose to 30 percent and real wages dropped in 1982. The budget crisis did result in a reduction in pensions in the old system, as a result of a freeze in the

18. Arrau (1992, pp. 51, 62).

Table 6-7. Fiscal Effect of the Transition, 1981–88, and Projections for Selected Years, 1990–2015

Year	Fiscal effect[a]			Percent of actual GDP	Percent of potential GDP[b]
	Old system	R bonds	Total		
1981	52,345	237	52,582	1.48	1.48
1982	124,162	3,345	127,507	4.19	3.46
1983	138,513	6,512	145,025	4.80	3.78
1984	146,520	7,903	154,423	4.80	3.88
1985	140,459	9,887	150,346	4.57	3.63
1986	150,809	14,106	164,915	4.74	3.83
1987	160,064	17,896	177,960	4.84	3.97
1988	163,392	19,436	182,828	4.73	3.92
		Projections			
1990	169,253	25,750	195,003	n.a.	3.87
1995	182,509	47,286	229,795	. . .	3.75
2000	175,158	63,841	238,999	. . .	3.20
2005	145,235	78,191	223,426	. . .	2.46
2010	108,633	73,461	182,094	. . .	1.65
2015	85,054	42,920	127,974	. . .	0.95

SOURCE: Ortúzar (1988, pp. 111, 124).
a. In millions of Chilean pesos of May 1988.
b. The last column was calculated for a constant GDP growth rate of 4 percent with 1981 as the base year. The prediction of a rapid reduction of the transition deficit by 2015 is currently under review because recognition bonds may cost more than projected here (Marcel and Arenas, 1991, p. 39). The projection in the last column can be checked with the numbers published by Marcel and Arenas (1991, p. 36). These figures indicate that the transition deficit was 3.5 percent of actual GDP in 1989. This is lower than our projection because we do not consider the positive effects of recovery on contributions to the old system. The conclusion is that the transition deficit can be expected to stay below 4 percent of GDP for the first fifteen years in a stable scenario and to fall subsequently. Not all of this is an addition to national saving because the initial effect on private saving was negative.

cost-of-living adjustment (COLA), but only in 1985, very late in the recession. Because of the reform, for those in the new system, the recession showed up as temporarily smaller contributions to the new individual accounts. Most affiliates have recovered contributions in the expansive phase of the business cycle. In contrast, the long-run effects of short-run adjustments in benefit formulas under conventional systems depend on the politics affecting the type of cut legislated and the type of adjustment (if any) once the fiscal crisis is over.

The incidence of financing a transition naturally depends on the sources of funds used to finance it. In the Chilean transition, a budget surplus close to 5.5 percent of GDP had been built up by 1980, and its purpose was to finance the transition. This meant that the primary balance did not have to move simultaneously with the reform. Although the authorities preferred to avoid issuing domestic debt, they did so in 1983, and they also issued recognition bonds.[19] At

19. Ortúzar (1988, p. 121).

times, the pension funds' holdings of government debt have increased. These increases should not be compared directly with the transition deficit, however, because the Chilean government also financed with domestic debt issues a cyclical deficit in 1982–87 and the accumulation of international reserves in the early 1990s. In 1985–89, the privatization of social security was synchronized with the privatization of other parts of the economy. Thus there was revenue from the sale of state assets, including state enterprises, part of whose shares were bought by pension funds. This was not a substantial amount. After the pensionable ages were raised to 65, the civilian SSIs themselves were expected to generate some cash surpluses from the delay in the payment of benefits under the old system.

Thus the four sources were general revenues (increased taxes or reduced expenditures), borrowing, sale of assets, and reducing benefits under the old system. Of general revenue financing, close to half was raised through a value added tax on consumption. As part of the diagnosis at the time was that total taxes on formal labor were excessive, a secondary purpose of the transition was to change the financing mix and the associated fiscal incidence.

A transition to a funded system (that is, not debt financed) represents an increase in taxes on current generations and an increase in capital (and so wages) of future generations. Thus on long-run considerations, the stock of savings must increase. In the short term there might have been a drop in consumption based on the same considerations.

However, the decision to reduce contribution rates in the new system immediately, from close to 22 percent to approximately 14 percent, had short-term macroeconomic implications in the opposite direction that appear to have been far more important in the short run. In fact, private consumption increased abnormally in 1981 as take-home wages increased extraordinarily. This short-term macroeconomic result could have been avoided by a gradual reduction of the contribution rate in the new system over a period of five years. More fundamentally, in light of the diagnosis that pensions in the old system were too low, contributions could have been reduced by less.

A critical element in the long-run funding of the social security system is the impact of this change on the rest of the government budget. Central is the question of whether the transition will be financed by tax or by debt. Although in Chile the maximum share of a pension fund's portfolio that may be invested in government securities is limited by law to 45 percent, the government could still achieve full debt financing by selling bonds to banks and companies that in turn issue securities to pension funds. That is why the critical issue for the long-term implications of this reform for the stock of savings is the effect it may have on the political incentives faced by subsequent finance ministers.

Table 6-8. Primary Fiscal Balance excluding All Pensions, 1980–91

Year	Percent of GDP	Year	Percent of GDP
1980	10.01	1986	8.25
1981	9.65	1987	10.01
1982	6.29	1988	12.45
1983	5.36	1989	11.39
1984	6.72	1990	10.18
1985	7.70	1991	9.58

SOURCE: Budget data for the general government published by Arrau (1992, table 7, p. 56) excluding the quasi-fiscal deficit of the Central Bank. All pension-related flows are excluded, including the defense and police SSIs, assistance pensions, and minimum pensions.

The reform appears to have important effects on political incentives because of the way in which budget accounting is done. As finance ministers dislike presenting budget deficits to public opinion, a pension reform like the Chilean one, which increases the reported deficit, may create political incentives to improve the budget balance. In the Chilean case, the democratic government installed in 1990 wanted to avoid populism, which required an austere public spending image. A shift to 100 percent debt financing of the transition would have looked definitely populist. The AFP industry, fearing nationalization, would have lobbied strongly against such a shift. Table 6-8 shows the fiscal balance up to 1991.

The reported budget surplus fell 4 to 5 percent of GDP between 1980 and 1991, so the government currently claims it has a balanced budget. The true story, shown by the primary surplus excluding pensions, which worsened during the recession of 1982–85, is that the general government returned to the same primary balance that was built over 1977–80 in preparation for the reform. Therefore, the Chilean reform locked in the primary surplus built in preparation for the reform. This may or may not be desirable, depending on the welfare value of this long-term fiscal saving program.

Another important transition has been the change in the incentive to raise pensions. Since 1981, legislated increases in pensions have been limited to the old system, to assistance pensions, and to minimum pensions. In the only exception, regarding the 1992 industrial conversion program for coal mines, the government proposed an early payment of the recognition bonds owed to targeted coal miners, but the amount was appropriately discounted, so it entailed no fiscal cost. Another interesting case arises from the election promise of the Aylwin government that early pensioning would be available under special conditions for workers in heavy and hazardous jobs (the ten-years-ahead pensions for copper miners found in the old system were abandoned in 1979).

Union leaders and politicians devoted substantial efforts to this issue, but they have not reached a consensus about the way to finance top-ups for the individual accounts of these workers—or even whether top-ups are needed, because a number of workers in these jobs earn above-average salaries.

Therefore, legislated redistribution has not been impossible but has required explicit evaluation of its fiscal cost. The need to use general revenue rather than implicit taxes on the balances of other affiliates has induced the government to be conservative, as in the case of coal miners. After the return of democracy in 1989, politicians and national union leaders adapted quite rapidly to this new setting, reorienting their attention to other policies, as pension policy ceased to be considered a specially rewarding area.

An important hypothesis is that during a tax-financed transition, those who remain in the old system are weakened politically because their pensions become a visible prime target for deficit reduction. This was not borne out in the Chilean case. During the early 1980s, the government did not follow the traditional practice of reducing real pensions when its budget worsened by merely avoiding a timely adjustment for past inflation. Only in 1985, after severe recession had reduced real wages substantially, was a COLA freeze applied to the earnings-related pensions paid by the old system. This can be compared with the timing of fiscal policy changes: general taxes were raised in April 1982 and public investment was reduced during 1982, early in the recession of 1982–85. This does not allow a rejection of the hypothesis, however, because it happened during a military government heavily influenced by economists.

The Pinochet government took advantage of the subsequent boom in economic activity to legislate a partial recovery of pensions paid in the old system. On the other hand, it allowed inflation to reduce assistance pensions substantially. The new democratic government that took office in 1990 continued taking advantage of the boom to legislate substantial increases in assistance and minimum pensions and a full recovery of pensions paid in the old system. It has recently upgraded the pensions paid by the old system to civil service employees.

Because pensions under the new system are paid by private companies, they have become largely insulated from the political process. The adaptation of affiliates to this change has been slow, because few believed in 1981 that pensions would stop being determined in the political arena. As experience has accumulated, a few affiliates have begun to make voluntary contributions to their individual accounts, suggesting that the perceived value of contributions has increased.

Economic Analysis of the New System

Individuals are free to select any approved AFP and to switch after at least four months in an AFP. An individual trying to select among AFPs, in addition to fund management, has to consider three services. The AFP provides both disability and survivors insurance. Government regulations leave little scope for differences among AFPs in this regard. A second service is the provision of information. AFPs do vary in the convenience of offices, the courtesy of staff, and the availability of explanations about the working of the system. This is particularly an issue in smaller towns distant from large cities. The third service is collection, payments, record-keeping of individual accounts, and mailing of account statements every four months.

Fund managers can compete in other ways, too. One is in the ability to select good investments—that is, to have stochastic dominance of returns of one fund over another. Not surprisingly, two studies of performance by the funds suggest that in the period 1986–90, no AFP was off the risk-return frontier that was available with the rules on portfolio limits.[20]

Another way managers can compete is to select a different point on the risk-return frontier. Legislated restrictions on portfolio structure limit the potential degree of difference among funds, although there are some differences. They may also compete by lowering their commissions (perhaps as a result of a strategy that generates low costs) and in the way that they divide the commission charge between a fixed part and a part proportional to wages.

Individuals will differ in their responses to these elements, just as they differ in the size of their funds relative to their current earnings, in the level of their earnings, and in their degree of risk aversion. For those with low funds relative to earnings, the commission charge is relatively more important compared with the rate of return on the funds. The division of the commission charge between fixed and proportional parts differentially selects across individuals of different wage levels. It also selects between people with different sensibilities about deductions from money going into the fund and out-of-pocket funds, since the fixed part of the commission is deducted from the fund, while the proportional part is paid out of pocket. One AFP makes use of the allowed option of charging a percentage of the fund for a worker who transfers an existing account into the AFP. (No such charge is allowed on exit from an AFP, nor is it allowed to charge a percentage of the fund that is being managed.)

To this description of the basis for choice for idealized demand behavior,

20. Walker (1991a, p. 29), and Zúñiga (1992, pp. 72–86).

Table 6-9. Total AFP Industry Costs over Time, Selected Years, 1982–91

Costs and contributors	1982	1983	1984	1986	1988	1990	1991
DI and SI costs[a]	n.a.	n.a.	n.a.	n.a.	32.80	30.14	24.23
Administrative costs[a]	17.18	16.88	18.66	18.79	23.88	30.55	33.51
Marketing costs[a]	8.55	5.46	5.45	5.00	7.30	9.37	11.58
Profit after tax[a]	−4.89	−0.46	0.58	4.91	6.07	15.45	17.31
Contributors in December for November[b]	0.91	1.05	1.14	1.49	1.77	1.96	2.49
Affiliates (December)[b]	1.44	1.62	1.93	2.59	3.18	3.74	4.11
Administrative cost/ contributor[c]	18.9	16.1	16.4	12.6	13.5	15.6	13.5
Administrative plus marketing cost/contributor[c]	28.3	21.3	21.1	16.0	17.6	20.4	18.1
DI and SI cost/contributor[c]	n.a.	n.a.	n.a.	n.a.	18.5	15.4	9.7
Profit/contributor[c]	−5.4	−0.4	0.5	3.3	3.4	7.9	6.9

SOURCES: Up to 1989, Habitat (1991, pp. 284–85). For 1990, Superintendencia de AFP (1990). For 1991, Superintendencia de AFP (1991b).
a. Billions of Chilean pesos of 1990.
b. Millions of persons.
c. Thousands of Chilean pesos of December 1990 per contributor.

we add two realistic features: inertia and the role of advertising and sales-people. With inertia, individuals who have made a previous choice may not be active in monitoring the alternatives and considering switching. They may prefer to direct their attention elsewhere. They may recognize that it is not easy to gather information and to evaluate alternative portfolio strategies in order to compare funds. They may be unfamiliar with the present-value calculations they need to compare a current commission with higher future benefits. Complementing this element is the role of advertising and salespeople. While some part of the role of salespeople is to overcome the inertia mentioned first, in practice, salespeople may be targeting individuals who are aware of the alternatives as well as those who are not.

Three dimensions of supplying AFP services need description. One is the structure of costs associated with providing insurance, providing information, and managing funds. Second is the selected structure of advertising, and commissions to attract and hold affiliates. Third is the potential for entry.

Table 6-9 shows the structure of costs (divided among insurance, administration, and sales) over time, along with numbers of contributors, numbers of affiliates, and profits.

Table 6-10 shows a cross section of scale, costs, commissions, and taxable earnings for the different AFPs. Some AFPs have a self-described strategy of keeping costs low. Others do not describe themselves in the same terms. From

Table 6-10. Cross Section of Costs, Scale, and Commissions for 1991

AFP[c]	Scale[a]		Costs per contributor[b]				Average taxable wage	Commissions	
	Affil- iates	Contri- butors	Adminis- trative[d]	Sales	Sales- people	Other workers		Percent of wage	Flat
Prov	1.198	0.782	11.41	4.07	786	1,863	88.7	2.50	230
S Ma	0.862	0.481	14.77	5.20	772	1,406	91.9	2.95	100
Hab	0.712	0.443	15.44	4.13	420	1,256	111.5	2.95	0
Unio	0.336	0.181	25.40	7.43	399	919	101.6	3.70	290
Sum	0.329	0.206	18.49	4.90	267	780	125.9	2.97	230
Inv	0.141	0.065	24.55	6.46	232	479	84.6	3.74	497
Con	0.140	0.063	16.38	5.46	290	440	59.8	3.48	230
Pla	0.100	0.046	17.04	10.00	276	396	85.6	3.70	280
Cup	0.098	0.080	17.76	14.60	265	445	235.6	2.99	0
ELib	0.083	0.052	23.81	8.50	155	328	110.5	3.40	178
Mag	0.065	0.046	24.24	7.11	114	318	87.0	3.40	220
Prot	0.038	0.033	30.06	18.73	122	285	203.9	3.27	0
Fut	0.007	0.007	38.86	11.0	36	74	226.0	3.24	0[e]

SOURCES: Superintendencia de AFP (1991–92) and (1991b).
a. Millions, December 1991.
b. Chilean pesos of December 1991.
c. Abbreviations for names of pension funds.
d. Note that administrative costs do not include sales costs or profits.
e. Futuro is the only AFP that charges an entry commission—1 percent of the outstanding balance in the individual account.

the table and the original sources, several conclusions are apparent. One is that there are significant costs associated with starting an AFP. This is revealed in the tendency for costs to fall in the early years of the system and after the entry of a new AFP. Some of the industry-wide decrease in costs presumably comes from learning by doing at the industry level. It is not clear that economies of scale go much beyond the level of 60,000 contributors. Although Provida appears to contradict this, it does not. Table 6-10 shows that in 1987–88, when Provida had the same scale that Santa María and Habitat have now, the average administrative cost of Provida was noticeably lower than those of Santa María and Habitat now. It is also clear that for the same scale, the differences in average costs are substantial. This is due in part to different clienteles. Because the commission rates are based on income, higher-income contributors pay more.

Entry by a new AFP requires approval by the government, although purchase of an existing AFP does not require such approval. In order to enter, a new firm must satisfy the minimum capital requirements, shown in table 6-11.

Without spelling out a specific model of equilibrium, we will refer to the outcomes that have occurred in this market as an equilibrium. In particular, it is

Table 6-11. Affiliates and Minimum Capital

Affiliates	Minimum capital[a]
<5,000	120,000
5,000–7,499	240,000
7,500–9,999	360,000
+ 10,000	480,000

SOURCE: Superintendencia de AFP (1991a).
a. Approximate U.S. dollars.

interesting to ask about differences in the distribution of earnings levels across different firms. Table 6-10 shows some data on differences in affiliate populations. There are two reasons to be interested in the patterns of affiliation in this market. First, they imply patterns of cross subsidization since both administrative costs and insurance costs are uniformly priced to affiliates. Second, one can consider what might happen to equilibrium if regulations were changed. This is a major issue because of the implications for income distribution of changes in allowed patterns.

A second issue is the pattern and level of charges made by AFPs. By law, firms are restricted in the pattern of charges that is allowed to uniform pricing, although they are free to select the levels. Table 6-10,which shows the patterns of charges in 1991, makes it clear that firms follow different strategies in the division of their charges between the two types of cost. The AFP pricing structure is regulated by law, which requires a single commission structure for all affiliates—they are not free to negotiate different commissions with different individuals or groups of individuals (such as the set of employees of a large firm). The latter condition is presumably relevant for the lack of interest in large firms in giving advice to their employees, in contrast with the widespread practice of giving advice on the selection of a health insurance company. In considering the implications of this restriction, one would like to know the separate effects of efficiencies of scale in administrative costs, efficiencies of scale in marketing, and simply market power. Those not in large groups would also be affected by group formation and commission negotiation.

Valdés-Prieto figures, on the basis of their financial statements, that AFPs in 1991 received a net commission income of 63.408 billion pesos, or 169.3 million dollars, for services excluding disability and survivorship insurance for the affiliates.[21] Dividing by 3.282 million effective affiliates (those covered—in other words, those that have contributed at least once in the last twelve months), we obtain an average annual cost of $51.6 per effective affiliate. This

21. Valdés-Prieto (1993b, p. 8).

is close to the costs in defined-contribution private pensions in the United States, but much larger than the costs in uniform government-managed conventional systems. Table 6-10 offers an additional breakdown, indicating the average marketing cost per contributor, the number of salespeople employed, the average nonmarketing administrative cost, and the number of other employees. The cost numbers seem to be roughly comparable to those one finds in the life insurance industry in advanced economies. For example, for the United States, approximately 14 percent of (stock) life insurance company income goes for operating expenses plus dividends to shareholders, with roughly one-third of this going for selling costs.[22] In the Chilean case, sales personnel seem to have increased in recent years.

The presence of a competitive market with individual choice is supposed to accomplish three goals. One is to encourage all firms to keep costs low and returns on the risk-return frontier. From this perspective the critical question is the balance between cost saving arising from competitive pressure and costs generated by marketing associated with many firms and individual choices. That is, this market resembles a monopolistic competitive market rather than a competitive market. The elasticities of demand relevant for the markup of price above marginal cost reflect both product differences and affiliates who are not very responsive to small price differences. With relatively easy entry, one would expect high costs as part of equilibrium.

The second goal is to have an array of alternative "products" in the market and to have a pattern of choices reflecting differences in preferences. It is not clear that there is much choice in the Chilean market, apart from the choice that is caused by regulations that make the portfolios of large AFPs different from those of small AFPs. Some of this lack of diversity comes from restrictions on fund portfolios. Some of it comes from the restriction that each AFP have only one fund. Some of it may come from the penalty imposed on an AFP if its fund shows a return that deviates too much from the ex-post average rate of return of all funds. In addition, it is not clear how much of the public has sufficient awareness and understanding of risk-return trade-offs to select reasonably. Therefore, the second goal does not appear to be important in Chile now.

The third goal is to insulate the pension accumulation process from political interventions. The privatization of provider choice seems to have yielded benefits in insulation from the political process, but to be costly in commission charges.

22. American Council of Life Insurance (1992, p. 76).

Disability and Survivors Insurance

Workers in the formal sector are forced to have insurance in the event of death or disability.[23] The insurance amount is a lump sum that is meant to supplement the balance in the individual accumulation account. The target balance is set by statute to finance a target pension equal to 70 percent of the average of CPI-adjusted taxable earnings over the previous ten years, with smaller legislated amounts for widows and dependent children.

In the accumulation of funds for retirement, the government specifies the fraction of earnings that must be saved, leaving the amount of retirement pension to be determined endogenously. In contrast, the government specifies the target disability and survivors pension that an individual must have and leaves the charge to be determined endogenously. In addition, these two insurance products are priced according to group principles, not individual principles. That is, the government requires that an AFP use the same commission structure for all affiliates. This contrasts particularly with the annuity market.

Thus this market does not allow pricing to reflect the amount to be received in the event of collecting insurance, but only an approximation of that amount. As the cost of providing these insurance amounts varies with the likelihood of death or disability, which varies in the population in a number of ways, it implies that AFPs will prefer some affiliates to others, leading to risk identification expenses.

The AFPs are required to purchase reinsurance from insurance companies. Frequently they engage in a risk sharing contract with insurers so that the (typically) excess of premium over benefits paid is partially returned to the AFP (not to the fund managed by the AFP, so that these return payments are part of the cost paid by the workers). In addition, the insurance companies typically reinsure the risk of unusually high claims in the London reinsurance market.

If the market for affiliates were a market where consumers were highly sensitive to price, there would be little scope for AFPs to convert higher premiums into income. With limited sensitivity, this is possible. This represents a profit opportunity that is no different from the profit from having commissions that exceed costs. In June 1992 the superintendency published a weighted average of the costs of these contracts of 1.06 percent of taxable wages. In contrast, Valdés-Prieto and Navarro estimate that from 1987 to 1990 the benefit rate was 0.84 percent of taxable earnings.[24] Taken literally, these numbers suggest a

23. Until 1987 individuals had the option of purchasing additional insurance from their AFP.
24. Valdés-Prieto and Navarro (1992).

charge of 0.22 percent of taxable earnings. This is divided up between the insurance company and the AFP—which receives back payments after claims have been settled. Multiplying by an average contribution of $25.0 a month, we get U.S.$6.7 a year for disability and survivors insurance. Taking the ratio of the charge to total cost, 0.22/1.06, we have an estimate of cost for premium of 21 percent. This is high compared with U. S. data on group insurance with which we are familiar.

From the risk-bearing perspective, one can ask who should bear the risk of aggregate disability and mortality in excess of that anticipated by the actuaries. A priori, there is neither gain nor loss associated with shifting this risk among large companies (insurance companies and AFPs), particularly those that are traded in the stock market. If it were desired to shift some of this risk to affiliates, there is probably no alternative to risk sharing with funds. No obvious case can be made, however, for allocating this risk to the affiliates rather than to the AFP itself or to the insurance companies.

A private market also creates the incentive to police claims of death and disability. In contrast to a government disability insurance system where the determination of disability is potentially disputed by the government, here it is disputed by insurance companies, with the government having the roles of organizing rules for disability determination and the framework for dispute resolution. It may be that this structure will avoid the fluctuations in standards of acceptability of a disability claim that have plagued some government systems such as that of the United States. In Chile, the superintendency has had a big role in standardizing medical evaluations of disability by regional medical boards and the central appeals board.

Annuity Market

Individuals accumulate their funds with an AFP until they (or their dependents if they die) are eligible to start receiving benefits. Eligibility can be achieved through disability (if it happens before pensioning) or through the death of a covered spouse, father, or other appropriate relative (if it happens before pensioning). Eligibility for a retirement pension is achieved by reaching the normal retirement age (65 for men, 60 for women). Eligibility for an early (also called anticipated) retirement pension is achieved at a younger age if a worker has accumulated an adequate fund, one such that the resulting pension is larger than both 50 percent of the individual's average taxable income during ten previous years, and 110 percent of the minimum pension. There is no age limit for an early pension. Thus the rules for early retirement are meant to assure both smoothing of apparent consumption by the retiree and protection of the government from claims for a minimum pension.

An eligible person is not required to start receiving a pension. The worker can choose between continuing to contribute and stopping contributions and starting a pension. When an eligible person requests a pension, the government requires a phased withdrawal if an annuity higher than the minimum pension is unaffordable, given the balance in the individual account. When an individual with sufficient funds requests a pension, there is a choice to be made. The individual can contract with an insurance company for a real annuity. This annuity need not begin right away, and it can have a guaranteed minimum number of payments. The government limits the structure of the allowable annuities, however, to protect spouses and children. Alternatively, the individual may choose a phased withdrawal of funds from the AFP. The maximum amount withdrawn is given by a formula. This option allows the individual to remove some money as a monthly benefit and to leave the remainder to accumulate with the AFP. The individual may change to an annuity at a later date.

Thus the annuity market involves two levels of competition. The first level is between AFPs that provide phased withdrawal and insurance companies that provide annuities. The second level of competition is between alternative AFPs to handle the phased withdrawal and between alternative insurance companies to provide an annuity. Both levels of competition are likely to be important in determining elasticities of demand, and so of markups.

In the first level of competition, the formula for programmed withdrawal is important. It sets the maximum amount that can be withdrawn each month. Every twelve months, the fixed real amount that will be withdrawn in each of the following twelve months is calculated. This amount is $P = F/UC$, where F is the current balance in the individual account and UC is the unit cost of an annuity pension. The unit cost UC is calculated from the official life table and a technical interest rate (TR), and it is essentially the reserve needed to finance an annuity that pays \$1 a month when investments yield TR. The return TR in turn is calculated according to a formula fixed by law. This formula specifies that for AFP i, TRi for year $t = 0.2*$ (average of past real returns of Fund i during the past five years) $+ 0.8*$ (average of implicit rate of return on all real annuities sold in calendar year $t-1$).

Programmed withdrawal offers no insurance for longevity risk. This can be seen in the fact that if the pensioner fails to die in a given period, the funds F are depleted faster than the fall in UC due to reduced life expectancy. Simulations show that a single male eighty years old who started withdrawals at age sixty-five would have a pension of less than 50 percent of the initial pension if the technical interest rate predicts actual returns correctly.[25] Since the phased withdrawal amount may fall below the minimum pension later on, such a person may end up collecting the minimum pension at that time. The technical interest rate formula has been criticized for being a backward-looking average that can differ significantly from current long-term market interest rates. This can give rise to either excessive or insufficient withdrawal compared with the performance of the funds.[26]

In the second level of competition, an individual with given demographic characteristics (including dependents covered by the annuity) and a given level of funds solicits bids from insurance companies. Insurance companies might differ in their creditworthiness, and so in the riskiness of their ability to pay the promised benefits. Insurance reserves are highly regulated to limit the extent of risk and, in any case, the government guarantees part of the annuity amount. One could imagine insurance companies differing in the quality of service to annuitants (such as promptness of payment), although we are not aware that this is an issue.

Otherwise insurance companies differ only in the monthly benefit promised (and perhaps in the array of different annuity contracts, including some with a minimum number of guaranteed payments). Since each individual is quoted an individual-specific price, the solicitation of bids is something that requires requests from each insurance company that a worker approaches (or the set of companies approached on his behalf by his broker). While one might expect this to be a market with a high degree of price competition, in practice the competition seems to rely heavily on sales effort, which must reflect prices noticeably in excess of other marginal costs. A regulation to require solicitation of at least three bids did not seem to help; alternative regulations are under study.

An industry of brokers has grown up to assist individuals in making their choices. Information on the numbers of brokers is shown in table 6-12. This information and other descriptions about brokers is taken from a thesis on this topic.[27] A problem with these numbers is that they include all brokers who participate in all branches of the insurance business, from casualty and liability to mandatory life. The growth in the number of brokers may be informative, however, since the growth in demand for retirement pensions is the primary change in this market. The market for brokers of real annuities is not concentrated. In 1990 the largest individual broker intermediated 4.51 percent of all

---

25. Díaz (1993, pp. 20–21).
26. Díaz and Valdés-Prieto (1992, pp. 27–38).
27. Frugone (1992, pp. 27–32).

Table 6-12. Number of Brokers, 1987–90

Activity	1987	1988	1989	1990
Brokers[a]				
Individuals	1,566	1,749	1,923	2,066
Societies	216	246	276	300
Gross inflow of new brokers to the registry				
Individuals	181	332	263	211
Societies	18	43	35	29
Gross outflow of brokers from the registry				
Individuals	101	149	89	72
Societies	4	13	5	5

SOURCE: Frugone (1992, tables 13–15, pp. 28, 30, 31).
a. December each year.

sales (in money terms), and the largest corporate broker intermediated 3.88 percent.

The existence of real annuities backed by private sector securities is peculiar to Chile. The extent of indexing is substantial. Table 6-13, for example, shows to what degree AFP portfolios are exposed to inflation surprises.

Insurance companies undertake two risks in issuing an individual annuity policy. One is the risk of interest rates different from those used in calculating the offered amount. This is an issue since no perfect hedging opportunities are currently available in Chile, although they are improving. In February 1993 the Central Bank changed its policy and stopped issuing only six-, eight- and ten-year (indexed) bonds. Now it issues a whole set of (indexed) bonds with maturities at four, eight, ten, fourteen, and twenty years. Over time, as the Central Bank turns over its domestic debt, the supply of long-term instruments will improve. The annual issue of real annuities, however, will treble in the next decade because of the maturation of the new pension system.

Second is the risk associated with life expectancy. It is useful to think of this risk in three parts. The first part is the risk associated with projecting a life table for the entire population. The steady but unpredictable improvement in mortality that has gone on for a long time makes this problem inherently risky. In the case of Chile, this risk is compounded by the absence of a life table giving the historic experience in detail. The second part is the adjustment of the life table that is appropriate for the set of people who select annuities rather than phased withdrawal. In addition, the life table needs to be adjusted to weight by accumulated funds rather than by lives. That is, insofar as mortality risk is correlated with income level (and so pension level), an unadjusted use of a single life table for all individuals will not be appropriate. The third part is the selection associated with the particular set of customers that an insurance

Table 6-13. Exposure of Chilean Pension Portfolios to Inflation Surprises, June 1992
Percent

Category	Share of portfolio
Total portfolio	100.00
Minus indexed bonds	
Government bonds	37.16
Long-term bonds issued by banks	14.43
Long-term bonds issued by firms	10.04
Net exposure	38.37
Minus equity	
Equity in firms	27.62
Other equity	0.40
Remaining exposure	10.35
Minus CPI-indexed bank CDs	n.a.
Final exposure	n.a.[a]

SOURCE: Authors' calculation from Superintendencia de AFP (1991–92), p. 163.
a. Probably less than 3 percent.

company attracts. This reflects both measurable elements that are correlated with mortality, such as region or past history of disability, and also individually unmeasurable factors that are still relevant in the aggregate as a result of the pattern of selling behavior of firms.

Brokers who advise on annuity selection are also regulated. Brokers must register and pass an examination. The extent to which they can use accumulated funds to pay for services up front, rather than paying only for the annuity, is also regulated. Since the insurance company converts the accumulated amount into an annuity, it is implicitly deducting any expense money, including the cost of sales personnel and payments to brokers, from the accumulated fund. Thus individuals are allowed to pay brokers out of their accumulation rather than out of pocket.

One way of measuring the extent to which these elements (and administrative costs) affect the equilibrium prices is by calculating the internal rate of return of annuities actually sold. Of course, such a calculation must be based on some life table. The government provides a life table and requires the insurance companies to report the average internal rate of return based on this life table. Since brokers and salespeople are paid out of the accumulation, these numbers reflect all the costs in converting from an accumulated amount to an annuity. Table 6-14 shows the rates of return that have been reported, two other interest rates in the Chilean economy, and a spread between the internal rate of return and the market rate on the closest hedging instrument. The average spread in the past eighteen months, after the last wave of entry, is 1.27 percent.

Table 6-14. Real Rates of Return on Fixed Annuities and Fixed-Income Bonds, 1987–91

Month	Annuities (A)	Bonds ESTX20 (B)[a]	ESTU12[b]	Spread B - A
1987:9	3.54	6.30	6.06	2.76
1987:12	4.01	5.97	5.50	1.96
1988:3	4.37	5.40	5.34	1.03
1988:6	4.14	5.75	5.58	1.61
1988:9	4.26	6.19	6.03	1.93
1988:12	3.76	6.61	6.37	2.85
1989:3	3.77	6.69	6.55	2.92
1989:6	3.48	7.16	7.07	3.48
1989:12	4.87	8.07	7.96	4.28
1990:3	5.27	8.83	9.20	3.56
1990:6	5.81	8.60	8.67	2.79
1990:9	5.67	7.07	7.63	1.40
1990:12	5.27	6.64	6.76	1.37
1991:3	5.05	6.35	5.93	1.30
1991:6	5.01	6.45	6.57	1.44
1991:9	5.09	5.89	5.97	0.80
1991:12	4.72	5.79	5.85	1.07

SOURCE: Díaz and Valdés-Prieto (1992).

a. The bond ESTX20, issued by the state-owned commercial bank, pays over twenty years equal amounts indexed to the CPI.

b. ESTU12 is issued by the same bank but pays over twelve years. Both are backed by the bank's guarantee and by a portfolio of mortgage loans. These are prices in the primary market.

As the life table is not checked to match the experience with those that choose annuities in Chile, and they may live longer than others, the expected spread may be smaller. On the other hand, the life table includes no adjustment for improving mortality.

These numbers can be compared with those in Friedman and Warshawsky, who compare the rates on twenty-year U. S. government bonds and on corporate bonds directly placed with insurance companies with the internal rates of return (IRRs) on nominal annuities based on using life tables (adjusted for projected mortality improvements) for the population purchasing annuities, as measured by actual company experience.[28] They report that for the period 1968–83, on average, the IRR on the mean policy from the ten largest insurance companies was 2.43 percent lower than the rate on government bonds.[29]

Now we turn to the charges levied on pensioners. At present, the AFPs do not charge for programmed withdrawal. This implies that active workers are

28. Friedman and Warshawsky (1990, pp. 135–54).

29. This gap varies from 0.80 percent in 1972 to 6.15 percent in 1981. The Chilean spread in the past eighteen months is considerably smaller, but still larger than it was in 1972 in the United States.

subsidizing retirees. Presumably this will change when there is a higher ratio of retirees to workers, or else the charge to workers will increase. Even after it is fully developed, the market for phased withdrawals will have significant differences from the market for annuities. Cost-based arguments and the difference in charges between mutual funds and annuities in the United States suggest that the charges in phased withdrawals could be smaller than in the annuity market. The two markets may have different degrees of competitive pressure, however, since one involves a single purchase while the other involves a continuing relationship, with the opportunity to change provider. We do not have evidence as to which of these will result in lower markups.

Drawing on the evidence that is available, we concentrate now on the cost of annuities. This charge can be estimated indirectly by the spread discussed above, which includes fees for the insurance broker and salespeople. As the duration of newly issued annuities is close to nine years and the average level of long-term real interest rates in Chile in the past two years has been close to 6.5 percent a year, the percentage reduction in pension benefits originating in the spread of 1.27 is 10.26 percent a year. To translate this into dollars, note that the average Chilean contributor reported an income of U.S.$325 a month in March 1992. As the contribution rate is 10 percent, and the flat commission is close to $0.34 a month, the average contributor adds to the account at the rate of $[0.10 \times 325 - 0.34] = \$32.16$ a month. As the average effective affiliate (the one that contributes at least once a year) contributes only 77.7 percent of the time, the average contribution from a life cycle perspective is only 25.0 dollars a month. Therefore, the dollar charge in the annuity option is 10.26 percent of $25.00, or U.S.$30.8 a year.

The published data report the total amount of commissions paid to brokers (independent) and to salaried salespeople. This does not include the salaries of salaried salespeople, only their commission income. These numbers are reported in table 6-15. The information Frugone gathered in interviews with brokers and marketing people in life insurance companies was that brokers received a commission of between 3.5 percent and 4 percent. During the first nine months of 1992, the average commission paid to intermediaries in annuities for old age, including early pensions, was 454,000 Chilean pesos, or U.S.$1,200, which is close to 4 percent of the average premium.[30] If 3.5 percent were a reasonable estimate, then 3.5/10.26 = 34 percent of the total charge would go to brokers and 66 percent to insurance companies.

As the Chilean annuities market has not settled into a final form, it seems important to call attention to two problems that have appeared in similar mar-

30. Superintendencia de Valores y Seguros (1992b, p. 9).

Table 6-15. Commissions to Annuity Brokers in Chile, 1987–91
Billion pesos of December of each year unless otherwise specified

Category	1987	1988	1989	1990	1991
Premium income					
Age and early pensions	8.3	14.0	27.1	62.8	133.4
Disability	. . .	2.6	10.7	14.8	6.8
Survivorship	. . .	1.4	5.0	13.7	10.5
Total	8.3	18.1	42.7	91.3	150.6
Commissions to intermediaries					
Total	0.21	0.42	0.67	2.67	5.12
Commissions/premiums[a]	2.47	2.32	1.56	2.93	3.40

SOURCE: Superintendencia de Valores y Seguros (1992, pp. 88–90).
a. Percent.

kets. One is adverse selection, which in this case can operate because many workers are free to choose between programmed withdrawal and annuities. The second is excessive research on risk identification, which in this case means that companies may spend substantial resources in building life tables based on health exams and family history and then seek those who have the most favorable traits. These problems may emerge in Chile in the future, and they may result in charges' rising above the current levels.

Redistribution within a Generation

The most visible element of redistribution in the Chilean pension plan is the provision of minimum pensions financed by general revenue. In considering this system, one should remember that general revenue finances the difference between the pension available from the mandatory accumulation with an AFP and the level of the minimum. This appears to be an implicit 100 percent tax on benefits. Since there is little or no checking on incomes outside the AFP system, however, the disincentive refers to savings within the system, not a disincentive to any savings.

The minimum pension itself may not play a significant role in disincentives since mandatory savings for workers with high discount rates are largely a tax anyway. For example, for workers with a personal discount rate at least as high as that observed in the mass consumer credit market, which is higher than the interest rate earned by pension funds, the net present value of affiliation is strongly negative, as shown in simulations.[31] This implies that a labor market distortion is present in any mandatory pension system, even if the minimum

31. Wagner (1991, p. 74).

pension does not exist. If these workers are dominant, the minimum pension is a method to help the elderly poor at minimum fiscal cost.[32]

Distributional issues also arise in the treatment of the costs of running the retirement system. That is, the allocation of administrative charges in excess of marginal costs is a form of redistribution. There are two aspects of this. One is the allocation of fixed costs along with marginal costs. The other is different AFP structure, designed to appeal to different clienteles. Insofar as this is a mandatory system, redistributions can occur within the system by choice of cost allocations or by direct redistribution of contributions.[33]

In the Chilean case, the most visible cost allocation is given by the equilibrium levels of the fixed and earnings-varying commissions, which are below and above, respectively, the fixed and earnings-varying costs. This implies that high earners are overcharged, while low earners are subsidized. In addition some of the costs are common. Such redistributions do have efficiency effects, but these effects must be evaluated in the context of the other government-imposed incentives. In particular, mandatory savings are a tax on labor for those valuing pensions below their present discounted value.

Such redistributions (together with general pricing in excess of marginal costs) create incentives for individual AFPs to spend on salespeople oriented to earners who have charges in excess of marginal costs. This transforms part of the redistribution into costs. In addition, there is an incentive to create new AFPs to serve just high earners, and entry in this segment can proceed even if economies of scale are far from being fully used. This also dissipates part of the rent into costs.

Labor Market

In evaluating the effect of this system on the labor market, we consider only workers earning enough to make the minimum pension irrelevant. The worker's earnings in the covered sector are taxed at the tax rate plus the commission charge less the perceived value of the future (and current insurance) benefits. It would be difficult to figure out how much of the tax plus charge is offset by the perceived benefits for different workers. Naturally the offset is based on the expected value of the future income to be received, adjusted by risk. For a

32. It seems useful to mention one implication of the minimum pension for a rational worker who anticipates receipt of a minimum pension in all years. For such a worker, the choice of AFP should be based solely on the goal of minimizing out-of-pocket expenses. These workers would not care how high the other charges were.

33. For example, Boskin, Kotlikoff, and Shoven (1988, pp. 179–206) consider a mandatory savings system that includes a redistributional element.

worker who would have saved the same amount anyway and who has the ability to rearrange his voluntary wealth to achieve the desired overall portfolio mix, the difference in the costs of carrying out the savings through AFPs or privately is an adequate measure of the implicit tax.

The issue becomes more complicated once one recognizes workers who do not value future income highly enough to be saving at least at this level. If we model myopic individuals as having very high discount rates, then current taxes that will be returned with 4 percent or 6 percent returns in the distant future are worth very little when the discount rate is at the levels of consumer interest rates, for example, 20 percent. Without trying to select a particular set of discount rates, we simply refer to the net tax and discuss its effects.

The presence of a net tax affects the choice of hours, the choice of whether to be in the labor force, and the choice of covered or uncovered sectors. Presumably, the tighter tie between benefits and taxes of a contribution-based system than is common with benefit-based systems and the greater transparency of the contribution-based system imply a lower net tax and so less of a distortion. However, if segments of consumers are high discounters, this may make little difference. We are not aware of any empirical work contrasting different systems and suspect that such work would be difficult to do. In any case, it may be illustrative that in Chile, independent contributors do not favor the new over the old system, as seen by the numbers that choose each.

Since individuals can claim benefits once they are eligible based on age or adequate accumulation only, there is no linkage between pensioning and retirement. This contrasts with systems that condition benefits on low or zero earnings, which generate substitution effects on labor supply. On the other hand, the lack of such linkages implies a lack of insurance for short working life, a form of insurance that measures actual earnings at retirement age. It is unclear how important this additional element of insurance would be since the minimum pension provides some insurance of this kind and already provides a disincentive to work through the lack of return on further accumulations. More generally, the ability to use an earnings test and the ability to redistribute accumulated amounts to lower earners (or workers with a short career) depends on the ability to measure earnings throughout the economy, an ability that may be lacking in economies that have large informal sectors. In Chile the government has always been unable or unwilling to prevent work by pensioners after retirement.

When the pension reform eliminated linkage between pensioning and retirement, it changed the legal rules that govern severance payments. In the old system, pensions originated from either age or years of service, but the issuance of the pension depended on showing a certificate of cessation of employ-

Table 6-16. Actual Returns Obtained by the Average Pension Fund, 1981–92
Weighted average annual percent in real terms, UF variation[a]

Year	Return	Year	Return	Year	Return
1981	12.9[b]	1985	13.4	1989	6.9
1982	28.5	1986	12.3	1990	15.6
1983	21.2	1987	5.4	1991	29.7
1984	3.6	1988	6.5	1992	5.2

SOURCE: Superintendencia AFP (1991–92).
a. UF variation refers to method of indexation.
b. July to December 1981. AFPs started operations May 1, 1981.

ment. This forced workers in the formal sector who wanted a pension to quit voluntarily and lose severance payments. Although in practice a pensioner could go on working elsewhere, this limited severance payments and forced job rotation at the age of retirement in the formal sector. With the reform, cessation of employment ceased to be a requirement for obtaining a pension, except for employees in the civil service. As this interaction with the labor law was overlooked, the change raised the cost of severance payments for employers, except the government, and reduced the incentives to switch jobs at the date of pensioning in the formal sector. The associated substitution effects have been that workers are extending their working life in the formal sector and employers are increasingly unwilling to hire older workers.

Performance and Regulation of the Investment Function

The very high real rates of return earned by the AFPs (shown in table 6-16) have attracted attention. In order to evaluate these high returns, it is important to compare this performance with market interest rates. Research has found that, as expected, Chilean AFPs almost never do better than a buy-and-hold strategy would allow.[34] Therefore, the high returns exhibited by pension funds reflect high returns in the Chilean economy generally.

Are these historic returns sustainable in the future? The answer can be gleaned from the yield curve observed today in the Chilean market for long-term CPI-indexed bonds, because AFPs can lock in those returns just by purchasing and holding the bonds. The forward rates observed today are close to 6.5 percent in real terms for the next four years, falling gradually along the yield curve to a level close to 5.5 percent in real terms in the period from sixteen to twenty years from now. Adding some risk premium earned in equity investments, a 7 percent real rate is reasonably expected by Chilean analysts.

34. Walker (1991a, p. 29); Walker (1991b, pp. 27, 29).

These returns are higher than the sum of population growth (1.6 percent now, falling significantly in the next twenty years) and real wage growth (in the 3–4 percent range). These returns are significantly higher than those that can be obtained currently in the OECD because investment opportunities in Chile are good and relatively risky, while international capital market integration is limited. One way of reducing volatility for pension funds is through investment outside Chile, which is expected to grow in the next years.

It is worth noting that Chilean AFPs obtain market return, after adjusting for nondiversifiable risk and for the effects of the investment limits that affect them. That result is superior to the result observed often in the United States and the United Kingdom, where the median pension fund consistently underperforms market indexes.[35]

Walker does find that different AFPs choose significantly different equity portfolios, with different exposures to systematic risk.[36] Zuñíga finds that a substantial part of differences in return in equity portfolios during the period from 1988 to 1990 can be assigned to the differential effect of portfolio limits on funds of different sizes.[37] Still, the hypothesis that one particular middle-sized AFP had special abilities regarding fund management could not be discarded. Thus we reach the unsurprising conclusion that most AFPs do not add substantial value by applying special abilities in their investment strategies, but rather do so by offering transaction and record-keeping services to affiliates.

The differences among pension funds along the risk-return frontier are limited by the incentives caused by a special regulation that forces AFPs to post a guarantee bond. That provision is intended to ensure that the ex-post difference between the return of their fund and the average of all the funds is less than MAX (2 percent; 0.5 average return ex-post) in real terms, measured every month for the past twelve months. This regulation gives a very large incentive to AFPs to hold portfolios that are "close" to each other. As the sum of pension funds hold the market, and the market belongs in the risk-return frontier, this regulation also encourages individual AFPs to move toward the risk-return frontier.

Anecdotal evidence suggests that affiliates seem to choose among AFPs according to the ranking of past returns. The public seems to have insufficient awareness of the trade-off between risk and return. We note that the superintendency does not arrange for a report on the standard deviation of past returns, so a ranking among AFPs in this dimension has never been reported to affiliates.

Chilean pension funds are subject to a variety of portfolio limits defined in

35. See Lakonishok, Shleifer, and Vishny (1992, pp. 339–90).
36. Walker (1991a, pp. 16–17).
37. Zúñiga (1992, pp. 67–71).

the law. These are maximum investment limits. There are no rules requiring a minimum investment in designated securities, except minimum rules that follow by subtraction. For example, until 1992, the minimum investment in Chilean securities was 100 percent, since investment abroad was banned.

Portfolio limits serve several purposes. Some are aimed at protecting affiliates, others are aimed at protecting the markets in which AFPs buy and sell. For example, equity holdings in Chilean companies are limited to 30 percent of the portfolio. For another example, no AFP can purchase more than 20 percent of a bond issue. AFPs can only invest significantly reduced amounts in securities issued by companies affiliated with the AFP. Another intent is to prevent dominance of any individual AFP in the shareholder meetings of a public company by limiting shareholdings to 7 percent of outstanding equity. Other regulations ban equity investment of pension funds in other AFPs, insurance companies, mutual fund management companies, and stockbrokerages. Regulation in this area is still evolving. A new proposal would limit a pension fund's investment in equity issued by each individual company to a number that is a function of a liquidity factor, an ownership concentration factor, and a ratio that measures the share of productive assets that are held directly by the issuing company and the volume of accounting information its subsidiaries have agreed to disclose. Life insurance companies are subject to similar portfolio limits. They are also subject to solvency regulations that limit their maturity mismatch.

The Effect of Fund Accumulation on the Capital Markets

The growth of pension funds managed by AFPs and of the investment reserves of life insurance companies has been substantial. Table 6-17 shows the holdings of pension funds alone. The pension funds hold a substantial share of domestic public debt, which increased significantly during 1990 and 1991. This public debt was issued by the Central Bank and invested in foreign currency reserves. The existence of fiscal balance from 1988 to 1992 has implied no issue of domestic debt by the treasury. The large increase in the equity share in pension portfolios between 1990 and 1992 was not due to large purchases by the pension funds, but to a 279 percent real increase in stock prices (IPSA index). This in turn appears to be due to a large reduction in the country risk premium and in international arbitrage. Large increases in value when a market is integrated into the worldwide capital market are common.[38]

38. Buckberg (1992, table 2).

Table 6-17. Share of Pension Fund Holdings in the Stock of Financial Assets, Selected Years, 1982–92[a]
Percent

Year	1982	1984	1988	1990 (September)	1992 (June)
Treasury bonds and Central Bank bonds	22.5 (26.0)	28.7 (42.2)	32.2 (35.4)	39.0 (44.1)	37.8 (37.2)
Bank deposits and bonds	4.5 (26.6)	6.0 (12.9)	23.7 (29.5)	19.9 (17.4)	18.2 (11.8)
Mortgage bonds guaranteed by banks	24.9 (46.8)	44.0 (43.1)	53.0 (20.6)	56.1 (16.1)	59.6 (12.9)
Corporate bonds	1.3 (0.6)	10.2 (1.8)	48.1 (6.4)	55.6 (11.1)	61.1 (10.0)
Corporate equity	0 (0)	0 (0)	8.4 (8.1)	8.6 (11.3)	9.6 (27.6)
Value of pension funds[b]	3.6	8.6	16.5	26.5	35.44

SOURCES: Up to 1990, Habitat (1991, pp. 82 and 86). The column for June 1992 was estimated by the authors from the Central Bank of Chile (1992) and Superintendencia de AFP (1991–92).
a. The numbers in parentheses are percent participation in pension fund portfolio.
b. As a percent of GDP.

Although it is impossible to prove that a major portion of share price increases were not a response to expected future purchases by pension funds, the hypothesis that AFPs are the source of a significant stock market bubble is doubtful. First, share prices rose so much that several pension funds violated their portfolio limits by much more than the existing 30 percent allowance, and some were forced to sell, limiting expected future purchases. Second, the prices of stocks that can and cannot be purchased by pension funds rose similarly. Real estate prices also boomed, even though pension funds cannot buy in appreciable amounts. Third, when a law that would relax investment limits for pension funds was proposed in January 1993, the stock market rose by 12 percent, suggesting that such laws had not been fully discounted previously. Experience has shown, however, that when pension funds are allowed to buy an individual share for the first time, its price rises 10 to 20 percent before pension funds are able to purchase.

Pension funds have had two main effects on the capital market. First, the large volumes invested have justified increasing specialization and the creation of new financial markets. The best example is the long-term corporate bond market, created in 1988–89, where most of the demand comes from pension funds and life insurance companies. Other examples are the appearance of a second stock market in Santiago and the creation of an electronic Central Custody. Of course, many developments in the Chilean capital market would have occurred anyway, even without pension reform. For example, during 1992, a substantial number of medium-sized companies have gone public and issued shares. This development appears to be driven by the 1991 increase in price/earnings ratios to international levels.

Second, in a small developing country, the introduction of private pension fund management makes imperative additional reforms to ensure transparency and efficiency in the financial markets. In addition, the growing volume of funds may stimulate the authorities to improve regulations to facilitate the appearance of new financial instruments. Both of these changes endow the economy with "institutional capital," which improves the operation of the voluntary capital market, yielding a positive externality.[39]

Examples of changed regulations include regulations forcing controlling shareholders of public companies to report on their share transactions (1986); introduction of risk classification agencies for bonds (1987); introduction of closed-end mutual funds (1989); extension of solvency regulations for life insurance companies to consider exchange risk (1985); bans for insurance companies on investing in the securities issued by affiliates (1987); creation of a new variety of mortgage bonds (1988); and adjustment of solvency regulations to consider duration mismatch (1989).

One aspect of the Chilean capital market that was essential for pension reform was the development in 1974–78 of a legal framework that permits the issue and purchase of a full range of CPI-indexed debt to all market participants, including banks, firms, and households. In table 6-13 we reported on the vulnerability of pension funds to inflation surprises. The tax collection system was also indexed in 1974, so real tax revenue apart from seigniorage is almost independent of the inflation rate, and the government can issue indexed bonds safely.

Government Guarantees

In the description of the pension reform, we mentioned a number of government guarantees. In this section, we bring them together to make clear their overall role. When a life insurance company that sells a pension system annuity becomes insolvent, the government guarantees, first, 100 percent of the value of the annuity, up to the level of the minimum pension, and second, 75 percent of its value above the minimum pension. In addition, implicit government guarantees may exist because of the mandatory nature of contributions and the fact that the solvency of life insurance companies is regulated. The only test up to now was the case of a medium-sized company that went bankrupt in

39. Valdés-Prieto and Cifuentes (1990, pp. 39, 44).

1984.[40] As prescribed by law, pensioners absorbed part of the loss, and the government has absorbed the rest with little pressure for more guarantees. After this experience solvency regulations on life insurance companies were improved in 1987 and in 1989. Currently, the regulation of insurance reserves limits the debt-equity ratio of insurance companies to fifteen, but they usually operate with a ratio near ten. As it is very unlikely that an insurance company can lose more than twice its capital without being taken over by the authorities, an estimate of the maximum loss to annuity holders is (Loss − capital)/Debt = (2-2)/10 = 10 percent of their promise. This means that the government guarantee is more likely to be called for those pensioners whose annuity is less than 1.10 times the minimum pension.

As explained before, a regulation forces AFPs to post a guarantee bond to ensure that the ex-post difference in return between their fund and the average of all the funds is less than MAX (2 percent; 0.5 average return ex-post) in real terms. The government guarantees this (stochastic) floor return in case the deviation in rate of return exhausts the posted guarantee. If there is a shortfall, the AFP must draw funds from its guarantee bond, which is 1 percent of the pension fund it manages. In addition, it must replenish the guarantee fund within fifteen days. If it does not, its license is revoked. The guarantee will involve government funds only if this bond is inadequate. Given the monthly frequency of evaluation, that is unlikely. In part, it is unlikely because the regulation gives a great incentive to AFPs to hold portfolios that are "close" to each other. Up to 1992, the guarantee bond had been called twice, and the government guarantee had never been called.

The third guarantee involves the minimum pension. The minimum pension implies that the treasury shares in the risks in both the rate of return and longevity when a phased withdrawal is chosen. For those workers who have chosen an annuity, an increase in the legislated minimum pension may force the treasury to pay the difference between the purchased annuity and the minimum pension.

Political Economy of Pensions

Consider a fully private pension system. The consumption levels of people who rely on this pension system for (at least) part of their consumption will depend on the rules and functioning of the pension system and the government tax treatment of such income. One would expect that the government would treat such income similarly to other incomes in the economy. That is, in times

40. Frugone (1992, pp. 95–98).

of government financial need, taxation of such income would increase, in keeping with the increase in taxation of other incomes. If government times are sufficiently hard that wealth as well as income is subjected to increased taxation, it would presumably extend, at least somewhat, to the wealth represented by pension accumulation. There would be no reason for the government to single out the particular good or bad health of this system as a reason for increased or decreased taxation (or implicit taxation), although any private institution in sufficient financial difficulty has an incentive to try to get the government to bail it out.[41]

In contrast with this pattern, consider a pension system whose finances flow through the government budget. In governmental hard times, there will be a strong impulse to cut benefits in excess of the cut of incomes generally. If the system appears particularly healthy, there will be a temptation to tap the resources for other spending, with the possibility of adjusted promises to the recipients. Thus the excessive growth of pension promises is often triggered by the ease of financing temporary increases that are then legislated as permanent increases. The question is whether the financing of pay-as-you-go pensions should be subject to the same vagaries of overall need as other government expenditures or instead treated like other sources of income.

Posing the question in this form raises the question of the extent to which government expenditures generally ought to vary with the fiscal health of the government. Presumably the answer should depend on the degree of intertemporal substitution in the services provided by the different government expenditures. Pensions have little intertemporal substitution since the recipients themselves may have little elasticity of substitution, and some of them will die before such a change can be reversed. Moreover, limited access to credit markets may make recipients particularly sensitive to changed timing of benefit payments. In contrast, both some public consumption and some public investment may suffer little from retiming.

As a matter of political economy, all of the government budget has a strong tendency to move together. This makes it appropriate to set up a pension system to be less subject to the vagaries of temporary budget position. This can certainly be done by the type of privatization that has been carried out by Chile. It can be done somewhat by a partially funded system, as in the United States. Possibly it can be done by earmarked revenues, provided the flow of funds is suitably automatic.[42] The record in Latin America suggests that this cannot

41. The desire for a bailout was part of the encouragement of the formation of the Pension Benefit Guarantee Corporation (PBGC) in the United States.

42. One does not hear much of short-run budget difficulties in the administration of central banks, which have direct access to seigniorage revenues.

adequately be done by the typical Latin American pension system in the setting of Latin American politics. In Latin America, there have been both kinds of abuse—excessive sensitivity to the state of the government budget and excessive sensitivity to the state of the short-run finances of the pension system. If a privatized system is expensive to run, then, from the perspective of the workers, the problem is to describe the benefit-cost calculation of political insulation relative to administrative costs. It is also appropriate to attempt to assess the degree of variation in both insulation and administrative cost as one varies the degree of both privatization and individual choice. The nature of insurance provided and the degree and type of redistribution are also parts of the comparison of different systems.

It is interesting to consider how the value of insulating disability insurance (DI) and survivors insurance (SI) from the political system is different from that of insulating the retirement income system. Both types of political abuse seem readily available for DI, less so for SI. Since DI includes a determination of disability, where standards are necessarily imprecise, the standards can easily fluctuate with political interests and short-run fiscal needs. In the United States during the Reagan administration, we saw people removed from the DI rolls who were then restored by court order. In several eastern European countries, DI is used in a discretionary fashion as a substitute for long-term unemployment insurance. These policies are less sensitive to political alteration in a setting where DI claims are covered by private insurers, with annually adjusted insurance premium charges set by the insurance companies.

Lessons from the Chilean Experience

Changing from an existing underfunded social security system to a fully funded system has major fiscal implications. The tax revenue currently flowing into the government that is used (at least in part) to finance the existing system will flow instead into individual accounts. Thus there will be a sharp fall in government revenue, without much change in the call on government expenditures in the short run. This was illustrated in table 6-7, which shows the deficit in social security expenditures that Chile experienced. The full effect of the change is smaller than it appears since a fraction of initial mandatory savings will naturally flow into government debt.

In considering the Chilean context and success, it is perhaps important to recognize that the Chilean government budget was put in significant surplus in preparation for the reform (although the crisis of 1982 put the government budget into serious deficit shortly thereafter). This surplus could have been used to finance tax cuts or other expenditure increases. Instead it was used to fund the social security system, that is, to increase public saving to retire hidden pension debt.

The credibility of the required future increase in the primary surplus in the government budget may be put into question by the shift to funding in the absence of such a surplus. Such a change adds considerably to an existing deficit. While an increase in the deficit may result in greater success in addressing the deficit, deficit pressures may derail the pension reform. We suspect that with a large deficit the politics of successful reform may be much more difficult than with the approach of building the surplus first. In the Chilean case, this sequencing occurred under a military government.

The presence of a large deficit will create an incentive to abandon the funding goal and restrict the reform to privatization. This may be done in ways that undermine the privatization goal, for example by restricting the investments of PFs outside government debt and forcing AFPs to accept government debt paying less than market rates, as in the Philippines.[43] After such a start, the political support for the development of a privatized system as a route to an insulated pension plan may be seriously undercut. It may be possible to privatize without shifting to funding, but this route is yet to be tried.[44]

The growth of the Chilean economy was accompanied by very high interest rates across the board. No doubt these high rates of return contributed to the popularity of the system with workers. One can wonder what would have happened had the rates been low instead. In a Chilean-style reform, workers bear the investment risk. It is our guess that a period of low returns in Chile in the near future would not generate irresistible calls for government contributions to pension (although it would increase the cost of the guaranteed minimum pension). In a system without such a history, however, one may wonder about the political economy of this risk. But partial government guarantees of the rate of return during the initial years may be very costly and may undermine the privatization aspect of the reform.

Considerable regulation of financial markets and financial intermediaries is a worldwide phenomenon, for good reason. The Chilean system needs regulations involving the soundness of the investment policies of two types of financial intermediaries—the AFPs and the insurance companies. Since large amounts of wealth are being accumulated under this system, there will be considerable incentive for taking advantage of these intermediaries. These range

---

43. Tiglao (1990, pp. 48–49).

44. For example this could be done by replacing at the outset all implicit pension debt with explicit public debt in the form of perpetual bonds, putting them in pension fund portfolios and allowing AFPs to trade and rearrange portfolios.

from furthering outside investment interests to outright embezzlement. As witnessed by the continuing development of capital market regulation in advanced countries and spectacularly visible periodic failures of regulation, these are not simple issues.[45] Thus it is clear that a country that undertakes a Chilean-style reform must strive to improve substantially its regulatory establishment.

The Chilean experience demonstrates, however, that reform can be started without having a sound regulatory structure already in place. Modern bank supervision started in Chile in 1980, just as the pension reform was adopted, and began to operate strongly only in 1982. Reforms to the securities and corporation laws were passed in 1981. Later, during the 1980s and 1990s, financial reform occurred at several times, many of them in response to the growth of pension funds. The range of allowed investments was expanded in step with the development of the regulatory process.

It seems to us that two conditions are necessary to imitate successfully the Chilean experience with regulation. First is a commitment of strong political support for continued regulation. The Chilean banking collapse, coming soon after the social security reform, may have added to the strength of the political will to continue tight regulation. Second is a close fit between the allowed investment instruments and those supplied safely by the local capital market. On this point, Chile seems to have compensated to some extent for the risks of starting its pension reform without a solid background in financial regulation by imposing stiff restrictions on the initial allowed portfolio, which was limited essentially to government debt and bank deposits. Over time, portfolio choice can be expanded as financial regulation is improved.

In Chile, the administrative expenses associated with the new system probably exceed those of the old system, even though the old system was viewed as expensive because of its fragmentation and its history of political appointments. Thus it is important to recognize that these expenses are part of the cost of adopting such a reform. In addition, the expenses may be higher than they would be under other reforms.

Further Reform in Chile

The Chilean social security system has been subject to nearly continuous reform and revision. Some additional reforms might include indexing of assistance and minimum pensions; improving the design of existing regulation; establishing an AFP clearinghouse; helping reduce the level of annuity fees; in-

45. Securities and Exchange Commission (1992).

troducing group purchases of annuities; and allowing AFPs to offer multiple funds.

INDEXING. Indexing of state-provided pensions over a long period is difficult to sustain without significant insulation from the annual budget process. Nevertheless, it is probably appropriate even with the recognition that there will be periodic adjustment of long-term benefit levels. Moreover, the issue of month-to-month indexing is still important. In Chile the only pensions whose real value is left to vary with monthly inflation (in between legislated cost of living adjustments) are those with redistributive character and those in the old system. Belief that the elderly, invalids, and survivors are less able to substitute current for future consumption explains why phased withdrawals are indexed monthly between recalculations and why only indexed annuities are authorized. There seems to be no reason to exclude the poorest among the old from the benefits of monthly indexation. Although this policy would fix real expenditure in assistance and minimum pensions, the tax system in Chile yields revenue that is relatively independent from inflation, so this reform would not increase the risk of a fiscal crisis.

REGULATION. The costs of the Chilean system can apparently be reduced by improving the design of existing regulation. In some areas additional tightening seems desirable. For example, the 1988 authorization to AFPs to issue voluntary savings accounts has resulted in offerings of these services at zero price, so the observed volume of these services is above the socially optimal one. The prospect of zero prices led politicians to entrust AFPs with additional tasks, such as the management of individual accounts where the employer deposits for severance payments (1991) and maybe other accounts where the employer deposits for unemployment insurance (under discussion now). One effect is that overall administrative charges rise too much because of excessive production of zero-price services.

In other areas, regulation seems excessive. For example, the superintendency specifies in detail how many administrative functions must be performed, leaving too little scope for firms to minimize costs.

CLEARINGHOUSE. Under the old Chilean system, the government collected payroll taxes for pensions along with other taxes (including payroll taxes for health benefits). The privatization of mandatory savings has meant that the government ceased to play a direct role in collecting the forced savings contributions. At present each AFP collects its own contributions separately, and many of them have service contracts with banks, so indirectly they have access to the bank clearinghouse. However, the cost and nuisance to the employer of making payments to multiple AFPs remains. This has been reported as leading some firms to encourage all their workers to select the same AFP.

One would expect that the payment of contributions by employers would have increasing returns to scale in the sense that each employer would prefer to make payment to a single agency rather than to several different AFPs and in the sense that the need for AFPs to check on the payments by employers would be cheaper for AFPs if checking were done by a single agency for each employer, rather than separately by many AFPs. There may or may not be gains from having a single collection agency in each region, rather than several in each region, although the former would probably be simpler for the AFPs to deal with. It is not apparent how large a region would minimize the sum of costs of single collection agencies for each region. Centralized record keeping may also be convenient, although computerized transfer of information is not very expensive.

To date no such collective arrangements have emerged in Chile, even though they would reduce costs for AFPs as a group. Two explanations are that AFPs are reluctant to set up institutions that might result in the sharing of information on their clients or that would make expertise on collection available to entrants for free. Another possibility is inertia. Thus there seems to be a role for the government to encourage the AFPs to set up a clearinghouse or some other institution. If a clearinghouse were created, it could also collect health insurance payments. It might also be used by the government to collect withholding payments on taxes. Such a clearinghouse should perhaps be owned by the AFPs (or the AFPs along with other users) to prevent the exploitation of monopoly power. (New entrants would be allowed to join as owners at a suitable fee.) The clearinghouse should probably not be allowed to make a profit for its owners, so that it does not become a vehicle for collusion.

FEES IN ANNUITIES. Concern has arisen about the high transaction costs associated with the start-up of the annuity market. In particular there has been concern about the level of fees charged by advisers to people selecting annuities. The start-up of any new activity often has high costs to customers until competitive forces are in full swing. However, as long as workers continue to be relatively improvident and uninformed, so that mandatory contributions continue to be necessary, totally free selection of annuities may continue to be expensive and subject to large fees. It is natural to explore alternatives to reduce these costs.

GROUPING. Purchase of an annuity, like selection of a fund manager, is designed to be done on an individual basis. This is in contrast with the provision of both disability and survivors insurance, which the AFPs do on a group basis. It also contrasts with the use of employer- or union-based private pension systems in much of the world. There the economies of scale associated with group purchase are exploited.[46] It is natural to ask whether an optional group purchase of annuities could not be introduced to offer a lower-cost alternative to workers and to increase competitive pressure to hold down costs on individual purchases. If such an institution can be successfully designed, then it would be natural to ask whether similar grouping might not be helpful for AFP selection as well.

In considering group formation, one approach would be to use employment as a basis for group formation and to have employers involved in the process. A different approach would have the government form the groups from all individuals reaching retirement age during that month.[47] No matter who sponsors the group, a supervisory machinery must be put into place to make sure that insurance companies cannot influence the bidding outcome through bribes or campaign contributions.

Discretion may be reduced through regulation. For example, each period the sponsor might form a group based on individuals reaching retirement age that period plus individuals announcing that they are considering an early retirement (with such an announcement allowed only once). The sponsor would solicit bids on this group each period. Thus everyone would receive a group quote before being allowed to accept an individual arrangement. A bid would necessarily be a formula for converting accumulation, age, and age of dependents into a benefit level, with the formula the same for everyone in the group. A board of trustees named by the sponsor must select one supplier for each group. This is tricky since the formula is not a scalar that is easily compared. But, in turn, the sponsor could be obligated to use a formula that is a weighted sum of benefits assuming everyone took a pension as the criterion for selecting a particular insurance company. The weights might be kept secret to limit adverse selection and gaming. Since there is no compulsion either to bid on a group nor to accept an annuity from the group, this does not seem politically unacceptable. There are two compulsions. One is to request the group bid before making an individual purchase. The second is that an individual can only be part of a group once.

MULTIPLE FUNDS. At present each AFP is restricted to managing a single pension fund. Allowing AFPs to have a short menu of other pension funds

46. For example, it appears that in the United States, individual choice of mutual fund is roughly three times as expensive as group choice. This tentative conclusion follows from a comparison of average fees for individual mutual funds of roughly 1.5 percent of assets with a figure of roughly 0.5 percent for investment management fees. The conclusion is tentative since the latter figure does not include the keeping of individual records provided by the employer. The first figure is from Sirri and Tufano (1992). The second figure is from *SEI Research Reports* (1990).

47. For a presentation of such an approach for health insurance, see Diamond (1992, pp. 1233–54).

that were clearly labeled is an alternative. There might be two, for example, labeled high risk and low risk. One advantage is that workers would not be forced to switch AFP when they are dissatisfied with the current portfolio chosen by their AFP, as they could merely switch funds within the AFP. As different funds would charge different fees for fund management, in addition to the fees charged by the AFP, there would be a transition period in which most workers might find it harder to choose among funds and among AFPs. In the long run, however, this reform should make choice easier than it is today, since AFPs would be compared on a commission-for-service basis and funds would be compared only on a risk-return basis. Any such change would require a reexamination of the structure of the guaranteed minimum rate of return.

Options Further from the Chilean Model

The Chilean system is based on private management of accumulated funds.[48] The Chilean system is also based on individual choice of fund managers. However, privatization of the demand side seems to be associated with substantially higher administrative and selling costs, as seen in Chile and in financial markets elsewhere. One alternative that would greatly reduce these costs would be to preserve private management of funds but to eliminate private choice of fund manager. This could be done by having one, two (high and low risk), or a few aggregate funds, with individuals having individual accounts with the aggregate funds. This would require the government to be placed between the individual accounts and the fund managers. Private fund managers would bid on managing parts of the aggregate fund. Incentive contracts could be designed for these fund managers.

This approach would put great power in the hands of the selectors of the fund managers. Therefore, this option requires a well-insulated, carefully audited, and transparent institution or group of institutions to fill this role. Such a public institution would need a high degree of independence from the political process, somewhere between the independence achieved by some central banks and the independence of private firms. This may be an impossible target in some countries. Political parties or the military would naturally affect or even control nomination to these boards. The presence of such a board or boards may alter the politics of restrictions on allowed or required investments.

48. Although a privatized system requires full funding from an individual's perspective, we can expect part of these funds to be invested in government securities, so privatization admits partial or little funding from an aggregate perspective.

In the end, the balance between cost savings and the risk of mismanagement may be unattractive in many political settings.

The Chilean system is based on individual choice by the worker. Again, contrasting this approach with the workings of some parts of private pension systems in the OECD, one might consider instead placing the choice of AFP in the hands of an employer. This could be restricted by allowing workers to have multiple accounts that are only consolidated at the time of retirement. Thus an employer would choose an AFP for the complete set of workers in the firm's employ. Workers would have the option of leaving their previous accumulation with the AFP that held them previously or combining the accounts in the AFP chosen by the employer. There is no reason to think there would be more of a problem with placing the choice of AFP in the hands of the employer than there is in having private pensions designed by employers, as in current practice in the OECD. In order for this arrangement to work, the employer must find it more profitable to act in the best interest of its employees rather than to seek compensation from the fund managers that it chooses, at the expense of workers. This requirement implies a machinery of surveillance and employers with reputations for benevolence to employees, both of which are costly.

Consideration of allowing group choice of AFP by employer raises the question of whether to allow group discounts. Since a major reason for allowing grouping is to affect the elasticity of demand, and so the markup, a critical question is the effect for other (smaller) groups and ungrouped individuals of allowing discounts on pricing for large groups. Limiting the size of discounts is one way of affecting elasticities generally. Not allowing discounts is one pole of the range of such limits. Without further research, or experimentation, it is not clear what the best policy is likely to be.

At present workers convert their accounts into annuities at a single time. This holds down the administrative costs, which would be higher with repeated purchases. In addition, selling costs might be higher with repeated purchases, although the selling costs associated with repeated small purchases are not necessarily higher than those associated with a once-and-for-all large purchase. With the single-time purchase system, workers are subject to considerable risk from possible fluctuations in interest rates in the long-term market at the time that they make their purchase.

A different route might be to convert contributions into annuities on a continuous basis. This is similar to a proposal made for the United States.[49] In

49. Boskin, Kotlikoff, and Shoven (1988).

order to have a functioning market, insurance companies would have to change the nature of pricing. At present price quotes are tailored to individual requests, and the costs are allocated to individual retirees. One could, instead, require firms to produce prices per peso of accumulation converted into an annuity from a planned retirement age. In this way one could allow the conversion into annuities of the actuarial value of the fund in the event of death before retirement. A particular worker would have to purchase a package of annuities to cover his spouse and children as well as himself. With continuous conversion, it would be natural to have a single institution, rather than the separation between AFP and insurance company that exists now.

Comparison of a Privatized and a Conventional Pension System

The Chilean system is built around mandatory savings and is thus similar to defined contribution private pension systems. Social security systems are commonly designed around benefit formulas. In this section we want to raise some of the issues associated with this choice.

CREATING A SYSTEM. Decisions about the creation of a social security system naturally fall into three areas: the pattern of intergenerational redistribution, the pattern of intragenerational redistribution, and the workings of the technical details. Conventional pension systems usually intermingle redistribution policy and benefit design. Contribution-based systems tend instead to isolate and make explicit the redistribution. This difference shows up in a difference in the agenda for legislation and affects both economic outcomes and the understanding of the effects of policy. This may improve or worsen outcomes, depending on the workings of the political system and on one's perspective. Let us consider two examples.

When a state is setting up a social security system where one does not exist (or there is one that gives small benefits), a critical question is what to do about those currently retired or close to retirement. Either type of pension system can redistribute toward this group. However, the two systems have different natural presentation of the issues and so tend to different political outcomes. With a contribution-based system, redistribution requires transferring assets to the accounts of older workers and retirees, which means identifying sources of financing. With a benefit-based system redistribution is more implicit, as it is achieved by applying the benefit formula to people who have less than full contribution histories, and financing is left in the background. As the system builds up its foreseeable fund after initiation and has a "short"-run surplus, political pressure to redistribute to current retirees arises.[50] This pressure is much larger with a benefit-based system than with a contribution-based system, since the people financing the transfer in the latter are currently present and more visible (as opposed to absentee "future generations" in a benefit-based system).

A second instance of foreseeable consequences is when a demographic transition is coming. The two systems have different incentives in managing a demographic transition. With a benefit-based system, the political process needs good management. For example, if a benefit-based system operates on the pay-as-you-go principle, demographic shocks require substantial foresight to change contribution rates and benefits and perhaps to introduce partial funding, preferably twenty or more years in advance. In a contribution-based system, part of the adjustment to a demographic shock is automatic, as retirees accumulate for their own retirements. There may also be changes in asset prices as the transition happens or as it is increasingly foreseen.

Similarly, benefit-based systems tend to produce implicit intragenerational redistribution, while contribution-based systems are more explicit. An instance in Chile that turns out to be bad for the poor is the structure of indexing clauses. In Chile the poor (those within the earnings-related pension system) are provided for through the minimum pension.[51] The minimum pension is not indexed, and adjustment is highly political and sensitive to the state of political balance and to the state of the overall budget balance. In contrast, a benefit-based system redistributes through the design of the benefit formula. Whatever indexing is chosen for the general system also applies to the redistributive component as well.

Another example that works in the opposite direction comes from different lengths of working lives and retired lives between rich and poor. Thus redistribution apparently incorporated in the benefit formula of a benefit-based system may be undone by the longer life expectancy of those with higher incomes. This may be somewhat offset by a tendency of those with higher incomes to work longer, provided the benefit design is less than actuarial. This issue is complicated by consideration of differences between men and women as well as differences between the earnings levels of each group separately. Similarly, if a benefit formula averages past earnings, assigning higher weights to earnings closer to retirement than a present value calculation would, benefits are less progressive than the formula suggests, since high earners are likely to have

50. The short run may be twenty to seventy years, depending on demographics and design.
51. Redistribution could have been done by (break-even) transfers at the time of contributions to funds, as was analyzed by Boskin, Kotlikoff, and Shoven (1988).

a steeper earnings path. In principle, these factors can be offset by suitable design of the benefit formula of the benefit-based system, but this does not ensure that it will be offset. In contribution-based systems, these factors are eliminated by design.

Consideration of life expectancy raises the issue that individuals at the same earnings levels may have different life expectancies. If they also have the same (ideal) working life, then those with longer life expectancy are poorer on the basis of their annual consumption over their life, although they may enjoy living longer. A difficult question arises about whether those with longer life expectancy merit transfers because of the need to finance a longer retirement. The conventional benefit-based system answers implicitly in the affirmative, because benefits do not depend on individual life expectancy. A contribution-based system may attempt to replicate this result, but the requirement of explicit identification of financing sources raises the political obstacles.

Now consider benefit seeking by special groups. In many countries, income has been redistributed by having different benefit-based systems for different groups. In some countries, uniform benefit-based systems have been successful in blocking such moves. A contribution-based system is presumably better at blocking such moves, since the required transfers must be explicit. A privatized contribution-based system has a tendency to be even better at resisting them, as both providers and trustees representing the workers facilitate representation of the losers.

Many social security systems are set up with benefit formulas that are highly inefficient. This is particularly true of formulas that multiply a number of years times an average wage based on a short averaging period. Such a poorly designed formula is not a necessary part of a benefit-based system, but it is very common. Some of the frequency with which it occurs may be attributed to the role of the formula in redistribution.

A major cost of privatized choice of provider—on either an individual or a group basis—is that administrative charges are likely to be considerably higher than without such reliance on the private market. The new institutions required by privatization of provision and selection of provider may have positive externalities, however. This seems to have been the case with the development of the capital market in Chile. In addition, up to now the Chilean government has left little freedom to design new products to the agreement of private trustees and private providers, so the scope of the gains from diversity is unknown.

The presence of new institutions also affects politics. As one example, the incentives for fund managers to vie for the risk-return frontier generates a built-in pressure group in favor of international portfolio diversification. The benefit for pensioners should be specially valuable in small, open economies where the local government's finances are risky.

RESPONSE TO SURPRISES. A contribution-based system is easy to place on automatic pilot and thus insulate from major political revision. While variations in long-term real interest rates might make changes in the contribution rate appropriate, this is not needed for survival and is probably an easy matter of political adjustment. In contrast, the usual structure of a benefit-based system has separate rules determining benefits and taxes, and so periodic adjustment in one or the other is necessary to respond to surprises. The lack of automatic adjustment keeps the political process involved in legislated changes. While these changes might be good or might be bad, historically, there is a high frequency of unsustainable changes.[52]

Thus one might consider how to put a benefit-based system on automatic pilot. It can be done parallel to the mandatory savings system: Legislate a tax rate and legislate an adjustment to the benefit formula that keeps benefits in line with available income, which might include interest on a fund as well as tax revenue. In the absence of any experience with such a system, it is difficult to speculate on how well such a system can insulate retirement income from short-run political forces.

To what degree should pension provision vary with the state of the government budget? Little response seems likely to be the ideal answer. That is, the fact that some pensions are flowing through the government does not make this source of income a better bearer of risks associated with budget problems. Arguably, pension income should adjust to government needs by less than other income, which would vary through tax changes. Similarly, a period of accumulation of funds for retirement within a nationalized system is no more of a reason to increase government expenditure than is private accumulation. Insulation of government expenditures from the state of the social security budget is also more easily done with a contribution-based system than with a benefit-based system. Restating, if the fiscal balance suffers a negative shock, pensions are shielded to a greater degree in the contribution-based system. If the pension system suffers a shock, the budget is better protected.

Another aspect of the political process is the existence of private companies handling funds and providing annuities, which have an economic interest in

52. Decisions about funding that are made without affecting sustainability are decisions about intertemporal income redistribution. A decision to redistribute to early generations, and so to have less capital in the future, is not necessarily a bad decision. In contrast, decisions that generate unsustainable systems with repeated fiscal crises are presumably poor decisions.

preserving their business and commercial image. In a sense, private interest groups provide a complementary channel of expression to the private interest of workers. In relatively open political settings like the Chilean one, the possibility of total capture of regulators by AFP interests is slight because individual politicians have a substantial electoral incentive to undo such collusion. The equilibrium that results from this competition between electoral and economic interests is not unlike that observed in other regulated multiprovider industries, such as banking. However, if the political and economic processes are in fact one, because the same persons control both, privatization will bring no change.[53]

It is interesting to compare the benefit- and contribution-based approaches on insurance dimensions. Both systems put some of the risks of fund accumulation on beneficiaries.[54] The exact pattern of risk bearing is probably different, but it would require explicit formulation and modeling to compare the differences. In general terms, a contribution-based system shifts some risk from beneficiaries toward investors in the capital market, both domestic and foreign, while a benefit-based system shifts risk among different generations of workers.

Another difference between the two approaches comes with risk sharing at different dates at which information about life expectancy becomes available. That is, an individual would like to transfer resources from the contingency in which he reaches retirement age with low expected need for expenditures to the contingency in which he has high expected need for expenditures. The easy case to consider is that of death before reaching retirement age (and assuming separate insurance of survivors). With no risk sharing, the estate goes to the worker's heirs. With risk sharing, there is no such bequest, and this money helps finance benefits for all workers surviving into retirement. This is automatic in a benefit-based system and not present in the Chilean contribution-based system.

Similarly, a contribution-based system with one-shot purchase of annuities at retirement does not provide insurance against the arrival of information before retirement age that affects the terms on which an annuity is available. Thus the combination of an annuities market that distinguishes among individuals on the basis of life expectancy and one-shot purchase tends to defeat insur-

53. This seems to have been the case of the Philippines under Marcos. See Tiglao (1990, pp. 48–49).

54. It is common to suggest that workers do not bear such risks in defined-benefit private pension systems. This is only correct if wages, benefit formulas, and firm viability are not affected by rates of return. All of these seem problematic.

ance as perceived at an earlier age. An ex-ante optimal system probably involves some move away from accurately priced annuities toward uniformly priced annuities (parallel with a similar result in the presence of moral hazard).[55] Conventional benefit-based systems provide this insurance by paying benefits that are independent of life expectancy, so they may produce too much averaging. Contribution-based systems can only give this insurance by arranging for partial purchases of deferred annuities at different ages, such as fifty, fifty-five, sixty, and sixty-five, but this leads to difficult issues of marketing costs and solvency regulation.

We have identified a number of different issues in choosing a basis for social security. The balance of these costs and benefits should be different for different countries, as it seems to depend on the institutional ability to design and operate regulations to limit inefficiency and fraud by private providers and trustees, as compared with the institutional ability to limit abuse and inefficiency when management is in charge of the political process. An important specific requirement of systems with private provision seems to be to allow private sector firms and banks to issue CPI-indexed securities.

This comparison may be misleading, however, if a third option is not considered: for countries without a system to continue relying on self-reliance and family and tribal insurance, avoiding mandatory earnings-related pensions altogether. That option is compatible with substantial income redistribution toward the elderly channeled through other institutions, such as government taxes and transfers. Of course, this option replaces the cost of abuse and inefficiency by private providers or by the political process, for the larger gaps in provision and risk of abuse within the family, and it does not take advantage of specialization. The fact that until recently Australia, New Zealand, and South Korea have chosen this option suggests that it should not be discarded out of hand.

Chile has given us a fascinating example to examine. It is interesting to study and important to consider imitating.

---

55. The optimal move is limited because the absence of correctly priced annuities tends to defeat rational choice between annuities and estates. We are not aware of any explicit modeling of optimal social design of such insurance. For an analysis of market equilibrium with repeated opportunities to buy annuities and information arrival over time, see Brugiavini (1993, pp. 31–62).

Comment by Nancy Birdsall

What lessons can other developing countries learn from Chile's experience with reform of its social security system?[56] The authors of this paper clarify the details of Chile's system within an incentives-grounded framework. But they could do more to draw out the potential replicability of Chile's reform, in whole or in part, for other countries.

Consider three questions about replicability.

First, is the Chilean approach—that is, a fully funded, contribution-based, mandatory system—a good idea for other countries? The answer to this first question is straightforward. The Chilean approach is a good one because it brings both greater equity and efficiency. Existing systems in most middle-income developing countries, which are benefit-based, pay-as-you-go (PAYG) systems, end up redistributing real income not from the relatively rich to the relatively poor, but the other way around. (Even the U. S. system does not succeed in redistributing benefits to the poor within cohorts, simply because the less poor live longer and collect benefits for longer periods). In most developing countries, old age security systems that are publicly funded provide benefits to a privileged group: those in the formal sector labor force who can document extended periods of full-time employment. Often the system is subsidized from general tax revenues—and tax systems are generally regressive, especially where they are still largely based on indirect and trade taxes. In some countries, including Brazil, generous provisions for early retirement provide to the privileged working class benefits that are much greater than are actuarially consistent.

The greater transparency of contribution-based, fully funded systems would also bring more efficiency by helping to insulate old age insurance systems from the predations of government. Governments in good times tend to establish entitlements that are not sustainable. As times turn bad governments tend either to subsidize the resulting system inappropriately from general revenues (with the perverse effects on equity noted above as well as perverse effects on efficiency, for example in the labor market) or to undermine the system's insurance function by allowing inflation to erode the real value of pensions.

The authors mention other benefits of insulation and independence from the

56. These comments are based in part on initial findings of a study of old-age security issues in developing countries being undertaken at the World Bank under the leadership of Estelle James. I am grateful to Estelle James for a useful discussion of the Chile example.

immediate administrative arrangements of government that also have obvious efficiency benefits compared with benefit-based pay-as-you-go systems: the greater likelihood of contributing to the development of financial markets and, in Chile, the related recent emergence of interest in international diversification of the holdings of insurers.

A second question arises. Is it possible to replicate the Chilean approach in Chilean form in other developing countries? Probably not. In the middle-income countries of Latin America with relatively large pay-as-you-go systems, the transitional burden on the fiscal system, which the authors emphasize, would be daunting. In some countries of South and East Asia, and in the middle-income countries of Africa, where pay-as-you-go systems are still relatively small, affecting primarily the civil service and parastatals, the fiscal burden of effecting a transition to a fully funded contribution-based system would be smaller. But in only a few of these countries is it likely that the necessary regulatory or supervisory apparatus to control the financial arrangements (even if the system were publicly rather than privately managed) could be effectively implemented.

Finally, a third question: are there aspects of the Chilean system that could be adapted in modified form in other developing countries? Yes. In many OECD countries, employer-based private pension systems that are fully funded and contribution-based are already expanding, partly in response to the change in public systems toward smaller, flatter, and more redistributive transfers. In middle-income developing countries, private demand for pension insurance is also likely to be increasingly channeled into similar, employer-based systems, as public pensions become smaller and flatter as a result of growing fiscal pressure and, with the demographic transition, the effects on increased payouts of the increasing proportion of the elderly in many populations. Over time these private systems are likely to be more and more subject to public regulation; governments will feel public pressure to fill in gaps for citizens who rely heavily on private systems by making the private systems more portable and to make pricing more transparent by forcing private systems to develop and provide uniform packages. In the extreme, such systems could become mandatory—thus mirroring even more closely the Chilean system.

In the poorer countries of South Asia and Africa, a mandatory, contribution-based system for formal sector workers could be appended to the existing public system; this would permit the public system to cover only a minimum and possibly flat-rate pension—which at lower cost would minimize the perverse efficiency and equity effects of the traditional public systems.

The authors do a good job of showing how the system even in Chile is being constantly adjusted and reformed. Perhaps the capacity to adjust the system is its greatest benefit—in contrast with the political difficulty of adjusting conventional benefit-based systems.

In summary, though difficult to replicate where benefit-based pay-as-you-go systems are large (if only because of the high fiscal costs of making the transition), Chile's mandatory, fully funded, contribution-based scheme does provide lessons that other developing countries could follow to effect a shift away from full reliance on the kind of system historically favored in OECD countries—the perverse efficiency and equity effects of which are worth minimizing even if they cannot be entirely avoided.

Comment by John Williamson

While this is an extremely informative paper, it raises several questions in the mind of a novice in the field of pensions like myself. My first question about this paper concerns the logic of limiting the equities that the AFPs (or pension funds, as I would want to call them) are allowed to hold. Even now they are apparently allowed to hold only 30 percent of their assets in the form of equities, despite the fact that one of the markets one would want to develop in a country like Chile is the equity market. To exclude pension funds from that market during the early stages of its development ensures that the capital gains that are likely to arise before the market matures are denied to the holders of pension rights, probably to the benefit of foreign investors.

A second question concerns the logic of institutionally splitting responsibility for the provision of pensions between the two phases of the life cycle, preretirement and post-retirement age. What are the relative merits of such a split compared with the procedure used by many private pension funds in the United States—for example, CREF—that purchase an annuity for someone who reaches retirement age and wants to take their retirement income in that form? Is this split one of the reasons why the Chilean system is relatively expensive to run? If so, are there compensating benefits?

It seems to me that the paper raises three key issues. The first is the effect of the pension arrangements on income distribution. Such an effect is inherent in mandatory arrangements that govern the provision of pensions, at least to the extent that it influences the distribution of income over the life cycle of an individual. Since, as mentioned in the paper, the absence of mandatory arrangements would be expected to lead to much less provision for retirement, those mandatory arrangements make people less happy ex ante but presumptively more happy ex post. The decision to have such arrangements therefore implies a social judgment that the ex post criterion is the more important one.

The paper focuses on interpersonal rather than on intertemporal redistribution, however. In that context the system has three potential effects. One arises from the cost of the system and the resulting transfer to the financial sector. The question arises whether there are offsetting benefits, but the only one that I found mentioned was the development of the capital markets. Another effect is to insulate the level of pension provision from the political pressures that often lead to pensions' being expanded when times are good and then cut back sharply when the economy encounters difficulties. Diamond and Valdés-Prieto present this as an unalloyed benefit: it seems to me that there is a case for arguing that pensioners should bear a part of the pain when it is necessary for society to curtail consumption, although I would not challenge the contention that the insulation of pensions would in practice be likely to bring a net benefit. The third effect is the transfer between rich and poor. Chile has instituted the system—private in preference to state pensions, and contribution-based in preference to benefit-based—least likely to generate such redistribution, although the continuing existence of the state minimum pension apparently retains some redistributive element in the total system. Nancy Birdsall has told us that the alternative to having zero redistribution is to have perverse redistribution, so I suppose I should be relieved to find that the Chilean system does modestly better than possible.

The second key issue is the effect on saving. Here the main effect in Chile came from raising the retirement age. An important secondary effect arose during the transition: in Chile this transitional effect increased saving, since the gap that occurred when the state system was still paying out pensions although it had ceased to receive contributions was financed by taxes rather than by debt. I suppose Birdsall is right to argue that it is unlikely that one would get a similar stimulus to saving in most other countries that chose to move to a private pension system, but it seems wrong to regard this as an argument against the move. It just means that liabilities that were previously being built up unrecorded under the state pay-as-you-go system suddenly start getting recorded on the government budget. This is more honest accounting, not a real worsening of the government's finances or any reduction in national saving. Of course, I prefer the Chilean route of higher saving, but I would not necessarily reject privatization just because it would not bring an associated benefit of higher saving. Perhaps it is possible that some governments would be tempted to exploit the ambiguities of the transition to relax fiscal policy, but that demands vigilance rather than a knee-jerk rejection of reform.

The development of capital markets appears to be the big benefit of privatizing pensions, and it was a major factor in Chile despite the limitation mentioned earlier on how much could be placed in equities. There is also an international dimension to this issue. When I visited Chile two years ago for discussions on liberalizing capital outflows, I was told that there were pressures to allow foreign investment by the pension funds. I expressed considerable skepticism about ideas of liberalizing outflows because experience seems to suggest that liberalizing outflows at a time of strong confidence typically brought a net inflow (induced by stronger assurance of the possibility of getting money out again if and when that should be desired) rather than relief from the pressures of too large an inflow. In retrospect I feel it was a mistake not to recommend an immediate liberalization of foreign investment by pension funds, since it is difficult to see how that step would strengthen the confidence of foreigners that they would be able to get their money out again, and foreign investments would obviously have helped diversify the portfolios of the Chilean pension funds.

But perhaps my pangs of guilt can be assuaged by the news that the Chilean pension funds are not rushing to exploit the limited freedom to invest abroad that they have now been granted, despite the presumption that any portfolio analysis would suggest that they should have more than half their assets placed outside an economy as small as that of Chile. My last question is: why are they so reluctant to move abroad?

References

American Council of Life Insurance. 1992. *1992 Life Insurance Fact Book.* Washington, D.C.: American Council of Life Insurance.

Arrau, P. 1992. "El Nuevo régimen previsional chileno." Chapter 2 in *Regímenes Pensionales.* Bogotá, Colombia: Friedrich Ebert Foundation.

Boskin, M. J., L. J. Kotlikoff, and J. B. Shoven. 1988. "Personal Security Accounts: A Proposal for Fundamental Social Security Reform." In *Social Security and Private Pensions: Providing for Retirement in the Twenty-First Century,* edited by S. M. Wachter, 179–206. Lexington, Mass: Lexington Books.

The Brick. 1992. *El Ladrillo: Bases de la Política Económica del Gobierno Militar Chileno.* Santiago: Centro de Estudios Publicos.

Brugiavini, A. 1993. "Uncertainty Resolution and the Timing of Annuity Purchases." *Journal of Public Economics* 50 (January): 31–62.

Büchi, H. 1993. "Social Security Reform in Chile." Interamerican Development Bank seminar paper.

Buckberg, E. 1992. "Emerging Stock Markets and International Asset Pricing." Massachusetts Institute of Technology.

Central Bank of Chile. 1952. "Ley No. 10,383 que deroga la ley No. 4,054 y crea el servicio de seguro social y el servicio nacional de salud." *Boletín Mensual* (July 1952): 200–09.

Chamorro, C. 1992. "La cobertura del sistema de pensiones chileno." Thesis 107. Santiago: Instituto Economía, Pontificia Universidad Católica de Chile.

de la Cuadra, S., and S. Valdés-Prieto. 1993. "Myths and Facts About Financial Liberalization in Chile: 1974–1983," in *If Texas Were Chile,* edited by P. Brock, 11–102. San Francisco: ICS Press.

Diamond, P. 1992. "Organizing the Health Insurance Market." *Econometrica* 60 (November): 1233–54.

Díaz, C. A. 1993. "Análisis crítico de las modalidades de pensión y propuesta alternativa." Working Paper 156. Santiago: Instituto de Economía, Pontificia Universidad Católica de Chile.

Díaz, C. A., and S. Valdés-Prieto. 1992. "La tasa de interés del retiro programado: critica y propuesta." Working Paper 149. Santiago: Instituto de Economía, Pontificia Universidad Católica de Chile.

Estadísticas Seguridad Social 1990. 1990. Santiago: Superintendencia de Seguridad Social.

Ffrench-Davis, R. 1973. "Políticas económicas en Chile 1952–1970." CEPLAN. Santiago: Ediciones Nueva Universidad, Universidad Católica de Chile.

Friedman, Benjamin M., and Mark J. Warshawsky. 1990. "The Cost of Annuities: Implications for Saving Behavior and Bequests." *Quarterly Journal of Economics* 105 (February): 135–54.

Frugone, J. P. 1992. "Análisis del mercado de rentas vitalicias previsionales." Thesis 106. Santiago: Instituto de Economía, Pontificia Universidad Católica de Chile.

Habitat. 1991. *Diez años de historia del sistema de AFP, 1981–1991.* Santiago: AFP Habitat.

Haindl, E., E. Budinich, and I. Irarrázabal. 1989. *Gasto social efectivo: un instrumento que asegura la superación definitiva de la pobreza critica.* Santiago: OPEPLAN and Facultad de Ciencias Economicas y Administrativas, Universidad de Chile.

Instituto Nacional de Estadísticas. 1992. "Indicadores de Remuneración y Empleo." *Boletin* (June). Santiago: Instituto Nacional de Estadísticas.

Lakonishok, J., A. Shleifer, and R. W. Vishny. 1992. "The Structure and Performance of the Money Management Industry." *Brookings Papers on Economic Activity: Microeconomics:* 339–79.

Larraín, F. 1991. "Public Sector Behavior in a Highly Indebted Country: The Contrasting Chilean Experience." In *The Public Sector and the Latin American Crisis,* edited by Felipe Larraín and Marcelo Selowsky, 89–136. San Francisco: ICS Press.

Marcel, M., and A. Arenas. 1991. *Reformas a la seguridad social en Chile.* Serie Monografías 5. Interamerican Development Bank.

Ministry of Labor. 1989. *Evolución de la seguidad social chilena en el periodo gubernativo 1973–1989.* Santiago: Subsecretaria de Prevision Scoial.

Ortúzar, P. 1988. "El déficit previsional: recuento y proyecciones." In *Sistema Privado de Pensiones en Chile,* edited by S. Baeza and R. Manubens, 105–28. Santiago: Centro de Estudios Públicos.

Piñera, J. 1991. *El Cascabel al Gato: La Batalla por la Reforma Previsional.* Santiago: Zig Zag.

Prat Report. 1959–64. *Informe Sobre la Reforma de la Seguridad Social Chilena.* Santiago: Editorial Jurídica de Chile.

Securities and Exchange Commission. 1992. *Protecting Investors: A Half Century of Investment Company Regulation.* Government Printing Office.

SEI Research Reports. 1990. 6 (December).

Sirri, E R., and P. Tufano. 1992. "Mutual Fund Services: Supply and Demand." Harvard Business School.

Superintendencia de AFP. 1991–92. *Boletín Estadístico* 103 (April 1991) to 113 (September 1992). Santiago: Superintendency of Pension Fund Managers.

Superintendencia de AFP. 1990. *Estados Financieros Anuales de las AFP 1989 and 1990.* Santiago: Superintendency of Pension Fund Managers.

Superintendencia de AFP. 1991a. *Decreto Legislativo No. 3,500.* Current version published in *Boletín Estadístico* 104 (May 1991): 105–56. Santiago: Superintendency of Pension Fund Managers.

Superintendencia de AFP. 1991b. *FECU: Income and Loss Statements of AFP for 1991.* Santiago: Superintendency of Pension Fund Managers.

Superintendencia de Valores y Seguros. 1992a. *Anuario de Seguros 1991.* Santiago: Superintendency of Securities and Insurance.

Superintendencia de Valores y Seguros. 1992b. *Revista de Seguros* 97 (September). Santiago: Superintendency of Securities and Insurance.

Tiglao, R. 1990. "Pinched Pensions: Government Institutions Called on to Help Philippine Cash Squeeze." *Far Eastern Economic Review* 48 (November 29): 48–49.

Torche, A., and G. Wagner. 1992. "La seguridad social en Chile: inventario de programas." Working Paper 142. Santiago: Instituto de Economía, Pontificia Universidad Católica de Chile.

Valdés-Prieto, S. 1993a. "Earnings-Related Mandatory Pensions: Concepts for Policy Design." The World Bank.

———. 1993b. "Administrative Costs in the Chilean Pension System: Evidence from an International Comparison." The World Bank.

Valdés-Prieto, S., and R. Cifuentes. 1990. "Previsión obligatoria para la vejez y crecimiento económico." Working Paper 131. Santiago: Instituto de Economía, Pontificia Universidad Católica de Chile.

Valdés-Prieto, S., and E. Navarro. 1992. "Subsidios cruzados en el seguro de invalidez y sobrevivencia del nuevo sistema previsional chileno." *Cuadernos de Economía* 29 (December): 409–41.

Wagner, G. 1983. *Antiguo sistema 1925–1980.* Volumes 2–3 of *Estudio de la Reforma Previsional.* Santiago: Instituto de Economía, Pontificia Universidad Católica de Chile.

————. 1991. "La seguridad social y el programa de pensión mínima garatizada." *Estudios de Economía* 18 (June): 35–91.

Walker, E. 1991a. "Desempeño financiero de las carteras accionarias de los fondos de pensiones: ¿es desventajoso ser grande?" Working Paper 137. Santiago: Instituto de Economía, Pontificia Universidad Católica de Chile.

————. 1991b. "Desempeño fnanciero de las carteras de renta fija de los fondos de pensiones: ¿es desventajoso ser grande?" Working Paper 136. Santiago: Instituto de Economía, Pontificia Universidad Católica de Chile.

Wallich, C. 1983. "Savings Mobilization Through Social Security: The Experience of Chile During 1916–1977." Working Paper 553. The World Bank.

Zúñiga, F. 1992. "Desempeño de los fondos de pensiones: impacto de las restricciones legales." Thesis 97. Santiago: Instituto de Economía, Pontificia Universidad Católica de Chile.

7 Privatization and Regulation in Chile

Eduardo Bitran and Raúl E. Sáez

IN MODERN corporations, ownership and management are separated. As is well known this creates an agency problem. In the case of state-owned corporations the solution to this problem is more difficult than in private enterprises because it is not only hard for the principal to exert control on the agent, it is also possible that the principal will have many voices. This will result in behavior that deviates not only from profit maximizing but even from the objectives for which the public enterprise was created. and may cause managerial inefficiency and inflexibility in adapting to changing external conditions.

Privatization has been seen as a solution to these problems. In certain markets, however, private profit-maximizing behavior may lead to allocative inefficiency as a result of monopoly power. In cases where ownership is widely diffuse, the agency problem may not be fully resolved because of shareholders' difficulties in exerting control. Therefore issues regarding the resulting patterns of ownership and market structures and the regulatory frameworks should be at the forefront in the design of a privatization program. This paper focuses on these issues in examining the Chilean experience with privatization and regulation.

Chile has pioneered in privatizations in Latin America and is one of the few countries that has undertaken a massive divestiture of state-owned enterprises in relatively short periods of time. Several episodes of privatization were undertaken between 1973 and 1989. Each of these episodes offered different types of enterprises and featured different methods of sale and mechanisms for financing the purchase of shares and buyers. This experience constitutes a valuable lesson for Latin American countries and perhaps also for reforming countries in eastern Europe that have privatization programs under way.

In the first privatization phase, from 1973 to 1981, a few emerging eco-

We are grateful to Patricio Arrau, Vivianne Blanlot, Dominique Hachette, William Maloney, and Enrique Méndez for useful suggestions and comments.

nomic conglomerates purchased the majority of the enterprises and financial
institutions that were privatized. With the economic crisis of 1981–83, most of
these enterprises and banks, together with the largest pension fund management companies, returned to the state. As enterprises became insolvent, they
ended up in the hands of their creditor banks, which were seized by the state.
As a result, a significant part of the productive sectors was indirectly renation-
alized.

The main mistake made during this process was to have allowed the formation of business conglomerates through the sale of state-owned assets, which
were purchased with soft financing provided by the state or with funds obtained by abusing the implicit insurance of bank deposits. The conglomerates
that owned banks created the larger pension funds when the pension system
was privatized in 1981. They deposited the majority of the funds in the banking
system, thus providing additional reasons for bailing out the financial institutions when they failed. The lack of appropriate regulation in the financial system accentuated the problems of moral hazard and adverse selection that arise
from implicit bank deposit insurance. Furthermore, the conglomerates were
structured in holding companies, with several layers of subsidiaries and affiliated enterprises without any consideration of their effective leverage by the
market and the regulators. By making loans to affiliated parties and issuing
securities without risk rating, the conglomerates were able to operate with extremely high levels of indebtedness. They also concentrated most of the large
foreign debt contracted between 1977 and 1981, pushed by strong government
signals that the nominal exchange rate was going to remain constant. All of
this made them, and the economy, more vulnerable to any external or internal
shock. When the first crisis occurred in 1981–83, the main conglomerates collapsed, with the resulting reversal of privatization and a fiscal cost equivalent
to one-third of GDP.

One lesson that can be drawn from this experience is that successful privatization must avoid schemes of soft financing by the state that allow the formation of conglomerates on the basis of debt. At the same time, lending by banks
to affiliated firms must be strictly controlled.

The trauma of the crisis, the perception that the conglomerates bore significant responsibility for the problems, and the search for political support for
divestiture led to an emphasis on diffusion of ownership in the privatizations
and reprivatizations undertaken after 1983. Privatization schemes such as
"popular capitalism" were designed to ensure that the ownership of several
enterprises was not concentrated. However, this could have created other problems by making it difficult for shareholders to exert control over management.

In addition, the original goal of avoiding the formation of economic groups was not accomplished since a system of widely diffuse ownership and relatively passive institutional investors makes it possible for minority owners to take control of the enterprise. Thus an emphasis on deconcentration does not inhibit the formation of conglomerates and may generate efficiency losses. The problem of conglomerates arises from the possibilities for abusing market power and when financial and productive activities are owned jointly but not properly regulated. If these aspects are properly dealt with, an exaggerated emphasis on the dilution or dissemination of enterprise ownership is not required.

One of the central topics of the paper is the relationship between privatization and the efficiency of resource allocation in markets that exhibit imperfections of industrial organization. Specifically, some lessons are drawn about the need to pay more attention to aspects of industrial organization in the design of the privatization program. In privatizing industries with characteristics of natural monopoly or public good, an effort should be made to restructure the enterprises and to strengthen the regulatory frameworks prior to divestiture. Because of the difficulties involved in regulation and the possibilities for opportunistic behavior, by both the regulated and the regulators, an attempt should be made to promote competition whenever possible. The way in which privatization is undertaken is crucial for the outcome in terms of market structure and performance. Overlooking these issues at this stage makes it difficult to promote competition once market structures are consolidated and property rights allocated.

The electric power and telecommunication industries are the most interesting cases for analyzing the relationship between privatization and regulation in Chile. In both cases insufficient consideration of the effects of vertical and horizontal integration and the inheritance of exclusive licenses granted to the state-owned enterprises have created barriers to entry and possible inefficiencies in resource allocation. Promoting competition must have priority in the privatization program.

With that goal in mind, we describe the different privatization episodes, emphasizing the type of enterprises sold, the methods, and the buyers in each of them. We also analyze the regulatory issues raised by the choice of divestiture strategy and suggest how the industries could have been privatized, what aspects of the regulatory frameworks should have been modified in those cases where competition is impossible, how efficiency could be improved after privatization by antitrust and regulatory measures, and how some of the remaining state-owned enterprises could be privatized.

Table 7-1. Number of SOEs by Legal Regime, Selected Years, 1970–90

Type of SOE	1970	1973[a]	1983[b]	1990
CORFO subsidiaries				
Enterprises	46	228	21	27
Banks	0	18	1	0
Seized firms	0	259	0	0
Created by law				
Enterprises[c]	20	23	22	13
Banks	1	1	1	1
Total	67	529	47	41

SOURCES: CORFO (1978); Hachette and Lüders (1993, appendix A); CORFO, Annual Report (1991); Budget Directorate, Ministry of Finance (1985).
a. Includes enterprises and banks in which CORFO had a minority or small share of ownership.
b. Does not include banks and enterprises taken over as a result of the economic and financial crisis of 1981–93.
c. Includes the Corporación del Cobre (CODELCO) beginning in 1973.

The Public Enterprise Sector in Chile

State-owned enterprises (SOEs) in Chile are under two legal regimes. One group of enterprises has been created by law over the years since the second half of the nineteenth century, and it operates under the supervision of a ministry. The state railways, the national airline, a commercial bank, insurance companies, the ports, petroleum extraction and refining, wholesale distribution of agricultural products, urban public transportation, and water and sewage services are or were part of this group. Another group of enterprises has been established since 1939 by CORFO (Corporación de Fomento de la Producción), the development corporation created in that year to promote the country's industrialization. The CORFO holding includes or included enterprises in steel production, electricity generation, sugar-beet refining, telecommunications, and cellulose, among others, many of them organized as joint-stock corporations. Until 1970 most of the SOEs were established as such, some of them having been taken over when they went bankrupt, some of them, in exceptional cases, having been nationalized.

In 1970 the Unidad Popular coalition was elected on a platform that called for large-scale nationalizations in all sectors of the economy, among other structural transformations, based fundamentally on considerations of distribution and political economy. Between 1970 and 1973 the size of the public enterprise sector increased significantly, both in its contribution to the country's product and in the number of enterprises. Between those two years the number of enterprises in which CORFO held some fraction of equity, alone or in combination with a subsidiary or other public sector institution, increased from 46 to 228, as shown in table 7-1. CORFO also acquired the majority of the shares of fourteen commercial banks and a minority in another four. The government also seized by decree, rather than acquiring through legal purchase, 259 firms.

During this period the government completed the takeover of the largest copper mines, which had already been partially acquired from foreign corporations. The largest SOE (CODELCO) was created to operate them.[1] The total number of enterprises under state control increased from 67 in 1970 to 529 in 1973, and the share of SOEs and government administration in GDP rose from 14 percent in 1965 to 39 percent in 1973.[2]

The Unidad Popular government was overthrown in September 1973 in a military coup. The new government's first actions were aimed at normalizing the operation of the SOEs, including those that had been seized, crippled by the economic and political crisis. To begin with, government representatives with ample powers of administration were named in all enterprises. Then financial support was provided through emergency credits and the rescheduling of debts.

In early 1974 CORFO created an office whose job was to supervise, manage, and name the members of the board of the CORFO enterprises, sell the shares of those enterprises to be privatized, and return to their previous owners the seized enterprises. In 1976 the function of selling CORFO enterprises and assets was transferred to a new office empowered to manage normalization.

The pressures that the SOE sector was exerting on the fiscal deficit required reforming the enterprises.[3] A decree issued in mid-1974 ordered a number of SOEs to reduce their personnel by 20 percent of the 1973 level before the end of 1975. Between 1974 and 1979, employment in a sample of thirty-six SOEs decreased by 25 percent.[4] The managers of SOEs were instructed to operate them with goals and methods similar to those of a private enterprise, to cover their operating and debt-servicing costs, to earn profits, and to transfer dividends to the government. At the same time, all preferential treatment of SOEs, such as income tax and import duty exemptions, was eliminated.

If the enterprises were to eliminate operating losses, then their price-setting policies also had to be reformed, phasing out any implicit subsidies. Initially prices and rates were increased to restore their real values after lagging behind inflation during 1970–73. Then price controls on tradable goods produced by SOEs were eliminated as the economy was being opened to international trade.

1. CODELCO is not part of the CORFO holding. Administratively it is under the supervision of the Ministry of Mining.
2. See Hachette and Lüders (1993, table I-2).
3. More details on the restructuring of public enterprises in Chile can be found in "Public Enterprise Reform in Chile" (n.d.) and in Alé and others (1990).
4. See "Public Enterprise Reform in Chile," table 14.

Finally, rate-setting procedures for public utilities were changed to avoid deficits. As a result of the reform of SOEs in the 1970s, the aggregate deficit of 10 percent of GDP for this sector in 1973 became a surplus of 0.6 percent of GDP in 1980, although some enterprises continued to have losses.[5]

Episodes of Privatization

Between 1973 and 1990 a large number of enterprises in practically all sectors of economic activity were privatized in Chile.[6] However, the process was not carried out in one single program. Each episode differs from the previous one in the type and size of the enterprises privatized, in the methods used to sell them, in the buyers, and in the implications for the role of government in the economy.

Some authors have defined the episodes differently, so that sometimes reference is made to two, three, or four phases of privatization, but in general the following sequence can be described.[7] Shortly after September 1973, the new government began the restitution of those enterprises that were illegally seized under the Allende government; then in 1974 it began selling firms and banks that had been legally nationalized during that administration. This process was concluded by 1981, just prior to the economic and financial crisis. Practically all these enterprises were in tradable sectors or in potentially competitive industries such as distribution and retailing. As a result of the 1982–83 crisis, a large number of the banks and enterprises privatized fell back under the government's control, but they were soon reprivatized in 1984–86. Finally, in 1985 the government started the privatization of the large, core SOEs created by the state over several decades. This time public utilities, which can be characterized as natural monopolies, were privatized together with large enterprises in tradable sectors. At the same time, the reforms that were introduced in the second half of the 1970s and early 1980s resulted in contracting out publicly financed services, privatizing the pension system, and partially privatizing education and health services.

5. See Larraín (1991, table 4.6).

6. More detailed descriptions of privatization in Chile, including aspects such as motivation for divestiture, methods of sale, pricing of enterprises, effect on public finances, and so forth can be found in Hachette and Lüders (1993), Marcel (1989a), Marcel (1989b), and Muñoz (1993).

7. For different definitions of the phases see, for example, Marshall and Montt (1988, pp. 281–307), Vickers and Yarrow (1991, pp. 111–32), and Hachette and Lüders (1993).

Privatization of Firms in Tradable and Competitive Economic Activities

In October 1973 the new government began the restitution of the seized enterprises and farms to their original owners. The enterprises were located in all sectors of the economy, but mainly in agroindustrial and manufacturing activities. The process was conducted quite rapidly; by the end of 1974 202 enterprises had already been returned, and by 1978 only 2 had not been returned. Since they had never been purchased by the state, they were not sold, but the owners had to renounce any legal action they may have been entitled to against the state. Because these enterprises and farms were never legally transferred to the state, the goal of this phase was to solve an abnormal situation.

The privatization of enterprises, banks, farms, and agroindustrial plants was initiated in 1974. The new economic team had diagnosed one of the problems of the Chilean economy as excessive intervention by the state in the economy, including the direct production of goods and services.[8] But the need to reduce the burden of SOEs on the budget weighed heavily in the decision to privatize and in the speed and method chosen to do it. The minister of finance declared that the sale of SOEs would reduce the pressures on spending and provide a source of revenue.[9]

The government decided, besides regularizing the situation of seized farms, to terminate the agrarian reform program, under which approximately 52 percent of agricultural land had been expropriated, and to privatize the legally expropriated lands still under state ownership. This process was practically completed by 1979: of the expropriated land, 30 percent had been returned to the original owners; 44 percent allotted or sold to private owners, mainly individual families and cooperatives; and 17.5 percent transferred to nonprofit institutions.[10]

At the beginning of the privatization round of the 1970s the government decided that the CORFO holding would retain eighteen enterprises considered at that time important for the country's development, although their divestiture could be decided in the future. These enterprises were mainly the larger ones in electricity generation and distribution, telecommunications (local and long distance) companies, coal mines, and companies involved in the production of nitrates and steel and in sugar-beet processing. With the exception of three

8. See Centro de Estudios Públicos (1992).
9. See Cauas (1979, p.96).
10. See Jarvis (1985, pp. 10–14). The percentages are based on agricultural land measured in physical hectares.

local telephone service companies and one electric company, all of them had been created by CORFO.[11] Among those to be privatized were a few enterprises that were subsidiaries before 1970, but all of them were in exportable sectors: forestry, cellulose, and fishing. Thus this privatization program was basically going to reduce the CORFO holding to the size it had in 1970. All of the SOEs not in the CORFO holding, including CODELCO, were also not going to be privatized. However, a number of these enterprises were closed down as part of the process aimed at reforming the state and reducing its size.

In 1975 the government put into force the legislation that regulated the divestiture of enterprises: the method of privatization, the conditions of the sale, the procedures to be followed, and other requirements that CORFO could impose before awarding an enterprise. The enterprises in which the public sector's share of ownership exceeded 10 percent were offered at public auctions in which domestic and foreign investors could participate. In most cases after the bidding process was finished, CORFO negotiated the sale directly with the bidders who had presented the most attractive offers. In general the purchase was not paid in full immediately. There was a down payment with the balance financed with a loan provided by CORFO itself. The loans were indexed, with annual real interest rates ranging from 8 percent to 12 percent, and they had a grace period and different maturities. The buyer had to provide guarantees, which could be the same enterprise's assets, equivalent to 150 percent of the debt. A few enterprises were liquidated and their assets auctioned separately.

The divestiture program advanced quite rapidly. By September 1978 most of the enterprises due to be sold had been privatized. The number of enterprises legally owned by the state decreased from 270 in 1973 to 47 in 1983, as can be seen in table 7-1.[12] CORFO valued the total sales of enterprises (excluding banks and other assets) between 1974 and 1978 at $700 million in 1991 dollars.[13]

According to a 1978 report by CORFO, of ninety-five privatized enterprises, almost half were purchased by other domestic corporations, 22 percent by forty individual domestic investors, 10 percent by foreign investors, one by a cooperative, and the rest by the firms' workers.[14] The process resulted in the concentration of ownership of the larger enterprises in a few conglomerates

11. See CORFO (Corporación de Fomento de la Producción); 1978, p. 19. In fact, in the early 1980s two regional local telephone service and two regional electricity distribution companies were privatized.

12. The figure for 1983 does not include the banks and enterprises taken over during the economic crisis of 1981–83.

13. See CORFO (Corporación de Fomento de la Producción); 1978, appendix 31.

14. See CORFO (Corporación de Fomento de la Producción); 1978, p. 35.

(the *grupos*). The lack of proper review of the bidders' background, for example, of their financial and ownership relationships, allowed the growth of these conglomerates. Moreover, the conditions of the sale facilitated the process because holding companies with small capital bases needed only to come up with the down payment; CORFO provided the loan, with the enterprise's assets used as collateral.

The simultaneous privatization of banks also contributed to this debt-led privatization by providing to the conglomerates an additional source of financing for the purpose of buying SOEs.[15] The result was not only a concentrated structure of ownership of enterprises and financial institutions but also highly indebted conglomerates, for which the banks had no incentives to write-down bad loans. Conglomerates' ownership of banks without restrictions on lending to affiliated enterprises exacerbated the effects of moral hazard and adverse selection of the implicit government insurance on bank deposits. The conglomerates' weaknesses, which were exposed as soon as the economy entered a recession toward the end of 1981, contributed to making the 1981–83 economic and financial crisis one of the worst Chile has faced.

After almost six years of growth, GDP began to decrease in the fourth quarter of 1981. As banks started to become insolvent, the government took them over and with them the parent holding companies and enterprises of conglomerates, which were also in difficulties. Of the enterprises and banks that had been privatized, 70 percent became insolvent.[16]

The process of reprivatizing these enterprises was started in 1984 and completed by 1986. Diffusing ownership and avoiding indebtedness for the acquisition of enterprises were explicit goals of this phase of reprivatizations. Again, the method chosen was public auctions, but this time the bidders were more carefully reviewed, and only those who qualified were allowed to enter the final stage of the bidding process. Also, the government did not provide credit for the purchase. The larger enterprises were purchased by domestic investors, some of them members of conglomerates, often in association with foreign investors, while the smaller ones were purchased only by domestic investors.

The significant participation of foreign investors was another important difference from the divestiture phase of the 1970s. Enterprises were purchased using the debt-equity swap program created by the Central Bank in early 1985. Since Chilean debt at that time (1985–87) was traded at 62 to 67 percent of

15. The term "debt-led" privatization was introduced by Marshall and Montt (1988). Descriptions of how the conglomerates grew out of the privatization program can be found in that paper and also in Larraín (1991) and in Hachette and Lüders (1993).

16. See Marshall and Montt (1988, p. 292). A list of enterprises in difficulties can also be found in that paper.

face value and redeemed at an equivalent 93 percent of face value, foreign investors obtained a capital gain in the operation. However, these investments were subject to longer terms before being allowed to remit profits and repatriate capital than those that used the direct foreign investment law.[17]

As a result of the crisis, the legislation on securities and joint-stock corporations was reformed. Regulations were introduced to protect the rights of minority shareholders, to limit insider trading, and to control transactions between affiliated parties.

Privatization of Financial Institutions

The government decided to privatize the banks in which CORFO had acquired a majority of the shares between 1970 and 1973 and to sell all minority shareholdings. Only the Banco del Estado, which had always been a state-owned bank, was to remain in the public sector. The conditions set for the sale were a minimum price equal to the book value of the shares and a down payment of 20 percent, with the balance to be paid in eight quarterly installments adjusted by the CPI with a real interest rate of 8 percent. Thus as in the case of enterprises, CORFO provided a loan for the purchase of the banks.

In July 1975, CORFO began to offer groups of shares at public auctions. Three years after the program started, all the minority shareholdings had been sold, and the divestiture of eight fully state-owned banks was complete. CORFO still held a minority of the shares in three banks and a majority in another three. Most of the shares were auctioned in 1975 and 1976, yielding a revenue of $450 million in 1991 dollars.

One of the banks still controlled by CORFO in 1978 had been privatized in September 1975, but when the conglomerate to which it had been sold and the bank itself became insolvent in 1976, its ownership reverted to CORFO. This could have been taken as a warning of the serious incentive problems that were leading to imprudent behavior by the conglomerates, which later had a responsibility for the magnitude of the crisis. That bank's sale to a conglomerate was not an exception; rather, it was the rule. Most of the banks became part, and even the base, of the conglomerates that grew out of the divestiture of SOEs. In fact, they used the privatized banks as a source of funds to purchase additional

17. The conversion mechanism is usually known as chapter XIX because that is the section of the Foreign Exchange Norms that regulates them. For a description of swaps and estimates of the difference between discounts in the secondary market and the redemption value, see Ffrench-Davis (1990). On debt conversion see also Fontaine (1988). A list of enterprises purchased with swaps up to mid-1987 can be found in Errázuriz (1987).

enterprises once they were awarded and later on for lending to their own enterprises. In 1974 a limit on the percentage of shares an individual (1.5 percent) or a company (3.0 percent) could own in one bank was established, with the purpose of avoiding the concentration of ownership of financial institutions. However, the regulation was easily bypassed by having several investment companies or individuals related to a conglomerate purchase shares in the banks.[18] In 1978 this limit was abolished. Between 1975 and 1979, the banks and other financial institutions were being deregulated and there was no appropriate prudential regulation by the supervisory body (the Superintendencia de Bancos e Instituciones Financieras).

The first wave of bank insolvencies came in November 1981, when the regulatory authorities had to take over the administration of four banks and four *financieras,* one of each belonging to one of the major financial conglomerates. Three of the banks had been privatized in the 1970s. A second wave occurred in January 1983, when five banks had to be taken over, two put under the direct supervision of regulators, and two others and a *financiera* closed down. Once again, three of the insolvent banks had been previously privatized. Included in these financial institutions were the two largest private banks, each belonging to the two largest conglomerates, and other financial institutions belonging to them. The capital and reserves of these ten institutions represented 45 percent of the system's capital and reserves.[19]

When the conglomerates collapsed, their enterprises came under the government's control. Among them were the four pension fund management companies (AFP), including the two largest, that belonged to the two largest conglomerates. These four AFPs had in December 1982, just before the intervention, 68.9 percent of the individuals affiliated with the new system and 71 percent of the total accumulated pension fund.[20] Thus less than two years after the reform and privatization of the pension system the state again controlled most of it. The main investment instruments for pension funds were bank time deposits, bank mortgage bonds, and government securities. Of the total, 66 percent of the funds were invested in instruments issued by private banks and *financieras.*[21] The failure of banks would have caused a dramatic fall in the value of the funds, creating a serious legitimacy problem for the

18. For a description of how this happened in the largest private commercial bank, see Hachette and others (1992).

19. See Arellano (1983).

20. Calculated from information provided in Superintendencia de Administradoras de Fondos de Pensiones (1983).

21. In December 1982. See Superintendencia de Administradoras de Fondos de Pensiones (1983, pp. 47–48).

newly reformed pension fund system. Given the priority that this reform had, the government had an additional reason, beyond safeguarding the payments system, to come to the rescue of the banks.

As in the case of the enterprises, the government decided to reprivatize the banks in 1984. In order to disperse ownership, the two largest banks and approximately half the shares of the two largest AFPs were sold using the mechanism of popular capitalism—small packages of shares were sold mainly to individuals. The conditions for buying the shares were very advantageous: a very small down payment, an interest-free loan provided by CORFO for the balance, discounts for timely payment of installments, and income tax deductions, among others. There was an upper limit on the number of shares that could be purchased, and the conditions were less generous for legal persons. It has been estimated that these incentives were such that a taxpayer with a marginal income tax rate of 30 percent obtained a tax deduction larger than the down payment.[22]

The banks were technically bankrupt, so they had to be recapitalized, in some cases by sizable amounts, with the privatization by issuing new shares, which were initially purchased by CORFO.[23] The sale of shares using this system of popular capitalism was completed by the end of 1986; 41,000 shareholders in total had acquired the two banks with this mechanism.[24] As to the other banks under government administration, two were absorbed by other institutions, and two were sold to groups of domestic private investors.

Two other crucial actions were taken prior to or simultaneous with the reprivatization of banks. First, the Central Bank purchased the nonperforming loans of all banks that needed help in this respect, whether they were taken over or remained private. The banks must buy back those assets with a percentage of their profits; this is called the subordinated debt of the banks to the Central Bank. Second, the reform of the regulation of financial institutions was completed in November 1986 with the enactment of a new banking law that, among other new restrictions, does not allow banks to take equity positions, strictly regulates loans to affiliated parties, strengthens the power for early intervention by the regulators, and introduces a system for evaluating the riskiness of assets.

Two of the four AFPs that belonged to the failed conglomerates were partially reprivatized with the same mechanism of popular capitalism, but they did not need to be recapitalized. The government decided to sell about 50 per-

22. See Piñera (1986).

23. In the case of the two largest banks privatized by popular capitalism, the new shares were equivalent to 141 percent of capital and reserves in one of them and to 96 percent in the other. See Rosende and Reinstein (1986, p. 262).

24. See Ramírez (1987).

cent of the existing shares to small investors with conditions similar to those offered for the banks, but the buyers had to be affiliated with the new or the old pension system. Again, the process advanced rapidly so that by 1986 the AFPs were back under private ownership—14,000 shareholders in total had purchased shares in both AFPs with this mechanism. The rest of the shares were sold in each case to a single foreign investor. The two other AFPs were merged into one and sold to a foreign insurance company.

The high level of concentration of the pension fund system has continued, however; three AFPs account for about 58 percent of total funds, which in turn are equal to 34 percent of GDP.[25] Such a high level of concentration creates distortions in capital markets. The previous government missed an opportunity to reduce the concentration in this key sector in reprivatizing the AFPs.

Privatization of Core State-Owned Enterprises

In 1985 the government declared that it was starting a new privatization program that would include the core SOEs, almost all of them created as such. The list included some of the country's largest enterprises and public utilities. Only 30 percent of the firms' shares were going to be sold to the private sector, with the exception of two enterprises in which divestiture was going to reach 49 percent. However, once the program was under way, those percentages were periodically raised as new enterprises were added to the list.

By the end of 1986, the goal had been raised to 100 percent in some enterprises, while in others it was approaching 50 percent. In December 1988 almost all of the enterprises were going to be fully privatized, and in 1989 the last enterprises were added to the list. In total thirty-nine SOEs were included in the program.

Although this number is small compared with the number of privatizations carried out in the 1970s, the type of enterprise made this privatization episode much more important in its consequences for the role of the state in the economy. First, some of the enterprises are among the largest in the country and were created to accelerate the country's development in areas such as metallurgy, long-distance telecommunications, information science, and electricity generation or as support for particular activities, such as helping farmers with

25. The share of the total pension funds held by the largest three AFPs was calculated for September 1992 using information provided in Superintendencia de Administradoras de Fondos de Pensiones (1992). The category "Pension funds as a percentage of GDP" was calculated in current pesos using the accumulated pension funds as of November 1992 and the 1992 GDP, both taken from Central Bank of Chile (1993).

the establishment of sugar-beet refining plants. Second, some of the enterprises are natural monopolies raising the issue of the separation of regulation and ownership.

The arguments given for this new round of divestitures were explicitly more ideological, as the speeches of the minister of finance in 1985 show. He mentioned four reasons: (1) "the importance of private property as the foundation of a free society and of a market economy"; (2) the gain in efficiency that was going to occur in these enterprises under private control; (3) the reprivatization and recapitalization of the banks and enterprises affected by the financial crisis; and (4) the stabilizing effect that a deepening of the stock market would have on the capital market. Then a fifth goal was added: the spreading of shareholding. In fact, in the annual reports of the finance minister between 1985 and 1989, the program is called "Ownership Diffusion" and not privatization.[26]

In 1985 the SOE sector had a surplus of 0.57 percent of GDP; thus the SOEs could not be accused of being the source of that year's government deficit.[27] However, the public sector faced financial constraints at the time, and the proceeds from privatization allowed the government to show smaller deficits or larger surpluses without having to raise taxes or to reduce spending.[28]

The government set the stage for this privatization phase by taking a number of policy actions in preparation for divestiture. First, the pension funds were allowed to invest in shares of joint-stock corporations in January 1985. The regulatory framework is designed to encourage investment in corporations with dispersed ownership; those in which shareholding is highly concentrated are not eligible for purchase by pension funds. Pension funds became active participants in the privatization of those SOEs whose shares were offered and traded on the Santiago Stock Exchange, becoming an important source of demand for the shares of the enterprises being privatized, especially the largest ones. In December 1985, the sum of all the accumulated pension funds was equal to 11 percent of that year's GDP, and the flow into them represented one-third of private savings.[29]

Second, the government reformed the regulation of public utilities in 1982, enacting new legislation for the electric power industry and telecommunications. The new electricity regulatory law set the procedures and formulas for

26. See Budget Directorate, Ministry of Finance (1985, p.23). The translation is by the authors. With respect to the third argument, it must be remembered that at the same time that the government was starting the new program in 1985, the banks and enterprises taken over during the crisis were being privatized.

27. See Larraín (1991, table 4.6).

28. This issue is raised in Marcel (1989a).

29. See González and Marfán (1992).

periodic rate-setting, the rules for obtaining licenses for the building and operating of generating plants and distribution systems, and the role of the regulatory authorities. In telecommunications, the new law opened the sector to competition by private investors in local telephone service and defined the role of the regulatory institution. In 1987 a new reform determined the rules and formulas for the periodic setting of rates and established the obligation for licensees to provide service in their areas. In 1988 the regulation of water and sewage services was reformed on very much the same model as the electric power industry and telecommunications.

Third, a number of SOEs were restructured prior to divestiture. The two largest electricity companies (ENDESA and Chilectra) were transformed into holding companies by separating distribution and generation-transmission into different subsidiaries. In the case of ENDESA, some hydroelectric plants were turned into subsidiaries operating only as generators. Other enterprises also created subsidiaries that were later privatized separately. Government services such as water and sewage and the postal and telegraph services were transformed into joint-stock corporations. More generally, the partial sale of most enterprises through the stock market required that they be incorporated if they were not already public companies. Large enterprises in tradable sectors were not divided prior to divestiture. However, since the economy was opened in the 1970s, significant competition from imports already existed.

The restructuring of enterprises to eliminate losses or to make them more attractive prior to divestiture occurred only rarely because, as explained above, the major reforms in the management of core SOEs had occurred in the 1970s or early 1980s. One case was the state airline, which had to be reorganized in 1985 in the face of heavy losses. The company was turned into a joint-stock corporation, transferred to the CORFO holding, and authorized to sell 30 percent of its shares. In this process, some of the company's liabilities were ceded to the government. Another case was ENDESA, which transferred a large foreign debt to CORFO in exchange for a new issue of shares, thus improving the company's financial condition.

Once again the program advanced quite rapidly; when the democratic government took office in March 1990, it was practically completed. Twenty of the twenty-three enterprises offered for sale in 1985 had been fully privatized, CORFO maintained a significant but minority percentage of shares in one, and no progress had been made in the other two. Among all the enterprises included in this privatization phase, private shareholders held more than 90 percent of equity capital in twenty-nine of them; in one enterprise that percentage was 68, in four others the private sector was a minority shareholder, and five were still fully state-owned.

According to CORFO's annual reports, the total proceeds from the sale of shares between 1985 and 1989 amounted to $1.5 billion in 1991 dollars.[30] Hachette and Lüders estimate that the contribution of public sector enterprises and administration to GDP decreased from 24.1 percent in 1981 to 15.9 percent in 1988.[31] Table 7-1 shows that the number of public enterprises decreased only from 47 in 1983 to 41 in 1991. This is misleading for two reasons, however: some enterprises were created out of government services and not all of them privatized (the water and sewage services being an example); and several enterprises were divided at the beginning of their divestiture, so the number of privatizations after 1985 is large relative to the number of SOEs shown for 1983 in table 7-1.

Methods of Privatizing Core SOEs

In this privatization episode a large number of sale mechanisms were used. Furthermore, because the larger enterprises were not offered in one package, several methods were used simultaneously in their divestiture. The result was more variety of investors than in the first episode and ownership of individual companies distributed among different types of owners (employees, domestic investors, foreign investors, institutional investors, individuals).

Public bids were again used extensively, but this time only small enterprises were offered as a whole in one bid. The buyers included domestic and foreign investors and employees of the enterprise. In larger enterprises, controlling packages of shares were sold in national and international bids, with the rest sold to other investors, employees of the enterprises, public sector employees, and pension funds and to the general public through the stock market. Foreign investors were awarded controlling packages of shares or the entire enterprise.

The mechanism most frequently used was the periodic auction of noncontrolling packages of shares on the Santiago Stock Exchange. These auctions contributed to the diversification of the buyers, and it permitted the government to capture in part the steep increase in the price of shares that occurred in this period. It was also the mechanism through which pension funds participated in this privatization phase.

The direct sale of shares to managers, employees, and workers, called "labor capitalism," was another new method used in this privatization program. Several mechanisms were used to provide financing for the purchase, with the

30. See CORFO, *Annual Report.*
31. See Hachette and Lüders (1993, table I-2).

advance payment of severance benefits and loans from the enterprise itself, CORFO, or the state-owned Banco del Estado being the more frequently used. When workers were offered the option of receiving in advance their accrued severance benefits as shares of the enterprise, two incentives were provided. First, a percentage (usually 20 percent) of the severance pay was given in cash, with no obligation to purchase shares with it. Second, if the employee keeps the shares until retirement from the enterprise, the enterprise must compensate him if a fall in the price of the shares results in a value lower than the original investment. In some enterprises, in order to buy additional packages of shares the workers and the managers created investment companies managed by the latter. These companies contracted loans to purchase shares, using the previously distributed shares as collateral.

Some enterprises or packages of shares were sold directly to specific types of investors. Beginning in March 1988, public sector employees and members of the armed forces were offered the option of receiving in advance their accrued severance pay in the form of shares in a limited number of SOEs, with the possibility of acquiring shares beyond what they could buy with their severance pay with loans from CORFO at highly subsidized interest rates.[32] Several regional electricity distribution companies were sold only or partially to individual investors of the region where the enterprise is located. This was called "popular regional capitalism." The purchases were also paid for with loans from CORFO with subsidized real interest rates. A percentage of the shares of the sugar-beet processing company (IANSA) was sold to beet farmers, for whom this company is the only buyer of their product. Finally, popular capitalism was again used to attract individuals as shareholders using subsidized loans from CORFO.

Another method of privatization, significant though used only in a couple of enterprises, was variations in the firm's equity capital. This type of transaction was very important in the cases of ENDESA and the steel company (CAP). The privatization of CAP was accelerated by the decision made in June 1986 to reduce its net worth. In that month CORFO, which still owned approximately 83 percent of the company's stock, decided to sell 65 percent of the total to the company itself. Then the company wrote off those shares. As a result, the private sector's percentage of ownership increased from 17 percent to 49 percent. This transaction was one of the most controversial because of

32. The real interest rates in the CORFO loans were 2 percent, 4 percent, or 6 percent, depending on the option chosen, while the average real interest rate charged on loans with maturities between one and three years (similar to that of the CORFO loans) in the financial market was 7.4 percent in 1988 and 8.9 percent in 1989.

the method chosen to push forward the firm's privatization and the price at which CORFO sold the shares to the enterprise.[33]

In the case of ENDESA, a U.S.$500 million foreign debt was transferred to CORFO in exchange for a new issue of shares in the second half of 1987. CORFO then sold the shares to the private sector. Differences in the valuation of shares in the swap operation and in the subsequent sale to the private sector again raised a certain amount of controversy about this divestiture. When sizable new investments required an increase in a firm's equity capital, the newly issued shares were sold to the private sector.[34]

Finally, the shares of some enterprises were also used as payment to settle legal actions taken against the state by former farm owners who sued when their land was expropriated in the agrarian reform program of the early 1970s.

Privatization of Electric Power and Telecommunications

The electric power and the telecommunications industries are the two major privatized sectors under regulation. Privatization of other activities subject to regulation now or when privatized, such as water and sewage and ports, has not advanced.

The privatization of the two distribution companies (Chilmetro and Chilquinta) and the generator (Chilgener) of the Chilectra holding started in the second half of 1985, when shares were offered on the stock market. Then the employees were given the option of receiving in advance 50 percent of their accrued severance pay, and pension funds were authorized to invest in the stock of these companies. The process continued in the three companies using two methods of divestiture: periodic auctions of packages of shares on the stock market (in which pension funds could participate) and the direct sale of stock to the employees of the company.

By August 1987, Chilmetro and Chilquinta were fully privately owned. Pri-

33. The private shareholders implicitly paid for the increase in their share of ownership since the operation is equivalent to purchasing 32 percent of a smaller corporation. See Marcel (1989a, appendix II), for a discussion of the issue of the valuation of the shares and an estimation of the implicit subsidy for the private buyers. For an opposing view of this transaction see Hachette and Lüders (1993, chapter 8).

34. Another form of transferring ownership to private shareholders through increases in an SOE's capital was the mechanism of "financial reimbursable contributions." The regulatory legislation for electricity, telecommunications, and water and sewage services introduced in the 1980s allowed the public utilities to request contributions by new clients to pay for the extension of service. These contributions had to be reimbursed at a latter date, and one way it could be done was with shares of the company. However, this method was never significant in the divestiture of utilities.

vatization of Chilgener was completed in January 1988. The controlling share-holders of these three enterprises are different; pension funds are the only shareholders common to all three with significant percentages of equity. These companies operate in the Central Interconnected System, which supplies electricity to 93 percent of the country's population. Chilgener has approximately 14 percent of that system's generating capacity; Chilmetro and Chilquinta represent 40 percent and 20 percent of the system's demand, respectively.[35]

The divestiture of Chilmetro owes much to the leadership and active involvement in the process of the executives of the enterprise. The executives and workers initially purchased shares with their severance payments. Later on, these shares were used to form investment companies that contracted loans with the state-owned Banco del Estado to acquire the last two packages of shares offered (each equivalent to 10 percent of the company's equity). The newly acquired shares were also used as collateral for the loans. These investment companies are run by the executives of the electricity distribution company. Because the statutes restricted the voting rights of the workers who are shareholders, the government-appointed executives were able to gain control of the distribution company.

In 1988 certain functions of the original distribution company were transferred to newly created firms (Synapsis, Manso de Velasco). A holding corporation was created, called Enersis, which owns the majority of the shares of the distribution company and of the newly formed affiliated suppliers. The opening up of Enersis and of the investment companies that are its largest shareholders as public joint-stock corporations allowed the aforementioned executives to strengthen their control of the subsidiaries and to expand Enersis to control ENDESA. Pension funds played an important role in facilitating the expansion of Enersis by owning 34 percent of its shares.[36] The resulting structure of ownership has had adverse consequences on competition.

In 1986 ENDESA initiated the divestiture of the subsidiaries created earlier in the decade through public bids or direct sales, through regional popular capitalism, and in settlement of legal actions. In 1988 the subsidiary operating in the Greater North Interconnected System was divided into three distribution companies, which were privatized a year later mostly through regional popular capitalism, and a generation-transmission company, which is being privatized in 1993. Of the two large hydroelectric generators that were separated from ENDESA after 1986, one (Colbún) remains in the public sector and the other (Pehuenche) was purchased by ENDESA in 1989.

35. For details on how the electricity supply industry is organized in Chile, see Blanlot (1993).
36. In September 1992. See Superintendencia de Administradoras de Fondos de Pensiones (1992).

The privatization of ENDESA itself began in July 1987, when the company offered a small percentage of equity to its own employees. It sold additional packages of shares through the stock market and directly to individuals with the system of popular capitalism, to its own employees, and to public sector employees. By the end of 1989, 90 percent of the company's equity was owned by private shareholders. As a result of the intensive use of popular and labor capitalisms and the auctioning of packages of shares in the stock market, the ownership of ENDESA is very diffuse. The largest shareholder holds 13 percent of the enterprise's equity, and pension funds hold 28.5 percent of the shares.[37] In 1991 Enersis, the owner of the largest distribution company, acquired significant control of the board of ENDESA.

Local telephone service and national and international long-distance service were separated in SOEs.[38] This separation was maintained in the process of divestiture. Until 1981 there were three state-owned local-service telephone companies: two small regional companies and one dominant company (CTC). CTC owns approximately 94 percent of the telephone lines and serves 92 percent of the population. The two regional companies were sold to private domestic investors in 1981. ENTEL provides national and international long-distance telecommunications, and at the time it was privatized it handled 80 percent of the minutes of domestic long-distance calls and 100 percent of those of international calls.[39]

In the course of 1986, 30 percent of ENTEL was privatized through the stock market. Pension funds were important buyers. During 1987 little progress was made in its divestiture, but in 1988 private shareholders took control of the company as CORFO's share decreased to 38 percent. Employees became an important body of shareholders when they purchased 12.5 percent of equity through an investment company, using their own savings and a loan from the state-owned Banco del Estado. The divestiture of ENTEL was completed in 1989. Additional changes in ownership have occurred since then; a subsidiary of the state-owned Spanish telephone company became the largest shareholder when it acquired 10 percent of the shares and then in 1990 another 10 percent from the Chilean army.

Throughout 1985 small packages of CTC shares were sold on the stock

37. The percentage of the largest shareholder is equal to the sum of the shares owned by Enersis (7 percent) and those owned by Manso de Velasco (6 percent) in December 1992. The latter is a subsidiary of the former. For shareholding by pension funds as of September 1992, see Superintendencia de Administradoras de Fondos de Pensiones (1992).

38. CTC, the largest local service provider, has long-distance service only between Santiago and Valparaíso, in competition with ENTEL, the long-distance supplier.

39. This percentage has decreased to approximately 70 percent because CTC has started to use another company to carry part of the international calls.

market. In March 1987, the company's employees were given the option of receiving their severance pay in advance by investing 80 percent of it in shares. A few months later, in August, an international bid was called for 30 percent of CTC's equity, with the condition that the winner would have to commit the subscription of enough new shares to attain 45 percent ownership. The company was awarded to Bond, an Australian investor, in early 1988, the transaction handled as a direct foreign investment and not as a debt-equity swap. The increase in the firm's capital was required to finance an investment program needed to eliminate the excess demand for service accumulated over several decades. From 1988 to early 1990, the privatization was completed mostly by selling shares in the stock market and directly to public-sector employees.

The two companies have continued to operate in different markets, with ENTEL providing the long-distance services for CTC customers. But the two companies have been constantly in contention, as each has tried to obtain a license for service in the other's market. In 1990 Bond sold all its shares in CTC to the Spanish state-owned telephone company; thus the largest shareholder of ENTEL became also the controlling shareholder of CTC. This prompted the antitrust commission to rule that the Spanish company would have to sell its shares in one of the enterprises. In April 1993, Chile's supreme court upheld that ruling. The other shareholders common to both enterprises are pension funds.

Privatization and Regulation of Natural Monopolies

The privatizations of the 1980s focused on public utilities with characteristics of natural monopoly, an area that raises interesting economic issues. In addition to the traditional concerns about managerial efficiency and distributive effects, there are issues regarding the allocative efficiency of divestiture.

In industries with significant economies of scale in the range of production relevant to the market size and with significant sunk costs (due to irreversible investments), it is efficient to have a market structure with a single producer that takes advantage of those economies of scale (natural monopoly). The traditional argument has held that the potential for the abuse of market power by the single supplier will justify some kind of government regulation to improve welfare. Only in the case of contestable markets will the existence of a natural monopoly not have adverse effects on social welfare.[40]

Market failures or distribution problems can explain the insufficient provi-

40. See Baumol, Panzar, and Willig (1982).

sion of certain goods and services. The most obvious example is the provision of public goods, but there also are some examples of services that have high positive externalities but in which low levels of income result in insufficient demand to justify supplying the commodity or service through private means. Examples are providing transportation services to isolated areas and providing drinkable water and sewer services in rural areas.

In most countries SOEs provide these goods or services with characteristics of natural monopoly or public good. The justification for the entrepreneurial role of the state was that it would limit monopoly power or provide basic public goods that are not privately profitable. Why should privatization even be considered if it raises such obvious questions about allocative inefficiency and distribution? The reason is that even if the state could restrain itself in exerting monopoly power or commit itself to providing unprofitable goods and services, society as a whole would be worse off with direct government intervention because of the huge difficulties in ensuring that SOEs operate efficiently.

The main reason to consider seriously the privatization of these enterprises is the deep belief that it is very difficult to solve the principal-agent problem that exists between the state as owner and the managers of the SOEs. Therefore, keeping these natural monopolies in the hands of the state will not be in the public interest because of the magnitude of operational and managerial inefficiencies.

Of course, the problem of firm behavior that does not maximize profits is relevant not only in the case of SOEs. The separation between ownership and management generates an agency problem in which it is always difficult to make the goals of management and the goals of the owners compatible without incurring some losses in efficiency. The principal has difficulties in monitoring the behavior of managers, and it is difficult to know whether their observed performance is the result of random events or simply poor management. Agency theory shows that in the presence of random events that affect the firm's results and of risk aversion on the part of managers, the profit-maximizing goal always suffers. In the case of natural monopoly this problem is more severe. In industries with several suppliers the results of one firm can be compared with those of others operating in the same market, since external shocks affect all firms equally. With natural monopolies it is not possible to find patterns of performance to make such comparisons.

In the real world, corporations are complex entities, and the problem of exerting control by shareholders to maximize profits is a multi-tiered principal-agent problem. The agency problem is repeated between top managers and second-tier managers, and so on. At each tier the principal reflects in an imperfect way the goals of the shareholders.[41] A partial solution to this multiple agency problem in private firms is to establish a system in which wages at all tiers are linked to performance. At lower levels, it is again not possible to make the goals of shareholders fully compatible with those of the workers. The optimal incentive contract will require that managers and workers be made the residual claimers of firm profits. However, risk aversion on the part of managers and workers will make this an inefficient solution. The problem is worsened by the difficulties involved in measuring individual performance at the lower tiers because of team production, which gives rise to free riding.

It has been argued in general that the state as owner has more difficulties in properly solving the agency problem than do private shareholders. As a consequence there is a higher probability of finding larger deviations from an efficient or cost-minimizing operation.[42] In SOEs the principal has several voices with different objectives that are not always consistent. This gives rise to great ambiguity in the contract between the principal and the agents. The mandate for the managers is unclear and responds to multiple demands with a great degree of conflict among them. It is commonplace to see in countries of very different idiosyncrasies and ideologies how SOEs are used as a vehicle for political action or to pursue goals that are unrelated to the justification for the entrepreneurial role of the state.

The permeability to political considerations will usually result in significant labor rigidity. Incentive schemes with punishments and rewards linked to performance, although essential in complex modern corporations, are almost nonexistent in a SOE. Political interference makes it almost impossible to fire workers for poor performance. In a world with rapid and continuous changes in the pattern of specialization and dynamic comparative advantage, due among other things to strong and continuous technological change, maintaining production flexibility and factor mobility is essential for reaching high levels of efficiency and sustained growth. This type of consideration is particularly important when SOEs operate in tradable sectors because they face more constraints in trying to adapt to changing conditions. The resulting serious rigidities in resource allocation imply allocative inefficiencies which, in turn, are larger as the economy is closer to full employment.

41. See Mayhew and Seabright (1992, pp. 105–29).

42. Private firms expand their capacity by raising resources in the capital market, which imposes some discipline in monitoring managerial efficiency. SOEs, however, frequently obtain their financing through the state; when they raise funds through the capital market, they have the explicit or implicit guarantee of the state. Thus the discipline imposed by the market is lost, and the government will face a severe problem in having an efficient investment decisionmaking process.

The difficulties involved in eliminating political interference in the management of SOEs has been evident, in different periods, even in developed countries such as the United Kingdom, France, Spain, and Italy. This belief has been behind the privatization process in several countries.

An option for improving managerial efficiency and limiting adverse effects in resource allocation is to move from the state as entrepreneur to the state as regulator. Nevertheless, regulation is not without its own problems. Some are of the same nature that arise when the state is an entrepreneur, especially in sectors with characteristics of natural monopoly. The issue then is how to accomplish the goal of privatizing natural monopolies with a regulatory framework that will enhance operational efficiency without detracting from the quality of service or creating the potential for abuse of market power.

The successful regulation of private natural monopolies poses a significant challenge, requiring the development of institutions that are hard to build in developing countries. The regulation of a natural monopoly constitutes the typical long-term contract between a principal and an agent in which the latter should make irreversible investments with significant sunk costs. The existence of high transaction costs raises the possibility for opportunistic behavior, by the agent or by the principal, that will impose significant inefficiencies on the resource allocation process.[43]

Then how have these regulatory problems been solved to obtain allocative efficiency? Several approaches, all of which constitute second-best solutions, have been developed in recent years.

RATE-OF-RETURN REGULATION. The traditional mechanism of regulation has been to set rates based on rate-of-return targets, a scheme that has been used broadly in the United States for a long time. The system operates under the following rules: when a company wishes to modify its prices, it must apply to the regulator, having previously calculated operating and capital costs and the amount of capital required to operate. The regulator audits the information and sets a reasonable rate of return over capital. In addition, with the information regarding sales, the regulator will set the rates that will provide the target rate of return. This rather simple scheme has serious problems since it does not provide enough incentives to reduce or minimize costs because the regulation method will validate any inefficiency by raising rates. This type of regulation induces an overexpansion of capital with the goal of expanding the flow of profits.

RPI-X REGULATION. An alternative regulatory scheme, developed and applied in the United Kingdom, attempts to correct the well-known problems

---

43. See Klein, Crawford, and Alchian (1978) and Williamson (1975).

of rate-of-return regulation. This new approach, known as RPI-X, allows an increase in rates according to general inflation discounted by a factor, X, which represents an exogenous ex-ante estimation of the increase in efficiency. Every four or five years, the parameter X is adjusted. The firm may appropriate as additional profit any additional increase in efficiency (beyond X).

A criticism of this scheme is that in the periodic adjustment of the parameter X it is difficult not to have in mind past returns on capital when setting the new value of X. Therefore, in practice, the RPI-X converges into a rate-of-return scheme over a longer period of time with the same flaws.

A second problem is that in a dynamic and complex environment the mechanism leaves open the possibility for returns on capital significantly higher than the normal return, considering the level of risk of the industry. These abnormal profits can arise in part as a result of incomplete contracts regarding quality of service or product diversification, which give rise to ex-post opportunistic behavior. The starting prices of the RPI-X scheme will reflect in some cases the high production costs that result from the inefficient operation of the SOE, which in turn is a consequence of the huge rigidities imposed by the government. The prices that greet consumers will not follow the reduction in costs that will occur as those rigidities are removed when the enterprise is privatized.

The experience in countries where this or a similar scheme has been introduced shows that incomplete contracts still allow a significant amount of discretion on the part of both the regulator and the firm. The possibility for ex-post opportunistic behavior on both sides has arisen because the regulation has not set objective rules that provide a framework for the operation of the firm accompanied by an efficient monitoring scheme. As a result, regulation has been rapidly transformed into a game with a broad range of solutions and with a continuous process of negotiation and renegotiation between the regulator and the firm.

The environment in which firms operate has led to the development of a new kind of industry, one that has rent-seeking as a goal, because it becomes profitable to devote time and resources to building influence with the objective of favorably affecting the actions of the regulator—lobbying. Also, an important amount of resources is devoted to settling disputes that arise in the ambiguous regulatory framework between the regulator and the firms and between the firms themselves. This process greatly increases uncertainty in the industry, significantly increasing discount factors, adversely affecting investment, and raising prices.

FRANCHISING NATURAL MONOPOLIES. An alternative to the privatization of an activity with natural monopoly characteristics or operation by the state is to franchise the natural monopoly for a period of time equivalent to the lag between each adjustment in the factor X in RPI-X regulation. The idea is to promote competition for the field instead of competition in the field, given the impossibility of developing the latter. The franchise is awarded through periodic competitive bids. Between each bid, prices are adjusted on the basis of past inflation. This scheme is known as the Chadwick-Demsetz bidding scheme, and it has been applied in the United States in the cable television industry.

The main advantages of this scheme are that it eliminates the incentive problem of the rate-of-return scheme and it reduces significantly the risk of arbitrary renegotiations of the X factor in RPI-X regulation. The main difficulty in implementing this scheme emerges when there are significant investments with a high component of sunk costs. Attempts have been made to solve this problem by finding different ways to compensate the outgoing franchisee for sunk investments. Nevertheless, the valuation of these investments again creates monitoring problems and allows room for discretion. The fear of losing the franchise and the uncertainty involved in the compensation for previous investments create disincentives for investment by the firm.

This conceptual analysis has shown that regulation also must deal with efficiency problems. The decision to privatize natural monopolies should balance the benefits in increased managerial efficiency against the expected cost of allocative inefficiency and expenditures associated with the regulatory framework. The balance between these benefits and costs will hinge on the specific institutional arrangements and development, as well as the political culture, of each country.

One of the main policy implications of this conceptual analysis is that the privatization process should be carried out with great consideration to the goal of maximizing competition. It should avoid situations in which activities with natural monopoly characteristics will extend the market power of the firm beyond the segment of the market where this characteristic exists, allowing it to create barriers to entry and to establish a de facto monopoly.

Issues regarding vertical and horizontal integration of firms should be addressed before privatizing, with a focus not only on managerial efficiency but also, and mainly, on preventing the consolidation of private monopoly in competitive markets.

It has been argued that vertical integration of firms does not affect the performance of the market since an upstream monopoly could extract all the monopoly rents by setting a monopoly price for the intermediate product without the need for downstream integration. Moreover, vertical disintegration could generate important inefficiencies resulting from vertical externalities in the presence of a chain of vertically disintegrated monopolists, from bias in the choice of inputs, from underinvestment because of the risk imposed by bilateral monopoly characteristics of the market, and so forth. Efficiency could, therefore, be a justification for vertical integration.

Even though one should not dismiss efficiency as a motive for vertical integration, in regulated industries with characteristics of natural monopoly, it could generate serious difficulties for the regulator. First, the integrated firm that is constrained in its opportunities to extract monopoly rents in the regulated segment can extend its monopoly power in the nonregulated segment, allowing it to abuse its monopolistic position. The natural monopoly can discriminate, sometimes in very subtle ways, in favor of affiliated firms operating in upstream and downstream competitive markets. This will significantly increase barriers to entry in the competitive markets, leading to the exertion of monopoly power.

Second, vertical integration through joint ownership of the natural monopoly and of the firms providing inputs and services in many cases represents an opportunity to transfer monopoly profits upstream by overpricing them, circumventing the regulation. It is sometimes important that the licensees of natural monopolies be restricted to providing regulated products. Otherwise the regulation process becomes extremely complex because it is very difficult to sort out the information regarding operating and capital costs of the regulated activities. However, these restrictions may impose inefficiencies by preventing a firm from taking advantage of economies of scope through horizontal integration.

A second issue to consider is that the regulatory framework must be spelled out before privatization. Otherwise, important equity problems and efficiency losses may result from the privatizations. The absence of a rate-setting scheme generates uncertainty over the property rights that are being acquired, and this has two effects. On the one hand, the value of the asset will be highly discounted as a result of the risk premium applied by the investors since there is room for ex-post opportunistic behavior by the government. On the other hand, adverse selection may attract those entrepreneurs with greater willingness to take risks or those who have greater lobbying power in the political system, maximizing the probability of capturing the regulator for their own advantage. Underinvestment will result from an ambiguous regulatory framework, and there will be significant investment in rent-seeking.[44] Another common condi-

44. See Paredes (1993) for further discussion.

tion is that the state-owned monopoly is privatized with the same exclusive, beneficial rights it had, creating legal barriers to entry that retain the monopolistic characteristics of the sector.

The strengthening of regulatory institutions is key to the success of the privatization effort. The specialized nature of the function and the fact that the better trained technical staff remains in the privatized firm creates a serious problem of lack of human resources with the qualifications required to perform this function. Under these circumstances the negotiating power will be unbalanced and the regulatory game will allow monopoly power to be exercised. Public sector wages in developing countries allow hiring capable young professionals, but their obvious career path is to move on to the regulated firms with much higher wages. This creates conflicts of interest and a lack of independence of the regulating authorities, further affecting the results of regulation.

A final point is the effect on market competition of significant participation in the ownership of enterprises by institutional investors. Even if horizontal and vertical integration of enterprises with natural monopoly characteristics are restricted, the fact that institutional investors are shareholders in several enterprises in the same regulated industry could result in coordination among the enterprises, even to the extent of having common directors on the boards. The resulting problems of monopoly power will not be in the public interest. Solutions to this problem include forbidding institutional investors to elect the same persons to the boards of companies in the same industry and not allowing conduct that leads to coordinated actions between the enterprises in a sector.

We have argued that exerting control in an SOE presents severe problems. Although there is mounting consensus that privatization will improve the agency problem, the degree to which this is the case will depend heavily on the resulting structure of ownership and the mechanisms of financing through capital markets.

When the ownership of firms is widely distributed among thousands of shareholders, with no one having a significant stake in the company, there are not enough incentives to invest resources in information gathering to exert control over management. The shareholders instead of exerting control have the right of exit by selling their shares. It has been argued that this right will discipline management by increasing the risk of takeovers. However, for this to be the case other potential shareholders must be available who could exert their control rights and appropriate a significant proportion of the benefits, and this is not always the case. As a consequence of this free-rider problem and the lack of discipline from takeovers, managers in corporations with widely diffused ownership will enjoy significant discretion to pursue objectives that differ from those of the shareholders. As Michael Porter has pointed out, fragmented equity stakes with limited information about individual companies will result in managers' emphasizing short-term goals instead of investing with a long-term perspective.[45] Shareholders with a transitory position in particular companies and shareholders who trade frequently will be looking for short-term returns.

The development of institutional investors has not solved this problem. Their fiduciary responsibilities as pension fund or trust fund managers require prudent diversification of investment, and this has meant that funds have stakes in hundreds of companies, with little incentive to exert control in any one of them. Besides, rules that restrict or even inhibit voting rights in corporations create passive investors, giving more discretion to managers.

Shareholding through institutional investors creates a double principal-agent problem since the portfolio manager reflects in an imperfect way the goal of fund owners, once again reducing the degree of control over the managers' behavior. This problem can be exacerbated by the way in which incentive schemes and the corporate governance have been designed for pension fund managers in the newly created private pension fund system in Chile.[46]

Regulations on insider trading in the United States, and increasingly in some countries of Europe, by limiting communications between the directors and managers on one side and the shareholders on the other, have made it even more difficult for shareholders to influence firms' behavior. This regulation makes owners outsiders.

Porter has argued that banks should take positions as shareholders in companies in which they hold debt as a way to increase their control over the firms.[47] The conflict of interest that arises from this double role as creditor and shareholder was an important ingredient in the financial crisis of the 1930s in the United States, and it gave rise to the Glass-Steagall Act, which separated investment banking from traditional banking.

In sum, if the alternative to public ownership of enterprises is diffuse owner-

45. Porter (1992).

46. The pension fund system does not have a performance fee. The only incentives come from attracting new contributors, who pay an initial load fee. Therefore, there is no direct link between the performance of the fund and the profits of the fund management company. Unfortunately, because of information asymmetries, contributors have serious difficulties in evaluating the performance of different AFPs. Empirical evidence shows that the main reason for switching AFPs is that the contributor is approached by a sales agent. This casts doubts on the rationality of the decisionmaking process involved in changing from one AFP to another. In addition, the AFP is accountable for significant deviations from the system's average, so what matters is not making good or bad decisions, but doing what the system does as whole. This problem leads us to conclude that the management company reflects in a very imperfect way the goals of the final shareholders (the contributors).

47. See Porter (1992).

ship, with shareholders who do not exert active control over management because of information asymmetries and high monitoring costs, it is not clear that privatization per se will better align the goals of managers and owners. Because of distributional or political reasons and concerns about systemic risk when the industrial conglomerates are linked with the financial sector, schemes such as the widespread distribution of shares or popular capitalism have been introduced. However, they raise the risk of myopic behavior on the part of firms, as Porter rightly points out in his analysis of the capital market allocation system in the United States.[48] Privatization should aim at having at least some shareholders who have a significant stake in enterprises and the perspective of a long-term involvement.

Regulatory Issues in the Privatization Process in Chile

During the 1980s, prior to privatization, legislation was introduced to develop a regulatory framework. This was done in 1982 for the electric power industry, in 1982 for local and long-distance telephone service (but reformed in 1987), and finally in 1988 for water and sewage services. The legislation mainly defines rate-setting schemes based on the principle of marginal cost pricing in simulated efficient enterprises and on the role of the regulating bodies. There has also been some effort to develop an institutional regulatory capacity. Examples of this have been the creation of the National Energy Commission, the Superintendency of Electricity and Fuels, the Superintendency of Water and Sanitation Services, and the Subsecretariat of Telecommunications. In general these agencies have the responsibility for granting licenses, calculating rates, and monitoring the quality of service. The Energy Commission has the additional responsibility of medium- and long-term planning for the sector.

The Electric Power Industry

The regulatory mechanism in the electric power industry assumes the existence of competition in generating electricity and in supplying it to large customers. In addition, it assumes that the distribution and transmission of electricity are natural monopolies.[49]

How reasonable is it to structure a regulatory framework based on the as-

---

48. See Porter (1992).
49. This section relies significantly on Blanlot (1993) and Bitran and Saavedra (1993).

sumption of competition in generation? There is no definite answer to this question. It seems inconvenient to structure a regulatory system based on competition in generation in a small country in which the demand for power ranges between 500 MW and 800 MW, as in Central American countries, and the supply of power is provided by hydroelectric plants that reach economies of scale at capacities over 300 MW and concentrated hydroelectric resources in a few river basins. In these cases, it will be preferable to design a regulatory scheme based on licenses granted by the government with long-term marginal cost pricing.

In Chile, demand for electricity exceeds 4,000 MW, and electricity systems in the central area and in the northern area of the country are interconnected, suggesting that competition might succeed. However, obtaining it depends to a great extent on the way privatization is accomplished, on the vertical and horizontal integration of the enterprises, and on the degree of incompleteness of the contracts established under the regulatory framework. Economies of scope in generation might justify the horizontal integration of generators with different technologies to adapt to fluctuating levels of demand. But the main thing is to coordinate the short-run operation of the system so that at all times the facilities that are generating are those that have the lowest short-run marginal cost.[50] In Chile such a coordination mechanism among independent generators and transmission firms exists; thus, at least in theory, horizontal integration is not necessary to obtain a cost-minimizing operation. A different aspect, discussed in this paper, is whether this coordinating mechanism effectively guarantees enough transparency in the functioning of the system to avoid raising barriers to entry.

The price system comprises regulated rates for consumers of less than 2 MW of power and freely negotiated rates for the rest. The final price to regulated consumers has two components: a node price at which distributors buy energy and power from generators and from the transmission grid, and the value added of distribution. The node price is the sum of the forecast average of the short-run marginal costs of generation, given the investment program proposed by generators for the next three years, and of the marginal cost of transmission between the generating unit and the distribution point. Given that there are significant economies of scale in transmission, the marginal cost of transmission is lower than the average cost; therefore, tariff setting in the regulated segment does not cover the total cost of transmission. The difference

50. However, in order to avoid incentives for horizontal integration, the coordination mechanism may have to be very complex.

between the average cost and the marginal cost is charged to generators according to their area of influence in the system, and they, in turn, pass it on to the unregulated customers.

The law specifies that the regulated price must be within a 10 percent band around the average price in the freely negotiated contracts. The spirit of the regulation is that entrepreneurs will invest in generation to the extent that projects provide a return on capital compatible with the level of risk. If investments are postponed, the future short-run marginal cost will increase, and this will be reflected in higher node prices. Higher node prices will generate the incentive to expand capacity when demand increases.

The regulatory agency has only an advisory role regarding investment. The entrepreneurs must present their projects to the National Energy Commission, which determines the optimal path of expansion, given the investment prospects, and provides this information to the private sector. Private entrepreneurs do not have to abide by this planning, however, and the commission has no legal tools either to prevent the realization of investments that are not consistent with the optimal expansion path or to force those that are. The existence of indivisibilities and economies of scale in generation will imply that the decentralized solution, according to the second-welfare theorem, will not necessarily be Pareto-optimal, requiring coordination by the state.[51] The question is whether this indicative planning role is sufficient to guarantee a global optimum or whether the government needs to take some additional mandatory role regarding private investment.

The value added of distribution is calculated every four years. The procedure consists of determining the costs of an optimally adjusted and operated firm and setting rates that provide a 10 percent real return over the replacement value of assets. These rates are then applied to the real companies, in order to check that the average return is within a band between rates of return on assets of 6 percent and 14 percent. If the average actual return falls outside this range, the rates are adjusted to reach the upper or lower limit.

The operating cost of an efficient firm and the replacement value of assets are obtained as the average of estimates obtained in studies done by the industry and by the regulatory agency.

For determining the transmission grid tolls, the transmission firm should establish the area of influence of each generating plant, in order to charge the difference between the marginal and the average cost of transmission.[52]

51. For decentralization to have a Pareto-efficient outcome, technologies should be convex.
52. The area of influence is the portion of the transmission grid used by a generator.

Regulatory Problems in the Power Industry

The regulatory framework is based on the existence of competition in the generation of electricity. However, competition practically does not exist in Chile. The electricity system of the central zone, where privatizations have been carried out to a greater degree, has three generating companies of some significance. ENDESA and its subsidiaries have approximately 65 percent of the generation capacity, and Chilgener (a private enterprise), the second generator, has approximately 14 percent. The state-owned Colbún also has 14 percent of the generating capacity. The water rights of the main hydroelectric projects to be built over the next twenty years have belonged mainly to ENDESA, since the time it was an SOE.

The largest generator thus has an incentive to appraise its projects, considering the effects that they will have on the profitability of its inframarginal capacity. It can obtain the monopoly equilibrium over time by postponing investment. New entrepreneurs will be unable to enter because they do not have the water rights to undertake the more efficient projects.

ENDESA also owns the transmission grid of the central zone. Therefore, it has a decisive role in determining the areas of influence of the generators and how the average costs of transmission are covered. Because the law is not precise enough about how these areas are determined, and the decision is made by the owner of the grid, there is room for discretion. This situation, in which ENDESA is the largest generator and also owns the transmission grid, in an ambiguous framework provided by the law on transmission tolls, creates the possibility for opportunistic behavior by the owner of the grid to charge most of the average cost of transmission to nonaffiliated generators. This structure of ownership and ambiguity increase the risk for new generators who wish to invest, raising barriers to entry.

Enersis, a holding company, exerts significant control over ENDESA and owns the distribution companies (Chilectra and Río Maipo) that operate in the country's main area of supply (the metropolitan area of Santiago). This allows it to favor ENDESA in its contracts for energy and power. To the extent that distribution companies can determine when they buy from each generator, the possibility exists that a distributor will favor one generator over others. Given that the price that the distribution company pays depends on the node price, which is an average over three years of all future short-run marginal costs, it will not matter from which generator it buys energy, but because actual short-run marginal costs have large fluctuations during the year, generators will not be indifferent about when to sell; they will prefer to sell in periods of low marginal costs. Thus it is possible to favor an affiliated generator by making contracts in which energy and power are mostly purchased in those times when marginal costs are lower and below the node price, and little is purchased when marginal costs are high and above the node price. In contract renegotiations conducted in 1991, Chilectra's contracts reflected different load factors over the course of the year for different generators in such a way that it benefited Pehuenche, the ENDESA generating subsidiary, and negatively affected Colbún. This led to legal disputes, which, after a costly litigation process, led to a modification of the agreements among the generators for the transfer of energy.

The risk of this type of behavior in the setting of contracts between generators and distribution companies is an additional ingredient of uncertainty that inhibits the entry of new generators.

Finally, the setting of value added for electricity distribution also has important problems that affect the efficiency of the industry. The recent (in the second half of 1992) experience of the rate-setting process provides valuable lessons regarding the negative effect of incomplete regulatory frameworks that leave room for discretion on the part of the regulator and the regulated. The costs of the simulated efficient firm are calculated as a weighted average of the studies of the regulator and the firms, and this gives rise to obvious incentives, for one and the others, to alter the estimates. The discrepancies found in calculating distribution costs and the replacement value of assets were, in some cases, more than 50 percent.

An aspect of the process that was particularly sensitive is the estimation of the actual cost of distribution that is required to adjust the rates to the band established in the law. Distribution companies have diversified their business activities, and an important proportion of their electricity business corresponds to unregulated activities. In certain cases vertical integration in the provision of inputs and services has taken place through affiliated companies. This process of diversification and integration makes it harder to estimate the actual cost of distribution, allowing regulated firms to charge to their customers business costs borne by the unregulated business, or even setting artificially high transfer prices with the affiliated suppliers to increase return on capital beyond the levels established by the law.

The return on capital of distribution companies and their affiliated input suppliers or holding companies in many cases has ranged between 20 and 40 percent, which is not consistent with the riskiness of the business.

The Telecommunications Sector

Long-distance and local telephone service have regulated rates, with rate-setting schemes based on the concept of long-term marginal costs. The rates are set so that the net present value of the expansion project equals zero, discounted at a rate that reflects the risk of the sector. The rates are recalculated every five years on the basis of a simulated efficient firm. The cost studies of such firms are carried out by the licensees of telecommunications services. Any dispute about the cost estimates with the regulator give rise to an arbitration process whose characteristics are defined in the law.

In practice the rate regulation has been ineffective for long-distance service, as demonstrated by rates of return on capital that on average exceeded 40 percent before the entry of new companies. The failure of regulation in long-distance service requires the development of a new approach in this segment of the market. Promoting competition in long-distance service should be the main goal of the regulatory agency, specially since technological progress has reduced the significance of sunk costs and economies of scale, eliminating the natural monopoly characteristics that existed in the past.

ENTEL, the monopoly long-distance carrier, after privatization retained exclusive licenses that raised legal barriers to newcomers to the industry.[53] The sluggishness of the regulatory authority in removing these barriers and in granting new licenses has retarded the development of competition. This, together with inappropriate rate-setting schemes, has maintained prices significantly above marginal cost, with negative welfare consequences for consumers.

Another issue that may endanger the development of competition in the long term is whether to allow the integration of local and long-distance services. As long as local telephone service is a natural monopoly, it will be able to discriminate in favor of the affiliated long-distance carrier. Effective regulation to prevent this situation is difficult because of the technical complexities involved and the absence of a sophisticated regulatory capacity. Even with a multicarrier dialing system, the presence of the local natural monopoly will deter the entry of potential competitors because of the risk of discrimination, in the context of a weak regulatory agency and a cumbersome legal system for dispute settlement.

53. For example, ENTEL was privatized with the exclusive rights of connection to INTELSAT that were granted to the enterprise when it was owned by the state. In October 1992, the Antitrust Commission ruled that the regulators should find ways to correct that situation. See Paredes (1993).

Recently the democratic government sent to Congress a new telecommunications law that will eliminate the legal barriers for competition in long-distance services, giving significant market access to new companies. However, at the same time it will not prevent the local natural monopoly (CTC) from entering the long-distance segment through a subsidiary. Unless the Antitrust Commission rules against vertical integration, we can expect that CTC will compete with ENTEL, the de facto monopoly in long-distance service. Although this might reduce monopoly pricing in the short term, the long-term consequences are uncertain, especially because newcomers may reconsider their participation in this market.

Privatization and the Promotion of Competition

The difficulties involved in regulation should generate a special concern for privatizing under conditions that will promote competition and limit, at a minimum, the need for government regulation. Failure to consider regulatory aspects in the privatizations created the conditions for the monopolization of activities that could have been developed under the discipline of competition. In the electric power industry, the restructuring of enterprises before privatization fell short of what was needed, considering all the problems of industrial organization that were involved. More attention should have been paid to issues regarding horizontal and vertical integration and to joint ownership of distribution and generation facilities.

The previous government had the opportunity to reduce concentration in generation by selling the new, large hydroelectric plant, Pehuenche, to owners not affiliated with ENDESA or Chilgener. Nevertheless, CORFO sold the plant to ENDESA, which already held more than 60 percent of the generating capacity in the central interconnected system. ENDESA could have been broken up among several firms that operate in that system. Moreover, the water rights should have been returned to the state prior to privatization, which in turn could have granted them as incentives for the timely development of new projects by the existing producers or newcomers.

The transmission grid should have been set up as a separate company. Two schemes might have been considered. One would have turned the grid into a common carrier jointly owned by all generating and distribution firms and open to any newcomers; the other would have set up a separate company with concentrated ownership but without links to the generators.

The way in which ENDESA and Chilmetro were privatized facilitated the control of both enterprises by Enersis. The widely diffused ownership of

ENDESA made it possible for Enersis, with less than 20 percent of the shares, to obtain significant control of ENDESA. Both popular capitalism and the participation of pension funds were essential in reducing the power of other shareholders. Doubts regarding the motivation of pension fund voting have led the new government to propose a new law that will force pension fund management companies to vote for independent directors.

In privatizing telecommunications, care should have been taken not to maintain monopoly positions through legal restrictions and exclusive licenses and to be more expeditious in granting licenses to new companies. It is also arguable that CTC, the large local telephone company, should have been allowed to operate a cellular phone company in its area of concession considering that for technical reasons only two companies can operate in the same geographical area and in the long run cellular phones may become an important competitor in the local and domestic long-distance market.

Regulatory Capacity

Experience has shown that rate-setting schemes, and regulatory frameworks in general, constitute incomplete contracts between the regulator and the firms. This gives rise to the possibility of ex-post opportunistic behavior by the regulators or by the firms. The regulatory process has increasingly turned into a negotiating game where the relative power and the influence of the political process and interest groups will have a great effect on the outcome.

In order for regulation to protect adequately the welfare of consumers and create fair and equitable conditions for investors, the institutional framework that governs the regulatory agencies must be independent of political influences. In the case of Chile, regulatory entities have a strong dependence on the ministries that have political and technical responsibilities. The regulatory body for telecommunications is the Subsecretariat of Telecommunications, which reports directly to the minister of transportation and telecommunications. The National Energy Commission comprises seven ministers, four in the economic area and three in the political area. The superintendencies of water and sewage services and of electricity and fuels are administratively part of the ministries of public works and economy, respectively. Thus they are not independent of the political system. It is necessary to move in the direction of further independence by constituting regulatory commissions that are not subordinated to the administration in power.

Another aspect of the system that weakens the regulatory capacity of the state is the low wages of the employees of regulatory agencies; as part of the public sector, the employees of the regulatory agencies are bound by public sector wage scales. Wage levels are so low that they allow the hiring mainly of professionals with little or no experience. Conditions ensure high turnover. The more productive workers quickly learn the nature of the business and then emigrate to the regulated firms, where wages are several times higher. This implies that the negotiating power of the regulating agency is not in balance with the professional capacity of the regulated firm. Moreover, since the regulators see their service in the regulating entity as transitory and as an opportunity for future development in the regulated industry, their independence is limited, and they run the risk of being captured by the industry.

As Vivianne Blanlot has proposed, in order to concentrate the state's technical and financial resources, the creation of a single regulatory commission for all public utilities should be considered.[54] The existence of common principles and problems in regulating public utilities in different industries justifies the creation of a single entity given the scarcity of highly qualified professionals and of financial resources. This commission should take the responsibility for setting rates, coordinating private investment plans, and controlling the quality of service. Promoting competition and protecting consumers should be transferred from antitrust commissions and from the consumer protection agency to the regulatory commission when the industry involved is regulated, leaving the Antitrust Commission as an appeals court for the rulings of the regulators.[55] The commissioners should be selected through a process that ensures technical capacity and independence, with their tenure going beyond and only partially overlapping that of elected governments.

Prospects for Future Privatizations

Since the democratic government took office in March 1990, there have been no significant privatizations of enterprises, although SOEs still account for around 10 percent of GDP. Gains in efficiency could be realized by continuing the privatization process with more consideration of regulatory issues.

The process has bogged down because the previous privatization programs, undertaken by an authoritarian regime with insufficient transparency (in some cases), had inadequate political legitimacy. This legacy makes it politically more difficult for future democratic governments to use this tool to increase efficiency. Nevertheless, it is likely that in some cases, when firms are extremely inefficient or need significant resources for expansion and moderniza-

54. See Blanlot (1993).
55. More details on these proposals can be found in Bitran and Saavedra (1993, p. 276).

tion, the government will be able in the end to complete a few important privatizations.

The privatization of the state railways shows greater concern about regulatory issues. The new government received this firm almost bankrupt, with a rapidly falling market share in overall transportation services, a desperate need for maintenance and investment, and a management that was very unresponsive to market signals. Because of the needs of the export sectors, the government decided to privatize the freight railroad and to keep the unprofitable passenger service and the tracks, the latter because of its natural monopoly characteristics.

Another interesting case is that of the electricity generating and transmission company in the northern interconnected system, EDELNOR. The enterprise is being partially privatized by both selling shares and increasing equity to finance new investment. In this process the government did not separate the transmission grid prior to privatization, repeating the mistake made by the previous government in the divestiture of ENDESA.

The area in which the government has been innovative in privatizations is public infrastructure. At the beginning of the government, the legislature enacted concessions laws that allow the private sector to participate in building, operating, and transferring (BOT) infrastructure projects. This opened a new area for investment by the private sector that had previously been reserved to the government. Simultaneously, the government developed regulations to allow infrastructure project financing through revenue bonds that can be purchased by institutional investors. The first project, a tunnel that cost $20 million to construct, was successfully auctioned at the end of 1992. In our view, these concession schemes raise important regulatory issues that have not been properly dealt with in the legislation. These concessions are granted for periods between twenty and thirty years, and the law does not establish an explicit mechanism to adapt the contract to changing conditions, even though the contract may be renegotiated. This leaves open the possibility for opportunistic behavior and the exercise of discretion. The Mexican example of concessions in the highway sector that have resulted in massive renegotiations of contracts that favor investors should serve as a warning of the risks involved if this issue is not properly considered.

In 1994 a new administration will take power, and it should give priority to issues regarding privatization and regulation. The government owns important companies in tradable sectors where there are no issues of allocative efficiency to justify keeping them in the hands of the government, and there are important operational inefficiencies and investment restrictions that limit the contribution of these sectors to stable growth. Some degree of privatization should play a role in improving efficiency and mobilizing savings toward investment in these sectors.

In the electric power industry, the government should modify the regulatory framework, using the privatization of the remaining SOEs as a mechanism to bring new players into the industry. The major changes in the framework should deal with the separation of transmission and generation, limit the vertical integration of distribution and generation, make available to newcomers the water rights, and force deconcentration of generating capacity. If all of this is not politically viable, a regulatory regime based on competition in generation, with short-term marginal cost pricing, will have to be changed to a system that acknowledges the monopolistic characteristics of the industry and sets rates according to long-term marginal cost.

One issue that must be reconsidered in future privatizations, because of the difficulties for shareholders to exert control, is the emphasis on the diffusion of ownership. The major banks, privatized through popular capitalism, are run by managers who were named when the government intervened in the banks. This complete lack of control by shareholders has given significant discretion to managers, which could have had consequences for efficiency that are hard to quantify. This situation has been exacerbated because the banks have a subordinated debt with the Central Bank, which allows the Central Bank to claim between 50 and 90 percent of profits. The emphasis on the diffusion of ownership came also from the regulations on institutional investors where investment diversification requirements severely penalize investment by pension funds and insurance companies in concentrated firms.

Comment by Dominique Hachette de la F.

This paper presents a succinct history of the different episodes of privatization in Chile since 1974, with emphasis on the electric power and telecommunications industries. The authors also discuss the principal economic issues involved in the privatization of public utilities with characteristics of natural monopolies. They apply their theoretical framework to two cases of privatization with regulation, the electric and telecommunications sectors, and they conclude with an observation about the prospects for privatizations.

The main theme of the paper—economic issues related to the privatization of natural monopolies and the need for proper regulation—is well chosen given its high degree of relevancy, especially in countries starting to divest state-owned enterprises. Conclusions reached with respect to problems and related regulations, timing, and the practical difficulties of optimal regulations are clearly and succinctly analyzed.

The authors ask how the regulatory problems have been solved with an eye to allocative efficiency. Recognizing that we should not expect to be in a first-best world, they offer three alternatives: rate of return regulation, RPI-X regulation, and franchising. Recognizing the system's main advantage and difficulty, they nevertheless propose franchising as an alternative to the privatization of an activity with natural monopoly characteristics. Franchising is allocated through competitive bidding. In these conditions, it is difficult to see how franchising can be carried out without privatizing the state monopoly. Natural monopolies are capital intensive, by nature, and consequently no one would even be willing to bid without assurances of recovering fixed (or sunk) costs. As far as I know, no practical system has been devised to allow the private sector to take over a natural monopoly on the basis of franchising, unless the period under which franchising is defined is a very long one, indeed. In fact, the authors recognize this point later on and cite as the only example the cable television industry in the United States, which is a private enterprise.

My major comment is related to the efficiency of the regulatory framework imposed on the electric and the telecommunications sectors before their privatization in Chile. First, I find some inconsistencies between the theoretical discussion of the difficulties of any regulatory framework and the authors' criticism of the rules established for the mentioned sectors. Second, I believe this paper raises a basic issue with respect to any regulatory framework that I would like to sketch here.

I agree with the authors' assessment of the shortcomings of the existing regulatory framework in both sectors, which inhibits allocative efficiency: insufficient guarantees of competition, the possibility for favoritism in contracts between generators and distributors, and the difficulties in setting the value added for distribution of electricity. I also agree with the authors' description of the difficulties faced by the regulatory bodies in Chile, difficulties such as the existence of incomplete contracts, the political influences, and low wages.

However, regulations were far from absent in the Chilean context and far from inefficient, as suggested by the authors: marginal cost pricing imposed on the electrical sector is only one example. Further, there is a confusion between the definition of size of the would-be divested enterprise and regulations to ensure competition. Though the two are certainly related, the definition of size cannot be mistaken for a regulation and represents only a necessary condition for competition, certainly not a sufficient one. Insisting on criticizing the size of ENDESA at the time of divestiture blurs the main issue. Further, if ENDESA were a natural monopoly, the question of size would be irrelevant. The problem is to ensure regulations that prevent monopolistic behavior.

Regulations are certainly required. We should, however, shoot for realistic regulations, not regulations that are perfect on paper but impossible to apply. Legislators, who are pursuing many objectives that may be inconsistent with regulations, should realize that privatization of a natural monopoly does not guarantee a lower level of allocative efficiency. Quite the contrary in most cases. Most natural monopolies in different countries are badly managed even by the state, which is not able to ensure allocative efficiency. An example is the unfortunate case of the Chilean telephone company, which underinvested for decades.

An increasingly interrelated world imposes ever more complicated ties among economic agents and greater difficulties for regulations to remain efficient. In Chile tragic cases illustrate this assertion: executives of holdings sent to jail in 1982 for wrongdoings in relation to regulations that Chilean law does not define and Chilean judges do not understand, so today those men still have not come to trial. Each set of regulations may be acceptable, but will they be acceptable when they are all taken together? Recently, the president of a major Chilean firm called attention to the growing difficulties in making a significant investment because of cumbersome impositions. A proposal mentioned by the authors to create a single regulatory body would perhaps be a step in the right direction, though only a minor step. Regulations are certainly required, but how much regulation is a relevant query. Enthusiasm to improve the existing regulations is welcome if it is accompanied by some grain of realism.

Comment by William F. Maloney

This paper provides a sobering counterbalance to some of the more euphoric literature surrounding the Chilean privatization experience. The principal theme to emerge from the analysis is that the manner in which privatization is implemented is critical to the eventual success of the program. First, the ownership structure of the transferred firms is important both for the overall functioning of the economy and for the disciplining of firm behavior. The pre-1982 wave of privatizations favored the creation and expansion of large conglomerates, which grew to dominate the economic life of the country, with eventual adverse consequences.[56] The government appears to have extracted the lesson, very clearly incorporated in the design of the 1980s privatization program, that ownership of former state property must be diffused. The success of a variety of mechanisms used to this end has left the authors concerned that Chile has now reached the other extreme, where no substantial block of shareholders has the interest or the power to monitor management.

Second, and the area where the paper contributes strongly, is that since many public corporations are natural monopolies, the success of the privatization process depends on establishing a transparent and credible regulatory framework before privatization. This point has emerged now in several different contexts. Spiller provides a case study of the telecommunications sector in Argentina, where the failure to set up such institutions, most specifically safeguards against ex-post renegotiations of tariff structures, resulted in little interest among prospective buyers.[57] We have discussed how privatizing pension funds in the manner done by Chile can be extremely risky if it is copied by countries in which regulatory capacity is relatively underdeveloped. In two studies of the Chilean telecommunications sector, Agurto and Galal have argued that the mistaken assumption of increased competition and the resulting inadequacies of the 1982 telecommunications law led to much poorer results than were seen in the electricity sector, where a more complete set of regulatory norms had been established.[58] Bitran and Sáez offer an extensive discussion of the limitations inherent in even well-articulated regulatory systems, They then outline the substantial deficiencies remaining in the institutions that regulate both the electricity and the telecommunications sectors in Chile, particularly in preventing vertical integration and abuses leading to barriers to entry. Their analysis reinforces the lesson emerging from the previously cited studies: the nature of the regulatory structure within which a privatized enterprise will function will critically determine the social benefits reaped from privatization and must be considered as important as the transfer of ownership itself.

This said, it is not clear whether they judge the Chilean case a qualified success to be emulated or fatally flawed. Some industrial organization economists give the impression that the regulatory structure of the electricity sector in Chile approximates the Platonic ideal. It sets prices close to marginal cost,

56. It is arguable that the unsound financial practices between these *grupos* and affiliate banks were as important as the sustained overvaluation of the currency and high interest rates to the collapse of the economy in 1982.

57. Spiller (1993).

58. Agurto (1991) and Galal (1992).

establishes a transparent tariff adjustment mechanism that limits administrative discretion, creates long-term incentives to invest, and devises mechanisms to insulate the regulatory institutions both from capture by the regulated industries and from tampering by the political process.[59] But the view that Bitran and Saéz present is so much less sanguine that one is tempted to doubt the feasibility of privatization efforts elsewhere. If Chile cannot put together a good regulatory system, given the capacity for policy continuity and emphasis on economic efficiency under the military government, then few other countries can expect to do better.

Providing a balanced evaluation would require some evidence on the magnitude of the distortions. For example, while I understand that Chile is blessed with the natural capacity to produce hydroelectric power at low cost, the numbers I have seen suggest that average electricity prices to the central region of Chile are below those for most industrialized countries; even in the desert north, they are below those of Japan, Belgium, Spain, Austria, and Germany.[60] How large are the monopoly profits accruing to the electric companies, and, in a regime where prices are regulated at marginal cost, how is this happening? Returns to capital are below 10 percent in ENDESA, Chilegener, and Enersis, although close to 20 percent for Chilquinta, so where are the excess returns showing up?[61] I do not have similar numbers for the telecommunications sector, though the return on net assets in the Chilean Telephone Company (CTC) is also a modest 10 percent, and graphs of telephones per capita, network expansion, and digitalization of the system all show first and second derivatives dramatically positive after privatization.[62] So how far are we from the best of all possible worlds? Will the current system get Chile modernized fast, albeit with some excess profits accruing? Should other reforming economies view the Chilean privatization of the telecommunications and electricity sectors as something overall worth imitating or not?

In a similar vein, I would have liked to see some attempt to bring together the conflicting literature on the actual efficiency gains experienced in the Chilean case. This issue has been central to the discussion surrounding the benefits of privatization and is one for which the preliminary results from Chile are surprisingly ambiguous.

Efforts to use financial indicators to measure efficiency are largely unconvincing. The sometimes-cited returns on shareholder equity are probably not helpful because a significant subset of privatized firms are regulated natural

59. See, for example, Spiller (1993).
60. Agurto (1991) p. 206.
61. Agurto (1991) p. 205.
62. See Galal (1992) and Agurto (1991).

monopolies and are allowed a specified return on net fixed assets.[63] Further, as the authors point out, when we see ENTEL yielding returns of 40 percent, what is occurring is not remarkable efficiency, but the unregulated side of the industry, especially incoming international calls, earning excessive profits.[64] But even when a broader set of financial indicators is used, Hachette and Lüders, using discriminant analysis, were unable to distinguish publicly owned from privately owned firms. They offer the provocative suggestion, supported by the theoretical section of this paper, that public and private firms perform similarly when operating under common rules and with profit maximization as the exclusive objective.

The story seems even more ambiguous, even perverse, when we look at "real" measures of efficiency. Hachette and others, in a study for the Interamerican Development Bank, provide some statistics for a few industries.[65] In ENDESA, output per man-hour rose until 1988, the year of its privatization, and then fell, leading the authors to conclude that "privatization has not caused significant change, at least for now, in this respect."[66] In the steel holding company, CAP, the important efficiency gains occurred in 1983, three years before privatization: costs per ton of steel fell 28 percent from 1982 to 1985, but remained more or less stagnant after that; tons per worker similarly showed gains of 30 percent from 1982 to 1985 and made less striking advances later. CTC after privatization *continues* to show dramatic falls in workers per telephone and per line with acceleration after privatization in 1986, but again, the process began before. The pattern, as Hachette and others remark, is that the big physical efficiency gains occurred in the late 1970s and early 1980s, when the government imposed a hard budget constraint and forced the parastatals to shed labor. This would also seem to explain the absence of notable employment effects from privatization in most industries observed in Chile: the housecleaning had largely occurred out of sample.

Both financial and real measures of efficiency seem to support to some degree one of the themes of the paper, that the similarity of agency problems in a publicly owned and in diffusely owned private enterprises makes ownership less critical than appears at first glance. So should Kazakhstan abstract from this the general lesson that privatization yields only an ambiguous, and perhaps negligible effect on efficiency? Probably not.

First, it may be that a country with a government that is politically insulated,

63. Once we know the debt equity ratio, the return to equity can be easily backed out yielding little information about efficiency.

64. Galal (1992, p. 21).

65. Hachette and others (1992).

66. Hachette and others (1992, p. 304).

resistant to capture by interest groups, and philosophically disinclined to use parastatals for social policy or as a means of contracting debt may have little efficiency to gain by transferring them to the private sector. But the military government in Chile was probably a regional anomaly in these regards, and a recent study by the World Bank, though confirming relatively small gains in Chile, documented larger improvements in welfare and efficiency in Mexico and Malaysia.[67] Even in Chile, the Pinochet era may represent a temporal anomaly, since we really cannot know what pressures future politics may bring to bear on the remaining parastatals.

Second, and a point that might have been brought out more in the paper, was that in Chile, as in most countries, privatization was a policy with shifting motivations that was called upon to serve multiple masters, only one of which was static allocative efficiency. Lying near the core of the Chilean privatization program was a public finance problem. Not only were the sales of parastatals critical to balancing the budget during the years when foreign debt payments had a strong negative effect, contributing an average of 2.5 percent of GDP from 1987 to 1991, but the state simply lacked the resources to undertake the necessary investment within the companies it managed. I think this must be one of the most important parts of the Chilean story. In the telecommunications sector, for example, investment plans are specifically dictated within the regulatory structure and, as I mentioned earlier, the results are impressive. CTC is particularly suggestive on the overriding importance of the public finance constraint, since it was first sold off to the Bond Corporation, a firm with no telecommunications expertise, and then to the Spanish state telecommunications company, another parastatal, but a relatively cash-rich one. The changes in performance that we have seen were probably less due to who owns CTC than to how much money they have available for investment.

Finally, while we are looking for lessons, the programs of popular capitalism and worker capitalism perhaps merit some discussion from a political economy point of view. Measured along Minister of the Economy Collados's announced goal of diffusing property throughout the population, the programs had minimal effect, reaching perhaps 2.1 percent of the adult population and 1 percent of salaried workers. The programs could be very expensive, implying subsidies of share prices, in some cases, of nearly 80 percent, and they were probably regressive in their direct effect.[68] Nonetheless, they seem to have served an important purpose, as they did in the United Kingdom, of mobilizing support for or at least reducing the opposition to the privatization program.

67. Galal and others (1992).
68. Maloney (1993).

They constituted the narrow edge of the wedge that would permit increasingly ambitious transfers as the 1980s progressed. Allowing the privatized pension funds to purchase shares in the transferred parastatals through indirect popular capitalism raised the returns on retirement savings and, it has been argued, created a broad constituency against renationalization.[69] The success of these programs in both Chile and the United Kingdom would seem relevant to countries, such as Uruguay, where privatization has met strong resistance.

References

Agurto, R. 1991. "Sector Telecomunicaciones." In *Soluciones Privadas a Problemas Publicos,* edited by Larroulet V. Cristián, pp. 215–44. Santiago: Instituto Libertad y Desarrollo, Santiago, 1991.

Alé, J., and others. 1990. *Estado empresario y privatización en Chile.* Serie Investigaciones No. 2. Santiago: Universidad Nacional Andrés Bello.

Arellano, J. P. 1983. "De la liberalización a la intervención: el mercado de capitales en Chile: 1974–1983." *Colección Estudios* CIEPLAN 11 (December): 5–49.

Baumol, W., J. Panzar, and R. Willig. 1982. *Contestable Markets and the Theory of Industrial Structure.* Harcourt Brace Jovanovich.

Bitran, E., and E. Saavedra. 1993. "Algunas reflecciones en torno al rol regulador y empresarial del Estado." In *Después de la Privatización: Hacia el Estado Regulador,* edited by O. Muñoz. Santiago: CIEPLAN (Corporación de Investigaciones Económicas para Latinoamerica).

Blanlot, V. 1993. "La regulación del sector eléctrico: la experiencia chilena." In *Después de la Privatización,* edited by Oscar Muñoz. Santiago: CIEPLAN.

Budget Directorate, Ministry of Finance. 1985. *Exposición sobre el Estado de la Hacienda Pública.*

Cauas, J. 1979. "Report on the State of Public Finance." In *Chilean Economic Policy,* edited by Juan Carlos Méndez, 45–74. Santiago: Budget Directorate.

Central Bank of Chile. 1993. *Boletín Mensual* 781 (March). Santiago.

Centro de Estudios Públicos. 1992. "El Ladrillo" ("The Brick"). Santiago.

CORFO (Corporación de Fomento de la Producción). *Annual Report* 1986–91.

———. 1978. "Privatización de empresas y activos 1973–1978." Report prepared by the Gerencia de Normalización de Empresas. Santiago: CORFO.

Errázuriz, E. 1987. "Capitalización de la deuda externa y desnacionalización de la economía chilena." *Documento de Trabajo* 57 (August). Santiago: Programa de Economía del Trabajo.

Ffrench-Davis, R. 1990. "Debt-Equity Swaps in Chile." *Notas Técnicas* 129, revised edition. Santiago: CIEPLAN.

69. Piñera (1991).

Fontaine, J. A. 1988. "Los mecanismos de conversión de deuda en Chile." *Estudios Públicos* 30 (Fall): 137–57.

Galal, A. 1992. "Regulation, Commitment and Development of Telecommunications in Chile." The World Bank, December.

Galal, A., and others. 1992. "Synthesis of Case Studies and Policy Summary." World Bank Conference on Welfare Consequences of Selling Public Enterprises, Country Economics Department.

———. Forthcoming. *Welfare Consequences of Selling Public Enterprises: Case Studies from Chile, Malaysia, Mexico, and the U.K.* The World Bank.

González, P., and M. Marfán. 1992. "Determinantes fiscales del consumo privado en Chile 1961–1990." CIEPLAN.

Hachette, D., and R. Lüders. 1993. *Privatization in Chile.* San Francisco: International Center for Economic Growth.

Hachette, D., and others. 1992. "Seis casos de privatización en Chile." *Documentos de Trabajo* 117 (March). Interamerican Development Bank.

Jarvis, L. 1985. *Chilean Agriculture under Military Rule: From Reform to Reaction, 1973–1980.* Institute of International Studies, University of California, Berkeley.

Klein, B., R. Crawford, and A. Alchian. 1978. "Vertical Integration, Appropriable Rents and the Competitive Contracting Process." *Journal of Law and Economics* 21 (October): 297–326.

Larraín, F. 1991. "Public Sector Behavior in a Highly Indebted Country: The Contrasting Chilean Experience." In *The Public Sector and the Latin American Crisis,* edited by Felipe Larraín and Marcelo Selowsky, 89–136. ICS Press.

Maloney, W. F. Forthcoming. "Privatization with Share Diffusion: Popular Capitalism in Chile: 1985–88," in *Essays in Privatization in Latin America: The Changing Role of the Private and Public Sectors,* edited by Werner Baer and Mellissa Birch. Praeger.

Marcel, M. 1989a. "La privatización de empresas públicas en Chile: 1985–88." *Notas Técnicas* 125 (January). Santiago: CIEPLAN.

———. 1989b. "Privatización y finanzas públicas: el caso de Chile: 1985–88." *Colección Estudios CIEPLAN* 26 (June): 5–60.

Marshall, J., and F. Montt. 1988. "Privatization in Chile." In *Privatization in Less Developed Countries,* edited by Paul Cook and Colin Kirkpatrick, 281–307. New York: St. Martin's.

Mayhew, K., and P. Seabright. 1992. "Incentives and the Management of Enterprises in Economic Transition: Capital Markets are not Enough." *Oxford Review of Economic Policy* 8 (Spring): 105–29.

Muñoz, O., ed. 1993. *Después de la Privatización: Hacia el Estado Regulador.* Santiago: CIEPLAN.

Paredes, R. 1993. "Privatización y regulación: lecciones de la experiencia chilena." In *Después de la Privatización: Hacia el Estado Regulador,* edited by O. Muñoz. Santiago: CIEPLAN.

Piñera, J. 1991. "Privatization in Chile." In *Privatization of Public Enterprises in Latin America,* edited by William Glade, 19–26. San Francisco: International Center for Economic Growth.

Piñera, P. 1986. "Las opciones al capitalismo popular." *Revista de CIEPLAN* 4 (July).

Porter, M. E. 1992. "Capital Choices: Changing the Way America Invests in Industry." A Research Report presented to The Council on Competitiveness and cosponsored by The Harvard Business School.

"Public Enterprise Reform in Chile." In *Public Enterprise Reform in Latin America,* vol. 2. Public Sector Management Division, The World Bank.

Ramírez, G. 1987. "El capitalismo popular." *Información Financiera.* Santiago: Superintendencia de Bancos e Instituciones Financieras.

Rosende, F., and A. Reinstein. 1986. "Estado de avance del programa de reprivatización en Chile." *Estudios Públicos* 23 (Winter): 262.

Spiller, P. T. 1993. "Institutions and Regulatory Commitment in Utilities Privatization." University of Illinois, Department of Economics.

Superintendencia de Administradoras de Fondos de Pensiones. 1983. *Boletín Estadístico Mensual* 19. Santiago.

Superintendencia de Administradoras de Fondos de Pensiones. 1992. *Boletín Estadístico* 113 (September). Santiago.

Vickers, J., and G. Yarrow. 1991. "Economic Perspectives on Privatization." *Journal of Economic Perspectives* 5 (Spring): 111–32.

Williamson, O. 1975. *Markets and Hierarchies: Analysis and Antitrust Implications.* Free Press.

8 The State and Economic Policy: Chile 1952–92

Andrés Velasco

FROM 1952 to 1970 the Chilean economy grew at an average of 3.8 percent a year and had an average budget deficit of 3.1 percent of GDP. Inflation, which had been a problem since the late nineteenth century, averaged 29 percent a year. By contrast, in 1984–92 growth rose to 6.2 percent, and what had been a budget deficit became an average surplus of slightly more than 1.5 percent of output. Inflation also fell—though less sharply—to 20 percent a year on average.[1] How did such a drastic change in economic performance occur?

What separates the two stages is a period of political upheavals and also of profound structural reforms. While some reforms, particularly mild trade liberalization and tax streamlining, had already been put into place in the late 1960s, the 1970s and 1980s framed Chile's drastic economic transformation from the classic import-substituting economy with heavy state intervention to one of the more open and market-oriented economies in the world. Such changes were not effected without cost. Two major recessions, sustained unemployment, and a worsening in income distribution occurred in 1973–83.[2] Yet in contrast to many other Latin American experiences—and in spite of the sharp political opposition they once gave rise to—the reforms do not seem to be a transient phenomenon: a broad consensus in today's democratic Chile supports the outlines of the new economic strategy and attributes to the change in policies the much-improved economic performance of the past nine years.

What political and economic forces made such a thorough transformation of the Chilean economy both feasible and (apparently) sustainable? Searching

I am thankful to my discussants, Arturo Valenzuela and Francisco Rosende, to Bill Maloney, and to other participants in the conference for useful comments. Logistical support from the C. V. Starr Center for Applied Economics at New York University is gratefully acknowledged. This paper is dedicated to Konrad Stenzel, who cared deeply about Chile, and who thought clearly about this subject long before the rest of us.

1. See table 8-1.
2. See table 8-4.

for possible answers to this question, this paper attempts to look into the black box—usually labeled by economists with the all-inclusive tag of politics—where policies are decided upon and their distributional consequences worked out. Not even dictators as powerful as General Pinochet operate in isolation. The drastic changes in economic policy that he pushed through must be understood as the result of shifting coalitions and new strategies in Chile's age-old distributive game.

A main conclusion of the analysis is that the economic reforms of the 1970s and 1980s constitute the final chapter in the gradual demise of a particular political economy arrangement that emerged in Chile in the aftermath of the Great Depression. Then, as happened elsewhere in the region, an alliance of rising business groups, middle classes, and state bureaucrats came together to pursue inward-looking industrialization, fostered by activist government policies. But the Chilean state, while being (at least initially) the powerful engine of industrialization, eventually became itself weak, fragmented, and highly permeable to the pressures of interest groups. Clientelism and political accommodation—expressed through the Congress, the state enterprises, or the official development agencies—acquired increasing importance as mechanisms for allocating resources. Economic policy was often the outcome of a convoluted process in which various groups with vested interests interacted.

The development strategy favoring import substitution industrialization (ISI) and the group alliances and distributional mechanisms that accompanied it provided some growth and industrialization, particularly in the 1930s and 1940s; they also proved capable of ensuring a modicum of social mobility and preventing social pressures from boiling over. As a result, Chile was an island of political stability from the early 1930s to the late 1960s. At the same time, the prevailing arrangements possessed a tremendous capacity to generate microeconomic and macroeconomic inefficiencies. Excessive and complex regulations proliferated. The country stuck with import substitution long after its initial benefits had been exhausted, and efforts toward liberalization in the 1960s proved largely fruitless. The tax system became filled with special regimes and exceptions, and spending could not be contained; the result was a chronic tendency toward budget deficits and inflation. Table 8-1 shows that overall economic performance (especially in the 1950s) suffered. Between 1950 and 1972 Chile had the lowest rate of economic growth among the major countries of Latin America.

This system reached a political crisis in the late 1960s and exploded in 1970–73. The timing of the trouble was somewhat peculiar, given that Chile was not on the verge of an economic collapse. Over the previous three decades per capita spending had been rising, however slowly. In 1967, at the midpoint

Table 8-1. Long-Run Performance Indicators, 1940–92

Year	Inflation	Growth	Fiscal deficit[a]
1940–53	18.11	3.84	−0.70
1953–58	48.35	2.23	−2.65
1959–64	27.13	4.33	−4.57
1965–70	27.32	5.07	−2.53
1971–73	295.90	1.20	−11.50
1974–83	115.52	1.65	0.77
1984–89	20.40	6.25	0.55
1990–92	19.57	6.17	2.53
1984–92	19.99	6.21	1.54

SOURCES: Inflation: for 1940–51, Zahler (1978); for 1952–70, Ffrench-Davis (1973); for 1971–78, Cortázar and Marshall (1980); for 1979–92, Central Bank of Chile. Corresponds to the December-December change in the CPI. Growth: for 1940–51, Zahler (1978); for 1952–70, Ffrench-Davis (1973); for 1971–92, Central Bank of Chile. Fiscal deficit: for 1940–69, Ministerio de Hacienda, cited by Zahler (1978); for 1970–92, Tesorería General de la República, *Balance Consolidado del Sector Público*, various issues. Data for 1970–85 were previously published in Larraín (1991).

a. Definition of government corresponds to the general government, excluding state enterprises and local and regional governments.

of the Frei administration, the country had just experienced three years of unusually good performance, with rapid growth in 1965–66 and sharply increasing real wages. Nonetheless, the prevailing political-economic arrangement was overwhelmed by two factors: the arrival of new players in the redistributive game—particularly rural laborers and urban slum-dwellers—whose demands the state apparatus had difficulty accommodating; and an attempt by the newly dominant centrist party, the Christian Democrats, to bypass the traditional avenues for settling conflicting claims on resources, eschewing accommodation in favor of more ideological policymaking.

Toward the end of the 1960s the number of strikes rose sharply, lines of political communication broke down, and Chile began a chaotic socialist-populist experiment. The Allende years, characterized by massive nationalizations, vigorous political mobilization, and macroeconomic collapse, confirmed in the eyes of all Chileans, and particularly the country's elite, the passing of the old way of doing business.

The policies adopted by the military government must be understood as a reaction to the events of the early 1970s, but the connection is subtle. An unsophisticated interest-group analysis might suggest that a conservative, business-backed government would inevitably favor business interests by removing state intervention. But such a view misses a crucial point: a great deal of the government intervention before 1970 (tariffs, subsidies, and so forth) had favored some business sectors. Removing such intervention—as well as bringing down its by-product, inflation—meant that business interests were hard hit in the mid-1970s by both the tightness of aggregate demand management and the drastic trade liberalization. A second round of large losses affected local business in the aftermath of the 1982 devaluation and financial crisis. How could a business-friendly government afford to follow such policies?

The answer is twofold. First, the breakdown of traditional politics and the fragmentation of civil society in the aftermath of the upheaval of the late 1960s and early 1970s afforded the military and their advisors unusual autonomy in designing and implementing policy. Weakened financially and politically by the socialist experience, business groups and their allies—the traditionally weak right-wing political parties—were in no position to offer an alternative to the government's policies. Others who might have been opposed to the economic changes, such as trade unions and the state-based middle class (government employees, managers of parastatal enterprises), had been politically embarrassed by the abject failure of Allende's policies and then (in the case of the union movement) devastated by repression. Hence the state could operate with relative autonomy from interest groups in pursuing a set of reforms that went far beyond a mere restoration of the status quo ex ante.

Second, and more important, the shock of the Allende experience made large portions of the country's establishment—owners and managers of larger business enterprises, parts of the academic community, and the conservative press—particularly receptive to policies intended to institute drastic changes in the rules of the resource-allocation game. The developmentalist state and its many redistributive mechanisms had served Chile's industrialists (and portions of its middle classes) well for several decades. But in the 1960s the collective inefficiency of the system had become too patently obvious. Even worse, the early 1970s had shown that the redistributive mechanisms of the state could be captured by others—the political left, labor, statist bureaucrats—and used for purposes other than providing a sheltered environment for private sector activity. The only way to avoid that in the future was to render the state less vulnerable to private pressures, no matter where they came from. Thus the need to prevent a recurrence of the populist experience led many interest groups to accept a curtailment of their own power to determine policy, creating new institutional arrangements and enlarging the sphere of action for technocrats inside the government. The main legacy of this period was the demise of the clientelistic state and the emergence of a more autonomous state, in which technocratic considerations have greater policy weight.

That change is expressed in the institutional arrangements that emerged from the reforms. The many changes include the uniform tariff, which limits the scope of private sector lobbying for import protection; the "technification" of the state's activities as a regulator; the privatization of social security and consolidation of changes in budgeting procedures, both of which limit the amount of lobbying on fiscal matters; and the independence of the Central Bank, which both ends the partial control that private sector interests had on credit policies and also limits severely the ability of the bank to finance fiscal deficits. Such reforms have received a great deal of attention for their conventional economic effects. Perhaps, however, their most lasting effect lies elsewhere: they changed the nature and policymaking capacity of the Chilean state and therefore the way resources are allocated in the Chilean economy.

This change remains in force today, under democratic government. The demands of interest groups have been more moderate, and the government has had more room to pursue sound economic policies than anyone ever anticipated. Technocrats (though of a brand that maximizes a welfare function very different from that of its military regime counterparts) continue to exercise great leverage over economic policy, and politicians of a technocratic orientation have also locked in key positions in the congress and in the party bureaucracies. The process of policy formation today is vastly different from that of the 1940s, 1950s, or 1960s. Thus far that seems to have had a highly beneficial effect on economic policy and performance.

Politics and Policy after the Great Depression

Though an 1897 law had already set up an incipient tariff structure, it was the onset of the Great Depression that violently pushed Chile in the direction of import substitution industrialization (ISI) policies.[3] Particularly hard hit by the collapse in the demand for nitrate—indeed, a League of Nations report characterized Chile as the hardest hit of any country—the country reacted to the Great Depression with a bout of instability that set in motion populist forces.[4] In 1931–32 Chile went through a succession of governments, including a twelve-day-long socialist republic.

Yet it was business and the middle classes, not the teeming masses, that constituted the main force behind the change in economic strategies. In 1931, SOFOFA (Sociedad de Fomento Fabril, the main business association) was already criticizing the Ibáñez government for insufficient protection and credit needed to displace manufactured imports.[5] Particularly after the return to

3. Behrman (1976, p. 13) reviews evidence on protection and industrial growth before 1930. That book and Muñoz (1968) and Mamalakis (1976) offer the best overall accounts of Chilean import substitution.

4. See Behrman (1976, p. 20).

5. Drake (1978, p. 62).

power of Alessandri in 1932 and during the Popular Front and Radical governments of 1938–52, import substitution was the policy of the establishment,
led by an informal alliance that included urban business interests and a rising
middle class linked to the state sector.

Chile adopted the usual array of tariff and nontariff barriers, exchange controls often coupled with overvalued real exchange rates, centrally allocated
credit, and fiscal incentives to domestic industry. The policies, at least for a
couple of decades, had their desired effect: between 1937 and 1950 industrial
output grew by almost 7 percent a year; the share of imports in GDP fell; and
economic growth was a reasonably brisk 3.5 percent a year in 1937–45 and
rose to 3.9 percent in 1946–52.[6]

The loose alliance that favored import substitution industrialization differed
in two crucial respects from the ruling coalitions that had preceded it. The first
was the preeminence of industrial over traditional landed interests, which had
held sway in national politics since independence. As is the case in most import
substitution processes, exchange rate overvaluation and other policies tended
to transfer income from commodity exporting sectors (agriculture and also
mining) to the urban sector.[7] Indeed, an analyst of the 1940–58 period has
characterized the process as one of "sectoral clashes"—from which industry
emerged victorious, obtaining important resource transfers and limiting agricultural output growth to 1.5 percent a year in 1940–60.[8] The share of agriculture in total output declined from 18.1 percent in 1940 to 13.8 percent in
1960—and to 7.5 percent in 1970.[9]

The political consequences of this economic shift were much less sharp
than the numbers might suggest. The main reason was the substantial overlap
between owners of land and owners of capital. Zeitlin and Ratcliff, after trac-
ing the property holdings and social and business links of a large number of
prominent Chilean families, conclude that kinship, social, and economic ties
among Chile's "landlords" and "capitalists" are so pervasive and intimate that
they can scarcely be thought of as two distinct groups.[10] Agrarian opposition
to the ISI project was also muzzled by the fact that farm incomes and profits
performed much better than farm output. Heavily subsidized credit and low

6. Muñoz (1968). Mamalakis (1976, p. 6).
7. Notice that unlike agriculture, the large mining sector was largely foreign-owned, so its
output could be taxed directly or indirectly without great domestic political upheavals. As a result,
resource transfers from mining to the industrial sector were particularly large (Mamalakis, 1965,
p. 57).
8. Mamalakis (1965, pp. 122–23).
9. Edwards and Cox-Edwards (1987, p. 4).
10. Zeitlin and Ratcliff (1988).

taxes tended to offset at least partially the effect of distorted relative prices.[11] Moreover, heavy political restrictions on union organizing in the countryside helped keep rural wages low. As a result, real wages of unskilled rural labor fell by 20 percent between 1940 and 1952, while the real earnings of unincorporated agricultural enterprises rose by 62 percent in the same period.[12]

The other remarkable fact about the social alignment that developed starting in the 1930s was its ability to incorporate rising middle and even labor groups into the political process, enabling them to vie for a share of state largesse. The accommodation of the traditionally powerful groups to the new arrangement was remarkably untraumatic. "Especially after WWI and then the Depression, they (the traditional elites) lost their direct monopoly over electoral and administrative politics to challengers representing the middle and lower strata and had to accommodate the industrialization, minimal mass desires and centrist reformers. These concessions safeguarded upper-class foundations and the overarching goal of social stability. . . . Contacts and cooperation between the established elites and the urban middle-class leaders of leftist coalitions fostered political tolerance and trading even when it did not breed alliances."[13]

The middle class that emerged from this process was in some respects peculiar. Chile became not a nation of shopkeepers, but a nation of government bureaucrats. The structure of protection (with low effective protection for imported capital goods) and the concentration of subsidized credit in few hands favored the rise of large, capital-intensive industry in the consumer goods sector.[14] Small businesses were slow in developing, hindered by poor access to credit and excessive bureaucratic regulation. Hence the real opportunities for upward mobility lay in government service and in working in the state-controlled enterprises. The corollary is that the rising middle class supported—indeed, depended on—the growth of state intervention and redistribution. Foxley writes: "Unlike other historical experiences, this middle class is not rooted in an industrial and commercial 'bourgeoisie,' so that its power depends only on the political system and is expressed through universal suffrage. Its eco-

11. Drake (1978, pp. 155–56).

12. CORFO (Corporación de Fomento de la Producción) data presented by Mamalakis (1965, pp. 144–45). Drake (1978, p. 115) writes: "Stated simply, the bargain struck in the 1930s involved ceding office holding to middle class representatives and encouraging industrialization, but preserving immunity for the countryside." Scully (1992, p. 109) describes the industrialization process as the result of "a complex set of explicit and implicit agreements between industrial and agricultural elites and even the leadership of working class parties to exclude the peasantry."

13. Drake (1978, pp. 25–26).

14. See Ffrench-Davis (1973, p. 119).

nomic weakness is evident. This explains the instability of its behavior and its dependence on the state as a protective entity."[15]

The role of organized urban labor in the process was also noteworthy. While clearly less politically influential than some of the other groups linked with the ISI strategy, labor did have a seat at the table. The labor-based Socialist party was a formal member of most of the government coalitions in 1938–52. The Communist party, whose links with organized labor were even stronger than those of the socialists, also participated in the Popular Front government of 1938—but was pushed into opposition and declared illegal by its former Radical allies in the mid-1940s.[16] Union membership swelled in the early ISI decades: less than one percent of the labor force was unionized in 1932, while the corresponding number for 1952 was 19.3 percent.[17] Real wages in industry rose 41.6 percent in 1940–52.[18] But to the extent that organized labor viewed itself as a representative of other underprivileged groups in society (unorganized workers, the unemployed, the rural poor), its bargaining power and redistributive achievements were limited: state resources were scarce, and clear preference was given to industrial subsidies, not to social spending or direct transfers to the poor. Thus one might conclude that urban labor was a partner, though perhaps a very junior one, in the ISI coalition.[19]

Overall, the political-economic arrangement that emerged during the ISI years showed a remarkable capacity for bargain and compromise. Political parties—particularly the centrist, middle-class-based Radical party—and their elected officials were the key intermediaries in the process: "Whether it was a particular business seeking tax relief, a union organization seeking the establishment of a pension fund, a professional association seeking legal recognition, or a municipality after a new dam, political leaders and officials were continuously besieged by an overwhelming number of petitions. Parties were without question the key networks for processing demands, often channeling them up through different levels of party hierarchies."[20]

In turn these competing claims were dealt with at the national level in the Congress, where legislators negotiated over "major policy matters such as

15. Foxley (1982, p. 145).

16. For detailed accounts of the evolution of the labor movement and its links to political parties, see Angell (1972) and Drake (1978).

17. Union membership declined during the more repressive and economically turbulent years of Ibáñez's second term (1952–58), reaching 14.3 percent in 1960. For all these numbers, see Valenzuela (1978).

18. Mamalakis (1965, p. 67).

19. Drake (1978, p. 218). See Garretón (1983, pp. 26–27) for an insightful discussion of labor's role.

20. Valenzuela (1978, p. 9).

agrarian reform or copper nationalization" and "reached compromises on less important issues of mutual benefit to constituents."[21]

Such a system helped let off some of the steam accumulated by the inevitable economic frustrations of life in what remained a poor country. It also offered a sense of political inclusiveness and some (albeit limited) social mobility. As a result, it helped give Chile social peace and democratic stability for the four decades from the onset of the Great Depression to the late 1960s.

Policy Stalemate and Deteriorating Performance

Such an arrangement was not without costs, particularly in the economic arena. The price was a state increasingly dominated by private interests and a weakening of the autonomous policymaking capability of government.

While the presidential system nominally gave the chief executive substantial power, the president's ability to conduct the day-to-day business of government was severely limited. Congress—where the government did not always enjoy a majority—proved capable of delaying legislation and, in particular, of commandeering each year's budgetary process. Outmoded laws and rigid institutions like the *Contraloría* (the comptroller general's office) set very strict limits on government and its ability to hire and fire employees. The very institutions of the executive power were infiltrated by vested interests: "Key areas of the economy were dominated by essentially 'private' governments. The boards of many government agencies included one-third representation from private interests, one-third from technical experts, and one-third from the government. According to one study, during the period 1958–1964 the four most powerful business organizations had voting membership in all the major financial and policy institutions, including the Central Bank, the State Bank and CORFO (Corporación de Fomento de la Producción). Each business group had voting power on the government bureaus relevant to their particular economic sector."[22]

The economic effects of this overall politico-economic structure were not hard to detect. At the microeconomic level, special treatment, tax breaks, and discriminatory regulations flourished, granted to specific firms, industries or economic sectors, and geographical regions. Many regulations were contradic-

21. Valenzuela (1978, p. 17).

22. Valenzuela (1978, p. 16). The study he cites is Menges, "Public Policy and Organized Business in Chile." See also Ffrench-Davis (1973, pp. 119–20) and Drake (1978) on the issue of special interests and government. The State Bank was a large, state-owned commercial bank, the main provider of agricultural and housing loans.

tory and simply arose as an effort to offset an earlier distortion. Both in magnitude and in complexity, such government intervention seems to have gone far beyond what was required to provide a healthy dose of protection to domestic industry.[23] Over time, regulations also became the source of large and often unjustified privilege. A few examples illustrate this point.

—Import licenses were common and arbitrarily assigned, and their holders enjoyed important monopoly rents.

—In the 1950s tax and tariff havens for the provinces in the far north and the far south became a fad, but they soon evolved into a source of many distorted incentives and substantial tax evasion.[24]

—Centralized allocation of bank credit at subsidized rates was substantial: Ffrench-Davis estimates that in 1964 the subsidies implicit in centrally allocated credit at negative real interest rates amounted to one-fifth of total government revenue.[25]

At the macroeconomic level, the arrangement resulted in remarkably lax fiscal and monetary policies, particularly in the 1950s and early 1960s. The budget deficit, which had been 0.7 percent of GDP on average in 1940–53, rose to 2.7 percent in 1953–58 and to 4.6 percent in 1959–64, under the stewardship of the "conservative" Alessandri administration. External and internal borrowing possibilities were very limited, so monetization was the order of the day. Zahler reports that money grew on average at 22.8 percent a year in 1940–53, 41.8 percent in 1954–58, 27.3 percent in 1959–61, 33.9 percent in 1962–64, and 42.7 percent in 1965–70—for an annual average of almost 31 percent in 1940–70.[26] The associated inflation tax revenue was not trivial, peaking at 5.5 percent of GDP in 1955.

Chilean inflation had a long history. As chronicled by Fetter, it dated back at least to the initial abandonment of the gold standard in 1878.[27] But it really became entrenched during and after the 1930s: the average annual rate of inflation was 3 percent in the 1920s, 7 percent in the 1930s, and 18 percent in the 1940s.[28] Hirschman singled out inflation in Chile as one of Latin America's three most distinctive and stubborn policy problems.

23. See Behrman (1976, chapter 4) for a description of some of the great complexity of the system of import restrictions.

24. Ffrench-Davis (1973, pp. 165–166).

25. Ffrench-Davis (1973, p. 139).

26. Zahler (1978).

27. Fetter (1931). Disputes between advocates of convertibility and *papeleros* (advocates of paper money) reached a climax in 1932 when (after Chile had left the gold standard for the last time) the short-lived socialist government masterminded a massive injection of liquidity to erode the value of outstanding debts.

28. Hirschman (1963, p. 160). The previous inflationary peak had been reached during the first decade of the century, when prices rose on average by 8 percent a year.

Yet not all of Chile's inflation was due to fiscal laxity. A couple of peculiar monetary practices—both of them reflective of the weakness of government authorities in general and of the monetary authorities in particular—were also to blame. First, state financial agencies (the several *Cajas* and CORFO) could in effect issue money, for their debt could be held by commercial banks as reserves with the Central Bank. Hence the money supply had the potential to vary pari passu with the lending activities of the state development agencies. Second, as one might expect from any monetary authority whose board is packed with business interests, a good portion of domestic credit expansion by the Central Bank went directly to the private business sector in the form of subsidized loans.[29]

In short, starting in the aftermath of the Great Depression, but especially in the course of the 1940s and 1950s, Chile developed a semicorporatist political-economic arrangement in which fiscal, monetary, and resource-allocation policies were largely endogenous to the demands and pressures of several interest groups. Industrial business groups with sufficient influence to claim state subsidies and transfers were the primary beneficiaries of this arrangement. With the passage of time, white-collar middle classes and some labor sectors, particularly those linked with the state apparatus, could also lay claim to a share of the spoils.

Such an arrangement had the potential to be highly inefficient, and in practice it was. Transfers are not without costs—they have to be financed through taxation, which is usually distortionary. If each group controls only its own demand from the state redistributive apparatus and takes other groups' demands as given, the resulting equilibrium is likely to be characterized by an underestimation of the collective costs of fiscal transfers—and therefore a flood of such demands, imposing excessively high levels of taxation (including the inflation tax) and a host of other microeconomic distortions.[30] Notice that such inefficiencies can be dynamic as well as static. If the resulting level of taxes and regulations affects the private return to capital, investment will be deterred and growth will suffer.[31]

29. In 1952, for instance, direct credit from the Central Bank accounted for 8.5 percent of all credit available to the private sector. Such practices were also influenced by the "commercial loan theory of banking" inherited from Professor Edwin Kemmerer of Princeton (who advised on the creation of the Central Bank in 1925), which held that "organic" emission aimed at private business is "self-liquidating, necessarily represents an increase in production and is therefore not inflationary." Hirschman (1963, p. 181).

30. See the appendix for a formal model in which this inefficiency occurs. See also Aizenman (1992).

31. See Velasco and Tornell (1991) and Tornell and Velasco (1992) for models in which interest group interaction affects the private return to investment, and (in the context of a linear production function endogenous growth model) growth is reduced accordingly.

In this environment macroeconomic performance was mediocre and tended to worsen. In the 1950s inflation rose to an average of 36 percent a year, exactly double the average of the previous decade. The import substitution effort also eventually began to lag: in the 1950s total industrial production grew at an annual rate of only 3.5 percent—in this case only half the rate posted in the previous decade.[32] The overall growth performance was woefully inadequate even when compared with other Latin American countries that were suffering from some of the same problems: between 1950 and 1972 Chile's real GDP grew at an average rate of 3.9 percent a year, while Argentina's grew at 4.1 percent, Brazil's at 7 percent, Colombia's at 5.2 percent, Mexico's at 6.5 percent, Peru's at 5.7 percent, and Venezuela's at 6.2 percent.[33]

In the 1950s and 1960s the economy also began to experience stop-and-go cycles and chronic balance of payments crises. The cycles were of the type well known to students of Latin American macroeconomics: aggregate demand expansion under fixed exchange rates leads to growing real exchange rate overvaluation and a deteriorating trade performance; eventually, the near exhaustion of reserves leads to a devaluation of the currency and the corresponding sharp acceleration of inflation; once inflation becomes excessively high, alarmed authorities enact emergency stabilization measures, which often tend to be merely temporary, thus serving as the preface to the next phase of unsustainable expansion.[34]

Two aspects of these cycles are remarkable: the weakness of the government in both resisting the pressures that lead to the upswing and implementing stabilization measures on the downswing. In the upswing portions, governments attempted to avoid devaluation because of its perceived effects on income distribution, which favored exporters of natural resources and holders of foreign currency assets at the expense of industrial labor.[35] Once devaluation became unavoidable, it was seldom accompanied by the necessary monetary and fiscal austerity. In 1957, in the midst of public protests, the Congress refused to pass basic tax reform legislation needed to complement the Klein-Saks stabilization program launched a year earlier. In the last three years of the Alessandri administration, the fiscal deficit remained substantially above 4 percent of GNP (see table 8-2), in spite of a balance of payments crisis in late 1961 and early

32. Muñoz (1968), quoted in Edwards and Cox-Edwards (1987, pp. 4–5).
33. Edwards and Cox-Edwards (1987, p. 24).
34. In 1952–70 there were three stabilization programs, each implemented at roughly the halfway point of the presidential terms of Ibáñez, Alessandri, and Frei. Stallings (1978) has argued forcefully that the political business cycle is very similar in all three cases. The three episodes are discussed in detail by Ffrench-Davis (1973) and Behrman (1976).
35. Behrman (1976, p. 35) discusses this point.

Table 8-2. Macroeconomic Indicators, 1960–73

Year	Growth of GDP	Inflation[a]	Budget surplus[b]	Trade balance surplus[c]	Real exchange rate[d]	Real wage[e]
1960	3.7	5.4	−4.7	−8.2	40.5	0.0
1961	6.1	9.4	−4.4	−9.6	37.4	6.8
1962	5.7	28.6	−5.5	−7.2	36.0	4.0
1963	4.0	45.9	−4.8	−6.6	40.9	−6.7
1964	4.8	40.4	−4.0	−7.4	36.7	−2.7
1965	6.5	27.3	−4.3	−7.0	38.6	13.3
1966	10.1	17.9	−3.1	−12.2	40.4	12.2
1967	1.2	22.8	−1.7	−9.3	42.5	15.5
1968	3.5	29.1	−1.8	−10.6	45.8	0.8
1969	5.5	30.6	−0.8	−12.8	48.2	9.1
1970	3.6	36.2	−3.5	−12.5	48.5	10.2
1971	8.0	22.1	−9.8	−13.3	45.2	17.0
1972	−0.1	260.5	−14.2	−15.9	41.9	−10.1
1973	−4.3	605.1	−10.5	−15.1	62.7	−32.1

SOURCES: Growth of GDP: for 1960–70, Ffrench-Davis (1973); for 1971–92, Central Bank of Chile. Inflation: for 1960–70, Ffrench-Davis (1973); for 1971–78, Cortázar and Marshall (1980); for 1979–92, Central Bank of Chile. Budget surplus: for 1960–69, Ministerio de Hacienda, cited by Zahler (1978); *Balance Consolidado del Sector Público*, various issues. Data for 1970–85 were previously published in Larraín (1991). Trade balance surplus and real exchange rate: Corbo (1993). Real wage: Central Bank of Chile, *Indicadores Económicos y Sociales*.
  a. December–December CPI change.
  b. Definition of government corresponds to the general government, excluding state enterprises and local and regional governments.
  c. Percent of GNP.
  d. 1977=100.
  e. Deflated by CPI, annual averages.

1962.[36] The Frei administration was more successful in obtaining legislative approval of tax reform, but the political flop of a proposed 1967 forced savings plan marked the end of Frei's stabilization attempt.[37]

As awareness mounted concerning the vulnerabilities of the ISI strategy, stabilization experiments incorporated elements of liberalization, particularly in 1959–61 under Alessandri and during the Frei administration. Alessandri's attempt was remarkable in its decision to substitute price for quantitative barriers and to reduce the overall level of protection.[38] Nonetheless, the experiment ended with depleted reserves and a maxi-devaluation in October 1962, following which the protective apparatus was restored. In an immediate sense scarcity of foreign exchange aborted the program, but politics also played a part. Pressures to undo the liberalization mounted as imports flooded in during 1960–61 and domestic industry felt the hit. It seems highly plausible that the

  36. A major tax-reform bill sent to Congress in mid-1962 was only approved (in a watered-down version) in February 1964.
  37. Ffrench-Davis (1973, p. 57).
  38. See Ffrench-Davis (1973, pp. 82–92).

program's lack of political credibility aggravated the balance of payments difficulties, leading agents to postpone consumption and imports of durables.[39]

The Frei technocrats enjoyed more luck in sustaining an effort at tariff reform. Nonetheless, reform was limited, aimed at rationalization and elimination of bureaucratic barriers rather than at wholesale import liberalization.[40] Extensive plans further to liberalize the trade regime and to enhance domestic efficiency were shelved after the political situation deteriorated in 1968–69.[41] As a result Chile reached the end of the 1960s still saddled with a predominantly inward-looking economy.

Breakdown of the System

In the late 1960s and early 1970s the political-economic arrangement that had prevailed since the 1930s broke down. Two deep changes that took place in 1965–70 were at the root of this breakdown.[42] The first change, emphasized by Valenzuela, was the demise of the pragmatic Radical party as the hinge at the center of Chile's political arrangement and its replacement by the more ideological Christian Democrats. The Frei team pursued novel and politically charged policies, such as land reform and the attempted trade liberalization. But a new style of politics, based on the rule of a single dominant party, proved most controversial.[43] "The Center had been taken over by a party which openly disdained the political maneuvering of clientelistic politics that for so long had kept the system going. . . . Arguing against the incrementalism that had impeded reform, government technocrats sought to institute more 'rational' planning schemes which would dispense with the 'distortions' of the political process. Opposition leaders and legislators were progressively excluded from the particularistic deals of the past."[44]

Far from removing political distortions or curbing the lobbying appetites of vested interests, this change in policymaking style stimulated them. Con-

39. See Calvo (1986) for a formal model of this process.

40. See Ffrench-Davis (1973, pp. 98–100). A fundamental change, nonetheless, was the adoption of a passive crawling peg to neutralize the systematic tendency toward overvaluation of the exchange rate.

41. Behrman (1976, p. 311).

42. Much academic research has been devoted to this period. Valenzuela (1978) has provided the most detailed interpretation of the process. See also Foxley (1982), Garretón (1983), and Tironi (1984).

43. Frei had been elected in 1964 with 56 percent of the vote (a large majority by Chilean historical standards) and had obtained majorities in both houses of Congress in the 1965 legislative elections.

44. Valenzuela (1978, p. 36).

fronted with the possibility that the Christian Democratic party would consolidate political power and change the rules of the game forever, both the left and the right raced to differentiate themselves and to steal support from the center; landlords, businessmen, and traditional politicians fought to retain their usual spheres of influence.

The second change was the arrival of several new guests (and the return of some old ones) at the dinner table of the distributive state.[45] Among them was the traditional (urban, blue-collar) labor movement, which, after suffering repression under Ibáñez (1952–58) and a political weakening under Jorge Alessandri (1958–64), went on a successful organizing and recruiting drive after Frei came to power in late 1964. That year there were 632 industrial unions with 143,000 members, accounting for 14.3 percent of the work force; by 1970 there were 1,440 industrial unions with 198,000 members, accounting for 19.4 percent of the work force.[46]

The political organization and mobilization of rural labor and urban shantytown dwellers, two groups that had been largely outside the existing political arrangements, also took great strides. Aided by the process of agrarian reform and rapid change in the countryside, rural unions grew particularly strikingly, from 24 legal unions with fewer than 2,000 members in 1964 to 476 unions with more than 130,000 members in 1970.[47]

At first such mobilization was the deliberate policy of the Frei administration—for instance, through a 1967 bill that created incentives for organizing in the countryside and in the government's systematic promotion of *juntas de vecinos* (neighborhood associations) in shantytowns.[48] But as was to happen repeatedly in the next half decade, the elites soon lost control of the process, and in the late 1960s Chile entered a period of hypermobilization.[49]

Strike activity, the most obvious indicator of mobilization, rose dramatically in the late 1960s. There were 245 strikes in 1960 and 416 in 1963; by contrast, there were 1,073 in 1966 and 977 in 1969. More than 88,000 workers had been involved in strikes in 1960; over 275,000 (12 percent of the labor force) were

45. See the appendix for a formal analysis of how this affects the outcome of a simple redistributive game.

46. Valenzuela (1978, p. 28).

47. Angell (1972, p. 258) and Valenzuela (1978, p. 30).

48. Several factors account for this policy. Social Christian doctrine emphasized the rights of the truly marginalized poor—in contrast to those of industrial labor, which was regarded as a somewhat privileged group. But observers also stress the Christian Democrats' need to develop centers of popular support outside traditional trade unions, which were controlled by the Communist and Socialist parties. See Angell (1972, chapter 8).

49. The phrase was coined by Landsberger and McDaniel (1976).

Table 8-3. Fiscal Indicators, 1964–70

Year	Spending			Revenue		
	Current	Investment	Total	Mining	Non-mining	Total
			Index 1969=100			
1964	61.6	59.5	61.1	46.7	52.2	51.4
1965	73.3	84.5	76.6	57.2	66.4	65.0
1966	82.8	100.4	87.4	91.4	77.3	79.5
1967	88.1	89.3	87.9	87.5	86.2	86.4
1968	94.6	97.6	95.6	84.2	93.6	92.2
1969	100.0	100.0	100.0	100.0	100.0	100.0
1970	121.2	102.6	118.2	123.5	111.4	113.2
			Percent annual change			
1965	18.99	41.07	25.37	22.48	27.20	26.46
1966	12.96	18.82	14.10	59.79	16.42	22.31
1967	6.40	−11.06	0.57	−4.27	11.51	8.68
1968	7.38	9.29	8.76	−3.77	8.58	6.71
1969	5.71	2.46	4.60	18.76	6.84	8.46
1970	21.20	2.60	18.20	23.50	11.40	13.20
1965–70	12.11	10.53	11.93	19.42	13.66	14.20

SOURCE: Ffrench-Davis (1973, table 67).

involved in 1969.[50] Valenzuela has correctly emphasized that the increase in mobilization and strikes was not an indicator of worsening economic conditions or of an impending economic crisis—indeed, according to many indicators the Frei administration's economic performance was the best in decades (see tables 8-1 and 8-2). In particular, real wages had been rising sharply in 1965–67.

The new political climate, however, had two devastating implications for the prevailing politico-economic arrangement. First, mounting demands put further pressure on an already overburdened fiscal apparatus. In spite of the attempt to introduce more rational economic management, and in spite of an important retrenchment in 1967–69, real current expenditure expanded at a remarkable rate during the Frei administration (see table 8-3), starting with an almost 19 percent increase in 1965, falling to a fairly high low of 5.7 percent in 1969, and then exploding in an election year extravaganza with a 21.2 percent increase in 1970.[51] Current expenditures on personnel accounted for 7.6 percent of GDP in 1965, on social security, 7.6 percent, and on transfers, 2.8

50. Valenzuela (1978, table 9, p. 31). He also emphasizes that the average length of a strike declined, so that total worker-days lost to strikes were no higher in the late 1960s than in the late 1950s.

51. See table 8-3.

percent; in 1970 personnel accounted for 9.8 percent, social security, 8.6 percent, and transfers, 3.4 percent.[52] The unprecedented increase in revenues—particularly copper-related revenues, which rose sharply because of higher world prices—helped preserve a semblance of fiscal balance in the late 1960s.[53]

Second, the state began to lose its capacity to manage social conflict successfully. Perhaps the clearest example of this was the Frei administration's long and acrimonious row with CUT (the main national union organization) over wage indexation procedures.[54] In an effort to reduce inflation without a recessionary squeeze, the government attempted to persuade unions to accept cost-of-living increases that were below the accumulated increase in the CPI, arguing correctly that real wages would nonetheless rise if inflation decelerated. Readjustments of the minimum wage and of the wages of public sector employees were to be used as guidelines in this process. Unions resisted, extricating from employers far larger nominal (and real) wage increases than the government had hoped for.[55] During and after 1967, an orthodox monetary squeeze proved the only way to hold the line on inflation.

Both the attitude of the government party in 1965–70 and the increased mobilization of pressure groups undermined the legitimacy and the efficacy of the traditional, clientelistic way of reallocating resources through the political process. Thereafter it was possible and acceptable to seek redistribution by means other than political bargaining in a highly institutional environment.[56] In some senses the populist experience that followed under Allende (1970–73) was the logical culmination of this process.[57] For all the government intervention of the previous decades, and the changes in private rates of return that implied, the legitimacy of private ownership of the means of production had never been challenged. That was no longer the case in the early 1970s. The Unidad Popular (UP) program contemplated the nationalization of large-scale mining, the financial system, foreign trade, transportation of all sorts, energy production and distribution, cement, petrochemicals, cellulose and paper, and a set of unspecified strategic industrial monopolies.[58] Such nationalizations

52. Data from the *Balance Consolidado del Sector Público,* Tesorería General de la República, reproduced in Larraín (1991).

53. See table 8-3.

54. On this point see Ffrench-Davis (1973, chapter 3) and Angell (1972, pp. 202–03).

55. See table 8-2.

56. In the appendix, this is interpreted formally as a fall in the subjective costs associated with swift (and possibly chaotic) social and economic change.

57. For thorough accounts of the economics of the process, see De Vylder (1976), Bitar (1986), and Larraín and Meller (1991).

58. De Vylder (1976, p. 112).

and many additional ones were soon carried out, with much social and political dislocation. Agrarian reform was also accelerated, with the UP expropriating as much land in one year (1971) as the Christian Democrats had in the whole period 1964–70.[59]

The demands on the fiscal apparatus mounted sharply, generating a "fiscal explosion."[60] Table 8-2 shows that the government deficit climbed to 9.8 percent of GDP in 1971 and to 14.2 percent in 1972. The rapid growth of the deficit was due largely to increases in current expenditures—spending on wages and salaries and social security rose to 13 and 11.9 percent of GDP in 1972, up from 9.8 and 8.6 percent in 1970. The deficits of state enterprises and of private enterprises recently taken over by the government rose even more quickly, taking the deficit of the consolidated public sector to 15.3 percent of GDP in 1971, to 24.5 percent in 1972, and to 30.5 percent in 1973.[61] Valenzuela writes, "The Office of the Budget and the Ministry of Finance lost not only the initiative over general economic policy . . . but substantial control over the budgetary process. In the crisis atmosphere of the Allende years, the already cumbersome and decentralized Chilean public sector became more and more unmanageable."[62] The bulk of the resulting fiscal gap was financed through money creation. Not surprisingly, Chile came to the brink of hyperinflation, with prices rising by more than 600 percent in 1973.

In this environment, labor and the radicalized left saw a chance to alter the traditional political-economic arrangements forever. Such groups had always had an uneasy relationship with the state-led import substitution industrialization strategy and its political expression, clientelistic democracy.[63] Now they set about radically undoing both.[64]

The government's fundamental early policies—stimulation of aggregate demand through wage increases, an increase in government spending, nationalization of large industry and banking, land reform—were aimed at deliberately gaining control of the commanding heights of the Chilean economy, cutting off control of the resource allocation mechanism from the business and middle class groups that had held it for the past fifty years. This was a political strategy as much as an economic one. Pedro Vuskovic, the Allende government's chief economic policymaker, wrote in retrospect: "The nationalization of the bank-

59. Larraín and Meller (1991, p. 186).
60. Larraín and Meller (1991, pp. 205–11).
61. Larraín and Meller (1991, p. 208).
62. Valenzuela (1978, p. 64).
63. In the words of Garretón (1983, p. 27), it was an "ambivalent" relationship because labor's participation in the process was "partial, segmented and necessarily subordinated."
64. In the formal setup of the appendix, this is interpreted as willingness to pay a short-term cost for the sake of permanently changing the rules of the distributive game in their favor.

ing system was not decisive in itself, but insofar as it was used really to control the access to land management by the bourgeoisie of large shares of credit supply; what we did in this respect was clearly insufficient. It was not enough to enlarge the state-owned productive sector, if necessary decisions were not taken to turn this sector into the dominant sector, in the sense that it would impose the basic terms for the functioning of that area of the economy that was and would remain private."[65]

As they had during the Frei administration, events quickly got out of hand, with followers moving much further, much faster than the leadership had anticipated.[66] Illegal factory and farm takeovers proliferated; realized wage increases exceeded even what government-backed unions had pushed for. In spite of the reluctance of President Allende himself, who vainly attempted to impose some discipline on the process, the parties and political operators of the government pushed ahead, encouraging strikes and mobilization to accelerate the takeover of industries.[67]

By 1972 the strikes extended to middle-class groups (truckers, shopkeepers) in opposition to government policies. Shortages and black markets mushroomed as political violence spread. The economic policy consensus and the mechanisms for settling disputes that had worked (however imperfectly) for the previous half-century had collapsed. Is was only a matter of time until the political institutions were brought down by the September 1973 coup.

The Autonomous Military Regime

If it was the left that delivered the lethal blow to Chile's traditional political-economic arrangements, it was the military government that buried the system for good. The regime led by General Pinochet (1973–90) carried out structural transformations that drastically changed the face of the Chilean economy. But, more important, it overhauled the way resources were allocated through the political-economic process.

The Chilean military regime was very different from the classical conservative regimes in Latin America and from previous conservative governments in

---

65. Vuskovic (1978, p. 52).

66. Bitar, Minister of Mining in the Allende administration, writes (1986): "It turned out to be very difficult to contain the forces unleashed in 1971. The sequential conception of redistribution followed by accumulation assumed that basic political and social conduct could be altered and popular expectations changed virtually instantaneously. In the next few months (early 1972) it proved impossible to apply this thinking with the ease that had been hoped for." Quoted in Dornbusch and Edwards (1991, p. 11).

67. Valenzuela (1978, p. 62).

Chile, such as that of Alessandri.[68] The Alessandri government's reformist zeal was limited, particularly when it came to fiscal policy. The government's economic team was staffed largely by businessmen, and the regime itself had a cozy relationship with the business community. It would have been a safe bet in 1973 to predict a similar course for the Pinochet regime. After all, business, both small and large, represented the government's most obvious source of political support. Moreover, the Chilean military had no historical link with liberal, free-market ideas—if anything, it had shown nationalist-populist leanings during its interlude in power in the 1930s and later during the constitutional rule of retired general Carlos Ibáñez.[69] "The admirals and generals who took over in Chile in 1973 did not have a defined blueprint for government."[70] Established economists with links to previous conservative governments were available for policymaking positions—some of them were among Pinochet's early appointments to his economic team. But gradually, and particularly after 1975, a cadre of younger, U.S.-trained technocrats was given substantial reign over economic policy.[71] They pursued—to the surprise of much of the country and even of part of the government itself—a path of radical economic change. The data in table 8-4 show what has happened during this period.

Economic policies during the Pinochet government have given rise to even more academic interest—and substantial controversy—than those of the Allende years.[72] Early stabilization efforts focused on closing the budget deficit inherited from the Allende government and pulling the economy back from the verge of hyperinflation. The government launched a comprehensive attempt to restructure the public sector, involving personnel reductions and spending cuts. A first privatization round (1974–78) sold most state-owned firms and also those enterprises transferred to the state during the Allende administration. By

68. It did share some similarities, nonetheless, with the bureaucratic authoritarian (BA) governments that came to power in Brazil, Argentina, and Uruguay in the 1960s and 1970s. What these regimes had in common was a developmentalist and technocratic approach to policymaking, unlike that of the traditional *caudillo*-based military regimes in the region. For one treatment of the BA model and its implications see Collier (1979). Yet at the same time, Chile's government went much further than the other bureaucratic authoritarian governments in implementing trade liberalization and fiscal reform (among other conditions). See Ramos (1987).

69. Such tendencies within the Chilean military survived throughout the military regime and led to repeated clashes between some of Pinochet's military aides and the Chicago-trained technocrats. See Fontaine (1988).

70. Valdés (1989, p. 12).

71. The story of how this came to pass is told, from very different perspectives, by Valdés (1989) and Fontaine (1988).

72. Good surveys are Corbo (1993), Foxley (1983), Edwards and Cox-Edwards (1987), Ramos (1987), and Meller (1990). This portion of the paper draws on Labán and Velasco (1993).

Table 8-4. Macroeconomic Indicators, 1974–92

Year	GDP growth	Inflation[a]	Budget surplus[b]	Trade balance surplus	Real exchange rate[c]	Real wage[d]
1974	1.0	369.2	−6.6	−11.3	95.0	−5.4
1975	−12.9	343.3	0.0	−1.2	123.8	−2.7
1976	3.5	197.9	3.0	2.1	111.4	10.8
1977	9.9	84.2	0.9	−1.8	100.0	21.5
1978	8.2	37.2	2.2	−3.2	119.3	14.3
1979	8.3	38.9	5.1	−5.2	122.9	10.9
1980	7.8	31.2	5.5	−6.7	106.5	8.6
1981	5.7	9.5	2.9	−12.9	92.6	9.0
1982	−14.3	20.7	−2.3	0.2	103.3	0.3
1983	−0.7	23.1	−3.0	4.1	124.0	−10.9
1984	6.3	23.0	−3.5	2.2	129.6	0.2
1985	2.4	26.4	−3.7	6.4	159.2	−4.5
1986	5.5	17.4	−1.0	6.5	175.1	2.0
1987	5.7	21.5	2.4	5.2	182.7	−0.2
1988	7.4	12.7	4.2	3.9	194.7	6.5
1989	10.0	21.4	4.9	2.0	190.2	1.9
1990	2.1	27.3	3.4	3.9	197.4	1.8
1991	6.0	18.7	2.2	5.3	186.3	4.9
1992	10.4	12.7	2.0	n.a.	171.8	4.5

SOURCES: Growth of GDP and inflation: Central Bank of Chile. Budget surplus: Tesorería General de la República, *Balance Consolidado del Sector Público*, various issues. Data for 1970–85 were previously published in Larraín (1991). Trade balance surplus and real exchange rate: Corbo (1993). Real wage: Central Bank of Chile, *Indicadores Económicos y Sociales*.

a. December–December CPI change.

b. Percent of GNP. Definition of government corresponds to the general government, excluding state enterprises and local and regional governments.

c. 1977=100.

d. Wage and salary index deflated by CPI, annual averages.

1980 the public sector remained in control of only 43 firms (including one commercial bank), compared with the more than 500 firms under state control during the early 1970s.

The sequence of liberalizing moves, aimed at increasing the role of market forces in the economy, began with the freeing of most controlled prices in late 1973. Deregulation of domestic financial markets and an extensive trade reform followed in 1975. In 1979 the government undertook a major labor reform, complemented by an overhaul of the social security system in 1981. Only in the early 1980s was liberalization extended to the capital account.

In the late 1970s macroeconomic policy had also shifted gears. The rate of depreciation of the currency was slowed down, and eventually the peso was fixed vis-à-vis the dollar in an attempt to bring down inflation (which had been remarkably stubborn until then) through a stabilization program based on the exchange rate. By 1981 Chile had an economy with domestic interest rates and prices determined by the market (except for public wages and the exchange rate), a unified exchange rate, a balanced budget, a uniform 10 percent import tariff (except for automobiles) as the only trade barrier, and a relatively liberalized capital market.

A final major change was the 1981 social security reform, which replaced the pay-as-you-go system with a fully funded one and privatized the management of pension funds. The reform contributed to development of the long-term capital markets and provided an important domestic source of long-term project financing: the funds had reached U.S.$12.2 million (30 percent of GDP) by 1992.

Macroeconomic performance was dismal in the early 1980s as a result of both external shocks and domestic policy mistakes. But in 1985 the economy started a sustained recovery, accompanied by a steady improvement in the external accounts, the latter the result of a combination of internal and external factors. The government implemented an outward-oriented adjustment program, designed to restore economic growth through exports, especially through a strong expansion of noncopper exports, and at the same time to continue servicing the external debt. This program relied on a series of devaluations to restore the loss in international competitiveness suffered during the period when the exchange rate was fixed (1979–82) and on a reduction of import tariffs from 35 percent to 15 percent.

A second round of privatization took place in the second half of the 1980s, with a total of forty-six firms—including a number of financial institutions in which the government intervened during the 1982–83 crisis—sold to the private sector for slightly more than U.S.$3 billion.

Economists have been preaching this kind of far-reaching reform for years but, until the past three or four years, the prescription was politically infeasible in practically all less developed countries. After all, such reforms clearly impose substantial costs on organized labor and the middle classes linked to the state apparatus. They are not necessarily in the short-term interest of business and other elites; the changes bring about firm closures, industrial restructuring, and quite often recession. Moreover, systematically mediocre economic performance by a country is insufficient evidence to conclude that such a system must eventually collapse and be replaced. After all, Argentina's performance since the 1930s is in many ways worse than Chile's, and (until very recently) deep economic transformations did not seem to be a possible outcome of the Argentine political process. Why were such policies politically feasible in Chile? And why at that particular historical juncture?

One answer is almost tautological: they were feasible because the Pinochet economic team enjoyed considerable and unusual freedom in designing and implementing policy. In the phrase coined by Karl Marx but still in use among political scientists, the regime seems to have been "relatively autonomous" from group interests, and from the interests of business in particular.[73] This is a feature that Chile's transformations share with other large-scale economic reform processes, particularly in the newly industrialized countries of Asia: "the autonomy required for successful reform rested on discretionary authority of state elites and a rupture of existing bureaucratic routines and channels of societal influence."[74]

But why were Pinochet and his economists afforded such freedom? Of the possible groups that would have been natural opponents of such policies, both labor unions and the top management of the government bureaucracy and state enterprises under Allende were devastated by the repression that followed the 1973 coup. In the mid-1970s, they were at the mercy of whatever policies the military commanders and their closest advisors chose. The business community, weakened by the economic onslaught of the Allende years and lacking an economic blueprint of its own, was also (at least in the early years of the military regime) in no position to oppose the government's economic policies.

The magnitude of the costs the reforms imposed on business and the facility with which government policymakers imposed them are indeed remarkable. A key example is trade liberalization. Between 1974 and 1979 effective rates of protection dropped precipitously for many of the traditional ISI sectors (see table 8-5). In the same period, and measured in constant dollars, total imports grew by 34 percent; imports of nonfood consumer goods (the main product of domestic industry) grew by 123 percent. In some sectors the effects were devastating. A 1978 survey by SOFOFA reported that 60 percent of firms in the textile, apparel, and footwear sector and more than 75 percent of firms in the nonmetallic and basic metals sector had been severely affected by the increased import competition.[75] Bankruptcies proliferated. For instance, thirty-one textile and footwear firms declared bankruptcy between 1978 and 1979; forty-two more followed in 1979.[76] The effects were not limited to specific industries. The share of manufacturing in GDP fell from 29.5 percent in 1974 to 21.2 percent in 1979 and to 18.9 percent in 1982. A total of 2,748 manufacturing firms declared bankruptcy in 1975–82.[77]

Another case in point is the crisis and intervention of much of the financial

73. For a discussion of the "relative autonomy of the state" in developing countries, see the excellent article by Evans (1992).
74. Haggard and Kaufman (1992, p. 23).
75. Cited in Edwards and Cox-Edwards (1987, p. 118).
76. Ffrench-Davis (1980, p. 66).
77. Stenzel (1988, p. 17).

Table 8-5. Effective Rates of Protection, Selected Years, 1974–79

Sector	1974	1976	1978	1979
Foodstuffs	161	48	16	12
Beverages	203	47	19	13
Tobacco	114	29	11	11
Textiles	239	74	28	14
Footwear	264	71	27	14
Timber products	157	45	16	15
Furniture	95	28	11	11
Paper products	184	62	22	17
Publishing	140	40	20	12
Leather products	181	46	21	13
Rubber products	49	54	26	15
Chemicals	80	45	16	13
Petroleum and coal	265	17	12	13
Nonmetallic minerals	128	55	20	14
Basic metals	127	64	25	17
Metallic industries	147	77	27	15
Nonelectrical machinery	96	58	19	13
Electrical machinery	96	58	19	13
Average	151.4	51.0	19.7	13.6
Standard deviation	60.4	15.7	5.3	1.7

SOURCE: Aedo and Lago (1984); cited in Edwards and Cox-Edwards (1987).

system in 1982–83.[78] In that episode, thirteen banks and other financial institutions (including the nation's two largest commercial banks) were taken over by the authorities. Managers lost their jobs, and bank stocks plummeted. At the same time, many of the business conglomerates owned or led by banks, and to which financial institution had lent heavily, were dismantled and went into receivership. The banks were eventually bailed out, in a package estimated to have cost the taxpayers more than U.S.$6 billion; moreover, enterprise debts were often rescheduled on subsidized terms. But the original bank owners lost effective ownership and, in some cases, ended up in jail. In the words of Carlos Díaz-Alejandro, Chile had "shown the world yet another road to a de-facto socialized banking system."[79]

The bank collapse is important, and the associated government response is revealing, for it shows that the government had the capacity to act not only against the interest of small and mid-sized (and furthermore, declining) ISI entrepreneurs, but also against large-scale capitalists: some of Chile's wealthiest and most powerful individuals were among the jailed owners of the banks in which the government intervened. This fact invalidates the view, popular

78. See Díaz-Alejandro (1985) and Velasco (1992) for accounts of this process.
79. Díaz-Alejandro (1985).

among some analysts at the time, that it was "large-scale financial capital" that stood behind and was to gain from the restructuring of the Chilean economy led by the Chicago economists. As Stenzel points out, "One would have a hard time to show that finance capital had lost both its equity capital and its (mostly nonperforming assets), had its institutions effectively intervened by the government, and still was the driving interest behind economic policy."[80]

But while relatively isolated from public pressures, the military government and its policies were certainly not politically neutral. Even if we accept the notion of this or any government as a maximizer of the welfare of the population, it is clear that not all groups were weighted equally in its utility function. And as is the case with any government, the Pinochet administration had an agenda of its own—and this agenda clearly included creating the conditions to keep itself in power, rewarding its political backers, and weakening its potential opponents. The upshot was that the costs of the structural adjustment were not spread equally. If the costs imposed on business were substantial, the costs imposed on labor—not a passive ally but an active opponent of the regime—were far greater. Labor suffered all the costs associated with trade liberalization and industrial restructuring, and the speed and manner in which the process was conducted made the costs particularly high. The unemployment rate, including those "employed" in emergency employment programs, was above 15 percent in every year between 1975 and 1987, reaching 21.9 percent in 1976 and 31.3 percent in 1982![81] Collective bargaining was banned until 1981 and severely limited by a global labor reform thereafter.[82] As a result real wages were the main cushion in adjustment policies; the purchasing power of wages collapsed in the aftermath of the 1975–76 and 1982–83 recessions (falling almost 11 percent in 1983 alone).[83] The absolute level of the wage index stayed below the prerecession 1981 peak until the end of 1988. Income distribution also worsened.[84]

We have argued, then, that the Pinochet regime had considerable autonomy in economic policymaking. But that does not explain why it autonomously adopted the policies that it did. After all, such room for maneuver could just as well have been used to push the country further down the road of ISI, as the

80. Stenzel (1988, p. 18).

81. Cited in Campero and Cortázar (1988, table 2, p. 124). Excluding emergency employment programs and other adjustments, the unemployment peaks are 14.8 percent in 1975 and 19.6 percent in 1982. See Central Bank of Chile, *Indicadores Económicos y Sociales*.

82. See Campero (1984) for an analysis of the labor reform and the trade unions' response to it. The official party line on the subject can be found in the book by Piñera (1990), who was minister of labor in the early 1980s.

83. See table 8-4.

84. See Meller (1990).

Brazilian generals had done just a few years earlier. To understand the policy choices made by the military regime, two additional factors must be considered. The first was the need—as perceived by important portions of the country (including much of the middle class, and not only elite groups)—to ensure that the leftist threat against private property would not resurface. Businessmen and landed interests in particular had been badly shaken by that experience. If they had regarded ISI (and its political expression, liberal democracy) as a benign if somewhat cumbersome environment in which to go about their activities, that perception changed to one in which the old system was a fundamental threat to their most basic interests. This change began building up with the land reform, labor unrest, and growing political upheaval of the 1960s, but it came to a head with the nationalizations, price controls, and forcible firm takeovers of the Allende period. Foxley writes: "The radicalization of the left made more acute the perception of threat on the part of business sectors and the right, which ended up seeking a political solution to replace the democratic regime."[85]

The implications for the business-government relationship were of great importance. Ensuring that the events of the late 1970s and early 1980s would not be repeated implied going far beyond a restoration of the status quo ex ante (that of the mid-1960s, for example). It implied drastically overhauling the system to create rules that secured private property against the intrusion of the state, but, just as crucial, creating rules that impeded the possible capture of state institutions by other social sectors. To achieve this, business elites were willing to pay a price in loss of political control and actual economic pain, which was not trivial.[86]

The positions of large and small business diverged somewhat.[87] Small businessmen had traditionally been closer to protectionist, neocorporatist ideas, and they were most vulnerable to the costs of the liberalization effort. They were the least inclined initially to support it and did mount some public opposition to prevailing policies in 1975–79.[88] Noteworthy is the upheaval in the traditional agricultural sector (mostly wheat, oilseed, sugar, and dairy farmers). Some of this opposition was quelled by the partial and localized undoing of across-the-board liberalizing moves. The establishment of a price-support system for traditional agriculture is a good example. In other cases, the authorities simply ignored discontent. In general, however, active mobilization against the

85. Foxley (1982, p. 148).
86. This cost, and the willingness of a group to pay it, is formally modeled in the appendix.
87. Campero (1984) and Campero and Cortázar (1988).
88. And again during the 1982–83 recession.

policies was limited. With time, "small and medium businesses ended up accepting the neoliberal policies as a 'second best' alternative."[89]

The final factor tipping the balance in favor of deep institutional changes was the external shock of 1974 and the massive domestic recession that followed. Economic management in 1973–75 was conventional, and the economic team was a mixture of old and new faces. But, as has happened elsewhere in the developing world, the crisis strengthened the hand of those arguing that something drastic had to be done about the economy.[90] The structural reforms began in 1975 as part of the package intended to deal with the external shock.

Toward a New State-Society Arrangement

What was the legacy of this period of reforms? In the first place, the reforms effected changes that protected private property from the state, rolling back government participation in economic affairs and reestablishing the primacy of the market as a means for allocating resources.[91] The 1980 constitution enshrined the primacy of private property rights and established requisites for swift and fair compensation in case of expropriation. Henceforth a smaller state, deprived through privatization of much of its role as producer of goods and services, would play a much more limited role in economic life. The state's role as discretionary regulator of private economic activity was also sharply diminished, both through constitutional provisions and through legislation that ensured competitive business operating conditions in areas such as foreign investment and utilities.[92] A private capital market (only one commercial bank remained in private hands), operating under highly liberal rules, would play the leading role in the allocation of credit, using privately accumulated savings resulting from the new pension scheme.

These were not simply temporary measures that could be reversed with a stroke of the pen. In all cases, legislation affecting private interests (as in the case of utilities) would prove difficult to change by a popularly elected parliament; in some cases (as in the prohibition against nontariff barriers) the new legislation took on a quasi-constitutional status that created large legal and

---

89. Campero and Cortázar (1988, p. 136).

90. See Tornell (1992), who has argued that the economic crises were essential in aiding the process of liberalization and privatization in Mexico. See also Fontaine (1988).

91. See Foxley (1983, pp. 22–23).

92. Through the well-known Decree Law 600 of 1975.

practical costs associated with attempted reversion.[93] Through privatization, the reforms created a constituency that would fight tooth and nail against a return to the traditional system.

 The result of these reforms was a smaller state, but not necessarily a weaker one. For the other legacy of the reform process was the restoration of the state's economic policymaking capacity. A regime that controls the executive and the legislature and that operates within the environment of a moribund civil society is bound to make economic policy in a less encumbered manner. But that is a transitory phenomenon, dependent on a particular political conjuncture. The changes that took place in Chile were deeper and more lasting, and they re-shaped the nature of the Chilean state and its relationship to interest groups and to society as a whole.

Trade policy is an example. Tariffs are no longer the domain of presidential decrees, but the subject of legislation to be approved by Congress. The prevailing regime consists of a uniform tariff across all goods and a ban against non-tariff barriers. Both of these changes severely limited the space available for producers to lobby for protection. The need to discuss tariff changes in Congress brings the issue out of the back rooms of bilateral political deals and into the open arena of competitive politics, where affected parties can become aware of the effects of a proposed barrier and lobby against it. And the existence of a common tariff makes it more difficult for given sectors to ask for special deals, for a common tariff ensures uniform treatment for all. Departing from the common tariff would be a major policy change, sure to attract a great deal of attention and opposition.[94] In the longer term, the reform limited the access of business groups to state protection and the benefits of relative price manipulation by the government.

Consider also the area of social security. Under a pay-as-you-go system, the incentives were all there for congressional representatives and pressure groups to demand (and often to obtain) increases in current retirement benefits to be financed through borrowing—and hence through taxes on future generations with no current political representation.[95] With the creation of an individually funded system, the range of social security issues on which the government can be lobbied is much narrower, and the political incentives point in the direc-

93. This prohibition is contained in the Central Bank Organic Law, any amendment to which requires a three-fifths majority in the Congress.

94. See Rodrik and Panagariya (1991) for a review of political economy arguments for a common tariff.

95. See Alesina and Tabellini (1990) and Velasco (1993) for models in which the possibility of borrowing creates incentives for systematic government deficits. See also Tabellini (1990) for an analysis of the politics of intergenerational redistribution through social security.

1980 Const

tion of preserving the accumulated savings of individuals, not spending them away.

Two other aspects of the current institutional environment are of great importance. One has to do with the budget process. While the 1925 Chilean constitution was quite presidentialist and endowed the executive with ample powers in many areas, governments often found it hard to negotiate and obtain approval, in a timely and reasonably effective way, of the government's annual budget.[96] Reforms introduced in 1970 at the end of the Frei administration and retained in the 1980 constitution and in current budget procedure legislation establish mechanisms that greatly limit the scope for vested interest lobbying on fiscal affairs. First, all bills involving the allocation of public resources can be initiated only by the executive; the role of Congress is limited to approving, amending, or turning down. Second, there are strict limits on the time allocated to congressional discussion of the budget. If sixty calendar days after the reception of the bill the legislature has not approved an alternative to it, the executive's proposal is automatically approved.[97]

The final change has to do with Central Bank independence. The 1980 constitution prohibits the Central Bank from financing government deficits by purchasing treasury securities. In addition, in December 1989, during the closing weeks of the Pinochet regime, an organic law was passed providing for the Central Bank to be governed by a five-person board, serving overlapping ten-year terms, to be appointed by the president and confirmed by the senate.[98] The minister of finance sits on the board but cannot vote; at most he can delay implementation of approved measures by two weeks. The measure may have been intended to guarantee the insulation of the monetary authority from pressures arising from the executive, and it does that. Yet at the same time, Central Bank independence put a definitive end to the Central Bank's age-old vulnerability to private sector demands for direct credit.

The politics of the process that led to this new state of affairs is somewhat paradoxical. In some cases, the political and economic goals of the military government dovetailed nicely. That is seen most clearly in the changes imple-

96. That was also because under the 1925 constitution governments often did not enjoy congressional majorities, but that is a matter outside the scope of the present paper.

97. The budget is usually sent to the Congress in late September or early October of the year prior to that in which it is to apply, so the sixty days are normally over by late November or early December.

98. At first Pinochet tried to pack the board with men identified with his administration. A last-minute compromise provided for the appointment of two of his men, two technocrats close to the opposition parties, and a neutral, highly regarded economist from the UN Economic Commission for Latin America and the Caribbean (ECLAC) as president.

mented in the labor market, a case in which the efforts to weaken a political opponent and to enlarge the role of the market as a means for allocating resources were clearly complementary. The authorities were not content with accomplishing a much-needed deregulation of the labor market. Labor was perceived not simply as one more group vying for its share of the overall pie, but as a political adversary of the regime whose influence had to be neutralized. The 1981 Labor Code contained provisions limiting union organizing and wage bargaining that were unknown in OECD (Organization for Economic Cooperation and Development) countries and that were subject to harsh criticism by international agencies such as the International Labor Organization.[99] The results were immediately clear: affiliation to unions declined from 33.7 percent of the labor force in 1973 to 11.2 percent in 1985.[100]

In other cases the paradox is more apparent. Market-oriented reforms are supposed to enhance the position of the private sector, and in many obvious senses they do. Yet in Chile they had the additional effect of closing down many avenues of private sector pressure on and manipulation of government policy. Businessmen are not the only ones affected by the new setup. Public enterprise managers, middle-class groups linked to the state apparatus, and certainly trade unions—the power of all these groups to lobby for special treatment has been curtailed. But as the prime beneficiaries of the old system of selective protection and negotiated benefits, businessmen (particularly larger manufacturers in the import-competing sectors and smaller producers everywhere) have found themselves adjusting to a new situation in which corporatist practices have become much rarer in Chilean economic policymaking.

Postscript: Economic Policy under Democratic Government

In Chile the year between the 1988 plebiscite and the 1989 presidential election was filled with dire predictions—by government officials, business leaders, and conservative economists alike—of chaos, populism, fiscal deficits, rampant inflation, and capital flight if the opposition ever reached power.[101] None of these terrible forecasts have come to pass. In 1993 the country is enjoying extraordinary political tranquility, and legislative cooperation

---

99. For an analysis of how unions were affected by economic policies and how they reacted, see Campero and Valenzuela (1984). For an analysis of markets and politics in the wage-setting process and in other labor issues, see Campero and Cortázar (1988).

100. See Campero and Cortázar (1988, table 3, p. 126).

101. This section draws on Labán and Velasco (1993).

between government and opposition is the norm. The basics of an open-economy, market-oriented model have been not only retained, but deepened. Macroeconomic management has been cautious, with systematic fiscal surpluses and declining inflation. Government-labor relations have been cooperative. Business confidence is at an all-time peak, as evidenced by the strength of the currency and of the local stock market and the bulging investment flows and international reserve stocks.

Three conflicts, whose noncooperative and welfare-inefficient outcomes set the stage for Chile's mediocre economic performance from World War I to the 1960s, are being resolved today in a way that bodes well for sustaining Chilean economic reforms and for the overall performance of the economy. The first conflict was about real exchange rates and protection for domestic producers. The political economy of trade protection and exchange rate policy has changed drastically since the 1960s. After almost twenty years of a very open trade regime, the constituency in favor of low tariffs and competitive real exchange rates—which includes not only academic economists and exporters, but also the bulk of the business community—is dominant. The majority of business people favor a nonprotectionist regime because in their view a market-oriented, private-property regime and an open economy go hand in hand.[102] Stated another way, lack of access to the protective apparatus of the state is a price that business leaders are willing to pay in order to sustain a system in which others (labor, bureaucrats, managers of parastatal enterprises) also have limited access to state resources and state power. Business groups also favor free trade because the center of power has shifted within the business community away from import competing interests and toward exporters. The rise of a new entrepreneurial class linked to fruit exports and services, for instance, is noteworthy.[103] These groups form an important lobby not only in favor of low tariffs, but also in favor of competitive real exchange rates.

The second traditional conflict was over the allocation of government expenditures and taxes. But in 1990–92 the battle over the budget has also been resolved successfully. Fiscal policy has been guided with a firm hand, and the temptation to subsidize the undeserving has been avoided. A sharply increased

102. The underlying tensions have not gone away altogether. A handful of sectors remain uncompetitive in world markets and continue to demand special protection. Foremost among these is traditional agriculture (wheat, corn, sugar, and oilseeds), which is subject to a price stabilization scheme inherited from the military regime that, at least in the past few years, has kept domestic prices systematically above international ones. Other declining sectors outside agriculture, such as textiles and coal, beset by either archaic technology or structural changes in world markets, regularly demand special treatment.

103. See Cruz (1988).

awareness of the costs of budget deficits and money creation has contributed to moderating the spending demands of ministers, legislators, and regional and local governments. The budget rules have also helped keep the process running smoothly. In 1992 the fiscal surplus averaged more than 2.5 percent of GDP, remarkable for a period of transition to democracy.

The government has tackled the conflict between macroeconomic stability and the need to devote increased resources to lower income groups by seeking and obtaining approval of the 1990 tax reform and by changing the composition of government spending: the share of social spending in the government budget was, in 1990–91, 3.4 percentage points higher than it had been in 1988–89. At the same time, fiscal social spending has risen an accumulated 20.5 percent real during 1990–91, and it is expected to increase even further during 1992–93. Per capita fiscal social spending in the 1993 budget law is 40 percent higher in real terms than that stipulated in the 1990 budget law inherited from the military government. Overall, a greater social effort has been compatible with the maintenance of fiscal surpluses.

The third traditional conflict was over wage policy. While Chile has never had a fully centralized wage-setting policy, government-mandated readjustments in minimum wages and public sector wages have long had an important effect on wage practices at the firm level. In addition, formal and informal indexation arrangements (all of them backward looking) have long endowed inflation with inertia. Today the wage-setting process is well on its way to becoming more cooperative and efficient. In April 1991 the government, the Confederación de la Producción y el Comercio (CPC), and CUT agreed that further real increases in the minimum wage should be related to gains in labor productivity, and that future expected inflation (as opposed to past inflation) should be used as the criterion for nominal adjustments. This is an important contribution toward breaking indexation to past inflation, which is still widely used in labor and financial contracts. And perhaps even more important, it is an indication of the trust that has emerged in government-labor relations, for the unions have agreed to use a forecast of inflation produced by the government itself. As inflation continues to fall and such practices extend to the private sector, inflationary inertia should subside as well.

In short, a political economy arrangement seems to have emerged in Chile in which the costs of government transfers and interventions are (at least partially) internalized, and therefore a sound fiscal policy becomes achievable; the return on private investment seems safe from the menacing and predatory behavior of other social groups; and groups face incentives to moderate their demands that the government manipulate relative prices in their favor. Such behavior, and the rules and institutions that help make it possible, have been shown to be the normal outcome of voluntary interaction among social groups, not simply the imposition of a military dictatorship.

The new equilibrium is certainly more efficient than (and maybe even Pareto-preferred to) the pre-1973 one. And insofar as one can judge from the events of 1990–92, it seems also to be stable. It may well be that for Chile the period of conflictual politics, inefficient policymaking, and economic stagnation, which lasted for more than half a century, is finally coming to an end.

Comment by Francisco Rosende

Possibly the most important shortcoming of this paper is that it does not consider the role of external forces on the Chilean economic and political evolution. In particular, it does not consider the effect of changes in the terms of trade on national income, at least not after the 1960s. Moreover, the interpretation of high unemployment rates and bankruptcy episodes between 1975 and 1982 is clearly incomplete without the inclusion of external shocks.

A second limitation is that analysis of economic policy design must take into account international experiences. For instance, the degree of approval currently observed with respect to the efficiency of market forces and export-oriented development strategies, at least among Chilean economists, could be quite different but for the huge failure of socialism worldwide.

One important thesis of the paper is that during Pinochet's government there was a sort of "autonomous economic management." Velasco suggests that Pinochet's economic policy and the role that the economic team had to play were clear and well defined from the beginning of the process. I believe the story was different.

At the beginning of the military government the economic policy orientation was closer to old conservative strategies than to the so-called Chicago school model. In particular, the stabilization policy undertaken in 1974 was quite mild given a rate of inflation that reached 375.9 percent and a fiscal deficit of about 10.5 percent of GDP. In particular, it was not until the oil crises that hit the Chilean economy in 1975, with a 40 percent drop in the terms of trade, that the implementation of a severe adjustment program was necessary.

The successful handling of the crisis made it possible for the economic team to undertake many important reforms afterward—the trade liberalization program, for example. The depth of the structural reforms implemented since the mid-1970s was small compared with experiences under way in countries like

Argentina or Bolivia. By 1981 the government held control over public utilities, most of the copper industry, and many other enterprises. The share of the public sector in GDP was higher in 1981 than in 1965.[104]

In spite of the fact that Pinochet's government was not democratic, it faced significant constraints in implementing a market liberalization program. For example, in some sectors labor unions retained tight control over the labor supply. An example of this is port workers, who for a long period of time had enjoyed monopolistic power given to them by an official license.[105] The government had to buy this license from them to achieve a greater efficiency in this sector as a key condition for increasing international trade. Approval of the labor legislation included an important cost for the economic team in the so-called *ley del piso* (real wage-floor law), which ruled out real wage reductions.[106]

This was a high price to be paid for a free market oriented economic policy, as was demonstrated a few months after the implementation of this policy, when the terms of trade experienced a new decline, and foreign interest rates rose dramatically. This adverse shock requested an aggregate demand squeeze that produced a sudden increase in the unemployment rate.[107]

Perhaps the most important conclusion of Velasco's paper is that political coalitions among different parties and groups contribute to better economic performance of governments. Moreover, in the historical review of Chilean economic developments, the author stresses the relationship between the structure of government's political support and economic stability. Currently there is an important empirical and theoretical support of this proposition, but Velasco goes further, distinguishing among different schemes of governments depending on the broadness of their political support.[108] He opts for a sort of coalition scheme based on broad general principles rather than a single-party formula.

Following this line of reasoning the author concludes that since 1990 the problems related to noncooperative and welfare inefficient outcomes are being solved in Chile because of a cooperative equilibrium that exists among differ-

104. Larroulet (1984).
105. Wisecarver (1986).
106. This regulation established that in every wage negotiation the resulting nominal wage adjustment had to be at least equal to the rate of inflation since the last negotiation.
107. Once the contraction in economic activity was clearly mirrored by the unemployment rate, the regulations that inhibited labor demand were lifted. However, the financial crises severely hit the level of employment, necessitating a sudden reduction in real wages, which occurred later when the real exchange rate rose significantly. On the relationship between real wages, real exchange rate, and unemployment in the Chilean economy see Rosende (1985).
108. For instance see Cukierman, Edwards, and Tabellini (1992).

ent sectors of the country. Velasco singles out three conflicts that are being resolved.

—The degree of openness to world trade. According to Velasco Chile has achieved a basic agreement in favor of low tariffs and competitive exchange rates.

—The achievement of a substantial consensus on the need for sound macroeconomic policies for development.

—A conflict about wage policy that is in the process of being solved. The gradual use of future inflation in labor contracts is certainly an achievement for economic policy design.

I agree in principle with the author about the existence in Chile of a greater degree of approval of the economic model. However, this has not been an easy task. Maybe it would be useful to search for an explanation of how the basic rules of the game came to be widely accepted. Let me try two possible explanations. The first refers to the good results achieved by the Chilean economy since its external debt crisis. The improvement of the model ever since, together with the signal failure of alternative strategies, has caused a significant deterioration in the position of the model's critics. Second, some institutional changes like the Central Bank independence, the rules that govern approval of the budget, and so on, reduced the probability of future changes in the system. In other words, the profitability of rent-seeking activities is currently quite low thanks to those reforms. So pressure on economic policy design has been sharply reduced.

The analysis of institutional limits on economic policy design takes us to the study of constitutional economics, whose inspiration comes mainly from the public choice theory. I think that the analysis of Chilean economic policy and its results in the recent past make it necessary to stress the role played by institutional constraints. Thus far, the fairly conservative macroeconomic policy implemented during Aylwin's government as well as the commitment assumed by authorities to maintaining the economic model could have been quite different without an independent Central Bank and the inability of Congress to increase fiscal expenditures imposed by current legislation.

Therefore I think that Velasco's paper does not give enough credit to the importance of institutional changes implemented before Aylwin's government for the recent performance of the Chilean economy. In other words, the so-called cooperative game that Velasco says Chile has achieved since 1990 could also be interpreted as effective enforcement of some barriers to external pressures by economic authorities. I think that this interpretation is consistent with Velasco's explanation of the frequent and large swings observed in the growth of GDP and in inflation for a long period in the Chilean economy.

Comment by Arturo Valenzuela

Chile has been something of an enigma. Located far from the centers of power, with no significant strategic importance, the small country on the west coast of South America has always commanded considerable world attention. In the nineteenth century foreign observers noted the country's remarkable institutional stability and its success in two international wars. In the twentieth century Chile evolved into a complex and politically fascinating multiparty democracy with a strong state capable of implementing a broadly based strategy of import substitution industrialization. By mid-century Chilean voters divided sharply into rightist, centrist, and leftist tendencies, electing three successive governments (Jorge Alessandri, 1958–64; Eduardo Frei Montalva, 1964–70; and Salvador Allende, 1970–73) that adopted substantially different policies to address the country's failure to create dynamic growth and to resolve severe social inequalities. Conservative, Christian Democratic, and Marxist blueprints for change were followed, after the military coup of 1973, by sweeping transformations carried out by an authoritarian regime intent on reversing the historic pattern of import substitution industrialization and state intervention in the economy. Today, after the seventeen-year military interlude, Chile is much admired for its dynamic, free-market economy and the ability of the democratic government of the Concertacin, Chile's ruling multiparty coalition, to maintain economic stability while further encouraging investment and export-driven growth.

Andrés Velasco's excellent paper attempts to explain the political and economic forces that made the transformation from a state-centered economy to an open economy possible. He aptly describes the politics of stagflation, stop-and-go cycles, and chronic balance of payments crises in much of twentieth-century Chile. Beginning with a Popular Front government in the late 1930s, the country embarked on a concerted strategy of import substitution and state-sponsored industrialization that produced between 1937 and 1950 an average yearly growth rate in the manufacturing sector of 7 percent. But the Chilean economy stagnated in the 1950s, growing at an average rate of 3.8 percent between 1950 and 1970, while inflation became a painful reality of daily life.

In an economy in which the state by the 1960s loomed larger than that of any other economy on the continent except Cuba, competing groups scrambled to obtain state protection and subsidies, while seeking to gain ground relative to one another in a Byzantine game of price and wage readjustments. This game was abetted by highly competitive parties unable to establish majority governments capable of pursuing stable policies and reining in antagonistic pressures. Minority presidents with minority support in the legislature often found themselves with little power, as groups and interests parceled out policy areas in the vast and unwieldy bureaucracy, and the politics of outbidding ruled the day.

It is not clear from Velasco's account whether it was the nature of Chile's political game that impeded economic stabilization and growth or whether the problem was far more intrinsic, involving the failure of the model of import substitution industrialization and state intervention. The economic advisers of the military government clearly subscribed to the latter view, holding that Allende represented a more determined phase of state intervention in economic life, but one that was bankrupt before the Marxist government came to office.

The evidence in support of such a thesis is not altogether clear. The performance of the Chilean economy in the middle and late 1960s represented a significant turnaround. Per capita growth rates, which had declined in the 1950s and early 1960s, grew steadily in the late 1960s, reaching a historic high in 1970. Average inflation (quite low by 1980s' standards for an indexed economy) dropped considerably by comparison with the inflation rates of the Carlos Ibáñez and Alessandri administrations (1952–64). Chile also experienced positive trade balances after a long period of chronic balance of payments difficulties. Finally, the Chilean state increased its efficiency and taxing authority and made significant inroads in addressing social problems without jeopardizing fiscal responsibility. State expenditures increased significantly, but so did state revenues. And while unionization and political mobilization increased, after a sharp decline in the 1950s, there is no reason to believe that new demands had exceeded the capacity of Chile's political institutions to process them. Indeed, the percentage of the work force unionized in 1970 was the same as in 1952, and the number of worker days lost in strikes was far lower in the late 1960s than in the mid-1950s.

Although economic factors such as the high price for copper exports help to explain the improvement in economic indicators, the success of the Christian Democratic government can also be understood in political terms. For the first time since the early 1930s a president enjoyed strong majority support among the voters and in the legislature, obviating the more negative aspects of Chile's political game. Had Chile continued to be governed by a reformist government that could maintain coherent policies, rather than shifting dramatically to an unstable minority coalition under Allende, would the Chilean economy have continued to improve? Under Allende's unwieldy coalition, sound economic policies were deliberately subsumed in short-term political ends in a desperate attempt to build majority support for the socialist government.

To what extent, then, can Chile's historic economic difficulties be attributed to the principal characteristics of the economic model of import substitution industrialization and state ownership? Or to what extent do they stem from the country's peculiar game of coalition politics, which degenerated during the Allende years into open political warfare with catastrophic implications for the nation's economy? The economic crisis of the Allende years has to be understood as resulting directly from Chile's political crisis, not vice versa. Had the Christian Democratic administration continued in office throughout the 1970s with strong majority support, it is legitimate to ask whether the dramatic shock treatments of the military years would have been necessary, whether Chile could have pursued a more gradual, although necessary, policy of structural reform.

It is instructive to compare Chile with Colombia in reflecting on this question. Colombia did not depart as sharply as did Chile from the import substitution politics of the past; it maintained far more predictable sets of economic policies over a long period, based on strong majority consensus between the two major parties. Chile and Colombia were the only South American countries to weather the 1980s without a decline in per capita income. But Colombia did not experience the extraordinary economic dislocations that led in Chile to the highest rate of urban unemployment on the continent and severe declines in the standard of living of certain sectors of the population.

In explaining the political and economic forces that made Chile's experiment in structural adjustment under the military possible, it is also worth pondering the extent to which reform was due to specific characteristics of the Chilean case—characteristics that would be difficult to reproduce elsewhere even under authoritarian conditions. Some of these factors were conjunctural, relating to the context of Chilean politics in the immediate aftermath of the Allende years. Others were of longer standing.

Among the most important conjunctural factors was that Chile's military coup did not result from a classic Latin American coup coalition of rightist and business elements pushing the armed forces to take over the state to protect their interests. After it had seized power, the military was far more impervious to political pressures than the military establishments of other countries. The military regime did not face much opposition from labor or popular sectors that were severely repressed. What is intriguing is the lack of effective opposition from Chile's business community, which had developed under the aegis of the state and was strongly committed to a model of state-supported capitalism.

By the time of the coup, Chile's private sector, including big business and the once dominant rural elite, had been severely weakened by the reforms and by the expropriations of the Frei and Allende administrations. Although the private sector enthusiastically welcomed the coup, it did not have the resources to flex the necessary political muscle to thwart or modify the extensive structural reforms advocated by the military's economic planners. The opening of the Chilean economy, and indeed the transformation of Chile's entrepreneurial class, would have been much more problematic had the traditional business sector been more powerful.

It is also doubtful whether much of the revolution in Chilean agriculture, which stimulated the boom in nontraditional exports, would have been possible without the fundamental changes in land tenure patterns and investments in timber production achieved by the agrarian reform measures of the 1960s and early 1970s. By the same token, it is legitimate to ask whether the recovery of the Chilean economy would have been as easy after the devastating collapse of 1982–83 had the state not controlled the significant resources of Chile's copper industry, nationalized by Allende but never privatized by the military government. The political capacity General Augusto Pinochet enjoyed to implement reforms and the ability of Chile's private sector to respond were due in no small measure to the unintended consequences of the profound transformations begun by his anticapitalist predecessors.

More broadly, the autonomy of the Chilean authoritarian state and its capacity to institute change was, ironically, also aided by several factors directly related to Chile's long tradition of democratic politics. Chile's armed forces were unique on the continent. For decades they were isolated from politics, enjoying few ties with the country's party-generated elites, which ran the country. Because of this clear separation between political and military worlds, civilian elites had little direct influence on the military establishment, which ably drew on the fear of a return to the confrontational politics of the Allende years as a weapon to implement policies that proved difficult for much of the business community to accept.

But it was not only Chile's tradition of an apolitical military that facilitated the implementation of dramatic reform measures. Chile's open and competitive politics had forged over several generations a relatively strong and efficient state, while fostering widespread respect for the rule of law among the citizenry. The important role of Congress and the comptroller general in Chile's political system had attenuated executive discretion, contributing to the acceptance of universal norms and procedures. Although the military regime was forced to take measures to cut back on the bloated size of state agencies, the high degree of probity, professionalism, and experience in Chile's public sector, including the courts and many state enterprises, contributed to easing the reform process. Chileans obeyed the rules drawn up by the new authorities, though many questioned the legitimacy of the rulers themselves. By contrast with the experience of many neighboring countries, privatization and reform schemes were executed with a minimum of corruption, citizens paid their taxes, and private-sector actors quickly learned to adjust to new regulations drawn up to correct the deficiencies of the early moves to open up the Chilean economy.

Undoubtedly Chile holds important lessons for other countries embarking on a process of structural adjustment and reform. However, the combination of immediate and long-term factors peculiar to Chilean politics, factors that contributed to the successful outcome in the Chilean case, should make policymakers wary of drawing exclusively on the concrete measures and strategies pursued by Pinochet's economic team in attempting to apply the Chilean experience to other contexts.

For Chile the challenge today is to build on both the strengths of its democratic tradition and the success of its economic reforms to ensure continued stability and long-term growth, while addressing the serious social inequities the country still faces. The administration of Patricio Aylwin has shown that a democratic government can be fiscally responsible, ensure macroeconomic stability, and promote savings and investment. The administration's success, however, is due to the coherence of Aylwin's multiparty coalition, which enjoys majority support in the country and has support among a majority of elected members of Congress.

It remains to be seen whether future leaders will be able to structure viable majority governments. Chilean politics continue to be multiparty politics in which no single party or even tendency (right, center, or left) can command a majority on its own. The discipline of the Aylwin coalition is due in part to the common history of leaders and parties who struggled to defeat the military government at the polls and the fear of authoritarian reversal should they fail in managing the country. As Chile moves away from the experience of military rule, it is critical that the country not fall again into the perverse logic of competitive politics so aptly described by Velasco in his paper. This will require not only a political learning process that stresses the values of compromise and consensus, but also the adoption of additional constitutional reforms to encourage the politics of coalition building. Principal among these is a reversal of the extreme presidentialism inherited from the military period, a reform that would establish the legislature as the premier institution for consensus building and compromise, endowing it with more real authority.

Appendix

The Basic Game

There are m groups in society, each one of which is constituted by a large number of atomistic agents.[109] The total income of group i is

$$(8\text{-}1) \qquad\qquad y_i = q_i (1 - \tau) + g_i,$$

where y is total income, q is the aggregate amount of output produced by all agents in the group, τ is the tax rate (assumed uniform for all groups), and g is the transfer received from the government. Only group leaders decide on the size of the transfer they will seek from the government; group members make output decisions taking taxes and transfers as given.

Of the m groups, only n are insiders, in that they can obtain transfers; the remaining $m\text{-}n$ pay taxes and get nothing in return. Therefore, the government budget constraint is

$$(8\text{-}2) \qquad\qquad \sum_{i=1}^{n} g_i = \tau \sum_{i=1}^{m} q_i.$$

Taxes are not neutral. Because individual agents are atomistic, output in each sector is a decreasing function of the tax rate, with the relationship assuming the functional form

$$(8\text{-}3) \qquad\qquad q_i = \bar{q}e^{-\alpha\tau},$$

where $\bar{q}$ is the "natural rate of output" and $\alpha > 0$ is the semielasticity of output with respect to the tax rate.

The game is as follows. Each insider group leadership maximizes group income by deciding how much to demand from the government, taking other groups' demands as given. Leaders do understand the government budget constraint, nonetheless, and do internalize the effects that their demands will have on the overall tax rate. Notice that the game is purely redistributive: government spending serves no other purpose, and taxes are levied exclusively to finance this spending.

One-Shot Nash Equilibrium

Consider first the Nash equilibrium to the game among the n insider groups. A group's first-order condition is

---

109. This appendix is based on work with Aaron Tornell of Harvard University.

(8-4)
$$\frac{\partial y_i}{\partial g_i} = -q_i[1 + \alpha(1 - \tau)]\frac{\partial \tau}{\partial g_i} + 1 = 0.$$

Using equation 8-4 in equation 8-3, and noting that output will be the same for all groups we can write

(8-5)
$$g_i + \sum_{j=1}^{n-1} g_j = m\,\tau\,\bar{q}e^{-\alpha\tau}.$$

Each group i can therefore compute

(8-6)
$$\frac{\delta\tau}{\delta g_i} = \frac{1}{mq_i(1 - \alpha\tau)}.$$

Finally, substituting equation 8-6 into equation 8-4 and rearranging we have

(8-7)
$$\tau^N = \frac{(m - 1)- \alpha}{\alpha(m - 1)},$$

where τ^N is the equilibrium tax rate and N stands for "Nash."[110] Notice that as α rises the equilibrium tax rate falls, since there are greater output costs associated with more government spending.

The resulting level of income for each group can be computed by using equations 8-7 and 8-3 in equation 8-1, plus the assumption of symmetry:

(8-8)
$$y_i^N = \bar{q}\,e^{-\alpha\tau^N}\left[1 + \frac{m - n}{n}\tau^N\right].$$

Insider groups clearly benefit from being able to tax outsiders—though the equilibrium tax rate is less than that ($\tau = 1/\alpha$) which would maximize revenue from the outsiders. This is because any tax that is imposed on outsiders must also be paid by insiders.

Notice there is also an inefficiency associated with the decentralized and noncooperative nature of spending decisions. This is most clearly seen in the case in which n = m (all groups are insiders). In that case equation 8-8 becomes

(8-9)
$$y_i^N = \bar{q}\,e^{-\alpha\tau^N} < \bar{q}.$$

This level of taxation is inefficiently high—in the case $n = m$ the optimal tax rate would be zero—and that lowers welfare. More generally, it is easy to show that a central planner maximizing the welfare of all n insider groups (for $n < m$) would choose

(8-10)
$$\tau^P = \frac{(m - n) - \alpha}{\alpha(m - n)} \leq \tau^N,$$

110. Notice that to ensure $0 < \tau < 1$ we must impose $[n/(n - 1)] < \alpha <[n-1]$.

where P stands for planner. Hence the externality among competing insider groups generates a tax rate that is at least as large as the one a benevolent planner would choose.[111]

The Possibility of Switching

Consider now the intertemporal dimension of this game. A forward-looking group will maximize

$$(8\text{-}11) \qquad V_{i0} \equiv \sum_{t=0}^{\infty} y_{it} R^t, \quad R \equiv \frac{1}{1+r},$$

where r is the real exogenous interest rate. If the Nash equilibrium prevails forever, the payoff to each insider group is

$$(8\text{-}12) \qquad V_i^N = \frac{y_i^N}{1-R} = \frac{\bar{q} e^{-\alpha \tau^N}\left[1 + \dfrac{m-n}{n}\tau^N\right]}{1-R}.$$

That outcome is predicated on the "open access" structure of the previous section in which, through the government budget constraint, each insider group has access to the output produced by the $m - n$ outsider groups and the remaining $n - 1$ insider groups.

Assume now that each insider group has access to the following political technology: by paying a once-and-for-all cost of c, it can shut off the access of all other insider groups to its own output. This is intended to capture reforms such as fiscal restructuring and abolition of tax breaks, tariff reductions, or labor code streamlining, which may bring short-run costs but which, in the long run, reduce open access. The cost can also be thought of as noneconomic—for instance, the cost in terms of subjective utility of political upheaval, adjustment, and so forth. When will it pay off for an insider to use that technology?

To answer that question we must specify what happens after an insider group i has paid the cost c. If i is the only group to do so—we will say that in this case it becomes a leader—then it has exclusive access to government transfers (and indirectly, to others' output). In that case, the leader's income is

$$(8\text{-}13) \qquad y^L = \bar{q} + g^L = \bar{q} + (m-1)\tau \bar{q} e^{-\alpha \tau}.$$

The level of transfers (and associated tax rate) that would be chosen by the leader can be found by maximizing g^L with respect to τ. That yields $\tau^L = 1/\alpha$

---

111. The inequality in equation 8-10 is strict as long as $n > 1$.

Figure 8A-1. Payoffs as a Function of n

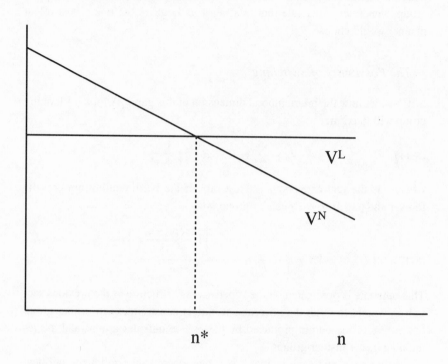

$$n^*\qquad\qquad\qquad n$$

—that is to say, the leader would predictably choose the revenue-maximizing tax rate. In that case, the leader's income is

$$(8\text{-}14)\qquad\qquad y^L = \bar{q}\left[1 + \frac{m-1}{\alpha e}\right],$$

where clearly $y^L > y^N$. The present discounted value of income for a leader is

$$(8\text{-}15)\qquad V^L = \frac{y^L}{1-R} - c = \frac{\bar{q}\left[1 + \dfrac{m-1}{\alpha e}\right]}{1-R} - c.$$

We are now in a position to ascertain when an insider will find it optimal to pay the cost c. Figure 8A-1 depicts V^N and V^L as a function of n, the number of insiders in the total set of m groups. Notice that V^L is independent of n, for under leadership all groups but the leader lose their access to government transfers. The function V^N, on the other hand, is decreasing in n—naturally, the

Figure 8A-2. Payoffs as a Function of q̄

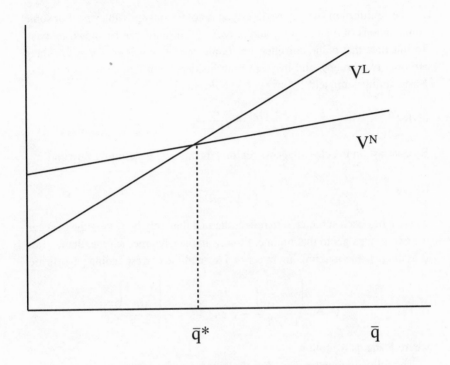

$$\bar{q}^* \qquad\qquad\qquad \bar{q}$$

larger the share of insiders in the total, the smaller the benefit of being an insider. For small n, the figure shows $V^N > V^L$, because of the fixed cost c of assuming leadership. But as n rises, V^N falls, and there is an n^* such that $V^N = V^L$.[112] At or above that point, it is optimal to pay the cost and become a leader.

Ceteris paribus, changes in $\bar{q}$ can also move the economy to the point where switching away from the open access regime is an equilibrium. Figure 8A-2 depicts V^N and V^L as a function of $\bar{q}$. Notice that because $y^L > y^N$, V^N is flatter than V^L. As before, because of the fixed cost c, $V^N > V^L$ for low values of $\bar{q}$. At $\bar{q}^*$, we have a level of $\bar{q}$ such that $V^N = V^L$.

In short, the equilibrium switch away from the open access regime could occur because outsider groups become insiders or because the natural rate of output rises. Both these cases are applicable to Chile in the late 1960s and early 1970s.

112. Ignoring integer constraints, that is.

Multiplicity and the Role of Politics

The equilibrium switch just described is not the only possible one. For some combinations of n and c, or $\bar{q}$ and c, two equilibriums can be shown to exist. To illustrate that point, consider the simple case in which $m = n = 2$—there are only two groups, and they are both insiders.[113] In that case, the one-shot Nash equilibrium yields:[114] $\tau^N = (1 - \alpha)/\alpha$ and

(8-16) $$V^N = \bar{q}\frac{e^{\alpha-1}}{1 - R}.$$

By contrast, in the closed-access regime, the tax rate is naturally zero and

(8-17) $$V^P = \frac{\bar{q}}{1 - R} - c,$$

where c has been subtracted to reflect the fact that only by paying the cost can the two groups get to that regime. Finally, in the asymmetric case, the tax rate is at the revenue-maximizing rate $\tau = 1/\alpha$, and the corresponding payoffs are

(8-18) $$V^L = \frac{\bar{q}\left[1 + \dfrac{1}{\alpha e}\right]}{1 - R} - c \text{ and } V^F = \frac{\bar{q}\left[\dfrac{\alpha - 1}{\alpha e}\right]}{1 - R},$$

where F stands for follower.

The following matrix describes the game in normal form:

		Player 2	
		Pay c	Not pay c
Player 1	Pay c	$\dfrac{\bar{q}}{1 - R} - c, \dfrac{\bar{q}}{1 - R} - c$	$\dfrac{\bar{q}\left[1 + \dfrac{1}{\alpha e}\right]}{1 - R} - c, \dfrac{\bar{q}\left[\dfrac{\alpha - 1}{\alpha e}\right]}{1 - R}$
	Not pay c	$\dfrac{\bar{q}\left[\dfrac{\alpha - 1}{\alpha e}\right]}{1 - R}, \dfrac{\bar{q}\left[1 + \dfrac{1}{\alpha e}\right]}{1 - R} - c$	$\dfrac{\bar{q}e^{\alpha - 1}}{1 - R}, \dfrac{\bar{q}e^{\alpha - 1}}{1 - R}$

113. Multiplicity of equilibriums also exists in the case of more than two groups, or in the case in which not all groups are insiders.

114. This can be computed by setting $m = 2$ in equation 8-7. Notice also that now, to ensure that $0 < \tau < 1$, we assume $(1/2) < \alpha < 1$.

With the help of this payoff matrix the possible equilibriums can be easily ascertained. If player 1 expects that player 2 will not pay the cost, 1's best response is not to pay the cost if

$$(8\text{-}19) \qquad \frac{\bar{q}e^{\alpha-1}}{1-R} \geq \frac{\bar{q}\left[1 + \dfrac{1}{\alpha e}\right]}{1-R} - c.$$

Conversely, if player 1 expects that player 2 will pay the cost, 1's best response is to pay the cost if

$$(8\text{-}20) \qquad \frac{\bar{q}}{1-R} - c \geq \frac{\bar{q}\dfrac{[\alpha-1]}{\alpha e}}{1-R}.$$

More than one equilibrium will exist if there is a $\bar{q}$, for a given c and α and all the other parameters, for which inequalities 8-19 and 8-20 can be satisfied at once. Those two expressions can be written jointly as

$$(8\text{-}21) \qquad e^{\alpha} \geq \phi(c,\bar{q},\alpha) \geq 1,$$

where

$$(8\text{-}22) \qquad \phi(c,\bar{q},a) \equiv e\left[1 - \frac{c(1-R)}{\bar{q}}\right] + \frac{1}{\alpha},$$

and where the first inequality corresponds to 8-19 and the second inequality to 8-20. There is nothing in the parameter space that would prevent such a pair of inequalities from holding. We conclude that if 8-21 holds, there are two equilibriums to the game.

To develop an institution for this result, it is useful to notice that $\phi_c < 0$, $\phi_{\bar{q}} > 0$, and $\phi_{\alpha} < 0$. Consider the effects of changes in $\bar{q}$, holding c and α constant. Suppose that initially the natural rate of output is very low—sufficiently so that equation 8-19 is satisfied, but equation 8-20 is not. In that state, the only possible equilibrium is for neither group to pay. As $\bar{q}$ gets larger, it will eventually satisfy both inequalities, as in equation 8-21; in this range one group pays if and only if it expects that the other will pay. One way to solve this indeterminacy is to appeal to politics; a political crisis can be interpreted as a situation where, starting from an equilibrium in which no one pays, the expectation that one group will attempt to switch leads the other to do the same. Such expectations may be driven by political factors such as ideology or mutual trust. Finally, there is a third possible case; if $\bar{q}$ gets so large that only equation 8-20 is satisfied, paying the cost and switching is the only possible outcome.

Notice that changes in c, ceteris paribus, can also move the economy in and out of the multiple-equilibrium range. Exactly the opposite story to the one just told can be constructed in terms of declining c. For sufficiently large c, $\phi(c,\bar{q},\alpha)$ is small, and only the no-switch equilibrium is feasible; for larger c, both equilibriums are attainable; eventually, if either parameter is large enough, only the switch equilibrium is attainable. Such comparative static exercises may be relevant to the Chilean story. If we interpret c as the subjective costs of political change (strife, upheaval), it is certainly arguable that the tolerance for such costs rose in the 1960s, when Latin America (and much of the world) was enamored of the notion of revolutionary (and perhaps necessarily violent) change. As this happened, Chile may have entered the range where a switch was possible (or perhaps inevitable).

References

Aizenman, J. 1992. "Competitive Externalities and the Optimal Seigniorage Segmentation." *Journal of Money, Credit and Banking* 24 (February): 61–71.

Alesina, A., and G. Tabellini. 1990. "A Political Theory of Fiscal Deficits and Government Debt." *Review of Economic Studies* 57 (July): 403–14.

Angell, A. 1972. *Politics and the Labour Movement in Chile.* Oxford University Press.

Behrman, J. 1976. *Foreign Trade Regimes and Economic Development: Chile.* National Bureau of Economic Research and Columbia University Press.

Bitar, S. 1986. *Chile: Experiments in Democracy.* Philadelphia: Institute for the Study of Human Issues.

Calvo, G. 1986. "Temporary Stabilization: The Case of Predetermined Exchange Rates." *Journal of Political Economy* 94 (December): 1319–29.

Campero, G. 1984. *Los Gremios Empresariales en el Período 1970–83.* Santiago: Instituto Latinoamericano de Estudios Transnacionales (ILET).

Campero, G., and R. Cortázar. 1988. "Actores Sociales y la Transición a la Democracia en Chile." *Colección Estudios CIEPLAN* 25: 115–58.

Campero, G., and J. A. Valenzuela. 1984. *El Movimiento Sindical y el Régimen Militar Chileno.* Santiago: ILET.

Central Bank of Chile. *Indicadores Económicos y Sociales,* various issues.

Collier, D., ed. 1979. *The New Authoritarianism in Latin America.* Princeton University Press.

Corbo, V. 1993. "Economic Reforms in Chile: An Overview." Paper presented at the Eastern Economic Association Meetings, Washington D.C., March.

Cortázar, R., and J. Marshall. 1980. "Indice de Precios al Consumidor." *Colección Estudios CIEPLAN* 4.

Cruz, J. M. 1988. "La Fruticultura de Exportación: Una Experiencia de Desarrollo Empresarial." *Colección Estudios CIEPLAN* 25: 79–114.

Cukierman, A., S. Edwards, and G. Tabellini. 1992. "Seigniorage and Political Instability." *American Economic Review* 82 (June): 537–55.

De Vylder, S. 1976. *Allende's Chile.* Cambridge University Press.

Díaz-Alejandro, C. 1985. "Good-bye Financial Repression, Hello Financial Crash." In *Trade, Development, and the World Economy,* edited by A. Solimano, 264–86.

Dornbusch, R., and S. Edwards. 1991. "Introduction." In *The Macroeconomics of Populism in Latin America,* edited by R. Dornbusch and S. Edwards, 7–14. University of Chicago Press.

Drake, P. 1978. *Socialism and Populism in Chile, 1932–52.* University of Illinois Press.

Edwards, S., and A. Cox-Edwards. 1987. *Monetarism and Liberalization: The Chilean Experiment.* Ballinger.

Evans, P. 1992. "The State as Problem and Solution: Predation, Embedded Autonomy and Structural Change." In *The Politics of Economic Adjustment: International Constraints, Distributive Conflicts, and the State,* edited by S. Haggard and R. Kaufman, 139–81. Princeton University Press.

Fetter, F. W. 1931. *Monetary Inflation in Chile.* Princeton University Press.

Ffrench-Davis, R. 1973. *Políticas Económicas en Chile 1952–1970.* CIEPLAN (Corporación de Investigaciones Económicas para Latinoamerica). Santiago: Ediciones Nueva Universidad.

———. 1980. "Liberalización de Importaciones: La Experiencia Chilena." *Colección Estudios CIEPLAN* (4).

Fontaine, A. 1988. *Los Economistas y el Presidente Pinochet.* Santiago: Zig-Zag.

Foxley, A. 1982. "Condiciones para una Democracia Estable." *Colección Estudios CIEPLAN* 9: 139–70.

———. 1983. *Latin American Experiments with Neoconservative Economics.* University of California Press.

Garretón, M. A. 1983. *El Proceso Político Chileno.* Santiago: Facultad Latinoamericana de Ciencias Sociales (FLACSO).

Haggard, S. 1990. *Pathways from the Periphery: The Politics of Growth in the Newly Industrializing Countries.* Cornell University Press.

Haggard, S., and R. Kaufman, eds. 1992. *The Politics of Economic Adjustment.* Princeton University Press.

Hirschman, A. 1963. *Journeys Toward Progress: Studies of Economic Policy-making in Latin America.* W. W. Norton.

Labán, R., and A. Velasco. 1993. "The Economic Policies of Chile's Democratic Government." Paper presented at the Eastern Economic Association Meetings, Washington, D.C., March.

Landsberger, H., and T. McDaniel. 1976. "Hypermobilization in Chile, 1970–73." *World Politics* 38(4).

Larraín, F. 1991. "Public Sector Behavior in a Highly Indebted Country: The Contrasting Chilean Experience, 1970–85." In *The Public Sector and the Latin American Crisis,* edited by F. Larraín and M. Selowsky, 89–136. San Francisco: ICS Press.

Larraín, F., and P. Meller. 1991. "The Socialist-Populist Chilean Experience." In *The*

Macroeconomics of Populism in Latin America, edited by R. Dornbusch and S. Edwards, 175–214. University of Chicago Press.

Larroulet, Cristian. 1984. "Reflexiones en Torno al Estado Empresario en Chile." *Estudios Públicos* 2(14): 129–51.

Mamalakis, M. 1965. "Public Policy and Sectoral Development: A Case Study of Chile, 1940–58." In *Essays on the Chilean Economy,* edited by M. Mamalakis and C. Reynolds, 3–202. Yale University Press.

————. 1976. *The Growth and Structure of the Chilean Economy.* Yale University Press.

Meller, P. 1990. "Resultados Economicos de Cuatro Gobiernos Chilenos, 1958-1989." *Apuntas CIEPLAN* 89 (October).

Muñoz, O. 1968. *Crecimiento Industrial de Chile 1914–1965.* Universidad de Chile.

Piñera, J. 1990. *La Revolución Laboral en Chile.* Santiago: Zig-Zag.

Ramos, J. 1987. *Neoconservative Economic Experiments in the Southern Cone of Latin America.* Johns Hopkins University Press.

Rodrik, D., and A. Panagariya. 1991. "Political Economy Arguments for a Common Tariff." The World Bank.

Rosende, F. 1985. "Tipo de Cambio y Salarios Reales: Consideraciones sobre el caso chileno." *Cuadernos de Economía* 22 (August): 343–55.

Scully, T. 1992. *Rethinking the Center: Party Politics in Nineteenth and Twentieth Century Chile.* Stanford University Press.

Stallings, B. 1978. *Class Conflict and Economic Development in Chile.* Stanford University Press.

Stenzel, K. 1988. "The Crisis as Blessing in Disguise." Yale University, Department of Political Science.

Tabellini, G. 1990. "A Positive Theory of Social Security." Working Paper 3272. Cambridge, Mass.: National Bureau of Economic Research.

Tironi, E. 1984. *La Torre de Babel: Ensayes de Crítica y Renovación Politica.* Santiago: Sur.

Tornell, A. 1992. "Are Economic Crises Necessary for Privatization and Liberalizaton? The Mexican Experience." MIT, Department of Economics.

Tornell, A., and A. Velasco. 1992. "Why Does Capital Flow from Poor to Rich Countries? The Tragedy of the Commons and Economic Growth." *Journal of Political Economy* 100 (December): 1208–31.

Valdés, J. G. 1989. *La Escuela de Chicago: Operación Chile.* Buenos Aires: Ediciones Grupo Zeta.

Valenzuela, A. 1978. *The Breakdown of Democratic Regimes: Chile.* Johns Hopkins University Press.

Velasco, A. 1992. "Liberalization, Crisis, Intervention: The Chilean Financial System 1975–1985." In *Banking Crises,* edited by T. Baliño and V. Sundarajan. International Monetary Fund.

————. 1993. "A Model of Endogenous Fiscal Deficits and Delayed Fiscal Reforms." Research Report 93-04. New York University, C. V. Starr Center for Applied Economics.

Velasco, A., and A. Tornell. 1991. "Wages, Profits and Capital Flight." *Economics and Politics* 3 (November): 219–37.

Vuskovic, P. 1978. *Una Sola Lucha.* Mexico City: Editorial Nuestro Tiempo.

Wisecarver, Daniel. 1986. "Regulación y Desregulación en Chile: Septiembre 1973 a Septiembre 1983." *Estudios Públicos* 4 (22): 115–67.

Zahler, R. 1978. "La Inflación Chilena." In *Chile 1940–75: Treinta y Cinco Anos de Discontinuidad Económica.* Santiago: Instituto Chileno de Estudios Humanísticos.

Zeitlin, M., and R. E. Ratcliff. 1988. *Landlords and Capitalists: The Dominant Class of Chile.* Princeton University Press.

Conference Participants

NANCY BIRDSALL
The World Bank

EDUARDO BITRAN
Ministerio de Hacienda, Chile

BARRY P. BOSWORTH
The Brookings Institution

ANDREA BUTELMANN
CIEPLAN, Santiago

ELIANA CARDOSO
Tufts University

SUSAN M. COLLINS
The Brookings Institution

VITTORIO CORBO
Catholic University of Chile

JOSÉ DE GREGORIO
International Monetary Fund

PETER DIAMOND
*Massachusetts Institute of
Technology*

RUDIGER DORNBUSCH
*Massachusetts Institute of
Technology*

SEBASTIAN EDWARDS
University of California, Los Angeles

ENRIQUE ERRARURIZ
InterAmerican Bank of Development

NICOLÁS EYZAGUIRRE
Central Bank of Chile

RAQUEL FERNANDEZ
Boston University

STANLEY FISCHER
*Massachusetts Institute of
Technology*

CAROL GRAHAM
The Brookings Institution

DOMINIQUE HACHETTE
DE LA F.
Catholic University of Chile

CHRISTIAN HOHLBERG
*Economic Minister, Embassy of
Chile*

ANNE O. KRUEGER
Duke University

RAÚL LABÁN
Ministerio de Hacienda

FELIPE LARRAÍN B.
Catholic University of Chile

NORA LUSTIG
The Brookings Institution

WILLIAM F. MALONEY
University of Illinois

MARIO MARCEL
InterAmerican Bank of Development

MANUEL MARFÁN
CIEPLAN, Santiago

JORGE MARSHALL
Minister of the Economy of Chile

431

RONALD I. MCKINNON
Stanford University

PATRICIO MELLER
CIEPLAN, Santiago

ALEJANDRA MIZALA
University of Chile

FELIPE G. MORANDÉ
Georgetown University

JOSEPH RAMOS
ECLAC, Santiago

FRANCISCO ROSENDE
Catholic University of Chile

RAÚL E. SÁEZ
CIEPLAN, Santiago

ANDRÉS SOLIMANO
The World Bank

SALVADOR VALDÉS-PRIETO
Catholic University of Chile

ARTURO VALENZUELA
Georgetown University

ANDRÉS VELASCO
New York University

JOAQUÍN VIAL
Ministerio de Hacienda

DENISE WILLIAMSON
Washington, D.C.

JOHN WILLIAMSON
Institute for International Economics

Index

Adjustment lags, 2, 12; in assessing reform effects, 17; causes of, 14, 27; income distribution, 19–20, 241; labor productivity, 107; significance of Chilean experience, 68, 70–72

Administradora de Fondos de Pensiones, 258–59, 263, 264, 265, 266, 267; annuity market, 291–97; capital markets and, 302, 303; in crisis of 1982, 339–40; current holdings, 341; development of, 276–78; disability and survivors insurance, 289–90; employer selection, 314; equity limits, 323; market conditions, 284–88, 312–23; performance of, 300–01; regulation of, 301–02, 305, 308–09, 310; reprivatization of, 340–41

AFP. *See Administradora de Fondos de Pensiones*

Agricultural sector: before reform period, 384–85, 417; exports since 1979, 97, 107; labor productivity, 176–77, 208; Pinochet government and, 404; privatization of, 335, 346

Airline industry, 343

Alessandri administration, 31, 220–21, 384, 388, 390, 390n, 391, 398, 415

Allende administration, 84, 217, 224, 225, 381; current account deficit, 34; economic development in, 5; economic indicators in, 223; election of, 395–96; income distribution in, 219, 220; inflation rate in, 43; policymaking in, 25; political goals of, 415–16; state-owned enterprises, 22; in success of Pinochet reforms, 417; trade policy, 31

Andean Pact, 155

Argentina, 246–47, 390

Arrau, P., 152

Artiagoitía, P., 178

Asian economies: Chile compared with, 180; labor scarcity, 202

Aylwin administration, 94–95, 96, 217–18, 276, 418; economic performance, 224, 413; income distribution in, 220; social programs, 228–29, 249–50; tax reforms, 222

Balance of payments crisis: before reform period, 390–91; 1982 crisis, 106

Banking system: capital inflow regulation, 156–58, 159; deposit insurance, 45; in divestiture of state-owned enterprises, 337; foreign borrowing guarantees, 156; nationalization of, 31, 154, 396–97; in 1982 crisis, 39–41, 48, 58, 110, 191n, 192, 401–03; privatization of, 338–41; purchase of nonfinancial assets by, 187

Barandiarán, E., 46

Barro, R., 202

Birdsall, N., 324

Bitran, E., 22, 24

Blanlot, V., 366

Boeninger, Edgardo, 95

Bosworth, B., 17, 107

Brazil, 120, 242, 246–47, 390

Bruno, M., 53

Büchi, Hernán, 41

Budget deficit: financing of banking system rescue and, 48, 58, 191n; in inflation control strategy, 51; in initiation of reforms, 5

Budget process, 407, 409–10

Calvo, G. A., 99, 136

Capital inflows: avoiding currency appreciation, 110–11; composition of, 122; crawling band policy and, 103–04, 134; debt vs. equity in, 123–24; domestic capital markets and, 140; domestic substitution, 160; exchange rate policy after 1989 and, 98–100;